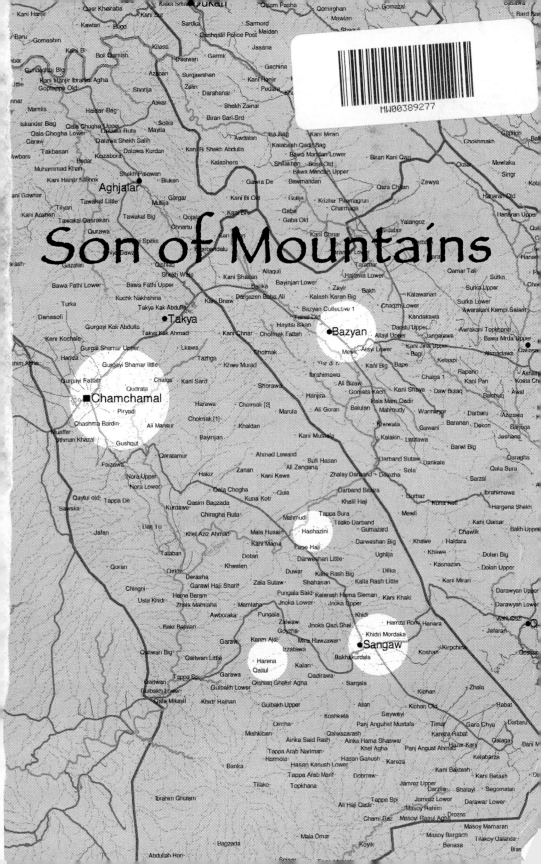

Son of Mountains

Son of Mountains

MY LIFE AS A KURD AND A TERROR SUSPECT

Yassin Aref

ياسين عارف

Cover and book design: Melissa Mykal Batalin

Front cover: Yassin Aref at Terre Haute Federal Correctional Institution, August 2007. Anonymous photographer.

Landscape in northern Kurdistan, Iraq, Sarrarush Mountains. Photo by Christine Osborne, www.copix.co.uk

Endpapers: Detail of map, "Northern Iraq, Chamchamal Area, SHS12." Map prepared by JHIC (United Nations Joint Humanitarian Information Centre), UNOHCI (United Nations Office of the Humanitarian Coordinator for Iraq), Erbil, northern Iraq, August 2002.
Note: Although Hashazini was destroyed in the Anfal operation in 1989, evidently by 2002 it had been rebuilt.

Title page: Author's name transcribed into Arabic by May Saffar.

Back cover: Yassin Aref after posting bail in August 2004. Photo by Will Waldron. Courtesy of Albany *Times Union*.

ISBN 978-1-933994-30-7

Printed in the United States in an edition of 750 copies.

Troy Book Makers
3 Third Street
Troy, New York 12180
(518) 689-1083
tbminfo@thetroybookmakers.com

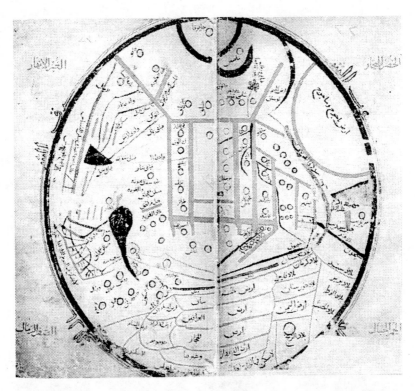

Map dated 1074 by Mahmud al-Kashgari, showing *Arz ul Akrad* (Arabic for "land of Kurds") located between *Arz ush Sham* (Syria) and *Arz ul Iraqeyn* (Iraq Arabi and Iraq Ajami). Original in Linden-Museum Stuttgart, State Museum of Ethnology, Stuttgart, Germany. Public domain.

DEDICATION

This book is dedicated to the many people who are in my heart:

To my devoted wife, Zuhur, who is the real victim of the government's unjust plot. She has been left to struggle, suffer, and live in pain to pay for a crime I never committed.

To my dear children, Alaa, Raiber, Kotcher, and Dilnia, who are not citizens of any country in this universe but who are paying for being my children and are losing their childhoods as victims of the government's plot.

To my family in Iraq:
My father, who by beatings and example taught me the importance of discipline.

My mother, who by her life taught me the importance of love and hope.

My brother Issa, whose philosophical arguments taught me to search and think.

My brother Ibrahim, who taught me to read and love poetry.

My brother Mohsin, who was my twin and best friend as we grew up together.

My sisters, especially Aisha and Nathifa, all of whom are victims of ignorant tribal customs.

My relatives and friends, including Arif Gull, who are always in my heart.

Nawzar Mazhar, my closest teenage friend (besides books), without whose friendship I would not have been able to keep my mind.

My teacher and Sheikh, Abo Saeed, whom I learned from and who changed me from an ignorant villager to an educated man.

To my family in the U.S.:
Kathy Manley, who cried for me and helped me more than my own sister.

Shamshad Ahmad, who takes care of me as though I am his son.

Abdulbarr Shuaib, my closest friend and big brother.

Abdulhaqq Hamzah, whose life in the U.S. was not much better than mine in Iraq.

Jabir Kareem, for his devoted care of my children.

To the local Muslim community, for their faithful support of my wife and children.

To Lynne Jackson, who was not deceived by the government's translation of the word *Kak*, who calls me Kak Yassin and says, They lied, you're Brother, not Commander. I am really honored to have such a sister and happy when I get her letters every week.

My special thanks to Jeanne Finley for her courage and sincere advice. Without her hard work as editor, this book never would have been completed.

And to all the peace seekers, justice lovers, truth speakers, and supporters who make me feel that I am not alone, who have been here for me and have become my best friends and real relatives and have supported me and my family in various ways:

The whole winter of 2006–2007, you challenged severe weather to participate in vigils every week in front of the courthouse.

You wrote letters to the judge to tell him to be fair, bring justice back, and free this innocent man.

You wrote and talked to the media about the government's tricky plot and the nonsensical verdict.

You visited my wife and children and supported them emotionally and financially.

You wrote letters to me and visited me to make me feel better.

Those who worked hard behind the scenes and helped me in a different way—no way to mention all of you, but here are all of you alphabetically, with my apologies to many, many of you whom I have not mentioned. You have all made me feel that justice and peace are still possible, and that the truth will finally be told.

Salih Abdullah, Faisal Ahmad, Huma Ahmad, Shazia Ahmad, Fa'izah J. Andrews, Sadik Astif, Petra Bartosiewicz, Ellie Bernstein, Sarah Birn, Jerry Bolduc, Cathy Callan, Dave and Cynthia Capone, Fred Arthur Childs, Sharifa Din, Barbara DiTomasso, Steve and Wil Downs, Marc Dudley, Priscilla Fairbank, Mohammed and Amina Faroque, Barry Finley, Jim Fulmer, Amy Goodman, Alice Green, Ghulam Haider, Moutasim and Taqi Hamayel, Mohammad Haroon, Abuhamza Hossain, Fatima Hossain, Connie Frisbee Houde, Jean Hynes, Dr. Muhammad Ismail, Adil Khalafullah, Imam Ahmed Kobeisy, Fred LeBrun, Joe Lombardo, Mickie Lynn, Joanne Mann, Abdulhamid Mansouri, Henry Matala, Lyn Miller-Lachmann, Abdul Mohsin, Margaret Murtagh, Tariq Niazi, Erin O'Brien, Paul and Katja Rehm, Michael Rice, May Saffar, Imam D'Jafer Sebkhaul, Brian Seymour, Mary Alice Smith, Sondra Sprinkling, Craig Stratton, Carl Strock, Nacer Tagziria, Steve Trimm, Islah Umar, Zia Usman, Daniel W. Van Riper, Grace White, Brahim Zaour.

Contents

Introduction

Between October 2006 and early March 2007, I wrote this book in the Rensselaer County Jail in Troy, New York while awaiting sentencing on my conviction for various terrorism-related charges. Since the guards keep me in solitary confinement twenty-three hours a day, I have had plenty of time to consider my life and the irony of my being jailed in America, the country that I fled to as a refugee in order to live free. So I would like to tell you the story of my life.

Under a UN-sponsored program, I came to America as a refugee from Iraq through Syria in 1999. After a few years, I became the Imam of a mosque in Albany, New York. As Imam, I worked hard to support the community of worshippers and help them build their faith. I married couples, counseled people in trouble, taught students, and tried to perform all of the many duties that are required of an Imam in an Islamic community. And I worked hard to support my wife and children.

On August 4, 2004, when I went home about 10:30 p.m. after night prayers to take my rest, the FBI was waiting for me in front of my family's apartment. The agents arrested me, took me to their office, and accused me of participating in a plot to attack New York City with a missile. I was astonished. I had never heard of such a plot, nor had I seen a missile, done anything to participate in, or shown my intention to participate in, such a crime. Later I learned that the FBI had tried to involve me in an elaborate sting. They promised leniency to a convicted Pakistani felon, Malik, if he could get me to say I supported a fake terrorist plot concocted by them. Malik posed as a wealthy businessman who wanted to loan money to a member of the mosque, and I was asked to witness a series of his loan transactions in accordance with the requirements of Islam. I had witnessed such transactions in the past, in a role similar to that of a notary public, and I had received nothing in return then, nor did I receive anything this time. I regarded this as a service that I could give to the community as an Imam.

Malik secretly tape-recorded our conversations in connection with witnessing the loans, and he tried to draw me into general conversations about terrorism. I told him that I did not know anything about the organizations he claimed to support, and that I had come to this country to raise my family and be an Imam in peace. I said that I did not think violence would bring any benefit in this country, and that suicide bombing is not allowed in Islam; that Muslims in America should obey American law; and that if he wanted to help Muslims in foreign countries he should give his money to women and children who were homeless and without food or shelter, and that way he did not have to help terrorists or other political groups. Malik's statements were just general talk, and he never gave any explanation or details about a specific plot, or asked me to participate in anything illegal. All of the statements, secretly recorded, are part of the record of the trial, and prove I did nothing wrong.

The trial record shows that I never said anything to indicate I supported terrorism, or that I was even aware of Malik's plot. To this day I do not know what the "plot" was, because it was never described to me. The government's theory did not make any sense, for it assumed that I would casually enter into a terrorist plot without asking any questions about it, or knowing anything about the organizations involved, or knowing any of the people involved or any details of what was planned. Why would anyone do this? What would be my motive?

To fill this gap, the government introduced days of evidence and testimony about my life in the Middle East before I came to America to suggest that my character was that of a radical who would willingly join any terrorist plot even without knowing anything about it. The evidence showed just the opposite, but because Americans are unsophisticated about Islam and the Middle East, and because the FBI mistranslated so many documents or took them out of context, there were many opportunities for confusion or misrepresentation. At the end of the trial, on October 10, 2006, two-thirds of the counts were dismissed by the jury, but I was convicted of money laundering; conspiracy in connection with a weapon of mass destruction (the missile); providing material support to a foreign terrorist organization; and lying to the FBI.

In April 2006, while I was awaiting trial, a volunteer lawyer, Steve Downs, visited me in jail to help with my defense. I was upset at that time because on September 30, 2005, the government had persuaded a judge to revoke my bail, based on a series of misrepresentations that supposedly showed that I was "dangerous." I suggested that Mr. Steve, as I called him, should help me draft a new bail application that would refute the lies that the government had put in its motion to revoke my bail. As we worked on it, the bail application became longer and longer, until one day Mr. Steve joked that after we finished he was planning to publish it as a novel. When we finally submitted the bail application, the court acknowledged that it was "well written," but otherwise was not moved to release me from jail.

After I was convicted, Mr. Steve visited me again in jail. I told him that I wanted to fire him as my lawyer. He looked surprised and hurt. I explained that I did not need so many lawyers now, but I would like to hire him as my brother because I did not have any family in this country, and it seemed to me that family would do me more good now than lawyers. He grinned and pushed a pile of blank yellow pads toward me.

"What's this?" I asked.

"Let's get started on your story," he said.

"Where should I begin?" I asked.

"At the beginning," he said. He wanted me to go back to Iraq—to the Kurdish part of Iraq where I was born—and to tell the whole story of what had happened, from then until now.

At first I did not want to write it. I did not think that anyone would get much benefit out of reading about my life, but Mr. Steve insisted that it would help people understand Kurdistan and its culture, and eventually the trial. I tried to write about myself and found that it was very difficult. I told Mr. Steve I would give him whatever information he wanted, and he could write my story as he wished. However, when he showed me what he had written, it was apparent that he knew so little about Kurdistan that he had everything mixed up. On some pages I had to cross out so much information that only a few sentences were left.

We developed a working relationship in which I would write out in longhand the story that I wanted to tell, and Mr. Steve would correct my broken English and make it into proper sentences. Sometimes he would add some sentences where he thought an American audience would be confused, and I reviewed his additions for correctness. He used to complain that I never spelled words the same way twice. I insisted that I was very consistent in spelling—I always spelled words I did not know phonetically, but the problem was I could not always pronounce them the same way twice. In this way we learned to adapt to each other's styles, and the writing progressed.

As I worked on the project, Kurdistan began to flow back to me, so that for hours at a time I was out of my jail cell and walking through the flowering hills of Kurdistan in the spring. People, places, and events I had forgotten or suppressed came back to me. Mr. Steve constantly encouraged me to write about personal events and add more details. I actually began to enjoy the writing, and to feel sad when it seemed that we were coming to the end of our work.

Because I did not have access to any notes or documents or relatives and their memories, I had to write this book from my own memory. I may have confused a date, or placed some events out of sequence, but I have written everything to the best of my knowledge. When I related a conversation, I generally could not remember the exact words that were used, but I tried to make the written conversation as true to the actual substance of the conversation as possible. I want readers to know that my story is not a novel, or a fiction, or an exaggeration, but is as close to the truth as I can describe without having other sources from which to check my memory.

When I finally read over the manuscript, I felt that it was good, and I was proud of what we had done. I hope everyone who reads this story finds it interesting and gets some benefit from it. I enjoyed the writing so much that after it was finished, I began writing the story of my life after I left Kurdistan for Syria, and then what happened to me once I arrived in America. The story would not have been written if Mr. Steve had not encouraged me. I do not think that a mere "thank you" is enough to express to him what his help has meant to me, but my gratitude is all I can give him in my present circumstance. He is my brother. He understands.

The writer Al Alim said, "We learned from messengers of the East that there is life after death, and we learned from the leaders of the East that there is no life before death." Because of these bloody leaders and ignorant dictators, life for people in the East is suffering and struggling. So brutal and inhuman are these leaders' corrupt regimes that people in the East move from disaster to disaster. My life is just one example. When you read this story, you may say that it is hard to believe I went through so much difficulty and suffering. But if someone from my country were to read this story, he would say, "Oh, Yassin—he lived the high life compared with mine."

The only way to change this situation—to stop the corruption and ignorance, and to promote peace and prosperity—is for scholars to speak out, tell the truth, and never blindly approve what the rulers do. As Imam Ahmad said, "If scholars don't speak the truth, and people don't know it, how will the truth ever come out?" The Prophet Mohammad, may peace be upon him, said, "The best *jihad* is to say the truth to an unjust ruler." Tell the truth to an unjust ruler; let him know how his misrule affects the people; and advise him and warn him about what disasters will flow if he does not stop the corruption and replace it with the rule of law. Only when justice replaces misrule will we know peace and see the peoples' lives improve.

Yassin Aref
March 2007

At our first meeting after his conviction, Yassin tried to put on a brave face. He told me that he returned to the jail from court with a smile and joked with the other prisoners. One of them asked him how he could be so happy when he had just been convicted. Yassin responded that appearing sad would bring no benefit to him, and would only make others sad. If he cried, it would be inside. He told me about his father, who said *"Okhay"* (I like it) whenever he injured himself because he did not want Satan to get any pleasure out of his suffering. But it was obvious that Yassin was now very worried about what would happen to his family.

He asked me to be his brother, since he did not have any family in America. I was very touched by this, and agreed without realizing exactly what was involved. Being a brother in Kurdistan meant that you were family and could be called upon to make sacrifices that only family members would normally consider. Thus taking care of Yassin's own destroyed family was just the first of the projects that had to be done to pick up the pieces after his conviction. Bills had to be paid, doctors' appointments had to be scheduled, immigration lawyers had to be consulted, money had to be raised, bank accounts had to be closed. The same was true for Mohammed Hossain's (Yassin's co-defendant's) family. As Yassin observed about the status of a convicted man, "He's not dead enough to forget and not alive enough to get any benefit from."

Fortunately, out of the wreckage of Yassin's and Hossain's lives, people rallied around. Cathy Callan and May Saffar, two residents of the Capital District, reacted to the injustice of the convictions by holding a public meeting that was attended by more than fifty people. From this meeting sprang the Muslim Solidarity Committee to help support both defendants and their families. The committee opened a bank account to receive donations from the public and raised over $14,000 as of sentencing day; it created a website to post information about the case; it organized weekly vigils outside the federal courthouse to keep the injustice done to the Muslim community from being forgotten; it circulated petitions asking Judge McAvoy to grant leniency to the defendants, and collected almost 1,000 signatures; it organized a campaign to write letters to the judge seeking leniency, and over fifty letters were sent; it held a number of forums and public discussions to draw attention to the cases; it reached out to other Muslims in other communities that had suffered similar frame-ups and bogus charges to create a unified front; and it helped writers and filmmakers with information. I participated in the Muslim Solidarity Committee and was inspired by the wonderful people I met there.

But the most satisfying project for me was helping Yassin write this book, with the editorial assistance of Jeanne Finley and Kathy Manley, between the time of his conviction and his sentencing on March 8, 2007. It was a simple mustard seed of a project that has bloomed into this huge tree. Through the book, I learned about a part of the world that few Westerners have visited or understood, and how important it is to Americans—who are only dimly aware of it. We fight in Iraq, but we do not understand why or what forces we are likely to unleash. Through Yassin's eyes I became a traveler in the magical world of Kurdistan, where nothing is quite the way you expect it to be, and I became a witness to the machinations of our own government, whose blunderings in Iraq have mirrored its blunderings in finding terrorists at home. And throughout it all I came to know a remarkable, brilliant man whose tragedy is the tragedy of the world, and whose compassion for the world may yet teach us the way out of such folly. I hope you enjoy reading this book as much as I have enjoyed knowing its author, who is now my brother.

Stephen Downs
May 2007

About the Editing of This Book

Editing is a matter of trust as well as grammar. The editorial process for this book was based on mutual trust between Yassin and us, the editors—but we want to make sure to establish a similar trust between us and you, the reader, with regard to the veracity of what you will read. You might wonder: since the book has obviously been edited for English spelling, grammar, usage, and syntax, what else did we change? How much of what you'll read is Yassin, and how much is us? And what kind of help did he receive from us on paper, in terms of making his story better?

That Yassin wrote this book entirely in English—and thus for a Western audience—is only one of the feats he accomplished here. He is not a native English speaker. Sorani Kurdish is his first language, Arabic his second, through his education and his study of the Qur'an; but his English, as Steve Downs characterizes it, is "evolving." So the first goal of the editing process was to render Yassin's stories into standard English. But this naturally caused a subtle change in tone, and made his first-person voice sound more Western and articulate in English than he actually is—an issue that is relevant, for example, to how he would have heard and understood conversations during the sting operation that led to his arrest and conviction.

Culture was another issue we had to consider. For example, when Yassin described a group of armed men fighting in the mountains of Kurdistan for their freedom, we were tempted to substitute the Western word "guerrilla" for the Kurdish word *peshmerga*. But are "guerrilla" and *peshmerga* synonymous? The former has connotations that may not completely apply to Kurdistan, while the latter invites the reader to explore and develop connotations unique to that country. Throughout the book, we made dozens of such decisions—whether to use a Kurdish word or concept that the reader might not understand except in context, or a similar Western word with possibly inappropriate connotations. In some places, whether right in the text or as a note, we added brief explanations of Islamic beliefs, Middle Eastern history, or other words or concepts that Westerners might not understand. So another goal of the editing process was to make Yassin's world more understandable and accessible to a Western reader, but not to change that world in any significant way.

For his part, Yassin embraced the editing process and seemed fascinated by it. He made us work hard, harder than we expected, because we could take no shortcuts. Once we had made changes to his stories, we always gave them back to him for approval or further revisions. (Access to him at the Rensselaer County Jail was accomplished through regular visiting hours.) Sometimes we exchanged drafts back and forth several times until we were all satisfied that we understood each other. If he added new stories or sections, he often gave us instructions as to where in the longer narrative to put them. His attention to accuracy was acute; each of us can recount instances when he firmly told us that he meant this and not that, and that we should "please to change" according to his explanation. Then he checked every word of the finished manuscript twice and made more corrections each time, some of them substantive. We were fortunate that Yassin is a naturally gifted storyteller who knew exactly where he wanted to go on paper. And we were Western "sounding boards" who could tell him how a Western reader would react to and understand his journey.

But trust was the main rule of engagement that enabled us all to go forward: Yassin's trust in us that allowed him to deposit his autobiography with Westerners, and our trust in him to tell the truth—which was, for him, a principle about which there could be no debate or compromise. He insisted on the truth down to every last detail because he could not do otherwise, because that is how he lives and what he believes in. Telling the truth was as important to him as the editorial bottom line of keeping the author's meaning intact was to us—or maybe our purposes were one and the same thing.

Steve Downs, who originally suggested to Yassin that he write this book, did the first typewritten rendition from Yassin's voluminous handwritten pages. During this process, Steve corrected grammar and spelling and made sentences where, on occasion, there were none. Since Yassin often spells phonetically and has acquired English mainly by speaking, not writing, it was both challenging and thrilling to see each story and chapter slowly emerge.

After Yassin approved the typewritten text, Steve then gave the chapters to Jeanne Finley, a Muslim Solidarity Committee member and a professional editor. She edited them line by line, continued to polish grammar and punctuation, checked spelling, names, and places, and rearranged sentences or whole sections where necessary to keep the narrative clear. She flagged items she had questions about, changed some story and chapter titles to better represent the material, omitted a few stories that were repetitive or didn't seem to fit into the larger story line, and arranged and assembled the book as a whole. The long lists of questions she presented to Yassin as she worked formed the basis for their continuing correspondence. He answered each question in detail, and regularly inquired where the questions were when she didn't have any.

Kathy Manley, one of Yassin's appeal lawyers, transcribed most of the poems in the book from his handwritten translations (he had written them originally in Kurdish, then translated them to English). She also did the first editing of the Syria and America sections; researched and checked items related to Islamic, Kurdish, and Syrian history; and cross-checked sections related to Yassin's arrest, trial, and testimony against the trial transcript, to be sure that both matched. At no time did she change or modify any facts or descriptions; Yassin has been unfailingly consistent in all his accounts of what has happened to him legally.

We are indebted to Dr. Shamshad Ahmad, our "secret source," for his help in explaining and clarifying points about Islam to us non-Muslims. At our (repeated) requests he also checked the spelling of individuals' names, and provided the correct spelling and translations of many of the Arabic words in the book, as did May Saffar, a native Arabic speaker.

In a September 2007 letter to Jeanne from prison, Yassin sent a note (quoted in full below) about any errors he may have inadvertently made in the book, and then added (in his unedited words): "I want you to write this note may be after preeface or any wher in the book but its important and I want to see it—feel free to fixed and formed in perfect English. Please write this and dont worry about any information <<name of place and people and events>> its my respanciblity."

So here's a "perfect English" version of Yassin's note to you, his reader:

> This is a non-fiction story. I wrote it while I was in jail, and there was no way for me to get books or contact friends for more information. I depended on my memory—perhaps sometimes I am not correct about an exact date—but certainly all the incidents are true, and I used the real names of everyone throughout the book. Most of the people are living, so it would be very easy to confirm what I wrote with them. This is a life story, however, so millions of people in Kurdistan could also be witnesses for these events, and I hope they will all see and read this book.
>
> At the same time, I ask everyone: please, if you find any errors or mistakes, take a minute to write them down, and another minute to send them to us [meaning the editors, as well as himself], so we can fix it in the next edition. Our goal is to tell people the truth, and only the truth, nothing else.

We invite you to do just as Yassin requests. You can write to him at the address given on page 488, or you can write to us in care of the Aref Children's Fund at the address shown on that same page.

Steve Downs
Jeanne Finley
Kathy Manley
October 2007

To my surprise, I am standing
on the top of a high mountain
I look back on my life
I can see it as though I am dreaming

                    —Kurdish poem

PART ONE:
KURDISTAN

Hashazini village in 1988, before the Anfal operation.
Family photo courtesy of Arif Gull.

Chapter One ❧
Land of the Kurds

My name is Yassin. (It is pronounced Ya-*seen*.) If I am being formal, I would add that my name is Yassin Muhiddin (my father's first name) Aref (my grandfather's first name). And if I am being very formal, I would add at the end Barzingi (the name of my tribe), and Garmian (the name of my region in Iraqi Kurdistan). In this way, my formal name carries with it enough information about my family, my tribe, and my region so that people who meet me for the first time will know something about who I am, as though I am carrying a letter of introduction. So my full name is Yassin Muhiddin Aref Barzingi Garmiani, and in that name is much of the history that influenced me as I grew up.

Our tradition uses the father's and grandfather's first names for what Western people call middle names and surnames. So my oldest son's name is Raiber (pronounced *Ray*-bur) Yassin Muhiddin; this system of naming also applies to daughters.

Western people sometimes try to show respect for me by calling me Mr. Aref, but in our tradition when people want to show respect, they say *Kak* before the first name, which literally translates as "brother," thus giving the same respect that they would show to a member of their own family. People very often use *Kak* when referring to someone else, because failing to show respect can have serious consequences in a culture that prizes honor very highly.

Strangely, the word that conveys the most information about me is not included in my name. I am a Kurd. Perhaps this word is not included because Kurdistan is a hidden land, and the Kurds are a hidden people. You will not find Kurdistan on a map today. It is not a recognized country. Kurdistan is divided into five parts, with approximately 20–25 million Kurds living in Turkish-ruled Kurdistan; 7–10 million Kurds living in Iranian-ruled Kurdistan; 5–6 million Kurds living in Iraqi-ruled Kurdistan; 1.5–2 million Kurds living in Syrian-ruled Kurdistan; and half a million Kurds living in Armenia near Yerevan. It is hard to get accurate figures about the number of Kurds living in Kurdistan, because after years of wars and repression most Kurds don't give their children Kurdish names or register their children with the government. In fact, many people use Arabic names to disguise the fact that they are Kurdish. My two sons, for example, have both Kurdish names and Arabic names: my oldest son Raiber's Arabic name is Salah, and my younger son Kotcher's (pronounced *Cot*-shur) Arabic name is Azzam. Being Kurdish is dangerous from the day of birth until the day of death, and so even as we cherish our Kurdishness—our language, our culture, our traditions; and our land—we also feel the need to hide our Kurdishness as we struggle to survive as a people.

We are the largest ethnic group that does not have its own free country. The rulers of Turkey, Iran, Iraq, and Syria have long tried to suppress the intense desire of the Kurdish people to be free. At various times, these governments have suppressed us by arrests, torture, and executions. They have made it a crime to speak the Kurdish language, to run our own schools, to express our own culture, and to live according to our own values. Since Kurdistan has rich oil and fresh water reserves, and the land is fertile, these governments believe that it is in their best interests to occupy and control our land, and have tried to make the Kurds believe that they are Turks or Persians or Arabs. As a result, some people are afraid that being identified as a Kurd may bring reprisals from the very government that is supposed to protect them. Other Kurds have fought back to keep our language and culture and land.

Our lives in Kurdistan are an almost continual struggle to defend and regain our homeland. But because there are few Kurdish journalists, because Kurdistan does not appear on maps, because Kurdistan is isolated, and because it was not in the interests of the superpowers to support Kurdish freedom, the governments of other countries have been able to define us to the rest of the world. We are not even allowed to travel abroad to visit Mecca on the *Hajj* pilgrimage, even though it is God's order and one of the Five Pillars of Islam, and even though it is a way, established for us by Prophet Abraham, for Muslims from all over the world to meet and know each other. Visiting journalists are prohibited from visiting Kurdistan, or else are accompanied by "security" people who let the journalists see only what the government wants them to see. Communications and Internet services are restricted. Because we are a hidden people, the world usually learns about us from how our enemies describe us.

The factor that most defines the Kurds is the landscape of Kurdistan—the mountains. There are many: the Zagros, the Hamreen, the Qandeel, Mount Ararat, Mount Handren…we are like people who live on a mountainous island. When storms come—and in our part of the world, violent storms often come—we seek refuge on our mountain island until the storms blow over. Only in the mountains are we truly safe. Throughout history this has been true. The mountains are harsh; the winters are cold. Roads have not been built or improved, villages are isolated, and people have to work very hard to scratch out a living. We depend for our necessities only on ourselves, and we import little. But life there is secure, and we live in dignity by our own hands. If you have a simple job and a small plot of land, invading armies will probably bypass your village on the way to somewhere else. Surrounded by your "brothers" and the walls of the mountains, you can resist and persist until conditions improve and the storms blow over. This understanding of history is in our blood. The Kurds express this by saying, "We have no friends, only mountains."

As a child, I learned that the history of Kurdistan was the history of the whole world. In Shanidar Cave, high in Kurdish Iraq in the Zagros Mountains, were found the homes and bones of Neanderthal people who had also sought shelter in the rock walls from encroaching danger. When God flooded the whole world so that all life would perish except Noah and the Ark, God brought the Ark to rest on the top of Mount Ararat in northern Kurdistan as the waters receded. So it seemed clear to me as a child that the survivors of the Flood started to repopulate the earth in the mountains of Kurdistan. There is a tradition that Father

Abraham, the father of three religions (Jewish, Christian, and Muslim), was a Kurd. Thus we are an ancient people, as proud and solid as the rocks on which we live, because we know that God brought us to the mountains to survive and that He sustains us there even through the worst calamities. Our enemies say that the Kurds have lived on the mountains so long they have rocks in their heads and have become rebellious, like wild animals. But for us, the mountains are a sign of our dignity, a castle of honor where fighters for freedom can find refuge, like children in a mother's care.

The mountains also contribute to another aspect of Kurdish personality: a love of beauty. As cold and harsh as the mountains are in winter, they are abundant with running water, flowers, birds, and animals in spring and summer—as though God, knowing what a hard life the Kurds must suffer during most of the year, allows them for a time to see a vision of Paradise. Kurdish tradition records this beauty in poetry—a form that can be remembered on cold winter nights to give hope for the season to come. So abundant is the poetic praise in Kurdistan that foreigners often claim that the Kurds are a nation of poets. A poet in Kurdistan will always draw a crowd to listen. A politician will not.

In 1989, I wrote a poem about our mountain home:

Mountains

To them our mountains are big and hard
Rocks and jungles for the criminal rebel
For us they are the lion's land
A castle of dignity for the strong
The mother protector of all *peshmerga* *
Fighting for freedom.

The land around our Kurdish island is troubled and dangerous. To the north is Turkey, a non-Arabic homeland for the Turkic ethnic people. To the east is Iran, a non-Arabic homeland for the Persian people, and to the south and west are Iraq and Syria, homelands for Arab-speaking

*Kurdish militia, freedom fighters

peoples. Because the region is a mixture of Turkic, Persian, Kurdish, and Arabic peoples, each with a different language and culture, Kurdistan's history is full of empires and dynasties, clashes and suppressions, as each group struggles against the other for supremacy. Always it seems that Kurdistan is dominated by some other culture, and always it is the Kurds fighting for their independence and freedom. But covering over all of these divisions like a beautiful emerald canopy is Islam—the one force that unites. Islam tells us that all of us—Kurds, Arabs, Persians, and Turks—are brothers. Islam forbids us to harm any of our brothers, but rather commands us to do good to everyone in the Islamic community and beyond. As bad as life is in our corner of the world, imagine how much worse it would be if not for Mohammad, peace be upon him, reminding us daily that only by complete submission to the will of God; by controlling our desires and acting mindfully; by educating ourselves and our children; by having always a pure heart filled with love; and by daily prayer and charity toward everyone, can we ever hope to achieve peace. Only by this submission and practice can we hope to end the violence, which is the result of hatred and racism.

I was born in 1970 in the Kurdish village of Hashazini, in the Garmian region of Kurdistan in Iraq. In 1970, Hashazini was a village of some 100 houses about thirty miles from the county center of Sangaw, which had approximately 2,000 houses. Sangaw was in a province that centered around the city of Chamchamal, with about 50,000 people. Chamchamal was originally in the State of Kirkuk, but in 1971 it was violently transferred to the State of Sulaimaniya by the Iraqi government so that the oil-rich city of Kirkuk could be "ethnically cleansed" of Kurds and the Arab government in Baghdad could steal the oil lying under this Kurdish land.

The relative importance of these cities and villages can best be expressed by describing the roads that connected them. From Baghdad to Kirkuk was a modern road, because Kirkuk was an important oil city. From Kirkuk to Chamchamal was a two-lane paved highway crowded with cars that struggled to pass slow-moving trucks while trying to avoid accidents with the oncoming traffic. From Chamchamal to Sangaw was a single unpaved road, full of potholes and washouts, and from Sangaw to Hashazini there was only a simple dirt lane that, in the early 1970s, carried almost no cars at all. I only saw a car in Hashazini a few times a month. Between most other villages in the area there were only footpaths, with no auto roads at all.

From the day of my birth in 1970 until the day I left Kurdistan in 1995, I did not see one year of peace. In 1968, the Baath Party took control of the Iraqi government in Baghdad and began fighting against the other parties. Soon after that, the Baath Party became a fascist police state that controlled the army and all sources of power within the state. In 1971, the Iraqi government began a campaign to remove the Kurds from Kirkuk by giving their homes and property to Arabs, who were promised good-paying government jobs if they would move to Kirkuk and replace the Kurds. The Kurds refused to accept this outrage, and although the tension had existed since 1945, between 1971 and 1991 there was continual violent fighting between the Iraqi government and the Kurdish *peshmerga*. At the beginning, the most important Kurdish *peshmerga* group was the Kurdistan Democratic Party (KDP), founded and led by Mulla Mustafa Barzani, whose son, Masood, is now the president of Kurdistan.

In 1974, Iran and Iraq formed an agreement at a meeting in Algeria that allowed both countries to attack the Kurdish areas inside their own countries. The war against us broadened and we faced new attacks. As a result, the Kurdish revolution collapsed in 1975, and in 1976 a new *peshmerga* group, the PUK (Patriotic Union of Kurdistan), founded and led by Jalal Talabani, was formed to defend Kurdistan. The violent fighting between the *peshmerga* and the governments of Iraq, Iran, and Turkey, which had begun during World War II, continued until 1991; when there was a lull, the KDP (the conservative nationalists) and the PUK (the liberal nationalists) would fight each other for control of what was left of Kurdistan.

In 1980, Iraq attacked Iran and set off a very violent war that lasted eight years, killed hundreds of thousands of people, and impoverished both countries. Tragically, both Iran and Iraq continued to attack the

Kurds while attacking each other. In 1988, Saddam Hussein, president of Iraq, furious at the Kurds for attacking his army at the same time that his army was fighting Iran, launched a genocidal attack against the Kurds. He first dropped poison gas on the Kurdish city of Halabja, killing thousands of Kurdish civilians. Then he launched the Anfal attacks (a sacrilegious use of the word that means "the spoils," taken from Surah 8 of the Qur'an) against Kurdistan, in which he obliterated 1,200 Kurdish villages, including my home village, and killed over 180,000 Kurds.

At the end of 1988, the war with Iran came to an end. In 1990, the dictator turned his attention to the south and invaded the oil-rich kingdom of Kuwait. In 1991 he was driven out of Kuwait by America and her allies in the first Gulf War, and his army was mauled. After this, the Iraqi army was so exhausted that Kurdish groups, encouraged by America, believed that they could successfully revolt and that America would protect them from the Iraqi government's retaliation. At first the revolt succeeded, but then the full fury of the army was turned upon the Kurds, millions of whom were driven into the mountains without food or shelter. After that, although the United Nations forced the army to withdraw its forces from most of Kurdistan except Kirkuk and the areas around it, life in Iraq did not improve.

Between 1990 and 2003, the United Nations imposed a strict embargo on Iraq, which the government simply shifted to the people. Everyone except the Iraqi dictator was impoverished. The government of Kurdistan simply collapsed, and fighting broke out between its various political groups. Food was scarce, medicine was impossible to find, and there were no services available: no mail, electricity, telephones, government offices. Then in 2003, America launched the Iraq War, which was followed by the present civil war in Iraq. As of today, there has been continual warfare in my country for my entire lifetime. God knows what else is coming, but there is no reason to believe it will be any better.

Even before Saddam came to power, it had been the policy of the Iraqi government to suppress the Kurds and keep Kurdistan poor and primitive. The government used the army to enforce a policy of slow genocide against the Kurds. The Kurdish language was not allowed in many schools or in government offices. Kurdish names for mountains, rivers, and villages were changed to Arabic. All signs referring to Kurdish influence were removed from Iraqi museums. Maps identifying Kurdistan were banned. Kurdish festivals were prohibited. No Kurdish-language newspapers, radio, or TV stations were allowed. Kurds in many areas were not allowed to wear their native clothing. Thousands were forced to change their names and nationalities on government papers in order to be allowed to stay in Kurdish areas like Kirkuk. Kurds who defied these rules were treated as suspicious, or were imprisoned, tortured, and even executed. Kurdish areas were not developed, roads were not built, agriculture was not improved, electricity and other services were not brought to the areas that needed them, and life was made as difficult as possible. The Iraqi government's war against the Kurds was only the culmination of a long campaign to eliminate the "Kurdish problem," following the example of other mass murderers such as Stalin in Russia and Hitler in Germany.

The violence that I grew up with as a child was a product of this long, slow genocide against the Kurds by all of the countries that surrounded Kurdistan. Now I understand that someone's childhood does not have to be like this. Children do not have to be exposed constantly to fear, starvation, and death, and they do not have to become adults by the age of ten in order to survive. But at that time I was only a child, and I thought my childhood was normal.

Chapter Two 🐦
In the Shade of My Family

My tribe, Barzingi, is one of the largest tribes in Kurdistan and traces its roots back to Hussein, the grandson of the Prophet Mohammad, may peace be upon him. The family of the Prophet is called Quraish. A distant descendant of Hussein living in southern Iraq had to flee to Kurdistan to escape from assassins, and settled in the village of Barzinga. (Barzinga was destroyed during Anfal, but has since been rebuilt.) Throughout history, the Barzingi tribe has played a special role in Kurdish society by making peace between rival tribes and families. Its traditional role has been that of a religious teacher who seeks the best and highest path and then tries to show others how to follow. Such a teacher is called a Sheikh. I have had several Sheikhs in my life who have had a big impact on me, from my grandfather and uncle to my high school teacher, whom I revere to this day.

My family was responsible for starting many of the schools in the area mosques where children could learn to read and write. My grandfather, Sheikh Aref, was a famous and much-admired Imam (teacher and religious leader), but he died some years before I was born. His son, my uncle Sheikh SayGul, was also a famous Sheikh and leader who succeeded Sheikh Aref as the Imam in the mosque and as leader of my grandfather's followers. I have heard many stories about what these two Imams did and the miracles that seemed to accompany them, but I tend to believe that religious followers often exaggerate, so I cannot confirm the stories.

Of my father's four brothers, two died before I was born. A third brother died when I was nine years old, but he lived in Kirkuk and I do not remember ever meeting him. Sheik SayGul died when I was thirteen years old, but I remember him well because he was living in my village, Hashazini. Sheik SayGul was the humblest and simplest person I ever met. He used to provide food for the poorest people in the village, and then he would sit and talk with them as though he was one of them. He never let people serve him; he would serve himself and do what needed to be done by himself. Sometimes after prayers he would keep his youngest son, Kareem, and me with him after the people left, and we would help clean the *masjid* (mosque). Often I saw Uncle cleaning the *masjid* toilet. He spent a lot of time praying in the *masjid*, and sometimes I saw him praying with tears running down his cheeks. When you met him for the first time, you simply could not believe that he was a famous Imam, or that he had even one follower. You might think he was a homeless beggar. His whole philosophy was about being simple: wear simple clothes, live a simple life, act like the simplest and poorest person, never show arrogance or pride.

In 1975, the first Kurdish revolution collapsed, and in 1976 the PUK (Patriotic Union of Kurdistan) began to assert itself in the Garmian region. Tension developed between the *peshmerga* of the KDP (Kurdistan Democratic Party) and the *peshmerga* of the PUK. My family was accused by the Iraqi government of supporting *peshmerga* activity against the government, and the KDP accused my family of supporting PUK *peshmerga* instead of the KDP's. At the end of 1977, the KDP arrested three of my cousins and tied them to the pillar of the Hashazini mosque for two days, waiting for the order to execute them. Uncle SayGul became very angry at this and criticized the KDP commander harshly; as a result, the commander ordered that my uncle be arrested and tied to the pillar also. But when they tried to arrest him, people from all over the area came forward to support him. In front of hundreds of people, the KDP leaders tried to tie Uncle to the pillar— and as they were doing it, the story goes that without any person near it, an old semi-automatic machine gun in the mosque fell from a high place and suddenly began spraying bullets into the crowd, killing the commander's gardener and wounding the commander himself, who had actually ordered the arrest. Some said it was just an accident, but for my uncle's followers it was a miracle. Even the wounded leader agreed that it was a miracle, and wrote in a book that Sheik SayGul's prayers had affected him deeply. Since this story was published and confirmed by the commander himself, there have been hundreds of other events like this. Thousands of people talk about them, but since they are all oral stories, I cannot confirm them.

After the incident of the gun, my three cousins and my uncle were released and the KDP did not bother us anymore. We had never supported one Kurdish group against another; the closest my father came to supporting a group was to name my younger brother Jalal, in honor of Jalal Talabani, the leader of the PUK. Once my brother turned two years old, Father used to call him *Mala* (Imam) Jalal, but the people in the village called him Mam Jalal—the same name as the leader of the PUK.

After Sheikh SayGul died, his son Sheikh Umar succeeded him. Sheikh Umar was a well-educated person, very religious, humble and simple like his father, and people respected him greatly because of his knowledge. They came to him from all over with questions, but he was living in Kirkuk and came to Hashazini mainly on special occasions like Ramadan, the month of fasting. Every year he used to enter one room in the mosque and stay there for forty days of intense prayer called *Khalwa,* in which the penitent cuts his relations with all worldly attachments and thus frees himself completely for God.

One day I was sitting with Sheikh Umar in his room in Kirkuk, which was packed with bookshelves full of books. I was wondering what he did with all those books and how he could read them all. I asked him if he could show me a simple way to learn to read all of them, most of which were handwritten. He responded by telling me a story.

Once, he said, there was a farmer who went to the Imam and saw that his room was packed with books. The farmer asked if the Imam had read all of the books. The Imam replied, "Most of them."

"Well, I have not read any of them," said the farmer, "but I know what all of them are about and what is written in them."

"How do you know?" asked the Imam "Tell me, what is written in all these books?"

And the farmer said, "It is written always to do good and never to do bad."

Sheikh Umar started laughing. In answer to my question, he said, all those books I wanted to read were about doing good and avoiding evil, which was simple and easy. "People by their nature know what is good and bad. You don't have to be a philosopher to figure it out. You just need to be honest, and when you know that something is not right, don't do it."

After that, he told me another story. A villager went to the Messenger, may peace be upon him, and said to him, "Oh Mohammad, I can't make long prayers like you. Please tell me something I can always ask God for."

The Prophet asked him, "What do you pray for now?"

The villager replied, "I ask Him to save me from the fire and to lead me to Paradise."

"That is all I am praying for too," said the Prophet.

Because Sheikh Umar was so seldom in the village, eventually Sheik Ismaeel (the son of my Uncle Mohammad, my father's deceased brother) became the Imam in Hashazini until the village was destroyed in the 1988 Anfal campaign. Sheik Ismaeel's home was like the village hotel, restaurant, and court combined. Every day he had guests staying with him, seeking shelter and asking him to solve their problems. He was such a model of generosity that people from other villages used to come to him for all kinds of reasons. Some simply wanted his blessing and prayers. Others had religious questions, or wanted advice on how to make peace, or how to find shelter for their families, or how to escape the poverty of their situation. Sheik Ismaeel and his wife seem to take their pleasure entirely from serving guests. His wife was my mother's best friend; I used to call her Mom too. Just one wall separated our houses, and the families lived together in Hashazini for at least thirty years until the village was finally demolished.

There were actually two Barzingi families in Hashazini: ours, the descendants of my grandfather Aref, and the other one, descendants of Sheik Sadiqs's family. Together our two families made up about half the population of the village. The rest were people from tribes that we considered inferior and so were unsuitable for marriage for our women.

There was a kind of "cold war" between our two Barzingi families for influence. Our side of the tribe was famous in religion because of Grandfather Aref and Uncle SayGul. Their side of the tribe was famous in politics. Sheik Sadiqs's son, Abdul Qadr, was the most important person in Hashazini, and indeed he was really the village "head" when I was growing up, especially after Sheik SayGul died. Sheik Abdul Qadr was my role model—a wise, pragmatic man respected by everyone. He was illiterate, but he was able to lead not only Hashazini but Kurdistan as well. People came from all over the country for his advice. Over and over again he was able to stop tribal fighting in Kurdistan, and people looked to him for leadership in keeping the peace. When he died, he left four daughters and six sons, all of whom were brilliant and lovely people. But none of them were able to take his place or play the same peacemaker role.

I learned history from my family as it was lived out in our daily conflicts and celebrations. In fact, I must say that as hard as my child-hood was, it was much better than the life of my father or grandfather, and indeed much better than the life of many of my friends. My brother Issa used to say that all we have been created for is suffering, and that we live as though we have fallen from the sky with no one to help us—to which my father would always reply, "Stop complaining and thank God. Life could be so much worse."

My Father

My father, Muhiddin, was a simple farmer and shepherd in a very isolated part of Kurdistan. He was fifty-eight years old when I was born. Father was a huge man physically—over six feet tall and 200 pounds. He was very strong, with a tremendous capacity to endure—his last child was born when he was sixty-six years old—but he radiated no joy in his life, which seemed always haunted by tragedy. To be honest, Father is still somewhat of a mystery to me. Before he married my mother he had three previous wives, all of whom died, as well as six or seven children from these earlier marriages, who also died. I know nothing about them. I do not know how old they were when they died, what they looked like, how they died, what their names were, or where they are buried. Nothing! My father did not talk about these tragedies. It bothers me a great deal that I know so little about him and his family, and it is one of the reasons that I am writing my own history down, so my children will at least know where they came from and can learn about life from my experience.

All of my father's four brothers were relatively rich and successful compared with my father. They had land and farms and big houses, and life was much better for them than Father's was. All of my uncles were educated; only my father had no education and was illiterate. Since Grandfather Aref was a famous Imam and Sheikh, it would seem reasonable that he would have educated my father along with the rest of his sons—but why he did not was never explained to me. Perhaps this is the reason: in our culture, a father will "direct" each of his sons toward a particular vocation, and so each son will have a different life. Of my father's brothers, one went to a regular school early on, to be educated with the intention of becoming a scholar or a teacher; one went to a religious school to become an Imam; one was educated for farm work and became a farmer; and one was trained in hotel-keeping, to be able to serve guests. Evidently my father was trained in sheep herding, since that must have been the life my Grandfather Aref wanted for him, and that may have been why my father was not educated.

But my father bore his limitations with humbleness and dignity, and people respected him for it. When people tried to kiss his hand or show him other signs of respect, he would always say, "No, please, I am not worthy of that." He often fasted for days because he did not have enough food, and whenever someone asked him what he wanted for his meal, he would say, "Anything softer than a stone I will eat, as long as it keeps me alive." Usually when I ate with him, our meal was bread and tea. I do not think we ever had meat, except perhaps at festivals or celebrations.

Although my father's pockets were always empty, he was not concerned about being poor—after all, most people in the village were poor. Instead he was worried that he must avoid anything that might disgrace the family. When people wanted to help him, my father used to tell me, "Son, people do this for us because they want to receive a blessing, but if they knew how sinful we are, they would run away from us as fast as they could."

I know little about my grandmother (my father's mother), or about the many relatives that preceded my grandparents. There is no written record of how they lived, and the oral stories about them are hard to confirm. It was as though life was so bitter in previous generations, nobody wanted to record what happened, though I believe it was simply because most people were illiterate and could not record the stories. But it may simply have been that my father was already an old man when I was growing up, and the pain of his many losses simply overwhelmed his desire to remember them. The only thing I really know about my relatives is that people always told me how much they loved my grandfather Aref and his son Sheikh SayGul. They were respected leaders, and because of that people respected me as well.

Because they were religious leaders who descended from the Prophet's family, people looked at us as a holy family. My brother Issa and some of my cousins stopped praying or going to the mosque, but still people would kiss their hands and old people would ask for a blessing from them. I used to say that we "lived in the shade of our forefathers"—otherwise, who were we to bless the people? This is true throughout the Muslim world: people descended from the Prophet are a special group, and most of the kings and important people come from this group. People who cannot even afford a meal will buy a whole sheep and send it to one of these special descendants of the Prophet as a sign of respect. It is our tradition. And it is also part of that tradition that such people as Grandfather Aref and Uncle SayGul were put here to serve and not to be served. It is the role of the family I was born into.

When my father was growing up, and also later, when he was caring for us, life was simple and hard. There was no electricity, there were no cars, no highways, no hospitals, no schools, and no social services in the region. Our whole family—six children and two adults—lived in a two-room house made out of sun-dried mud bricks mixed with straw. The floor was also mud, pounded hard. In summer we often cooked rice outside over a small fire, but in winter it was too cold to cook outside. Then we would pile wood on the fire in a stove made out of a large metal drum, and cook next to that. The drum would quickly turn red-hot, and the heat was so intense even on the coldest days that we would begin to sweat and had to back up against the farthest walls to stay cool. Then a few hours later when the fire had died down, everyone would shiver in the cold that leaked in under the door. It was so cold that we hung blankets over the door, and when we, or visitors, left the house, we were supposed to close the door before we pushed away the blanket so that no cold air would come in.

There was always the danger of toddlers burning themselves on the red-hot drum. People used to take a child's finger and purposely burn the end of it on the drum so that the child would cry and be afraid of the great heat. After a number of burns, children usually learned to avoid the drum at all costs.

There was no furniture to speak of in my father's house, or in any house in the village. There were so many people living in the small houses that there was really no room for furniture. At night we placed sleeping mats on the floor and slept under thick blankets to escape from the intense cold; these were our beds. In the morning we piled the mats and blankets in a corner. We also ate sitting on the floor; there was a mud-brick oven called a *tandoor*, which was used to bake bread. A fire was built inside the *tandoor*, which heated the bricks around the fire chamber. Then round, flat wheat cakes were plastered against the hot inside bricks and baked until they were cooked. This dry flat bread was the most common food eaten at meals. Rice was expensive and had to be imported. My father had several cows and some sheep that my mother milked, and from this milk she made yogurt and a kind of cottage cheese. We all ate a lot of butterfat from the milk, and this helped give us the calories that we needed to survive. We also had chickens and eggs.

In the months of December and January we could expect snow, sometimes a great deal of snow—enough to block the roads out of the village and even bring down the whole roof of the house if the snow was not quickly raked off. (The Kurdish name for December is *Bafran Bar*, which means "snowing month," and the name for January is *Reban Dan*, which means "no pathway," since snow blocks the roads and everything is cut off in the mountains.) The roof was made of sod, rich in clay to repel the rain, but if the snow was not removed it might melt and leak down between the cracks, causing drips inside. In summer we did not have to worry about leaks because it seldom rained, but before winter came people used to roll their roofs with heavy concrete rollers to pack the sod and fill in all of the cracks so there would be less chance of leaking. In some parts of Kurdistan the snow was regularly very deep, sometimes completely covering the doors of the houses. In our area it was not so severe, but there were usually some heavy snowstorms every winter. The women spun sheep's wool into yarn and made warm winter sweaters; without these, we would have had difficulty surviving the cold.

During the winter we all had to live and sleep in the single room with the stove, because we could not heat the other room. We even had to bathe in the same room. My mother would bring out a tub next to the stove because the other room was freezing and wash my brother Mohsin and me. As soon as we were five years old, we both wanted privacy to wash ourselves, but Mom would slap us if we protested, and she washed us until we were almost ten. We had to stand together in the tub while Mom poured hot water over us. We shouted and cried, but none of our pleas helped us.

In summer we could go down to the small creek that ran through our village and swim, so we did not have to submit to the indignity of Mother washing us. None of us had shirts; we had only a pair of pants, often ripped, to cover our nakedness, but we didn't care because we were free to run and swim outside rather than be cooped up in the house all day under the eyes of our parents.

Rooster Eggs

It bothered my father that he had no education, and he always told us that we should not be like him. So impatient was my father for me to be educated that when I was five years old he took me to the local school and asked the principal to accept me into first grade, since there was no kindergarten. But the principal said that by law, he had to wait until I was six years old. My father would not accept this refusal, so the principal said that he would test me, and if I passed he would accept me.

"Yassin," he said, "if your rooster lays an egg in your neighbor's yard, will the egg be yours or your neighbor's?"

"Ours," I said.

The principal said, "But it is in their yard."

"It still is ours," I said.

"But the egg is on somebody else's property," the principal said.

"But our rooster made the egg!" I exclaimed.

The principal laughed and said, "Yassin!! Come back next year!" So I failed my first test because I did not say that roosters don't make eggs.

Father was also a deeply religious man, but without direct knowledge, since he could not read the Qur'an. Once I was two years old, almost every day he would take me to the mosque for prayer. He made me pray five times each day, as was the custom, until I grew to like the inner strength and peace that prayer gave me. Father was most excited when he saw his children praying, or reciting from the holy book, or cleaning the mosque. We children knew this, and we tried our best to show him how devout we were so that he would forgive us if we had irritated him—or to perhaps get a piece of candy, or perhaps to protect ourselves from his slap, which he was always ready to apply for any infraction of the rules. That was how I first learned to pray, but eventually prayer became the most important thing in my life. Those of us in the East survive because of prayer and because of the peace and tranquility that it brings to our hearts to balance the survival actions that our minds are always demanding. Now, living in solitary confinement twenty-three hours a day, the inner strength of prayer has literally saved my life.

Gold Ring

During my childhood, people in Kurdistan seldom used money—they had little money to use. Instead they bartered goods, especially the farmers. One day when I refused to eat my lunch, which always made Father angry, he told me a story of just such a barter.

Once he and some friends went to Kirkuk with ten horses loaded with grain to trade for food and clothing. He was also looking for some gold to give my mother, since tradition required that she receive at least a gold ring on her wedding day. It took them two days to get to Kirkuk, where my father bought a very beautiful gold ring. However, on their two-day journey home they had to pass through a rebel-held area. Normally if people returned from Kirkuk with food and clothing for the winter, the rebels might take some of it as a "tax" and let them continue; but if they had some gold, the rebels might kill them for it.

On the first night of the return journey, my father and his friends were caught in a rebel ambush. My father did not know what to do. If he threw the ring away, he would probably never be able to find it again, but if the rebels found the ring on him, they might kill everyone to try to find more gold. He asked one of his friends what he should do.

"Throw it," the friend said.

But Father said, "I can't."

The friend said, "Swallow it, then."

"How?"

"You don't know how?" the friend asked. "Just do it!"

So my father swallowed the ring.

The rebels asked if my father and his friends had any gold or money, and they denied it. The rebels said that they would check everything, and if they found any money or gold they would kill everyone.

"OK, check," Father said.

But while the rebels were going through the packs they heard gunfire, and demanded to know what the party had seen on the road.

"Nothing," said Father.

The gunfire came closer. The rebels became nervous, took some food, and ran away. After Father had put all of his things back in his pack, he asked his friend what would happen to the ring.

"You mean you've never done that before?" asked the friend.

"No..."

"Well, I used to do it all the time when I sold stuff for money." He laughed. "Go shit and get your gold back."

That night Father tried hard, but nothing came out. The next morning he searched what he had been able to produce, but still found nothing. The same thing happened at noon. Finally, late in the day, Father found the ring, and it was exactly as it had been—only shinier.

His friend said, "So now you've learned."

"I have, absolutely," Father said. He was very excited that the rebels had not taken their clothes and had run away with only a small amount of food. If the rebels stopped them again, now he knew just what to do. Father told me that this was one of the most important things that he had ever learned in his life. He said it gave him peace of mind that he knew what to do when surrounded by robbers.

I have no idea why Father told me this story, what the point of the story was, or what important insight he learned from the experience. Was it just something he wanted me to know? Or did he want me to learn something about the gold that he gave to my mother on their wedding day? Or was it something about self-reliance? Or about not giving in to fear? Or about the importance of friends? Or was he just joking with me by telling me a funny story that had no point? Or was it something else? I do not know. But for some reason it was important to him, and so it was important to me as a small child hearing it from him for the first time, and I have remembered it ever since. Perhaps he just wanted me to appreciate how many hardships and sacrifices were necessary to put food on the table so that I would not complain. Now my children will be able to read about my experiences and might wonder why those experiences were so important to me, just as I wonder about the importance of Father's experiences. Fathers are often such a mystery.

Okhay

Our cattle were kept in a low, dark barn without any windows. There was a hole in the wall that we stuffed with cloth in the winter to keep out the cold; it was open at other times to let in light and air. When the hole was closed it was very dark in the barn, and I had to grope my way blindly through the straw and manure to find the hole and remove the cloth so that I could get some light. When I pulled out the cloth, a shaft of yellow light stretched across the barn; because of all the dust particles in the air, it appeared to hold up the roof, like a solid golden beam.

The roof of the barn was actually held up by a large wooden beam less than five feet above the ground, from which smaller rafters radiated. My father was a very tall man, and he had to bow down each time he entered the barn to avoid hitting his head. After bending down to do his work, many times I saw him straighten up and hit his head forcefully on the beam. Or he would be walking through the barn, concentrating on something else, and run his head right into the beam.

One day when I was with him, he hit the beam so hard with his forehead that the skin broke and blood ran down over his face. But the only thing he said was, "*Okhay*," which means "I like it" or "That's good." I was surprised at his reaction, and asked him what there was about hitting his forehead on the beam that he seemed to like so much.

He said, "Son, if I complain, Satan will be happy and laugh because I did not accept God's decree. But now, since I said I liked it, Satan is sad at his loss because he did not stop me from thanking God."

"But you did not mention God or thank him," I said. "You just said it was good."

"*Okhay* means, 'Oh God, I accept what you have given me,' and God certainly knows my heart and what is in it. Son, never complain or cry when something bad is given to you. You will get no benefit from your complaints, and it will only make you sadder and weaker. Instead, if you look at your situation as though it is a test and thank God for it, it will make you feel good and strong."

Since then I have seen the wisdom in my father's words. I saw him struggle against hardship and suffering all his life, and yet he was always ready to joke, always acting as though he did not have a care in the world. If it were not for such faith, few people would survive the conditions in the Middle East. Now, confined to my jail cell twenty-three hours a day, I have time to consider the wisdom of his words in relation to my own life, and I can also say, "*Okhay*, I accept it"—it is a test that will only make me stronger. If I don't say *Okhay*, how else can I be patient with being convicted for crimes I did not commit? Satan will derive no pleasure from my suffering. I will thank God always for what he has given me, and pray only that this is the last test I will have to endure.

Calling Dates

Every year Dad would buy two or three big packs of dates to last us for the whole winter. Dates were very cheap in Iraq, but we were allowed only a few per day so they would last. It was decided that everyone could have five dates a day: two in the morning, two in the afternoon, and one at night. But after awhile Mom saw that the dates were disappearing faster than that, so she started watching us children closely. One day she caught Mohsin with a handful.

"What is this?" she demanded.

"Mom, it is not my fault," Mohsin said. "The dates were calling to me to take them and eat them!"

Mohsin was lucky—Mom let him have the dates. One day when I took a date and ran out the door, I saw my father. I quickly put my hand behind my back and said, "I took nothing."

"So why are you hiding your hand?" he asked.

I quickly dropped the date and showed him my empty hand, but he heard the sound of the date as it hit the ground and slapped my face so hard that my ear was ringing for ten minutes afterwards.

My Mother

My mother, Fatimah, was from a very poor family of the Jaff tribe, a very old tribe with a long history in the Garmain region. They were noted for being simple, strong shepherds. She had three brothers: Majid was single all of his life and homeless for part of it, and died in 1985. Uthman loved our family too much, and at a young age went to the mountains to fight with the *peshmerga* and died there. Umar is my only maternal uncle still living. Mom also had four stepsisters and one full sister. These women were like angels. It sounds extreme, but they lived in total poverty and yet they seemed to embrace their suffering, as though their strength came from some divine source. They worked hard to support themselves and their sick father, and they also were able to educate themselves at a time when women were not supposed to be educated or depend on themselves. They were also so religious and generous in the community that people began to regard them as examples of purity. Though they died in silence, I remember them now as great, heroic women who were self-sufficient in the hard, dark times of Kurdish suffering. They proved that women can live with dignity, even in a third world country.

I learned obedience and endurance from my father, but I learned suffering and patience from my mother. Women in the East work very hard and get little for it except suffering. I could see it in my mother's face. She did all of the housework, raised six children, helped my father on the farm, milked the cows and sheep, and received no credit for anything. On top of that she was sick for my entire childhood, and her sickness was never diagnosed or treated. There were no doctors in the region at that time. She complained of rheumatism and headaches, which were so bad that whenever she went to take water from the well she did not put the pail on her head like most women, but carried it on her shoulder.

In 1979, Salma, my seven-year-old sister, died; in 1981 my five-year-old brother Jalal died; and something inside my mother died with them. Her mind was never the same afterwards. Whenever I saw her there was a tear in her eye, and sometimes she would grab me and hug me and kiss me and cry for my dead sister and brother.

It is odd that I cannot remember how Salma died. I was nine years old at the time of her death. I don't even have a picture of her, and I have difficulty remembering what she looked like. Perhaps I was away from home at the time, since the circumstances of her death were never clearly described to me. With all the grief and problems in our family, such sad stories were not often repeated. But my sister's death had a great effect on my mother because Salma was the only daughter my mother had. My mother badly needed a daughter to help her, because in our tradition men may not help women with housework. My mother was sick and we could not afford servants. So Mom had to do all the housework alone.

My Brother's Death

I remember very well my youngest brother Jalal's death in 1981. Both my parents believed that Jalal would be the last child they would ever have, and so they gave him more love and attention than any of us. He was a very happy child, active and healthy. He was always talking to people and playing with them in an innocent way. Now all I have left of him are two or three black-and-white photographs. When he was four years old, I remember how much he loved a French cheese snack called *Abo walad* that they sometimes gave us at school. I used to hide the snack at school and bring it home for him, and he would always ask me, "*Glay matti?*," meaning, "A small thing from school?" He was always so happy when I gave it to him. I have liked that cheese since then. All my children love it too, and I have made *Abo walad* many times for them to take with them for their school snacks. But I have never told them the story of Jalal and *Abo walad* until now.

One night in 1981, Jalal complained that he had a pain in his stomach, but he was big and healthy and we did not think much about it at the time. Two or three times he had to go outside to relieve his bowels behind a wall. This was the custom, since we, like most villagers, had no bathroom. After midnight I woke up to find that Jalal was not sleeping near me. So I went outside calling "Jalal *Gian!*" ("Dear Jalal!"), and he responded, "Kaka, I am here." He said his stomach hurt. I asked him why he did not ask Mom for help, and he said that Mother had brought him outside twice already that night and he did not want to wake her up again. I brought him back to bed and he gave me a big kiss—the last thing I would ever receive from him. Then I fell asleep.

I woke up to a great wailing. It was still dark, but everybody was awake and the house was in turmoil. Jalal was lying unconscious with white foam coming out of his nose and mouth.

"Take him to a doctor!" I shouted.

"What doctor?" everyone shouted back at me. "There is no doctor!"

And that was true. There was no doctor, nurse, clinic, hospital, or anything else in the village or in the whole region.

My brother Mohsin said, "We have to get him to a doctor in the city."

Mother was crying. Father wanted to know how we could bring Jalal to the city.

Suddenly I remembered something. "My cousin has a guest from the city staying with them, and he has a car!"

Father said, "Thank you, God," and ran out of the house. He came back with my cousin and the car—but they did not carry Jalal to it.

"What are you waiting for?" I asked.

My cousin said that we could not take Jalal to the city in the dark because there was a curfew on any travel after sundown, and it was still night. If we tried, the Iraqi army that patrolled the area would think that we were *peshmerga* and would shoot us.

Throughout the rest of that long, horrible night, all we could do was remove the foam from Jalal's mouth and try to help him breathe. But only God can give breath. Like all villagers in this situation, we were essentially helpless except to cry and pray and wait for the sunrise.

The car left at dawn, and Jalal was still breathing white foam. Half an hour later the car returned. I was so happy I ran to Father and told him that the car had returned. But he suddenly exploded with grief.

"What is wrong?" I asked, dumbfounded.

"If they brought him back now, it can only be because he is dead,"

Father moaned.

I thought Father was wrong and I ran to the car, but I saw the stricken look on everyone's faces, and then I knew it was true. Mother could not even walk, she was so broken.

"What happened?" I shouted.

"It is Allah's decree," my cousin said as he carried Jalal's body to the house.

Father took Jalal from my cousin and began to cry and kiss him and chant, "Oh Allah, I know this is the test I accepted!"

Finally my cousin took Jalal's body back and said to us, "Don't be sad. He is sinless, and he will be in Paradise where we will see him again, *insha-Allah* (by God's will)." To this day I pray to see Jalal again, and I believe it will happen as it was promised. But never afterwards did my mother and father live a normal life. Hope in their life, and peace in our home, died with Jalal.

After he died, Mother used to cry a lot. This made Father angry because he said she was not accepting the will of God. He would shout, "Cry, cry, cry all you want. Never will that bring him back!" The situation became so bad that the rest of us children told her that if she kept crying, we would all leave home and leave her too. This is what villagers always did in such a situation, but we did not realize that we forced her to cry privately in her heart and to hide her tears from us. We were ignorant and too young to be able to help her. We even added to her burden by saying, "They died, they died. We are going to die too. So why do you cry so much?"

She became weaker. Mother was a Sufi and had many religious songs to express her feelings and her love of God and his messengers, but she was not allowed to sing if men were present. So she used to go out late at night to my grandfather's grave and sing. Unfortunately she sang loudly enough that many people heard her. One day my cousin Hasan told me about Mom's late-night singing, and even played a tape recording of it that he had secretly recorded. I told Mom that if she did it again I would tell Dad and my older brothers, and after that I think she stopped. She was very scared to lose us. She believed that someone had cursed us. Some people's eyes were worse than weapons, she told me. I told her only God could harm or benefit us.

Mom's Amulet

One day Mom brought me an amulet to wear that she said would save me from the evil eye. "It is a prayer, a protection, and you should wear it," she said.

"I don't believe in it," I said.

Mother was immediately fearful that something bad would happen to me for what I had said. "No, no, please, my son, ask forgiveness and put it on."

"Mom! I'm not going to wear that."

She begged me all the harder. I said I wanted to open the amulet and see what was written on it. I told her that if it were a verse from the Qur'an or any prayer, I would wear it, but if not, why should I wear it? She said that the Sheikh who had given her the amulet told her that anyone who opened it would be blinded, since he did not want anyone to know how it was made.

I said, "Mom, nothing in that amulet is going to hurt me. Is this thing more holy than the Qur'an?"

"No," she said.

"So why, when I open the Qur'an, does nothing happen to my eyes?"

"The Qur'an is for reading."

"So what about the amulet?"

"Nobody can open it."

"Why not?"

"Because that is what the Sheikh told me!" Mom said.

I told her that the amulet was just a paper with pictures of eyes and triangles and stars and other things, and that it meant nothing.

"How do you know?"

"I've seen these things before."

"Where?"

"Dad got one for our cow last year."

"Ehhh!" Mom let out an exclamation of surprise. "Did you open it?"

"Yes," I said. "And then I threw it away."

"But the bag is still tied on her horn."

"It is empty," I said. "I opened it and I threw the contents away."

"But why did you put the bag back on the cow's horn?"

"Because I did not want Dad or even you to know."

"What was written on it?"

"Nothing," I said. "Just pictures of eyes, stars, boxes, things like that."

"What about verses from the Qur'an?"

"Nothing from the Qur'an was there, Mom!"

Mother thought for a moment. "But this amulet that I brought you has Qur'anic verses and prayers in it."

"So then if I open it, nothing bad is going to happen to me."

"If you open it," she said, "you will go blind. That is what the Sheikh told me."

"Let me try." I reached for the amulet but she pulled it away.

"I will wear it myself on your behalf," she said.

During the day I saw her wearing the amulet, but at night I used to wake up and find it under my pillow or on my chest. One morning when I found the amulet in my bed, I decided to open it. There was nothing inside that I could read. Later my mother came in and innocently began to look around the room.

"Did you see something lying around here?" she finally asked.

"Like what?"

"The thing."

"What thing?"

"Your prayer."

"Yes, Mom, here it is. I opened it."

"Ehhhh!" She took a deep breath of surprise. "You opened it? What is written in it?"

"Nothing, Mom!"

She looked at the paper full of strange lines. "What are all these verses?"

"Just lines, like cuneiform."

"You don't know how to read it?"

"No, Mom, I don't know how to read it because nothing is written. The one that Dad got for our cow was much better than this. At least that one had pictures of eyes and stars."

She blinked. "How are your eyes? Can you see?"

"I can see fine. Nothing happened when I opened it. I did not go blind." I gestured toward the paper. "Why don't you give it to someone you trust and have them try to read it for you? They will tell you that there are no prayers here."

Mother looked confused and said nothing for awhile. Then she said, "Let's go to the schoolteacher."

"Fine," I said. "We will see what he says."

I asked the teacher to read the paper for my mother.

"Nothing is written here," said the teacher.

"But what are all these things?" asked my mother.

"Just lines and dots," said the teacher. "Nothing more."

"Maybe it is Arabic?" said my mother hopefully.

"There is not even one Arabic letter written here," said the teacher. We thanked him and left the school.

My mother was very confused and scared by all of this. She was still afraid that something bad would happen to us. I told her that we believed in God and the Qur'an, and that the paper with the strange lines was nothing. She kissed and hugged me, recited some verses from the Qur'an, and then blew them onto my face.

"God protect you, my son," she said.

"This at least is good," I said. "I believe in it. Amen."

Mom smiled at me, and I could tell that she felt relieved

Because my mother was from another tribe, the Jaff, she felt herself to be a stranger in Hashazini. She mostly stayed at home and did not even tell her own family what she was going through. Perhaps she felt it would be a shame on the family to say how unhappy she was. In our tribal tradition, a good woman never complained about her husband or her miserable life. And in any event, she knew that there was nothing anyone could do to help her because the situation in her parents' family was no better. Her father was old and sick and lived with Mom's stepmother; complaining to him would have accomplished nothing except to make her father sad. So she suffered in silence and waited for us children to grow up and give her some measure of relief. But none of us were able to give her any help when we grew up, until it was too late.

With My Mother

Since I was one of the youngest, I was often alone with my mother, and in her loneliness she would pour out her story to me. She would place my head on her leg and talk for hours, then cry silently. My mother was a source of kindness and love who balanced the hardness and discipline of my father. Unfortunately my father did not always appreciate this. While my mother was softening my heart, my father was trying to toughen it. Dad was a really strong man and was quick to anger. When he was angry, he would beat me. He was so rough and slapped so hard that we children would sometimes mess our pants in fear. Such beatings were common in the East. Children were beaten in the home, in school, and at work. They grew up in fear and saw violence continually. Eventually fear became part of their personalities. It was not much better for wives. My father would yell at my mother and sometimes humiliate her. She always returned his anger with patience, but she paid a big price for that.

Strangely, my mother was an optimistic person. Her life had been nothing but hard work, problems, sadness, and abuse, and still she looked forward to a better future— not for herself, perhaps, but for her children. Now I see that she really only lived for us children. She took no pleasure for herself and gave us everything that we needed first, before she took anything for herself. Since there was not enough to go around she was always short-changing herself, and so she became weaker and weaker. Now I feel guilty when I think of the number of times I was hungry and demanded food, and she told me to take any food I liked from her plate. But as a child, I did not understand that a person—a mother—would give up her life so that her children could live. I was so focused on surviving in the violence all around me that I did not understand that the person I loved most was slowly giving up her life for me.

Mother's only real desire was to see us obtain an education, develop careers, and give her grandchildren. She wanted us to have all the things she did not have. She died before she was able to see any of the dreams she lived for, but perhaps she had already seen them. She used to say to me that God would do everything for us, even if now we could not see how. In her heart I think she knew that God would protect us.

The most beautiful times I remember from my early childhood with my mom were the sunny winter days when she used to place a blanket in the backyard in the sun with a basket of dates. I would lie on the blanket with my head on her leg, and she would tell me traditional stories and talk to me about what she wanted me to be in the future. Sometimes she would even give me a piece of candy that she had saved from the Eid celebration at the end of Ramadan. My two older brothers, Ibrahim and Mohsin, were in school, and Father was at work, so it was just the two of us.

While Mom talked, she worked on patching a pile of old clothing. Or she spun thread out of raw cotton. And eventually, after I had fallen asleep on her leg, she would kiss me many times very softly, and I would pretend that I had not woken up because I did not want that warm, soft, safe, beautiful moment in the sun with her to end. Never have I found a bed as comfortable as that blanket in the sun. The love that Mom gave me, the concern that I read in her eyes, the suffering that I saw in her face, taught me without any words being spoken many things that I needed to know about life.

In 1989, I wrote a poem about the strange contrast in our lives between innocent maternal love and continual violence.

Tableau

The beautiful Kurdish baby
Was nursing at his mother's breast

Under the warm rays of the sun
While his mother quietly watched him
Thinking of his future
Hoping he would grow up faster.

Like a sudden crash of thunder
An army of hatred and evil
Rushed into the village
Kidnapped the baby
And dragged the mother with them,
Away to prison.

After my brother Jalal died in 1981, both my parents became weaker. The war with Iran had started, and food was hard to get. Their health was poor, and without their strength to work we all sank deeper into poverty. They began to fight more. If it were not for their belief that they were being tested by God, I think they would have lost their minds completely. Neither my brother Mohsin nor I were able to do anything to help them. If we opened our mouths to say anything, Father would beat us. When they started to argue, Mohsin would begin to cry and tell them, "Please! Please! Stop!" Sometimes I used to pull Mom away and take her outside the house. Now I understand that it was not really their fault. Grief, especially when it is hidden, causes anger, but so does hunger and stress and poverty and illness. But at the time, our lives as children were in turmoil because our parents' lives were in turmoil, and there was nothing we could do to stop the violence. And there was no outside help: no doctors, nursing homes, or health care.

Separation

In 1984, my mother left my father and went to live with her sister in her village, Harena. I was fourteen at the time, and I stayed with Father, who was sick, to take care of him. But I was angry with my mother for leaving us. In our tradition, a mother never leaves her husband or children, so it was a scandal when she did. It brought shame to the whole family. I did not understand that she was very sick, and that perhaps she wanted to save me from the pain and the continual arguments every day. She knew that we were teenagers, that we understood what the arguments were about, and that the anger would remain with us and would eventually shape us. And perhaps she just could not take it anymore.

About a year after Mother left, my brother Mohsin and I got a promise from Father that he would forgive her. Father said that if we brought her back home he would not bother her anymore with any bad words and would not blame her for anything that had happened in the past. So Mohsin and I left for Harena, which was about a ten-hour walk from Hashazini, to get Mother and bring her home.

We started before sunrise and arrived in the late afternoon. But when I finally saw my mother, I did not recognize her. She was sitting outside on the ground, leaning against a wall, looking at the sun. Her face was as white as a piece of paper, and she did not appear to have any blood in her. She was not even fifty years old but she could not have weighed more than sixty pounds. She was nothing but bones.

I looked at my aunt, and she said it was Mom, so I went to her and said, "Peace be upon you, Mom." She turned her face toward me in surprise and gave me a big smile of recognition. She reached out her hand so I would sit beside her, and for the next ten minutes she did not stop hugging and kissing me, or crying. Finally I said, "Mom, Mohsin is here also," and then she let go of me and began kissing Mohsin. Eventually we both said, "Mom, please! Enough!"

"Thank God I saw you before I die," she said.

We wanted her to stand up but she could not, so we had to help her inside.

"How did you get here?" she asked.

"We walked."

"Who brought you?"

"We came ourselves."

"How did you find this place?"

"We asked directions."

"Thank God," she said.

I told her, "Dad promised never to bother you again, and he will not ask you to do anything, and you don't even have to speak with him. All you have to do is come back home with us."

And Mohsin said, "You just have to promise to come back with us, but if you don't we will turn around and go back right now."

Mother said, "Sit now, Mohsin."

"Only if you promise us," Mohsin said.

"I'm sorry," Mother said. "I can't."

Mohsin angrily said that he was going back, and told me to come with him.

"How will you go by night?" asked Mother.

We told her we would just go.

She began to cry and called out to her sister to stop us from going back.

I did not know what to do. We had been walking all day. I did not know the way home in the dark, and it was not safe to go. But our tribal custom required that we leave if she would not promise to come back with us. We were still angry at her for leaving us and breaking our custom and for bringing shame on the family. We were ignorant and did not try to understand her broken heart and health. We did not show any feelings or mercy to her. We did not even acknowledge that we were her children. Instead we tried to show that we were men now, real tough villagers.

We said, "If you do not come back with us, you are not our mom."

She just looked at us. And I suddenly realized that she could not speak words anymore. She could only speak with her eyes. Her eyes were saying, "This is not fair. I *am* your mother. Look at me! I can't walk. I can't take any more of this. Enough is enough!" I saw all of this in her eyes, and I knew in my heart she was right, but my training in tribal custom told me to cover my mind, kill my feelings, and enforce the tradition—to be proud and ignorant. After my aunt interceded, Mohsin and I agreed to stay the night, but we refused to talk any more with Mother.

I woke up in the middle of the night. Mohsin and I were sleeping together on the floor, as was our custom, but Mother was sitting between us, with one hand on my head and the other on Mohsin's. I looked at her and she smiled at me, but I turned my face away and closed my eyes, pretending to be sleeping. All night she sat between us with her hands on our chests, praying. I was listening, but I did not want her to know I was awake. She did not sleep all night, she did not stop praying, and she did not stop crying. From time to time she would put her head on my chest, or on Mohsin's, and kiss us.

When we woke up, Mother was on her prayer rug. She looked at us with eyes full of tears, but she smiled and said "Good morning!" We did not answer her, and instead asked if she was coming back with us or not. The only answer we received was more tears and the look in her eyes. My aunt called us to breakfast. We said we did not want any; we were going back. My aunt begged us not to go. Mother came to the door and opened her hands to give us a hug and say goodbye. We just stood there looking at her, and then we turned away and started walking home. The last words I ever heard from her were, "God be with you. God protect you."

Later that year, we brought my sister Aaisha back to Hashazini to take care of Dad. At that time I was a student in Chamchamal, but because Dad was sick and it was during the Iran-Iraq war, our poverty became so heavy that I left school and went to southern Iraq to work and support the family. Every two or three months I would come back to Hashazini and bring them whatever money I had saved. I would stay there one or two weeks and then go back to work.

In 1986, on my way home from southern Iraq to visit the family, when I reached Chamchamal I saw my neighbor Kak Najat. He came over to me and said, "I am very sorry. God forgive her!" I didn't know why he'd said that, and I asked who had died. He realized that I didn't know. At first he did not want to tell me, then he tried to conceal it, but I begged him to tell me the truth. So he said that he heard my mother had died.

I was shocked. I asked when this had happened. He said that she had died two months ago.

I was astonished. Nobody had told me. I never participated in her funeral. I never had a chance to say goodbye. Perhaps her family was angry with us because of the way we had treated her. Or perhaps they had tried to tell me and the message did not get through. There were no telephones we could use in those days, no post office or telegraph. Messages were passed along from one person to another, but they were not always delivered.

That night, instead of going home to Hashazini, I took a bus to Sulaimaniya, where my Mom's half-sisters and her stepmother lived. When they saw me, my aunts started crying. I asked, "Where is my mother?" and one of the aunts said, "If you had a mother, you should know where she is. Don't cry now; it is too late." But another aunt stopped her and said, "Yes, she was his mom. She loved him a lot." We all started crying again. She told me that my mother's last words were that she loved us, forgave us, and asked our forgiveness. Mom had wanted us to finish college, get our degrees, and to marry and have children. She had asked my aunt to kiss us, and asked that we visit her grave.

I stayed that night with my four aunts, and in between the tears they told me about my mother. They understood our hard situation, and they realized that I was still too young to be blamed for what my father had done. But to this day, I do not know exactly where my mother's grave is. My aunts only said that she was buried in Saywan Cemetery, a big, famous cemetery in Sulaimaniya, but many years later when I went to find her grave, I searched for a long time but could not find it. Afterwards, I wrote this poem:

> O Saywan Hill —
> I am here looking for my mom's grave.
> Please tell me where it is.
>
> I am really sorry.
> I have all the stories,
> I want to tell them to my mom.
>
> Mommy, can you hear me?
> I am very glad,

Thanking Almighty God
That you have lain down
In Saywan,
The hill of dignity,
The home of Kurdish poets,
The land of the murdered *peshmerga,*
The place of great scholars.

When I went back home, my dad was even sorrier than my aunts. He cried like a woman when he saw me; I was surprised that my father would cry like that. He said that he was sorry, and that he forgave my mom.

Now I have a great deal that I want to tell my mother: how sorry I am that I could not have helped her more; that now I understand how difficult life was for her; that I wish she could have seen some of her dreams come true; that I pray to God to forgive her and take her to Paradise. God willing, I will see her again and we can be reconciled. She used to say to us that only when you get your children will you understand what it means to be a mother or a father. She was right. Now I know; but it is too late.

The Rest of My Family

Some of my older brothers and sisters had different mothers. All of them have stories in their own right. Let me introduce them to you.

My Sisters
Aaisha

Aaisha, my oldest stepsister, was born in 1935 and was the daughter of my father's first wife. She was thirty-five years older than I. Hers was a typical woman's life in a tribal society at that time, and she became a victim of tribal law, which forced her to live her life in sorrow. (I often think that we should call it "trouble" law, not tribal law, because of all the problems it gives the people, especially women.) Aaisha was a very quiet, clean, kind, helpful woman and hard worker. At that time no education was available in the villages for most children, but if anyone had an opportunity to send his child to school, he would send a boy rather than a girl. Aaisha had absolutely no opportunity for education, and she never even learned to read or write.

When her mother died, and my father remarried, she had to live with her stepmother, my father's second wife. In the custom of our tribe, stepmothers are very hard on stepchildren, to the extent that you can say stepchildren are actually tortured and punished for having lost their mothers. And under tribal law, no woman from the Barzingi family was allowed to marry a man from another tribe; she could only marry someone whose roots went back to Quraish, the family of the Prophet Mohammad.

Because of all the violence and killing in Kurdistan at the time, there were fewer men than women, and the number of Quraish men available for marriage was very small. Our tribe was also prouder and richer than other tribes, and the women were expected to marry a rich man with a house and an education. If a suitable rich Quraish man could not be found, women in my family and in the tribe were forced to stay single all of their lives. The custom was even more unfair because Barzingi men could marry women from another tribe, and the Quraish men who did this reduced the number of men who could marry women from our tribe. Many of my female cousins, who are now old, never had an opportunity during their lives to marry. Instead they were exploited as laborers, sometimes in the fields, but in our tribe more often as home servants.

While she was growing up, Aaisha became sick. Her health was so bad that my father finally sent her to my cousin Sheikh Umar, who lived in Kirkuk, so she could go to the hospital there. At that time there was no health care in the villages. Many children died young from malaria or other such diseases, or simply from cold weather and lack of proper food. After two months of better food and care Aaisha's health improved, but she did not want to come home because of the hard life in the village, and also because of the abuse she received from her stepmother.

My father was very rigid about tribal rules, and under normal circumstances he would not have permitted his daughter to stay in someone else's house. However, because Sheikh Umar was his nephew, and a very religious man and an Imam, my father accepted the arrangement. So until the death of my mother, Aaisha stayed in my cousin's home and served his family. After my mother left my father in 1984, we needed Aaisha to come back and help my father and cook for us, which she did.

To this day I do not understand why Aaisha was not given an opportunity to marry. Sheikh Umar should have been able to find a suitable husband for her. I think she was just a victim of the custom that she could only marry someone from the Barzingi family. It bothers me that people do things in the name of religion that in reality are simply matters of custom. In fact, many tribal traditions and customs are completely contrary to the practice of Islam. It is just ignorance. Like many women, my sister had to pay for this ignorance all her life.

Nathifa

Nathifa is my next-oldest stepsister, the daughter of my father's second wife. She was born in 1950, and her life was not much better than Aaisha's. Nathifa was lucky to be married, but her husband was a strange, violent, mentally unstable man with two small children from a prior marriage. In 1970, he had divorced his first wife, who also happened to be his cousin, and he then had to take care of his two small children (in our Kurdish custom, when a man divorces his wife, he, not she, takes the children). My father wanted to help him take care of his children by giving Nathifa to him, and in return Nathifa's husband gave his three-year-old daughter Nasreen to be married to my eight-year-old brother Issa. But when he got older, Issa refused to marry Nasreen, even though my father tried hard to persuade him. He was living in Sulaimaniya and looking for an educated, modern wife, not a villager.

This practice of exchanging girls for marriage existed in Arabia before the time of Mohammad, and somehow it must have been brought to Kurdistan by the Arabs. Mohammad, may peace be upon him, prohibited the practice in Islam, but unfortunately our Kurdish customs were never changed to reflect the teachings of the Prophet. It was very unfair to the women because they were given in marriage as children without having any say in the matter, and they did not even receive any gold or a house or clothing for the marriage because the bride price had already been paid by the exchange of the women. It was really just a way for two poor fathers to marry off their daughters cheaply. This is another example of how ignorant traditions prevent Islam from reaching the people. It is like the buying and selling of slaves, or cattle. Worse than that, people would give women to another family as ransom for an injury or murder. For example, if you killed or injured someone and your family wanted to prevent a blood feud, you would give one or more of the women in your family to the family of the victim as a form of payment. You can imagine how these women were treated—they were lucky if they were treated merely like slaves, instead of like the enemy. This practice still goes on in various forms today, where poor families try to give a daughter in marriage to someone living in Europe so they can get some money from her and maybe one day be allowed to go to Europe. There are too many sad stories of what ultimately happens, and in each case it is the woman who is the victim.

So Nathifa was given to her husband in a sort of "bargain and sale," and she suffered all her life as a result of it. Even my mother had a better situation with my father than Nathifa did with her husband: he was extremely religious, but with no knowledge. It is my experience that religion practiced by ignorant people can be very dangerous. Every day he abused my sister. Under tribal rule, a man had to prove he was a man by how harshly he treated his wife. It was considered a shame if he spoke softly to her or helped her in any work around the home. A man never cooked or washed a dish or cleaned the house. He sat like a king and ordered his wife around by yelling at her and insulting her, and by this he proved he was a man! And the woman had to pretend that she enjoyed this abuse and had to accept an occasional beating like a child, because if she did not, people would say she was a rebel.

Nathifa was much more obedient than my mother. She worked all day on the farm to take care of her husband and his two children. She milked his sheep, fed two or three cows, took care of the chickens, cooked and made bread, catered to his guests—all without benefit of any machines, and all she received for it was abuse. Yet no matter how badly her husband abused her, Nathifa never complained or tried to leave him. Whenever people talked about her violent husband and his mental problems, Nathifa would get mad and defend him. If not for her, the villagers probably would have stoned him to death. But for her part, staying married might have been the best of her alternatives. In our Kurdish custom, it is almost impossible for a divorced woman to remarry, unless the man is very old or sick, and a single woman has a very difficult time surviving unless she is willing to labor for some other man.

Nathifa lived in Hashazini, so I saw her fairly often. She was the closest person to me. Whenever I was hungry I used to go to her, and she always had an egg or a glass of milk for me. Sometimes when my father was really angry, I used to run away and stay with her for days until my father calmed down.

In 1989 during the Anfal attack, the government's troops overwhelmed our village and demolished it. Nathifa, her husband, and their five children between the ages of one and fourteen had to flee to Chamchamal, and they lost everything—all their animals, the farm, their house, their possessions. They all had to hide in a small house belonging to one of my Uncle SayGul's followers, because the government would have arrested them if they had found them in Chamchamal. Nathifa's husband had no work, and it was very difficult for women to find a job, since our culture frowned upon this. Fortunately, Nathifa was both a clever woman and a professional seamstress. She went to five or six tailors and obtained customer orders that she could bring home for sewing. She also made bread to sell in the market. In this way she supported her family while hiding out from the government—until 1991, when the Kurds revolted against the Iraqi government. After that time, Nathifa opened a store in the back of the house. She ran it with her children. By that time she had three more children, so the family now numbered ten. In 1994 her husband died and left her with the eight children, three of whom were under five years old. She struggled on as best she could, and I think she hoped that when I came to the U.S. in 1999 I would find some way to lighten her burden. But I was not able to do anything to help her miserable life. She gave me so much, and I gave nothing back. The last time we spoke by telephone, she cried and told me that the only thing she needed was to see me back in Kurdistan again.

Aisha

After Father's second wife died, he married another woman who already had a daughter, Aisha, so she is my third-oldest stepsister. (Eventually Father's third wife had a son, my stepbrother Issa. Soon after Issa was born the third wife died, and father married my mother.) Aisha was actually like a real sister. It became a joke among my friends that I had two sisters by the same name, and they asked me why that was. I told them to figure it out: "Aisha is not my Mom's daughter; she is not my father's daughter; she is not my foster sister; and she is not an adopted sister. So who is she?" They would laugh and say, "She must be your sister in Islam" (since all men are already brothers in Islam). All of my brothers and I had a great deal of affection for Aisha; we called her *Dada*, which means "big sister."

Aisha eventually married Ishmail Barzingi, who is a famous actor in Kurdistan. He produced what I believe was the first Kurdish film in Iraq. Aisha has eight beautiful, smart children. There is a funny story about them. Once they all were watching a film on TV that starred Ishmail, their father. Aisha was sleeping in the back room. The movie was very dramatic, and at the end Ishmail's character was killed—and all of the children started to cry. Aisha woke up and ran in to find out what was the matter.

"What's wrong? What happened? Why are you all crying?" she asked.

"Our dad, our dad!" they cried.

"What happened to your dad?"

"They killed him."

"What!!" hollered Aisha. "Who told you this? Did someone call?"

"We saw it ourselves."

"What did you see?"

"They killed our dad!"

"Where did you see this?"

"On the TV!" the children shouted.

Aisha started to laugh so hard she could hardly talk. "But that is not real."

The children insisted, "By God, it *was* real! We heard him shout and saw the blood. His friend pulled his body up and started crying too. We saw it!"

Aisha had to kiss and comfort them and explain to them over and over that it was just a film, and that it only *looked* real.

We used to wait for Aisha to visit Hashazini; even more, we wanted to visit her in the city. When she came she always brought us clothes—which made us all feel proud, because none of our friends in the village had such clothes. Even after we grew up, she continued to be our beloved sister, and her children called my brothers and me "Uncle."

My Brothers
Issa

Issa, my oldest living stepbrother, was born in 1962. He was two when his mother died and Father married my mother. This left Issa at the mercy of a stepmother. Stepmothers in our culture have a reputation for being very mean. Kurds say that according to religion, an orphan is someone who loses his father before adulthood, but the real orphan is the child who loses his mother. But my mother truly loved Issa, and he loved her. Mom would always praise Issa to me, telling me what a pure heart he had and how kind he was, and how he was going to help us all when he grew up because he had so much mercy in his heart.

I was two years old when Issa finished primary school in Hashazini. Since there was no higher education available in the region, he moved to Sulaimaniya at the age of eleven so he could live with his sister and uncle and attend the middle school and high school there. Eventually he finished high school in Sulaimaniya and went for a time into construction, where he was quite successful. Later he graduated from the health institute in Sulaimaniya. In 1981 he married, and that same year he took me into his house after I had finished primary school in Hashazini so I could continue middle school and high school in Sulaimaniya as he had done. I stayed with him only one year, to finish seventh grade, and then I moved to Chamchamal to continue my education.

I remember one time around 1978, when Issa came home to Hashazini to visit. We always woke up early because Father would beat us if we slept after sunrise. But there was Issa sleeping beside me, and it was well after sunrise; evidently Dad had let him sleep as though he were a guest in the house. Jaleel, one of Issa's friends from down the block, called to me. "Yassin! Is Issa home?"

"Yes," I shouted back.

"Call him for me!"

"No, he is still sleeping!"

"Well, wake him up. It is almost noon."

"No!" I shouted as loudly as I could. "I am not waking him up!!"

Just then Issa opened his eyes and laughed. "Sky's Son! You are not going to wake me up?" After that, whenever he joked with me he would always shout at me as loudly as he could: "No, by God, I am not waking him up!!" He called me Sky's Son because he believed that we have all fallen from the sky onto the earth, and we have no one to help us.

Gas in the Car

When I first went to live with Issa in Sulaimaniya, he was going to college and owned a taxi. One day he gave me a gallon of gas and told me to put it into the taxi before I went to school. I was excited to do something like this, something I had never done before. I opened the hood and poured the gas into the engine—where the oil is supposed to go. I went into the house and told Issa I had done what he'd asked, and then I went off to school. But when I came back from school, Issa was still at home.

"Why are you still here?" I asked.

"The car is not working, and I don't know what's wrong," he said. "It doesn't run, and black smoke is coming out everywhere."

"I told you this was not a good car."

Issa gave me a stern look and said, "So buy me a new car, wise guy. I'd like to have a nice car too. Did you put in the gas I gave you?"

"Yes."

"Where did you put it?"

"I told you earlier, I put it in the car, as you asked."

"I know, but where in the car did you put it?" he said.

I opened the hood and showed him.

"You put the gas in *there*?" he asked in surprise. "Are you joking?" Then he raised his hands and beat his head as hard as he could.

"No, by God, I did," I said.

"Sky's Son, how could you have put gas in the engine?"

"Well, where else am I supposed to put it?" I retorted.

And then Issa realized that in all my eleven years in Hashazini, I had never been in a car before; I had never even touched a car; and he felt sorry for me and hugged me and said, "It is my fault. I never showed you what to do. I thought that you knew." And then he showed me the gas tank and engine, and where oil is taken out and where gas is put in, and how to check the oil level, and all sorts of other details about car maintenance. I told him what Father used to say, that what you learn from your mistakes you will never forget, and Issa smiled at me and gave me a kiss.

As Issa went through college, he was exposed to intellectuals, writers, and publishers, and was affected by both Marxism and nationalism at the same time. In 1982 he started work with the PUK and abandoned anything having to do with Islam. My father was very sad when he heard about this and pleaded with him, saying, "Dear son, when will you return to God and start your prayers again?" Issa used to laugh at Father and would answer in Kurdish, saying, "The wolf's return is its death," which made Father laugh too, because it meant that we will never give up the struggle until we die. It also meant that the wolf is alone in the world, and dangerous, and will never change or give up its character.

But in 1996, Issa gave up the struggle and left Kurdistan to seek refuge in The Netherlands. He hoped to be given permanent status there so he could bring over his wife and two sons. Instead he ended up in a refugee nightmare. For eight years he was denied status, kept in a series of temporary camps, and not allowed to work or even own property. So once again he gave up the struggle and returned to his family in Kurdistan. He was a large fat man when he left, but I was told that he returned skinny. He now runs a hospital in Sulaimaniya, where he lives with his family.

But still there was a bit of the wolf in Issa that refused to change. He and some of my cousins got together to prevent one of my female cousins, Mzda, from marrying a man who was not from the Barzingi tribe—notwithstanding that she wanted to marry him. They beat the man and threatened him until he was too afraid to go through with the wedding. When I refused to support them in suppressing my cousin's right to marry, they accused me of not respecting my family's values and claimed that I was not a real Muslim! In modern Kurdistan, it has become fashionable for "educated" people to deny Islam and to claim that Islam is the reason for all the tragedy and ignorance of our country. But here you had "educated" people—and Socialists, no less—perpetuating ignorant customs that brought tragedy upon people, while Islam would have liberated their thinking.

Ibrahim

Ibrahim, my mother's first child, was born in 1966. I did not see much of Ibrahim in my early life for the same reasons that I did not see much of Issa. After Ibrahim finished primary school around 1978, he left our village and went to Kirkuk for higher education, where he lived with my sister Aaisha while she was serving in my cousin Sheikh Umar's house. Eventually Ibrahim moved in with Issa in Sulaimaniya, finished high school, and graduated from the health institute there. People respected him and called him Dr. Ibrahim. I don't know why both he and Issa went to the health institute; perhaps it was because of all the children who died for lack of health facilities in the villages.

Ibrahim always had a book in his hand, and he was always reading. When he finished with a book he would give it to me to read, and he even bought some books just for me. It was from Ibrahim that I learned to love reading and to love poetry. He later published many articles in newspapers and magazines. He was very smart, but he was a loner. He did not like to talk to people or to joke or have fun. Instead he was serious, always reading alone, always thinking. People thought he was arrogant, but I knew him better, and I realized that in books he could enjoy worlds in his head that his eyes could not see in reality.

As he ignored people and the reality around him, he began to drift away from our customs and traditions. I used to argue with him. "You have to deal with reality!" I would say. "You have to talk to people and understand their lives, otherwise you will not be able to change anything. Nobody gets any benefit from your reading if you don't share it." But Ibrahim did not change until after he graduated from the health institute. After that, because of his job in the clinic and hospital, he became the best friend of the villagers and eventually moved back to Hashazini.

One night around midnight I was awakened by a knock at the door. When I answered it, two people with guns were standing there and asked if this was Dr. Ibrahim's house. They said that they were *peshmerga* and that they had an injured brother who needed treatment. They asked me to please get Dr. Ibrahim.

I did not know what to say. Should I even say that this was his house? How did I know who they really were? Perhaps this was a trick by the government to see what we would do. If I said no, perhaps they would come in and search the house. So I said to them, "Where is the injured man?"

"Outside on the donkey cart," they said.

"Take him to the clinic," I told them. "Wait outside and Ibrahim will come in ten minutes."

When they left, I tended to believe they were *peshmerga*, but still I told Ibrahim not to go right away. I told him I would call my cousin Sherzad, who had a gun, and he would come with us to protect us. Eventually we set off for the clinic—Sherzad and I in front with the gun, Ibrahim behind us.

When we arrived, I recognized two of the people as being *peshmerga*, and so I felt better about the meeting. The injured man had a big hole in his leg, and his belly was slit open. We had no anesthesia or antiseptic, so Ibrahim just started sewing up the man's belly so his guts would not fall out. The man opened his eyes at one point and said, "Doctor, you look just like you are sewing up a shirt." I couldn't help myself and started to laugh. To this day, whenever I see Ibrahim I tell him, "Doctor, you look like you are sewing a shirt."

In 1987, Ibrahim joined PUK and became a *peshmerga* himself. In 1988, when Saddam launched his genocidal Anfal attack that destroyed our village and over 1,200 others, many of the *peshmerga* were killed, and others laid down their guns and surrendered to the *Jash* (border guard units organized by tribal leaders). Some sought refuge in the mountains of Iranian Kurdistan. Ibrahim was one of those who went to the mountains. We did not know where he was from 1987 until 1991, and we did not know if he had been killed or not. If the government found out that he was with the *peshmerga,* our whole family could have been arrested. But in 1991, when the Kurdish uprising drove the Iraqi army temporarily out of Kurdistan, Ibrahim suddenly appeared in Chamchamal one day, where we were living, and only then did we finally know he was safe.

I was very proud of what Ibrahim had done. The four years that he had lived with the *peshmerga* in the mountains and treated their wounds as their doctor was the most dangerous and difficult period in the whole Kurdish revolution. I never believed that Ibrahim was strong enough to do that, but he was, and he did.

My Uncle Uthman, my mother's brother, was also *peshmerga,* but he died in the Anfal operation. A friend sent his mother a letter telling about his death. His mother refused to believe that he had died because she never saw his body, never got it back, and never was taken to his grave. The friend only said that he had been buried somewhere in the mountains at the beginning of the Anfal campaign. Like so many other Kurds, he lies in an unmarked grave in the mountains of Kurdistan. We say in Kurdistan that under every single rock there lies a Kurdish body, and every flower grows there because of our blood.

In 1992, Ibrahim married and moved to Chamchamal. I was also living in Chamchamal at the time, so I moved in with him. My brother

Mohsin and my sister Aisha joined us. Suddenly we were all living together as a family again, free in our city, with Ibrahim playing the traditional family role of big brother and father. It was a beautiful time in my life. This had been the hope of Mom and Dad, and now we had achieved it. But both Mom and Dad were dead, and we felt their absence, just as we missed Jalal and Salma. Without all of them, we knew that the family could never really be complete again.

Mohsin

Mohsin was the only brother I really grew up with as a child. He was only one year older than I was, and we did everything together: cried, laughed, ate, played, fought, suffered, and grew together, because we shared the same parents, home, and village. My father never called him Mohsin, but always called him Mussa, which means Moses.

In 1979 we had a very old, ugly, sick goat whose nose was always running, and we kept waiting for it to die. One day my father called us to help him slaughter the goat; we had to hold it while Father slit its throat. Then we had to hold it again while he skinned it and cut it up into pieces. Then Mother cooked some of the pieces. Mohsin and I were shocked by all that we saw, and after that we could never eat red meat. If children ever knew how animals were slaughtered, they never would eat meat. No matter how hard father punished us, he could never get us to eat red meat again.

Both Mohsin and I loved to play soccer. But Mohsin was a much better player than I was. He was usually the captain of the village team. Both of us were always coming home late. Whenever Father needed us, or it was time to pray at the mosque, we were out playing soccer. We were punished so often that one punishment ran into the next. Sometimes we were not allowed to play for a whole month. But soccer was worth all the punishment. Some of my best memories are of our village team winning a game because of Mohsin's goal, with all the villagers clapping and chanting "Mohsin! Mohsin! Mohsin!"

Mohsin was very vain about his appearance (although I didn't care about mine). He liked to have nice clothes, and he even carried a mirror with him to check on his hair, to which he applied oil. I think he was embarrassed to walk with me because we looked so different. He was thin, while I was plump. He liked to eat things that tasted sour, such as lemons, while I liked sweet things. I loved to read books, but Mohsin avoided them.

Extended Family
Marf

Marf was the son of my cousin Sheikh Umar (who was himself Sheikh SayGul's son). Once Marf gave Mohsin a book of short stories to read.

"Why should I read this?" asked Mohsin.

"So you can learn something," Marf replied.

"I don't want to learn and become blind like you from all your reading," Mohsin replied. "What is the benefit?"

Marf just shook his head and said, "I wish I was ignorant like you." Marf and all well-educated people knew that in Iraq, the more knowledge you had, the more trouble you would have, and the less peace of mind, because you would always see the huge gap between how things should be and how things really were. Only guns and money seemed to get things done. Ignorance protected us from stress and despair, while thinking always brought us back to reality and all its problems. This reminds me of what the Persian poet wrote:

> In this world, no one is without sorrow and compassion.
> If there is such a man, he would not be human.

Another Arab poet, Ahmad Matar, wrote:

> In any Arab country,
> If an educated person
> Shows any sign of his intelligence,
> He is a fool!

He is a fool because the authorities will arrest him and he will "disappear." Instead, an educated man should close his eyes and shut his mouth and carry a gun, rather than a book and a pen, and speak the truth in order to be safe.

Marf played a big role in our family. He was highly educated, having graduated from college in Baghdad, and was a well-known poet who published a few books and articles. He was arrested while he was in college for his poetry and subversive activities. While in prison, he wrote a collection of poems that was later published as a book, *Prison Sun*. Later he went to the mountains to support the *peshmerga* and founded a magazine, *Qandeel*, to support the Kurdish revolution. Eventually, because of his political opinions, he was forced to leave Kurdistan and went to Ukraine in what was then the Soviet Union, where he obtained his master's degree in 1990. For his degree, he wrote about Anfal, the Iraqi government's Kurdish genocide. In 1994 he received a Ph.D. in international law. But he found conditions in Ukraine so horrible, with suffering everywhere and no freedom, that he left both the country and Marxism and went to Belgium.

As a lawyer, Marf played a big role in proving the Anfal genocide against the Kurds, and he participated in many conferences in the U.S. and Europe. Now he lives in Sulaimaniya and teaches at the university there. It was Marf and another cousin, Ahmad (who also taught at the university), who insisted that our family send us to school and who made sure that all of the children of our generation were well educated. By Marf's courage, he made our education possible, allowing all of us to escape the poverty of our villages.

Insane Hussain

I must also mention one of the most notable and unusual members of my extended family, my cousin "Insane Hussain," the son of my Uncle Saeed. Hussain was a brilliant student and was always first in his class. But it was his tragic mistake to fall madly in love with a girl named Garibah from another village. He told his family that he wanted to marry Garibah, but they would not permit it because she was from another tribe and the daughter of a poor and insignificant man, and his parents thought that he would be marrying below his level. His father wanted him to marry someone from the Faumas tribe, a big family in town. Hussain tried everything to change their minds, but he was unsuccessful. He made his plea worse by claiming he was in love with Garibah, which was a completely unacceptable argument for marriage in those days. By refusing permission, his father may have been punishing him for his presumption in appealing to love.

But when Garibah was finally convinced that Hussain could never marry her, she committed suicide, taking with her Hussain's heart and mind. Hussain went insane. He did not know the difference between hot and cold, clean or dirty, good or bad. He began to wander the streets, a cigarette always in his hand, singing in a very beautiful voice for Garibah and her love:

> Oh stranger, Garibah, please don't go
> My dear, don't leave me alone
> Stay here and sit down
> Let me put my head on your leg
> Allow me to look in your eyes
> Let me tell you my whole story.

We used to see Hussain daily as he wandered in Hashazini, and we would listen to his song of forbidden love destroyed. Some people cried to hear him and gave him cigarettes so he would sing more. To us young men, there was something wonderful about Hussain's escape from reality, and we were drawn to him the way teenagers today are drawn to music and parks and tea shops. Hussain in his insanity was free to dream, to live in another, sadder, more beautiful world, while we always had to work and suffer in the misery all around us. Many people in the village used to say to him that they wanted to be like him—no more concerns! Spending time with Hussain was a chance, for just a few minutes, to experience his enticing dream and to thrill with the romantic idea of remaking the world. For us young people, Hussain and soccer were the only two pleasures we had in life. The rest was just struggling.

Suicide is not allowed in Islam under any circumstances, and so, notwithstanding the harsh conditions of that time, it was uncommon for someone to commit suicide. The only suicides that people knew about were usually caused by some kind of sexual abuse, so most were women. A woman might commit suicide if she could not marry the man who loved her, or if she was forced to marry someone very old and sick, or if she was pregnant from or had lost her virginity by rape.

Sheikh Sadradin

The present leader of our tribe is Sheikh Sadradin, the son of my Uncle Mahmood. Sheikh Sadradin is an example of a true Kurd—simple, strong, and generous. He is cultured and educated and an excellent communicator. When he is in Kirkuk, where he normally lives, he lives as a modern man, but when he is in the village he is a tribal leader who can really relate to the people.

Unfortunately, Sufism has had a great influence on him. My family is Sufi, and so are many other people in our tribe. The Sufis are a spiritual, mystical branch of Islam. The Sufi poet Rumi is well known in the West for his ecstatic poems of praise to the one universal God. But at the other extreme, Sufis often hold strange or even bizarre ceremonies to induce a spiritual or mystical trance or atmosphere. The whirling dervishes of Turkey, for example, spin rapidly around in a mystical dance until they enter a trance. I know of Sufis who carry snakes, or eat glass, or beat themselves with a sword to prove that they have been saved by a miracle. Sheikh Sadradin has tried to hold onto some of these old traditions in modern life, but they have not helped him to lead our tribe in the way my Uncle SayGul did.

One day in 1983, Sheikh Sadradin took me with him as he drove to the village of Kripchna, where the most famous Sheikh in all of Iraq was living. With us in the car were three Sufis. Mostly the Sufis spoke Arabic, which I did not understand, but Sheikh Sadradin did and was joking with them. At the last checkpoint before we reached Kripchna, soldiers stopped us and asked for our identity papers. The Sufis said that they were followers of Sheikh Abdul Karim Kaznazani, and that they had put a green flag on the car and the Sheikh's picture in the car's window to identify themselves this way, but the soldiers still insisted on identity papers.

I was sitting in the back seat with two of the Sufis, and the other one was in the front seat. The Sufi on my right put his hand in his pocket, apparently to take out his identity papers, and retrieved a small bag. The soldier rested his arm on the car's window and leaned his head into the car to examine the contents of the bag.

The Sufi opened the bag and drew out—a snake, which he handed to the startled soldier, saying, "Take this! It is my identity! I am Darwesh!" (which means Sufi). The soldier immediately jumped back, well away from the car, and waived us frantically through, saying, "Please go! Please go! It's OK. For God's sake, for Sheikh's sake, just go!" As we drove off, the Sufi was hanging out the window, still trying to hand the snake to the soldier, saying, "Take it, please, it is my identity." Sheikh Sadradin laughed for the next ten miles until we arrived at Kripchna.

We Kurds have paid a very high price for our ancient customs and traditions. Ignorance was forced on us as a religion and made a part of Islam, although true Islam is always opposed to such ignorance. The uprising in 1991 was the beginning of a new life for the Kurds in Iraq. After much struggling we now have a measure of freedom, and life in Kurdistan is changing—changing very fast. Finally we have access to the outside world. We have satellite TV, radio, and telephones. We have the Internet and books, Kurdish newspapers and magazines. Foreign influences are pouring in and tribal influences are weakening. People no longer blindly follow tribal customs, and many nonsensical rules have been left behind.

But for all of these changes, crime and suffering are increasing, and the war is still going on. Political parties have taken the place of tribes, and with politics taking the place of ignorance, life can only get harder; people are troubled now in a different way, which prevents them from enjoying democracy and freedom. Yesterday it was tribal customs and ignorance; today it is party politics and corruption. The result is the same: suffering and difficulty for innocent victims, especially women and children.

Chapter Three ❧
My Childhood That Never Was

There is a beautiful American expression that "a child should be a child," but in the village in Kurdistan where I grew up there was no way for a child to be a child. Children were born weak and malnourished and often died of simple diseases that could have been treated. But no medicine was available, and food was hard to come by. It is estimated that some 2.5 million Iraqi children died during the ten years of the embargo and UN sanctions from 1992 to 2002. Everywhere people were hungry and searched for food. Children started to work as soon as they could, without ever having a chance to be a child. When I was eight years old, I put a big tray on my head and walked through the village selling candy and cake to help feed my family. All the children worked.

One of my father's cousins had a tea shop on the road between Chamchamal and Sangaw, and in 1980, when I was ten years old, my father sent me there to work. The place was called Basara, named after the small river that the road crossed, and it took me about forty minutes to walk there from Hashazini. There was a bridge over the river near the tea shop, and an army base had been built on top of a big hill overlooking the river to protect the bridge and the road from *peshmerga* activity.

Working

My first job was to clean the tables and wash the dishes. I also had to make the tea. My cousin used to sell some "fast food" like boiled eggs, potatoes, bread, and yogurt. The road did not have much traffic—each hour, maybe only two or three cars passed by. Sometimes as many as ten cars would pass without stopping. When drivers did stop for tea, I would ask them if they wanted me to wash their cars as well. If they said yes, I'd bring some water from the river, wash the car, and split the money I made with my cousin.

The thing that made the tea shop successful was the army base on the hill. Many army officers and soldiers would come down to the tea shop from time to time for a break to drink tea, talk, and sit. Most of the soldiers were Arabs from the south, but since I could not speak Arabic I could not talk to them, and so they would just sit in the tea stall and relax.

One soldier used to come several times a day. While I worked around the shop, I felt his eyes following me. When I looked up, I saw him staring at me. I became very uncomfortable and scared. Why was he always looking at me? Had someone told him that I had *peshmerga* friends? Perhaps he was looking for an opportunity to kidnap me? But he always smiled at me and seemed friendly. Nobody in those days ever talked about child molesters, and I had no idea about such things, but still it seemed creepy that he was always watching me and smiling.

One day I decided that I had to do something to find out why the soldier was always staring and smiling at me. So I told my cousin about him and said that he was scaring me. What did he want from me? But my cousin said he was a very nice man and not to worry about him. I asked him to please ask the soldier why he seemed so interested in me. My cousin spoke to him for five or ten minutes, and then the soldier pulled out a photo and showed it to my cousin, who looked very surprised and then began to smile.

"The soldier loves to look at you," my cousin said, "because you look just like his brother. It is five months now since he has visited his family, and he misses his brother very much. He said even your movements remind him of his brother." He showed me the photo, and I was surprised to see myself with the soldier and a lady.

I looked at my cousin, perplexed. "When was I ever with this soldier and that lady? I don't remember this at all. When did I ever wear Arabic clothes like those?"

My cousin laughed. "That isn't you, Yassin. That's the soldier's brother."

The soldier was watching my reaction with amusement, and asked my cousin to ask me if I thought I looked like his brother.

"Exactly," I said.

"That is why he keeps looking at you," said my cousin.

"Tell him I can be his brother too," I said.

When my cousin told that to the soldier, he stared at me and then he started to cry—softly at first, and then big sobs, as though a great pressure was being released from within him. Then he came over and hugged me and kissed my head. "I have only one brother, and no sisters," he said to my cousin, who translated into Kurdish for me.

"So now we are three," I said.

The soldier, whose name was Raid (pronounced *Raayid*), was very happy and excited and said he would tell his mother and father about what had happened.

After that, every day whenever he had a chance to come from the base, Raid would run down to see me, even if it was just for a minute, and sometimes he would give me candy before running back to the base. I learned a lot of Arabic words from him. That was the first time I had ever tried to communicate with someone who did not speak Kurdish. And I had not eaten as much candy in all my ten years as I ate during the two months that Raid visited me. Sometimes he visited me four or five times a day, and often he used to bring canned food for me from the army base. Sometimes he brought a whole bag of canned food and told me to take it to my family. Suddenly we were rich in fish and meat and beans! He even took a picture of me and sent it back to his own family.

One day after I finished my job, I came home with a bag of canned food—and found three *peshmerga* in our house. I told my mother that she did not have to cook anything because I had enough food for everyone.

"How can there be enough?" she said.

"I brought back a lot today," I said as I showed her the bag. "Raid gave it to me."

"Good. Let the *peshmerga* eat meat tonight."

When Mom started serving the cooked meat to the *peshmerga*, I started laughing.

"Why are you laughing?" one of them asked.

I did not answer.

"If you laugh again, you'll go out," warned my dad.

After the *peshmerga* ate they talked, and then said they wanted to go. I walked them outside. One of them, whom I had known for a long time, took me aside and said, "Since I joined the *peshmerga*, I never ate food like this."

I started laughing again.

"What's so funny? Why are you laughing?"

"That was Saddam's food you were eating."

"What??"

"That food was from the army."

"How did you get it?"

"At the place I work there is a soldier who is my friend, and he keeps bringing me food from the base."

"He is your friend?"

"Yes."

"How can that be? They are our enemy."

"Not Raid. He is a very nice guy."

"So why is he in the army? To kill us?"

"No...you know how it is. In Iraq, serving in the army is not a choice. He is not Baathist. He is just serving his time."

"So why doesn't he flee?"

"Where would he go?" I said. "They don't have mountains to go to, like we do. If he got out of the country, they would just arrest his family."

"I know. Most people in the army hate what they are forced to do, but they have no choice."

"Especially Raid. He is very nice."

"Tell him the *peshmerga* ate his food."

"I can't! Never have I joked with him about *peshmerga*."

"I have to go," my *peshmerga* friend said.

I whispered in his ear, "You better not tell anyone that you ate Saddam's food." I laughed, but I kept a close eye on him, and was relieved to see that he laughed back.

Since that day, whenever I see this *peshmerga* he always jokingly asks me if I have any more of Saddam's food, and I always say, "No, they moved my friend." In fact, they did move Raid from that base, but I kept him in my heart and mind. He was my first Arabic teacher and my first and best non-Kurdish friend. He really was like my brother in a way, always taking care of me and always worried about me. I never found out what happened to him, except that they moved him to a battlefront during the Iran–Iraq war, and then probably to some other front in some other war, because wars never stop in Iraq. I hope Raid is still alive, and if he is, I am sure that he still has my picture with him.

No Fun, No Education

The most important element missing from my childhood, and from most Kurdish children's childhoods, was fun and play. We were hungry for it, the way a starving person is hungry for food, but the daily pressure of survival made play and fun impossible. Even if you took a few minutes to play with something or to follow your heart, you felt guilty about it and expected a beating when someone else found out what you had done. We were fearful of our parents and our teachers and the Iraqi army and just about everything else. Our parents told us fearful stories about wolves and *jinni*—dangerous, invisible spirits—and darkness and monsters, and snow and floods, to frighten us into behaving. We were taught to be afraid of the moon and the sun and the stars and the rain. Where fear is always present, it is impossible to just have fun and play—like a child.

Proper education and real learning were also missing from my childhood. When parents brought their children to primary school for the first time, it was traditional to tell the teacher that it was not necessary to return any of the child's flesh—just the bones would be sufficient. Beatings were given almost daily, and it was assumed by everyone that a child would not learn without them.

In my school we had over 100 students from grades one to six, and all of them were taught by just two teachers. We were lucky—some schools had only one teacher. Often two whole grades were combined, one on each side of the classroom. With such a large number of students per class, the teachers could maintain order only by the most brutal methods. I became used to beatings from the teachers, but I hated it when the beating left a visible mark because then my father would see it and would give me another beating for disobeying the teacher. Once a teacher hit me so hard on the side of my face that his four fingers were clearly visible on my cheek for weeks afterwards.

    And father did not need much of an excuse to give beatings. The whole society was like that. As a child, you were beaten for almost everything that went wrong, even if you were not at fault or had no understanding of why you were being beaten. Maybe you were beaten one day for leaving something out that should have been brought in, or for bringing in something that should have been left out. So the next day you tried to do the opposite, and you were beaten for that also. If you were the oldest child in the family, at least you had the right to discipline the younger children, but if you were the youngest child, like I was, then the whole family—indeed, the whole society—had the right to beat on you for any reason, fair or not. If a neighbor beat you, your parents would never ask why or if it was fair. It was just assumed that you had done something wrong, and your parents were likely to give you a second beating because you had brought shame on the family. My mother used to sing the Kurdish song for me, "Adult beatings make the child grow up fatter and healthier." It was as though beatings were a form of medicine.

    One of the most beautiful aspects of America is the way adults talk to children, and let children talk with them, and actually listen sympathetically to what they say. This never happened during my childhood in Kurdistan. We were treated like soldiers from very early on. We were given orders, scared into acting by threats, and not allowed to question or even understand the orders. We just had to do it, and if we failed, even if it was not our fault, we were punished, glared at, cursed, or slapped in the face. We could never express how we felt about an order, or even ask why. All of us kept our feelings hidden, and eventually these feelings became part of our personalities and shaped the way we grew up.

We were often beaten for simply having too much energy—for jumping or running or talking, or worst of all, for laughing at school or at home or in the mosque when a guest was present. In our tradition, it was important to leave a beating mark on the child's body so that he would see the mark and remember to improve his behavior. Only God could help you if you still had a mark on your body from the last beating and you repeated the misbehavior.

Students learned at school by memorizing without any understanding, so that even if they went to school they did not get a proper education. I often saw with my own eyes how a teacher would slap a student in primary school for not memorizing correctly, and the student would be so scared and hurt that he would wet his pants. Then the teacher would send the student home to change, but the student would be too afraid to go because if he came home with messy pants his parents would beat him again for bringing shame to the family by acting like a baby. If he explained that he couldn't control his bladder because the teacher hit him, he would get a double beating for disobeying the teacher.

As students, we never had the right to express our own feelings or to ask questions in order to get the explanations that we needed to understand. And we had no playground or place just to be kids and use our energy. Most of the day we were so crowded together that any movement or sound would earn us a good beating. We used to call one of our teachers The Butcher because he would beat students' feet until they were swollen, and then he would force the students to walk around the room on them. It was like we were in Abu Ghraib prison, not school!

Our primary school was an old building with broken windows that made the classrooms feel like ice in the winter. The books were old and everything was rundown. At the end of the year, all of the students had to give their books back so they could be used again by the next class, and anyone who failed to return his books would not get a book next year. Students sat three or four to a desk, and if you were restless, or you damaged your book, or forgot what you were supposed to memorize, you were in big trouble. I never looked at the teacher—I only saw the big stick in his hand. We were as scared of the teachers as we were of the government's forces.

After I came to America, I happened one day to see a bumper sticker that said, "If you think education is expensive, try ignorance." It really caught my attention, and I preached about it at Friday prayer. I said that Muslims are paying for 800 years of ignorance. It is costing us our freedom and dignity among the nations of the world, but even worse, it is costing us hundreds of thousands of lives. We have to understand that, and educate our children. If we fail, our children will not even have the future that we wanted and were denied.

Karra

One notable man in Hashazini was Karra. He was thirty years older than I was and had never married; he lived with his mother and father. When the government finally opened a clinic in Hashazini, he became the janitor. He was also a very good farmer and a hard worker.

I never knew his real name, but everyone called him Karra, which means "dumb." Karra was both deaf and dumb. He could not speak at all except to make noises like "Ua, ua, ua, ua" whenever he became angry. People in Hashazini learned to communicate with him by moving their hands, and eventually some of his friends became very good at this "hand talk."

One day when I was about nine years old, I went to the mosque early. Karra was the only person there. I greeted him like a soldier saluting his commander, and he smiled at me and returned the salute. Then he started "talking" to me by moving his hands. I thought he was asking me something, but I did not know what. Perhaps it had something to do with the prayer that would begin soon? I tried to tell him that it was not time yet for the prayer, but Karra just shook his head right to left, which meant "No." He kept talking to me with his hands, and sometimes I nodded "Yes" when I thought I knew what he meant, and sometimes I shook my head "No" when I did not know, but never did I understand what he was trying to tell me. I was just excited to be "talking" to him.

At one point I tried to communicate something, but Karra seemed confused. I responded by first pointing at him ("you"), then pointing to the temple of my head ("understand"), then giving the negative sign with my hand ("not")—meaning, I thought, "You don't understand." But Karra began to make angry sounds—"Ua, ua, ua, ua"—and those I understood. I thought he was getting angry because he did not understand me, and so I repeated the same hand movements that I had just made—and this time he slapped me hard on the right side of my face. His hand was heavy, like my father's. I grabbed my face and ran crying from the mosque all the way home.

My father asked me what happened.

"Karra beat me in the face."

"Why?"

"I don't know. I went to the mosque and he was there, and I tried to ask him how he was doing, and then he beat me and kicked me out of the mosque."

My father's face turned red, which I knew meant that he was really mad. If an adult beat a child, parents did not even ask why—but kicking me out of the mosque was against our tradition. My father took my hand and said that we were going back to the mosque.

When Karra saw my father, he came over to him and kissed his hand in greeting. My father asked with his hands, "Karra, why did you kick my son out of the mosque?"

Karra began talking with Father using his hands, but I did not know what they were saying. At one point Father turned to me and said, "Did you make a hand gesture like this?" And he showed me with his own hands.

"I don't know. Maybe."

"And did you repeat it again?"

"Maybe. I was only trying to talk with him."

Suddenly my father slapped me on the left side of my face harder than Karra had. I ducked my head down, and Father grabbed my head with one hand while he beat on the back of my head with the other. Suddenly Karra began to say, "Ua, ua, ua, ua!!" and, taking hold of my hand, pulled me away from my father.

"What's wrong? What did I do?" I cried. I was completely confused.

"You are a little Satan!" my father said to me.

"Why, Daddy? What did I do?"

"You would make a joke about Karra, huh? He is a hundred times better than you and your father combined."

"No no no," I said. "I did not make any joke about him!"

"Suppose God made you like him and also blind?"

"But I did nothing wrong! I was just trying to talk with him."

"Why did you tell him that he was insane?"

"Me??"

"Yes, you. You said that twice. The first time he thought maybe you did not know what you did, but you repeated it again, so he beat you."

"Daddy, I swear by God I did not know, and I never meant that."

Father told Karra that I did not know that my gesture had meant "insane." Karra had been holding my hand since he had pulled me away from my father, but now he wrapped me in his arms, kissed my head, and gestured that he was sorry. He said to my father through gestures that he loved me, and that he knew I prayed and respected everyone in the village. He said that he found it hard to believe that I had called him insane, and that he'd hit me only because I repeated it. Now he realized that I did not understand.

My father told me to kiss Karra's hand and tell him I was sorry, which I did. Karra kissed me again, gave me some candy, and we all managed to laugh in relief that everything was forgiven.

Living with Nature

Growing up in a Kurdish village forced you to live close to nature. You had to live in harmony with it, or you did not live at all. At night there were no electric lamps; we moved by moonlight and starlight. Black clouds meant heavy rain, and we hid ourselves from the thunderstorms and covered our ears when the lightning flashed. We took shelter from the wind and rested in the shade of a tree during hot weather. We woke up with the first light of morning by the cry of the rooster, telling us to pray. Birds brightened our lives, giving us different songs and telling us different stories about what was happening in their lives. I used to stop periodically during the day to watch the sun creep slowly across the dome of the sky and down toward the mountains, until eventually it hid itself behind the mountains and another day had gone.

Father never had a watch and never had a calendar in the house, but he knew from the position of the sun in the sky all that he needed to know about time. He knew which hour it was with only a few minutes' error. He could tell the exact date by the moon's size and location in the sky. He knew from the calls and movements of birds and animals if it was going to rain or snow, or how hot it would be.

Throughout the whole cold, dark winter we waited for spring and anticipated the beautiful flowers that would soon cover the hills, especially the *nergz*, the simple white lilies, or the wild roses. These flowers bloomed in such profusion that they literally changed the color of the land itself and filled the air with a perfume that brought joy to every face. We eagerly anticipated summer when we could pick bunches of grapes and all the other fruits that we had not eaten for almost a year. The days were long, for extra swimming and fishing. When autumn came we were almost in despair, thinking of the cold barren months ahead with no beautiful flowers or birds to relieve the gloom of winter.

We ate whatever we could grow from our fields or raise from our own animals. Everything was done by hand, without power tools. It was hard work, but in a way more satisfying—even more beautiful—than work done by machine. We had no alcohol or drugs or television to divert us from this harmony. It was a simple, hard, natural life, and while it would be wrong to say that we liked it, it would also be wrong to say it was completely bad for us. The villagers learned from their experience with nature. Those people who survived were stronger and wiser for it.

In winter we just put on more clothes and shivered. In the high mountains of Kurdistan, whole villages would be under deep snow for two or three months. In some places the snow was so deep that the villagers could not open their doors, and they literally dug tunnels from one house to the other. Many of the fruits and vegetables of autumn were dried and saved for the cold months, and people lived like ants on what they had stored from the autumn.

Hashazini was in a warmer area, so we were not buried completely in snow, but most villagers had little to do outside during the winter. The cattle stayed in the barn. People said that winter was like a jail sentence—except there is more to do in most jail cells in the West than there was to do in a house in Kurdistan: no books, radio, electricity, telephone, hot water, TV, movies, computer, Internet, toys, or mail. Five to ten people lived in one room because it was the only room that was heated. The only activities were feeding the animals and milking the cows and ewes. The women cooked and sewed. For entertainment, we told stories and jokes.

In such a state of isolation, almost anything unusual would be exciting, and for me it was when I found a newborn baby goat in the barn. I would scoop the baby goat up in my arms and carry it into the room and hold it close to the warm fire, and kiss it, and put milk in its mouth with a spoon. The most exciting moment was when I put my little finger in its mouth so it could suck on it and I felt its scratchy tongue. I would laugh and laugh at the feel of it. Once when I was four years old, I went with my father into the barn and we found three baby goats. I brought one into the house and my father brought the other two. My mother was mad at me for bringing the goats into the house, but to my surprise Dad said that I could keep them. Every baby animal was beautiful in my eyes. Chicks, calves, donkeys—I loved them all. I picked them up, I fed them, I hugged them, I kissed them, I followed them around. In the long winter months, these little helpless babies were always entertaining.

But winter months were particularly hard because there was too little room for any physical movement. Since children were not permitted to speak when adults were present, it was hard to even share ideas. All the time we had to be silent and unmoving, until our very muscles ached to cry out and run. It was also common for us to catch colds in winter and to lie in bed with a cough and fever. Sometimes school would be closed for weeks because of the snow and bad weather. In 1979, school was closed for a whole month because the teacher could not get any transportation from the city to the village.

Still, I was lucky. My school was closed only because of snow and bad weather; now schools in Iraq are closed because of bombings and civil war. We were scared of monsters and soldiers, but now children are scared of friends and neighbors. We got sick from diseases, but now children die from cluster bombs, white phosphorus, and toxic chemicals. And still there are no playgrounds or special programs for them. After thirty years, many modern things have come to the village—and now life for an Iraqi child is actually far worse than it was when I was growing up. We are sliding backwards.

I Wish I Was an Orphan

In the summer of 1977, when I was seven years old, I was playing with two of my neighbors in the village: Rizgar, who was six years old, and his brother, who was four. They were orphans. A man from another village stopped and called to them, and the two brothers ran to him. He kissed them and gave them both a piece of candy. When they came back to me, Rizgar wanted to give me some of his candy, but I refused and told the younger brother to go back to the man and ask him for another piece of candy for me. The boy ran back to the man saying, "Uncle, Uncle, can you give me one more piece of candy for our friend? Please?"

"No," said the man. "Because he is not an orphan."

The boy came running back. "I'm sorry," he said. "No candy because you are not an orphan."

I was really sad, and wished that I could be lucky enough to be an orphan so I could get a piece of candy.

Bridge

In the spring of 1978, when I was eight years old, I was coming home from visiting a friend in a nearby village. Spring is the season of changes in the weather; first it rains, then it shines. There were no weather reports for the village, however, and even if there had been we did not have a radio or newspaper from which to receive them (and even if we'd had a radio, there were no broadcasts in Kurdish). On this particular day, when I reached Hashazini a small brook just outside the village was flooding over its banks. Hard rain in the mountains seemed to be causing the flood. My mother and four of my friends were waiting on the other side of the brook for me because it was close to sunset. I did not see any way to cross the brook, and I asked my mother if I could go back to my friend's village.

"No! It is getting dark." She was crying.

"So I will wait until the flood goes down."

"Suppose more rain comes and the flood gets bigger?"

"I don't know," I said.

"I will get a big branch," said one of my friends on the other side. "When I put it across the brook, you can climb across."

"Suppose he falls?" asked my mother.

"I'm not going to fall," I said.

"We'll tie a rope around his waist so that if he falls in, we can pull him out," said the friend. My mother cried harder.

My friend went to find a large branch, brought it to the brook, and gently stretched it toward my side. But just before I could reach for it, the end got so heavy that it dipped into the swirling water. The pull of the water was so strong that my friend could not hold onto his end, and he had to let go. The branch was immediately swept away.

"What can we do?" my mother wailed. The sun was now in the process of setting, so it seemed unwise for me to go back to my friend's village.

"I'll bring a ladder," said another friend.

"But how will that work better than the branch?"

"I'll tie a rope to the far end and throw it to Yassin. Then when the ladder gets near the far shore, Yassin can help hold the end up and pull it to his side."

They tied a rope to the ladder and threw the end to me. I began to pull the ladder toward me little by little. Even my mother was starting to like this idea. But just like the branch, as the end approached my side it became heavy and dipped into the water. Everybody immediately shouted at me to pull. I pulled as hard as I could. But instead of my pulling the ladder, the ladder pulled me toward the brook.

"LET GO!" shouted my mother.

I looked down, realized that I was almost in the water, and let go. The ladder immediately disappeared in the swirling flood.

"Now what do we do?" we all asked each other. And then we were quiet, except that I could hear my mother crying.

Suddenly I shouted, "Mom! Mom! Stop crying. I know what to do. Give me five minutes and I will find the way to your side."

"How?" she asked.

"I'm going to the big tree that overhangs the brook and I'll climb onto the branches that hang all the way over the brook. I'll just crawl over the branches and drop down on the other side."

"You can't do that!"

"Yes, Mommy. We do it all the time. If I can do it when the brook is not flooding, I can do it when it is."

I ran down to the tree, but my mother got there first.

"Stop!" she said. "Wait for my friend to come with a lantern so you can see where you are going."

I waited until he came. Then I climbed into the tree, found the largest branch, and crawled along it until I was over the other bank. From there I could look down to where my mother was standing ten feet below me with her hands raised to the sky, praying. She looked up at me and smiled, but then she looked worried again.

"How can you get down? You can't jump without breaking your leg."

"I've done this before."

"Wait. I'll get my friend to bring mattresses."

"The ground is soft from the flood."

"No, WAIT," she said.

Suddenly I pointed behind her. "Oh look, look! Is that Father coming?"

She turned to look, and I jumped. When she turned back she looked right into my face, and I said, "No, Mommy. I was joking. My father is not coming."

Her face lit up. She hugged me and laughed and said, "Thank you, God. I got my son back!"

Tarzan

In the summer of 1979 one of my cousins, Kak Qadr, bought a TV. It was the first TV Hashazini had ever seen, because the village had no electricity. But the TV worked by car batteries. It was just black and white, but Kak Qadr's home immediately became the village cinema.

He had a big back yard, and he put out two or three blankets for people to sit on. He made rules for the children to follow, and if they did not, they were sent home. The first rule was that you could not touch the TV at all; you could not even go near it. The second rule was that you had to be quiet and listen, no talking. The third rule was that you could not fight with your friends. The fourth rule was that you could not get up and run around; you had to stay in your place. The fifth rule was that if you had to go to the bathroom, you had to go home and come back the next day.

During the day, there were programs for children for two hours, and at night there were three hours of programs for the adults. So every morning between 8 and 10 a.m., twenty or twenty-five children went to my cousin's house. I was nine years old. This was the first time any of us had ever seen a TV. We were completely amazed and wanted to know how it worked. How did they put all of those people, cars, houses, trees in the small box? How did they move? How did they talk? Some of us said that the images were *jinni*; some said it was magic; some said it was a miracle. Some of us thought that if we went around to the back of the TV, we would see the other side of the scene that was on the screen.

We went every day, but we didn't understand anything in the programs because all of it was in Arabic. There were no Kurdish cartoons or programs. During the second week, the Tarzan show began, and for almost two months after that we could watch thirty minutes of Tarzan every day. During this time the whole village changed. Many adults stopped going to see adult shows at night and came to watch Tarzan with us kids. Everyone was talking about Tarzan. In the homes, in the mosque, on the farms, the only subject discussed was Tarzan. Many of the kids began to imitate Tarzan's monkey sounds. The village became like a Tarzan jungle. We ran to the trees, hung from the branches, and jumped from limb to limb. We were Tarzan!

Some people were upset with the influence that the TV had over the village, and asked my cousin to get rid of it. He would laugh and say to them, "Don't come, and don't let your children come, if you feel it is bad." But not only could our parents not stop us from coming, even the critics kept coming to watch the TV at night. Nobody could resist the power of the tube. Tarzan changed our lives and made us feel good. We finally had some fun.

Every morning for ten or fifteen minutes before the TV came on, one of my neighbors would climb on his roof and make Tarzan monkey sounds: Eh Eh Eh, Oh Oh Oh. It was our signal that the show was about to start and we needed to get ready. We were very emotional afterwards, especially if Tarzan was in trouble or had lost his monkey.

Summer in the Village

As much as winter was hard, summer was fun and beautiful, with long days outside to work, swim, fish, and play soccer. Whenever we got tired there were many trees to shade us while we rested. When night came, all the people of Kurdistan slept on the roofs of their houses, where it was cool. Soon after the sun went down, people went to their beds, but there was often such a beautiful light show going on in the heavens that it was impossible not to enjoy it and ask questions about what it all meant. Mohsin and my cousin and some friends and I all slept on the roof together, and we always started the night by telling stories.

"How many stars are there?"

"There are as many stars as there are human beings—each human being has one star."

"How do you know?"

"My father told me. When somebody dies, his star turns off, and that is why we see shooting stars. Every shooting star means someone died."

"But how many stars are there?"

"I don't know exactly."

"Let's count them."

We promised each other that no one would go to sleep until he had counted 5,000 stars. The next morning we asked each other how many stars we had counted, and each time we had to confess that we had fallen asleep before we got to 5,000. We complained that the stars were very close together—sitting on each other—and that's why we couldn't count them.

One night Mohsin started talking about soccer.

"But yesterday we did not finish counting the stars," I said.

"No one can count all the stars," said Mohsin. "They're too close together."

"So why don't we just find out how many people died today?" my cousin said.

"Good idea," I said.

We agreed that we would not go to sleep until we had counted ten deaths. We lay on our backs with the cool breeze blowing over us and looked in the beautiful sky for a shooting star that ended its life because a human had died. Once again sleep overtook us.

One night I noticed that one star was much brighter than others. "Why is that?" I asked.

"Because that is Agha Dara's star." (Agha Dara was our tribe's leader.) "Just like Agha Dara, that star is richer and more powerful than any of the other stars, and so it is bigger."

"Why are those seven stars all clumped together all the time?"

"Those stars are Sheikh Ali's family, Sheikh Ali, his wife, and his five children—because they love each other and they are very religious, and so God put them all together."

"Why is that star so far and so high?"

"Because that star is for the people who live on top of the high mountains of Qandeel, which are so far from us."

"Why does that one star shine so brightly?"

"That one is the star of a beautiful girl."

And so we kept asking questions and making up answers until we all fell asleep.

One night Mohsin said that we should look at the stars to decide how many people had moved that day. Because we did not know about airplanes, rockets, or satellites, we believed that when we saw stars moving slowly it meant that the people to whom the stars belonged had moved on that day, and now their stars were following them. Wherever you lived, your star would be there. If the stars moved slowly to the north, people were going to Dhok, the Kurdish city close to Turkey. If the stars were going south, people were going to Kirkuk. East-moving stars were going to Sulaimaniya. We all agreed that we could find the number of people who moved by counting their stars.

"I see a star going to Dhok. I must find ten before going to sleep." The next morning I said I had counted four, and nobody had more than I did.

One night while we were looking up at the sky, we became aware that the full moon, which a few minutes ago had been shining at full brightness, was slowly getting red and dark. It was not dimming the way it did when a thin cloud passed in front, and in any event there were no clouds in the sky that night. The moon was simply changing color and dying out. We were amazed. We had never seen anything like it before. As the red area spread across the face of the moon, the night grew dark and threatening, and people in the village began to run out of their houses to see what was happening. When they saw the dying moon, they ran to the mosque. We came down off the roof and followed them.

At the mosque, some people were crying and some were praying.

"Why is the moon getting red?" we asked.

"It is the blood from all the people who have been slaughtered," they said. "It is going to the moon."

"Some part of the moon looks black."

"That is from the sins of human beings."

"What is going to happen?" I asked.

"It is a sign that God is mad about all of the blood and the sins. He is going to destroy all of the sky and the earth. It is the end of the world and the beginning of the hereafter."

All of the people began to cry harder and pray more intensely as they waited for the sky to fall down and the earthquakes to start. But the Imam said that if God would accept our prayers, He might give us another chance.

I saw my mother in the mosque. "Mommy," I said. "We did not kill anyone. We did not shed any blood. Why should we die?"

Mom kissed and hugged me. "Just pray and ask God to have mercy on us."

"I will, but we never shed any blood."

"It does not matter who shed the blood. Too many people have been killed—so many that their blood covers the whole moon."

"How did the blood get on the moon?" I asked. "Since they were killed on earth."

"God will not allow anyone's blood to be lost. He collects it all and saves it on the moon."

I started to pray. "Oh God! Please don't kill us. We love you. We love the sky. We love the moon. Don't destroy us!"

Mom hugged me and held my hand. I believed that we would be OK as long as Mom smiled on me.

The moon became darker and redder until it was very dark and scary. We stayed for about an hour, waiting to die and praying and crying. All of a sudden the Imam began crying, "*Allahu-akbar*! *Allahu-akbar*! (Allah is the greatest!) See, see? It is getting clearer."

And sure enough, little by little, the red blood began to leave the moon. Everyone started smiling, and I believed that we would be OK. God had given us another chance. When the moon was nearly clear I went home to bed on the roof, and I sent a couple of kisses to the moon. "I love you," I said. "I am sorry for what happened to you. I hope no one ever again will shed blood so that we will always have your beautiful light." And I also said, "Thank you, God, for saving our lives," and then I covered my head and slept.

Adult Certification

The tradition in Kurdistan is that boys do not become adults simply by age. Rather, the child must prove that he is an adult by his ability to suffer hardship. When boys are nine or ten years old they are often tested by adults: they are sent alone on a dark night in the snow or rain to another village to take or bring something. And to make the test even scarier, they are brought up with stories of *jinni* and wolves and bandits on the road at night. As they get older, more difficult tests are devised to see what kind of a man is developing inside the child, and whether he will be able to handle the responsibilities of home and marriage. Adults might send an older boy on horseback to buy and sell goods, and before he leaves they will ask him questions: suppose this or that happens, what will you do?

By age fifteen, boys are usually married but are still living with their families. By the time a man is twenty years old with two or three children, he has been set free from his parents and can speak and give opinions without being beaten. The ability to suffer hardship is like a Ph.D. in Kurdistan. No other degree is as important to the future of a child.

My father approached tribal tradition like he approached religion: as a sort of military exercise. I was required to follow orders, and I could not ask why. Perhaps he did not know himself, or perhaps he was not able to explain it to me, or perhaps he believed I would understand when I was old enough. For example, it was tradition that children were not allowed to speak in front of guests or adults: it was a shame on the parents if the children broke this rule, so it was difficult for us to ask why a rule existed or even to seek explanations for our questions about the world around us. But for whatever reason, we had to follow the religious and tribal rules: don't talk, don't ask, don't move, don't eat too much, don't laugh out loud, don't scratch yourself, don't stretch your feet, don't lay down in front of guests, put shoes on the shelf, respect elders, and always serve water when guests are present by bringing a single glass of water and serving each of the guests from the same glass, one after another.

Before we did anything at home, we had to ask father's permission. My father sometimes would force me to sit for three hours in an uncomfortable position to train me to sit in the tribal way on the floor. He wanted to be sure that if he took me to another house I would sit properly on the floor, remain silent, and follow all of the rules so that he could be proud of me. If I didn't, I would bring shame on him. He was a tough father, yet his simplicity and humility allowed me to see that he loved me and wanted only to train me for the difficult trials that I, and all young Kurds, would face in the years ahead. Without that training, would I have survived?

I attended the Hashazini primary school until 1981, but when I graduated that year there was no middle school for me to go to the next year. My brother Issa lived about 100 miles away in Sulaimaniya, a big city with many good middle schools. So my parents arranged for me to go and live with Issa. Coming from Hashazini to Sulaimaniya was a big change for me. I was lucky to have a chance to stay with my brother and go to middle school at all, and so I escaped having to get married or join the *peshmerga*. But life did not get easier.

Chapter Four ✎
A Student in the City

New Year

In a way, I felt that I became an adult on March 21, 1982, when I was twelve years old. Our greatest Kurdish national festival is Nawroz—the Persian and Kurdish New Year—which takes place on March 21. Our tradition is that the evening before, we must go to the highest point of land we can find, light a bonfire at sundown, sing Kurdish patriotic songs, and dance Kurdish dances. During Saddam's time it was very dangerous to celebrate Nawroz because the army or security forces would arrest people who participated in this celebration, and yet I do not remember a single Nawroz that I did not celebrate in some way or another.

There are many myths and legends associated with Nawroz, some of which may go back to the Persians and the Zoroastrian fire worshipers. The Kurds believe that at one time long ago there was a tyrant named Zuhak who hated the Kurds and wanted to kill them all. Two large snakes grew out of his shoulders that ate only human brains, and to protect his own brain from being eaten Zuhak killed two Kurds every day and fed their brains to the snakes.

There was a Kurdish blacksmith named Kawa who had three sons. Zuhak took two of his sons and fed their brains to the snakes. When Zuhak returned for the last son, Kawa refused to give him up, began to beat his hammer on the anvil, and called out to the people in a loud voice, "Come out! I need you!" When the villagers came to him, Kawa said, "Listen, Zuhak is going to kill all of us and feed our brains to the snakes. Let us cut off his head before he can finish us off."

"But how can we kill Zuhak?" the villagers asked.

"If we go together we may kill him, or at least we will all die together," said Kawa, "but if we don't try, we will certainly all die one by one. What do we have to lose?"

The villagers agreed to try, if Kawa would lead them. They went to Zuhak's castle, where Kawa, being a strong blacksmith, easily broke down the iron gate. The servants, seeing how easily Kawa broke the gate and observing the large crowd of people with him, ran away, and the crowd went into the castle, seized Zuhak, dragged him out, and killed him.

Once Zuhak was dead, everyone wanted to spread the good news, but they had no radio or telephone to announce the victory. Instead the people went to the top of the nearest mountain where everyone could see them from afar, built a bonfire, and began to sing and dance in victory. The defeat of Zuhak occurred on March 21, and from that day on it has been regarded as the start of the Kurdish new year, as well as the Kurdish day of victory that must be celebrated by dancing and singing around an open fire on the top of a mountain. Every Nawroz celebration is a challenge to the government: that we are a Kawa nation, that a dictator's end will be no better than Zuhak's, that we know our history, and that our victory is coming!

In 1982, the first year that I stayed at my brother Issa's house in Sulaimaniya, I told him that I wanted to go back to Hashazini to celebrate Nawroz. Issa said that it was going to rain, and anyway they were going to celebrate Nawroz in Sulaimaniya, so there was no need to go to Hashazini. But I knew that the government's security forces would be watching the celebrations in Sulaimaniya, and so we could not freely express our desire for a free Kurdistan, nor could we sing patriotic songs and wear Kurdish national costumes. Sometimes modern city people just light a lamp or have an indoor party for Nawroz, but the real celebration is a bonfire at the top of a mountain shouting out defiance of a government that wants us dead. I felt that I had to go back to my village because there the *peshmerga* would participate, and I would be with my friends. There we could read all the anti-government poems we wanted, or just express our love for Kurdistan in the rich, raw way that free people are able to do. I kept insisting that I wanted to go home until Issa finally agreed that I could try, although he did not think I could get there by sundown, since Hashazini was over 100 miles away. I asked him for an old car tire to take with me, and he asked if I was crazy: how was I going to get to Hashazini with a car tire? But I kept insisting, and finally he laughed and gave me one.

I walked out of the house with the tire on my shoulder like a weapon and ran to catch a bus. I had to change buses four times. People looked at me like I was crazy, but some said "Happy Nawroz!" The closest bus station was a forty-minute walk to Hashazini, so I started to walk. It began to rain and night was coming on, but I had to get there. A thunderstorm broke, and the sky became completely black, with wild wind and blowing clouds everywhere. I remembered stories that my mother used to tell me about wolves, and I managed to scare myself half to death, as only twelve-year-olds can, by imagining how hungry wolves were about to jump out of the swirling clouds and eat me up. I was so scared that I began to run, and I made the forty-minute trip in fifteen minutes. I was so relieved to finally see my home.

My mother was shocked to see me walk through the door and wanted to know who had brought me. When I said I came by myself, she began crying and laughing at the same time. I changed into dry clothes, and she told me to sit down and relax, but I told her that I had to get to the top of Segrdan Hill to the festival. She told me that it was raining and that nobody was going to go. I begged her to please let me go before my father came home, because I knew that he would not let me go. At first she refused, but eventually I wore her down and she agreed. Then I asked her for a bottle of gasoline. She knew why I needed it and so she just gave it to me. "I love you," I told her, and then I ran toward Segrdan Hill with my tire as fast as I could because there was less than an hour to sundown.

I stopped at a friend's house on the way, and he was very happy and surprised to see me, but I told him we had no time to talk, just that he should tell all our friends that Yassin had gone to the mountains for Nawroz and that they should all come as soon as possible and bring fuel for the fire.

As I climbed the small mountain, in my mind I could hear Issa laughing at me, telling me that he had been right—that I could not make it to the top in time for sundown. I forced myself to go faster so that Issa would be wrong. I began singing, *"Amrozi sali to zaya bahar hatawo* (Today is the New Year and the spring has come back! Nawroz brings happiness and blessings.") It was still raining softly, and I saw nobody else on the hill.

When I reached the top, there was no one around. I put my tire down and poured gasoline on it in the rain. Then I lit it on fire, and watched as the little flame spread a protective wall of warmth and light a few feet around me.

Suddenly I heard two people coming. Thank God I was not going to be alone. Then I heard two more—and then more—five, six, ten. People began to appear from everywhere. The rain stopped and the fire burned higher and brighter. Everyone had brought something with him—wood, paper, clothes—and one of my friends had brought a big tape recorder with Kurdish patriotic songs on it. We all talked excitedly together about how Nawroz would not pass this year without a celebration.

One of my friends said that he had cried for three hours until his mother pointed to the top of Segrdan Hill and said, "For heavens' sake, stop crying. You will have your Nawroz. Come look. The fire has started on the mountain." Another friend told me he had been very sad, and said that if Yassin were here, there would be Nawroz even if it was snowing, that last year it had rained hard and Yassin had started the fire even then.

Usually the Nawroz celebration takes one or two hours, but this night nobody wanted to leave. We stayed on the mountain for three hours, even after our parents began calling us from the village to come down. It was one of the best nights of my life. I was so happy and proud. Everyone was glad to see me and praised me for keeping the traditions alive. I felt as though I was no longer twelve years old, but had become a leader whom others followed.

Finally I had to tell everyone to go home, because I believed that they would have stayed on that mountain as long as I did. We came down singing *"Jazna Jazna Jazni Kurdistana, Jazni Nawrozn!* (It is

Kurdistan's festival, it is the Kurds' day! It is Nawroz! By the fire's light I will wish you a happy celebration.") When I got home, my father refused to believe that I had been on the mountain. I just kissed his hand and hugged my mom and started eating dinner with my brother Mohsin.

In 1986 I wrote my first poem, and it was about Nawroz:

> Behold the lily (*nergz*)
> With the sweet scent of spring.
> How wonderful the spring
> That starts with Nawroz.
> Nawroz tells me of history
> Shows me the way to victory
> Teaches me the meaning of freedom
> And of living proudly with dignity.

We Are Marxists

In 1983, while I was still living with Issa in Sulaimaniya, the PUK made a peace agreement with the Iraqi government. Sulaimaniya was full of *peshmerga* at that time, and people went out daily to demonstrate in the street in favor of the peace agreement. One of my friends, Shazad, took me to a demonstration, and as I watched the crowds and the chanting I became more and more emotional and pushed my way to the front of the line so I could shout louder than anyone else: "*Ema naway Marxisin la se dara natrsin!* (We are Marxists, we are not afraid of death!")" I kept shouting this over and over until my throat was swollen and I could barely speak. I saw Issa in the crowd, and he had a strange smile on his face that I took to be approval for what I was doing.

I was so excited by the demonstration that I stayed to the end, and then I ran home. Issa asked me what the rush was.

"My prayer! My prayer!" I gasped. "The time for it is almost over." When I had finished praying, I saw Issa laughing at me.

"What's so funny?"

"Your prayer."

"Why shouldn't I pray?"

"All day you were out in the street shouting 'We are Marxists!' and now you pray!" Issa said.

"I was at the demonstration, but then it was time to pray, so I prayed. Why not?"

"Marxists don't pray."

"But I do."

"Then you are not a Marxist."

"Why not? What are Marxists?"

"You tell me."

"I...I don't know."

"So why were you shouting that you were a Marxist?"

"Everybody else was."

"What do you think being a Marxist means?"

"That we are Kurds and that we love Kurdistan and we want our freedom," I said.

"That is not what Marxism means."

"Yes it is. That is what the demonstration was all about."

"Do you know who Marx was?"

"One of the *peshmerga* leaders, maybe?"

Issa just started laughing, and it made me angry.

"Why are you laughing?"

"Because Marx was not *peshmerga*. He was not even a Kurd."

"So why did people carry his picture at the demonstration and say that they were his followers?"

"Because they follow the ideas of Marx."

"What ideas are those?"

"His ideas about God and society and the economy."

"So I believe in God, too."

"But Marx doesn't."

"WHAT?" I yelled. "Why not?"

"Because he says God doesn't exist."

"*Astaghfirullah*," I said (which means, "I ask God's forgiveness for this impiety.") "Is Marx so ignorant that he does not know that God exists? If God does not exist, how is it that we exist?"

"Marx will tell you how."

"You tell me."

Issa handed me a book entitled *Dealikty Marxi* (*The Marxist Dialectic*), published by the Communist Party of Iran. "Read this," he said.

This incident, and this book, were the starting points for me to search and read. I read *The Marxist Dialectic* a couple of times and got nothing from it. I found nothing in it that I was looking for. Then I started reading about what other people thought of Marx, and what Islam said. Whenever I went back to Hashazini, I used to argue with the *peshmerga*. Many of them prayed, and yet they had Marxist signs on their bags and weapons. But none of them knew anything about Marxism.

In our area was a very old man named Haji who was a *peshmerga*. Usually the name Haji means someone who has made a pilgrimage to Mecca (the *Hajj*), and in his case he had actually made a *Hajj*, but afterwards he joined the *peshmerga*, stopped praying, and became interested in Communism. But he was illiterate, and he knew nothing about it. Everyone made jokes about him and asked him why he did not pray. He replied, "I am Martilinism," which meant that he was a Marxist/Leninist, except that he could not pronounce the words correctly.

One day the army surrounded the village and blocked all the escape routes. They started to bomb the village with helicopters and rockets. The *peshmerga* were trapped inside.

Haji asked his friend, "What shall we do?"

"Nothing. We are *peshmerga* and we should be ready to die."

"Yes, but how can we get some help? Who can save us?"

"We fight until we die or we can escape."

Haji said, "Before when I had any trouble, I used to ask God to help me. And I used to feel good because I believed I got some support. Then you tell me that there is no God. So now who am I supposed to call on—Marts?" He began to yell. "Marts! Marts! Can you do anything for me? Can you hear me?"

"He can't hear you," said his friend. "Marx died a long time ago."

"Listen," Haji said, "let's go back to praying to God. Only He can save us." And after that, Haji started praying again.

I had many dialogues with the *peshmerga* about Marx, sometimes lasting the whole night. And in school in Sulaimaniya, and later in Chamchamal, we discussed Marx all the time. The issue was whether Kurdish liberation would come through a nationalistic movement like KDP, or through a Communist/Marxist revolution, or through Islam. Which one of these ideologies would spark the Kurdish revolution that would lead to freedom?

The question was literally a matter of life and death. Pamphlets were written, books were published, debates were argued, all on this issue, everyone responding to someone else's arguments. I read as much as I could to educate myself on the issue, and took many notes. My sister Aaisha thought I was insane. Sometimes I stayed up the whole night reading a book and trying to understand the problem. Some books I read ten times. All of us became very familiar with what Marx, Lenin, Engels, Darwin, Freud, Sartre, Rousseau, Nietzsche, Hegel, and all the others said. It was as though they were not just authors of books, but were actually members of our village with whom we were having a dialogue. Sometimes we just joked about the absurdity of it all by telling stories.

Once the son of the Imam came home from school crying because his Marxist teacher had told him that nothing existed unless you could detect it using your five senses—sight, sound, smell, taste, touch. As an example, he asked the students if they could see God, hear God, smell God, taste God, or touch God. Since the answer in each case was no, he said that God did not exist.

The Imam told his son to tell the teacher that he was crazy and had no mind. If the teacher disagreed, the Imam said, ask him if he could see his mind, or hear his mind, or smell his mind, or taste his mind, or touch his mind. Since the answer in each case was no, the Imam said that the teacher's mind did not exist.

The son did as his father instructed him, and proved to the class that the teacher's mind did not exist. All the children started laughing.

At first the teacher was silent. Then he said, "No, this is different from God, because even though I cannot detect my mind directly using my five senses, I can detect it indirectly by the power of reasoning and thought that it produces."

The Imam's son responded, "Yes, but the same is true of God! Look at life; look at the sky; look at the earth. Everything in the universe sings and proclaims God and God's power."

After that, the teacher did not return to the subject again.

Army in the Village

From 1983 to 1987, my brother Mohsin and I lived for the school year in a government house in Chamchamal (called a *Qismal Dakhly*, or dormitory) that had been built in 1982 for students so they could go to school or college in that city. The government built such dormitories in other cities too. I had been living in Sulaimaniya and going to middle school there since 1981 because there was no middle or high school in Hashazini, or in many other villages at that time, but Chamchamal's school was much closer to home, and now both Mohsin and I had a place to live in that city.

On the other hand, the government's army had a fortified base on a high point near Hashazini, and from there they could look out over the countryside, including our village, for signs of *peshmerga* activity. Whenever they saw signs of such activity, they called in the helicopter gunships to bomb, rocket, or strafe suspected *peshmerga* positions. During my childhood, whenever we heard the sound of helicopters we had to run to the creek that meandered through the village and hide in caves that were carved out of the rocky riverbank. During some periods, we had to hide out in these caves almost daily, since the fear of attack by the government was always present.

In addition, we lived in a *peshmerga*-controlled area. During the day the *peshmerga* kept out of sight from the government troops on the ridge, but at night they came into the village for food and other necessities. They would visit friends, and often came to our house. My mother would quickly fry them an egg on a piece of bread as a kind of guerilla "fast food," and then they would often go to the mosque so they could sleep together in case of attack. I knew many of the *peshmerga* because I had grown up with them, and as I grew older more and more of them became friends.

Because my family helped the *peshmerga*, we were always in danger of being "found out" and arrested by the government. At a very early age, I knew that I could never say that I knew someone who was *peshmerga*. Whenever we had to pass through a government checkpoint, the soldiers would always ask us if we had seen any sign of *peshmerga* activity, and as a child I learned that I had to say no, even if a *peshmerga* had spent the evening at my house the night before. So the pressure of having to lie convincingly, and the knowledge of what would happen to you and your family if you did not, gave substance to the scary tales told by my parents of bad children who were carried off and eaten by wolves and other wild beasts.

There is a story of Saddam himself visiting a Kurdish city. As part of tradition, beautiful young girls carried bunches of flowers to give to him when he arrived. After he took the flowers and kissed one of the girls, Saddam asked her if she knew who he was.

"Yes," the girl said.

"Who am I?" he asked her.

"You are Saddam," she said.

"And how do you know me?"

"Because every time you are on TV," she said, "my dad spits on you and turns the TV off."

Immediately the army took her father, and he disappeared forever.

During the Iran-Iraq war, Saddam was on TV every night for two or three hours "honoring" the soldiers. In Iraq, there were no other channels besides the two government channels, and when Saddam wanted to speak, both channels, and even the radio, broadcast only him. For almost eight years, there was nothing to see on TV—only Saddam.

All males over eighteen were required to serve two years in the army, but when the Iran-Iraq war started in 1980 this two-year period of service was extended for all practical purposes to twenty years. There was no way to escape military service except to be killed or to flee to the *peshmerga*. Many soldiers left the army to join the *peshmerga*, and these groups grew much stronger during the war. The government in

Baghdad realized that the policy had created a bad situation, and so to stop desertions to the *peshmerga* they created guard units organized by tribal leaders. If a tribal leader could organize 100 Kurds into a unit, the government would give them weapons and training and count their time as required military service, even though the men did not leave their region or go to fight in Iran. The tribal leader who organized a unit was called a counselor or adviser, and the force was a border guard unit, but we called both leader and men *Jash*, which means "donkey."

The *Jash* were a popular way of avoiding the unpopular Iran war. One of the most active advisers was a tribal leader named Tahsin, who controlled 600–700 *Jash* from his headquarters in Chamchamal. The government used this force to attack the *peshmerga* because the *Jash* knew their Kurdish countrymen better than the army units did; besides, it suited the government policy of allowing the Kurds to turn tribes against each other and kill each other.

Once in 1983, I paid a visit to the house of my uncle, Sheikh Abdul Qadr. He was the head of Hashazini and was also a person whom I greatly admired, even though he was illiterate. His son Samad was my closest friend at the time. Around noon, while Samad and I were on the roof, we heard gunfire near the road that connected Chamchamal with Sangaw, about three miles from our village. Sheikh Abdul told us to come down. "If they see you outside, there is a danger they will think you are *peshmerga* and attack with rockets or helicopters."

"Sorry, Uncle. We will come down."

"Did you see anything along the highway?"

"There was fighting all along it."

Just then the gunfire got louder and came nearer. I said I wanted to go home, but Sheikh Abdul told me to stay where I was. Samad and I waited. Just as things seemed to have quieted down, suddenly there was a noise outside and ten or fifteen *peshmerga* gunmen burst through the door.

"Salaam, Sheikh Abdul."

"Salaam. Be welcome here. We heard fighting outside. What happened?"

"We were crossing the highway to get away from the army when the *Jash* ambushed us. We fired at them, but they hit two of our men. We have come here with the two wounded men, but the army and the *Jash* are right behind us."

"Where are the two men?" the Sheikh asked them.

"Right here."

"Leave them in my house and I will look after them. The rest of you quickly leave the village."

"But what will you do with them? The army is coming right behind us."

"They are my problem. I want you to go."

The *peshmerga* quickly ran out of the house, leaving the two wounded men behind.

"Yassin, Samad, quickly take some blankets and get these men to the basement. Make them comfortable."

The Sheikh followed us down to the basement to make sure that the two injured men were comfortable. Just then people outside began to shout, "The army is here! *Jash* is here! What should we do?"

"Nothing," the Sheikh called out to them. "No one should run, or the army will shoot. Everybody come with me."

When he got outside, thirty or forty men lined up behind the Sheikh, including Samad and me, and we walked down to the village entrance to welcome the *Jash*. Army cars pulled up and some officers jumped out.

"Who is your advisor?" asked Sheikh Abdul.

"Kak Tahsin," they replied.

"Let me speak to him."

"You can't."

"Kak Tahsin knows me. Just tell him that Abdul Qadr wants to talk to him."

The officers went away, and very soon Kak Tahsin appeared, accompanied by two army officers.

Kak Tahsin said, "I'm sorry, Sheikh, but the army commanders have orders to search your village house by house."

"That is no problem," said the Sheikh. "No problem at all. Let us go to my house first, and then you can send your soldiers to search all of the houses."

So Kak Tahsin, the two army commanders, and about twenty or twenty-five soldiers went to the Sheikh's house, while the rest of the soldiers began to search the village.

Sheikh Abdul took his guests to his living room, which was right above the basement where the two injured *peshmerga* were lying. The Sheikh welcomed his guests and asked them about the gunfire.

"We were trying to catch some rebels," one of the commanders said, "but they escaped and ran toward your village. We are looking for them." While the conversation was going on, Samad and I were serving the guests fruit and tea. On my uncle's instruction, we also told people to slaughter about ten of the sheikh's lambs and prepare a barbecue.

After about an hour and a half, the soldiers returned and reported that the whole village had been searched and nothing had been found. An army commander said that they would all go now.

Sheikh Abdul said, "Impossible. The food will be ready soon. This is your first time visiting our village. How can you even think of leaving before we have an opportunity to serve you?"

"No, please," said the commander. "You have already served us fruit and tea. We have a job to do and we must start right away and do it."

"But we have slaughtered all these lambs for you. Just give us half an hour more and it will be ready for you." Sheikh Abdul turned to Kak Tahsin. "You must tell them that there is no way in Kurdish tradition that you can come to a village for the first time and go away without tasting food. It would be an injury to us."

The army commanders laughed nervously, but they accepted the invitation to eat.

"Now tell the guards and the soldiers to come to the barbecue," said Sheikh Abdul. "Tell them to go to the mosque. We will eat there."

The army commanders objected that there was no need to go to such trouble, that the guards and soldiers already had their food.

Sheikh Abdul smiled. "Tell them that we will not become poor if they eat our food. There is enough for everyone. Let them go to the mosque and eat, and then they can take some rest."

The two army commanders said that they would also like to see the mosque. My uncle knew that the Iraqi army had been told during their training that the Kurdish people were wild barbarians and Communists who could be killed without violating Islam because they were not real Muslims. So these commanders, who had just received great hospitality from Sheikh Abdul, were undoubtedly curious to see the mosque and the kind of prayers that were performed there.

"We will go in a few minutes when the food is ready," said the Sheikh, who then began to tell the army commanders about Kurdish customs. The Sheikh called me to his side.

"Kak Tahsin, this is my nephew, Yassin, who is studying in Chamchamal. Yassin, this is your Uncle Tahsin, who also lives in Chamchamal. Whenever you need something, go and visit him. Don't be shy, just ask him. He is your uncle."

Kak Tahsin said to me, "Yes. You should come to my home." Then apparently thinking of the Arab Iraqi commanders, he asked me, "Can you speak Arabic?"

"Only a few words," I said.

"So talk to me," he said in Arabic.

I tried to reply in Arabic but it came out all funny. Everybody laughed. Then Sheikh Abdul introduced Samad. The two army commanders loved us. They brought out their cameras and had their pictures taken with us. Eventually, when we went to the mosque, one of the commanders held my hand and the other held Samad's hand, and they stayed with us until they finally left the village.

The half-hour that was needed to start the barbecue became three hours. The army commanders were surprised to see how many villagers were serving food to the Iraqi army soldiers and being very friendly with them. Everyone was joking and having a good time. Probably the commanders were beginning to feel some guilt for having shot at these same villagers from helicopters almost every day, and for believing that the villagers were hostile, ignorant Communists who just wanted to kill Iraqi soldiers. It was obvious that the villagers did not hate Arabs, as the officers had been told. So why was the army attacking the villagers every day?

The commanders had also probably been told that there were Iranian soldiers being hidden in the village, and yet this obviously was not true. They had searched the village, but they had found no Iranian soldiers. Perhaps the commanders and their soldiers began to doubt the truth of the propaganda they had been given about the Kurds, and began to even doubt why they were fighting the Kurds at all.

Evening was coming on, and all the villagers prayed with the soldiers in the mosque. Soon it would be dark, and there would be no time to continue the search for the *peshmerga*. At night the *peshmerga* had the advantage over the army, so the commanders decided to stop the search and go back to their base. Before they left, the commanders gave Samad and me their home addresses and promised to send us pictures from Baghdad.

So ended the great *peshmerga* raid. Samad and I really loved the two army commanders even as they loved us, because we believed that after this day they would never again send their helicopters to bomb our village. "*Ma'Assalamah*," we told them, which is Arabic for "goodbye with peace and safety."

We all went back to Sheikh Abdul's house, went immediately to the basement, and told the two injured *peshmerga* not to worry anymore, they were safe. We brought them up to the living room where Kak Tahsin and the two army commanders had been sitting. We gave them some of the dinner that had been served to the army.

"Now is it *peshmerga* time," I said to Samad.

"No, it is not yet sundown," he laughed.

"Why don't you ask your father what he would have done if the soldiers had searched the house and found the two *peshmerga* in the basement?" I said.

"Oh, he has hundreds of ways to get around that," said Samad.

"Like what?"

"Well, last year when the army came with *Jash* to our home, two *peshmerga* were in the house and we had no time to even get them out of the room. My father told them to quickly put their guns in the corner and cover them with a blanket. Immediately afterwards the soldiers came into the room. My father introduced the two *peshmerga* to the *Jash* soldiers as his two nephews. They all shook hands, sat down, drank tea, and joked and talked until the soldiers left."

I told Samad, "I hope your father will become the Iraqi president some day. He will bring the country together, Kurd with Arab, *peshmerga* with *Jash*. They'll all talk and joke and eat and pray together instead of hate and fight and kill each other."

Qum

One day, one of my friends who was a *peshmerga* told me that they had captured a government soldier. They gave the soldier to my friend to take care of. My friend took the soldier into a room and told him to sit down. The soldier did not speak Kurdish, and my friend did not speak much Arabic, but he tried his best to communicate.

My friend said, "I told him to sit down in Arabic by saying, '*Qum.*' But he immediately stood at attention. I slapped him and said, '*Qum!*' again. The soldier stood even straighter. Then I began yelling '*Qum!*' at him, and I beat him when he would not sit down. But he only stood straighter and straighter."

Finally my friend grew tired of beating the soldier and went outside. "How's your guest doing?" a friend of the *peshmerga* asked.

"He is the most obstinate man I have ever met!" replied my friend. "He does not listen to anything I say, and he does just the opposite no matter how hard I beat him."

"What is he doing?"

"Well, when I tell him to sit down, he refuses, and he just stands straight even when I beat him."

"What did you say to him?"

" 'Sit down.' "

"No, what is the word you used?"

"*Qum.*"

"But *Qum* means 'stand up.' "

"What?"

"Go tell him '*Ijlis*.' That means 'sit down.' "

My friend went back and said "*Ijlis!*" to the soldier, who was standing as straight as a rod. Immediately the soldier collapsed onto the floor. The friend could not control his laughter, and ran outside again. "You were right!" he said to his *peshmerga* friend. "He sat!"

Torture

Torture was part of the tradition on both sides. Once I was arguing with a *peshmerga* friend about the use of torture. He defended the practice by saying that the government tortured *peshmerga* captives, and so it was only justice that the *peshmerga* should be allowed to do the same to government captives.

I told him, "Acting the same simply makes you the same. You are no better than the government."

"But we do not torture even one percent of the amount that the government tortures our family and friends."

"So what? You should prove that you are a freedom fighter struggling for human rights and dignity, rather than just being one percent as bad as the government."

He laughed. "You read too much. Life is different than all the books in the world."

In 1983, the government captured my cousin Shabaz while he was putting a poster for the *peshmerga* on a wall at night. They took him away, and nobody knew what happened to him. He just disappeared. In 1987, a prisoner was freed from jail and said he had known Shabaz in jail, and that Shabaz had died under torture about three years earlier. His family, however, did not believe this, and still waited for Shabaz to be released.

The government would arrest someone with no court order and never tell the family. Then they would torture him to get him to say he had done what the government wanted him to acknowledge, even if he had nothing to do with it. If the person denied doing it, the government would keep torturing him. If he died, the government would

never acknowledge that they had even arrested him. But if, under torture, the person acknowledged that he had done something wrong,
they would take him to a special court, where he would get the death
penalty. In this instance, because the government kept the person in
what they called a "court," they would inform the family and allow
them one visit before they hanged him.

One of our neighbors in Hashazini, Jawhar, was a *peshmerga* and
was captured by the Iraqi army and taken away. Sixteen other *peshmerga*, including my cousin's son, Dr. Alaadeen, were killed, but
Jawhar was the only one to survive. His family searched for him for
seven months until one day they received a letter from the government
and brought it to me to read, since they were illiterate. The letter said
that Jawhar was jailed in Abu Ghraib prison and that the family could
come and visit him on a particular date at a particular time. At the top
of the letter was written in red, "Aeen." The family asked me many
questions about this red notation, but I knew nothing about it. Then
someone said that the notation meant that Jawhar would be hanged,
because the first letter of the word was the same as the first letter of the
word for "hanging." I told them not to jump to conclusions.

On the day specified in the letter, ten or fifteen people from Jawhar's
family went to see him. When they got back to Hashazini, we went to
see them. They were all crying.

"They let us see Jawhar," the family said, "because they are going
to hang him next week. He showed us the court's order of execution."

"How is he holding up?"

"He was strong. He even tried to stop us when we cried. He is
proud he will give his life for Kurdish freedom. He told us to give his
salaam to every one of you and to ask for your forgiveness."

Three weeks later, Jawhar's family received a package containing
his clothes as a sign that he had been hanged, and a letter stating that
the family was not allowed to have a funeral for him. They never got
his body back.

These were the conditions in which I grew up.

All during this time, the adults were watching the children in primary school, deciding who would become a farmer or a shepherd, who they should send to the city to work in a restaurant, or who should go on to middle school or even high school. By the time you were ten or twelve and had finished primary school, society had decided what would become of you, your childhood was essentially over, and you became a responsible adult. If you stayed in the village, by the time you were fourteen or fifteen you were the man the family depended on, and you had two basic choices: get married, or carry a weapon for the *peshmerga*. If you refused to get married, people humiliated you to such an extent that joining the *peshmerga* and carrying a weapon was the only way to prove that you really were a man. Whichever route you chose, trouble was waiting for you.

Summer Job

Most summers during the 1980s, Mohsin and I used to go to Kirkuk to work so we could save some money for school. There was no way to make money in Hashazini, because if there was anything that needed to be done people would just do it themselves, and if more than one person was needed, people would help each other. Nobody ever paid for labor. In most Kurdish cities it was hard to find work because the economy was so depressed. So we used to go to Kirkuk because many construction jobs were available there.

In Iraq at that time, you did not find a job by submitting an application. Most jobs in an office, a hospital, the electric company, the phone company, the media, or any other big company all belonged to the government. This kind of employment required that you be a member of the Baath party, and you had to know someone in the government who would help you get a job. Mohsin and I were only students, however, and we had only three months in the summer to make money.

I went to Kirkuk with Mohsin for the first time in 1983, when I was thirteen. Mohsin was fourteen and had already gone the year before, but he said that this year was not like last year. It was really hard to get a job because many Egyptians were coming to Iraq looking for work. Kirkuk was literally full of Egyptians—they slept on the streets like strangers. I never thought I would see a group of people poorer than the Kurds, but the Egyptians were poorer and would work for almost nothing. For this reason, wages for labor were very low. Mohsin and I also had a problem because we were so young: people either wouldn't hire us, or they would give us only half-pay, especially since Mohsin was really skinny. People thought that we were both children and couldn't do a full day's work.

For accommodations, we went to Findq Abas, the same hotel that Mohsin had used the previous year. Ninety-five percent of the people there were Kurdish workers. It was the cheapest hotel in Kirkuk, and it was very dirty. There were about twenty-five rooms, each about ten feet by ten feet, on two floors. Two to three people occupied each room. For all of these people, there were just three bathrooms and two showers; it was like a cattle stall in our village. But we didn't care; we were there for only seven or eight hours a night, and everyone slept on the roof anyway. The owner of Hotel Abas was Turkish, but he spoke some Kurdish and was really a nice guy. To keep his customers, he would sometimes help them get jobs; if they could not find work, he would let them stay for two or three nights as a loan.

Every day before dawn we all left the hotel and went to a place in the city called Mayan, where we waited for contractors to hire us. We had to wake up at 3 a.m. to make preparations and walk to Mayan, which was about forty minutes from the hotel, so we could arrive there between 4 and 4:30, which is when the contractors came—before sunrise, so they could start the workday early. A workday usually ran from 6 a.m. to 5 p.m. We had to work ten hours, with only one hour for lunch. If we did not get picked by the contractors by 6 a.m., we probably would not get a full-time job that day, but we might get a part-time job until about 8:30. After 9, though, those who weren't picked knew that there was no hope, and they might as well go back to the hotel. Sometimes contractors came after sunrise, but then they would only offer half-pay, even if someone was willing to work eight or nine hours. But many students (like us) had come from outside the city and were living in hotels and needed money to pay their expenses, and so we had no alternative but to take any job that was offered, since otherwise our time was wasted and no money could be saved for school.

When the contractors did come, we all stood up, hoping to be hired, and the contractors checked everyone over as though they were buying an animal. They examined your muscles, and if they liked you they asked you some questions. If you gave the answers they wanted, perhaps they would pick you. The contractors usually just gave Mohsin and me a stern look because we were too young, and picked someone else.

We did not know Kirkuk well, and we could not speak Arabic. Even if a contractor picked us for a job, we still might lose it: after we worked five or six hours, our employer might say that he was not satisfied and give us no money for our work, and might not even bring us back to the hotel. We might have to walk for hours to get to the hotel. But what could we do? If we objected, they would just beat us, since there were no police to call and no cell phones to use to call them.

Mohsin and I tried to get jobs where we could work together, or at least where we could work with someone else we knew. Many times we turned down jobs where we could not be together. And even if we found a good job, the work was very difficult.

Between 10 a.m. and 4 p.m., the temperature in Kirkuk was always at least 90 degrees, and sometimes it went as high as 115 degrees. Often throughout the whole day we carried black pails or buckets full of cement, and the contractors were always yelling at us to hurry... hurry...hurry! They made us carry two pails at a time. They were always cursing. They wouldn't give us even a one-minute break. Most of the time our only food for the day was bread and an egg, which we brought with us. They never fed us. We lost so much weight that we could count our ribs one by one, especially Mohsin, who looked like a victim of starvation, all bones and no flesh. Often I got nosebleeds, and I would have to take a break and lie on my back until it stopped. Then it was back to hurry...hurry...hurry.

Once after a nosebleed stopped, I stood up and started carrying my bucket again—and collapsed and passed out. I don't know how long I was out, but when I woke up I told the contractor that although

I had worked two-thirds of a day, I just wanted him to pay me for a half-day and I would go back to the hotel, since I could not continue working because I had a very bad headache. The contractor, however, said that if I stopped working I would get nothing. I told him just to take me back to the hotel, that I didn't want any money. He refused. I begged him for bus fare. He said no way. So I forced myself to go on and finish the day. At the end, the contractor still wanted to pay me only half-pay because I had been unconscious for an hour. But all of the workers got together and told the contractor to fear God and give me my money—and after that he gave me 75% of it, cutting 25% for the hour that I was unconscious.

Once I started working with a contractor who said that he liked my work and that he would employ me on a regular basis. I was happy because I did not have to go to Mayan every day. However, I still had to get up at 4 a.m. because I had to walk two hours to get to the job site. I would work there until 5 p.m., and then I had to walk two hours back to the hotel. I could not take a taxi because it would be so expensive that I would not have enough money left over to pay for the hotel, or to save for school. It was a fifteen-hour day, but I was really happy.

For the first two weeks, the contractor paid me for my work every day. By the third week we knew each other pretty well, and the contractor said that he would pay me for the third week at the end of the week, and after that the job would be over. But it became ten days, and I still wasn't paid. Finally the contractor told me that although the job was over, the homeowner still had not paid him for the job, but that if I came to his house tomorrow he would pay me. He gave me the address, but then he told me that he did not know what time the homeowner would pay him, and so he told me it would be better to come back sometime after tomorrow. He was going to take a week's vacation from work, and would be home the whole week. He brought me back to my hotel, which he had never done before, and he shook my hand and hugged me and said, "I will see you after tomorrow."

On the day after tomorrow, I went about noon to the address he gave me. I found the block, but there was no such number. So I asked people if they knew Wasta Hashim. Nobody knew him. Finally one man said he knew him, and said he was a thief who lied all the time. I told him what had happened and he said that I would never find him, that he did this to many people. The only way I would find him would be in Mayan, but he generally worked for a month and then disappeared for several months.

Three weeks later I saw Wasta Hashim in Mayan. I ran to him and tried to shake his hand, but he denied that he knew me. He said it must be someone else that I knew. I went to collect some of my friends who were waiting on another corner, but when I brought them back, Wasta Hashim had disappeared. People told me that he had done this hundreds of times. No one worked for him unless the worker was paid in advance. I was disappointed to have been so badly cheated.

On another occasion, Mohsin was sick and had to stay in the hotel for a whole week. For three days in a row I went back to the hotel crying in the morning because I could not find any work. I was afraid that we would not be able to pay for the hotel. Mohsin became really angry and started cursing the Egyptians.

I said, "Please stop. They are poor and hard workers like us."

But Mohsin said, "Before they came we used to get good jobs that paid ten dinar a day. Now we can't get work for even five dinar a day, because the Egyptians will do everything for one dinar a day. Wherever we go—to restaurants, construction jobs, cleaning jobs—everywhere there are Egyptians. They even sleep on the street."

One day I asked one of the Egyptians why they did everything for such low pay. He said that they were coming here only to work. If they made even one dinar, it was better than nothing, which is what they had. They didn't want to stay for even one day without work. He also said that when they changed Iraqi money to Egyptian, they could get a good exchange rate: at that time one dinar was equal to two dollars. (Ten years later, in 1993, one dollar was equal to 700 dinar.)

Mohsin said that we should both go out and find—something. I told him he was still sick, but he said he felt better. We went to the tea shop where most of the Kurdish workers congregated when they couldn't find work. Sometimes people would come to the tea shop when they had a small job, and hired people for only a few hours.

While we were sitting and talking, Kareem, a friend of Mohsin's, came over to us. When we told him about our situation, Kareem said that he never worked with contractors. He said there was another place like Mayan, but for one-time jobs only. For example, if someone was moving to a new apartment he might hire some workers to help him carry his furniture. Or sometimes people were hired just to clean a backyard or to empty trucks, small things like that.

The best thing about those kinds of jobs, Kareem said, was that after you made an agreement, nobody yelled at you or humiliated you. You were responsible for getting the job done, but you didn't have to work with anyone. You were your own boss. If you worked one hour or ten hours, you got the same money because the pay was per job. You could earn good money for even simple jobs, and rich people would give you good tips as well. You might have several days in which you earned nothing, but then you would get a day in which you earned enough for the whole week.

We said this sounded good to us, and so Kareem took us with him. We ended up standing on a street corner with nobody else around. I did not believe we could get jobs just standing on a street corner, but Kareem assured us that he had a number of other friends who did this, and that they were not here because they had all gotten jobs.

Eventually a big truck stopped. The driver said he had twenty-five tons of cement—500 bags—that he wanted us to unload from the truck. Kareem asked for 10% of a dinar for each bag, or fifty dinar for the whole job. The truck driver wanted to pay twenty-five dinar. Kareem refused. I was surprised he said no, because twenty-five dinar was a lot of money. If Mohsin and I worked together for three days, we could make about twenty-five dinar—and now we could probably make that in three hours! We also had no money left to pay our hotel bill, and we needed a job that day so we could eat. So Mohsin said that he and I would unload the truck. Kareem refused again, so Mohsin and I got in the truck and the driver drove us into the city for about twenty minutes.

When we finally stopped, the driver told us to take the cement bags into a building some distance away. We objected that he had only asked us to unload the bags from the truck, not carry them to another building. We asked for more money. The driver refused. At this point we were completely lost and had no idea how to get back to our hotel, even if we could walk that far. But we had to have some money, so we agreed to do what he wanted.

We started lugging the bags out of the truck and into the building. It was really hot and we had no equipment. Soon we were covered with cement dust, which reacted with our sweat. The concrete, curing on our bodies and in our noses, burned our skin. The bags were as heavy as stones. Mohsin was still sick, and neither of us had eaten much in the last few days. Soon we were exhausted.

We thought that we could finish in one or two hours, but it took us seven hours to unload the last bag. We were half-dead. By that time it was night, and we sat down to wait for the driver to come back. He had come back two hours earlier, saw that we still were not done, and left again. We were somewhat afraid. Suppose the driver did not come back that night: where would we go? Suppose the driver came back, beat us, and chased us away: where would we go? We couldn't speak the language; how would we find our way home? We did not know anyone.

Mohsin had worn all the skin off his shoulder, and he said that the cement dust was making the raw sore burn. Our noses were so full of dust that we could barely breathe. I said, "We made 25 dinar, but it almost killed us."

Eventually the driver came back. "Oh good," he said, "you are finally done. You took too long, but at least there were no problems."

"Please give us our money and take us back to our hotel," Mohsin said.

"How many bags did you rip?" asked the driver.

"We put the ripped bags to the side."

The driver counted the ripped bags. "You ripped twenty bags," he said. "You will have to pay for them."

"What!!" I said

"I intend to sell the bags," said the driver. "I cannot sell ripped bags, and so they are of no use to me."

"But most of them were already ripped on the truck."

"Then why didn't you leave them on the truck?"

"You did not tell us to!"

After a long argument, the driver said that we had to pay for half the bags. He said that each bag was worth three dinar, so ten bags were worth thirty dinar. After subtracting our wages of twenty-five dinar, the driver said we owed him five dinar. Mohsin showed him his injured shoulder, pointed out that we had we worked for him for seven hours and practically killed ourselves, and still we should pay him five dinar?

"Oh, you can take the ten bags of cement for yourselves," said the driver. He knew perfectly well that there was no way we could carry away ten ripped bags of cement. At that point, we could not have carried even one. And even if we could have, where should we have taken it—to the hotel?

I told the driver that he should fear God and give us our rights and our wages, and bring us back to our hotel where we could take a shower and rest. He ignored me. Finally, after more arguing, we asked him to give us half of what we had agreed on—twelve dinar. Then I started crying. I raised my hands and began to address God, saying, "Oh God, You know this is unfair. Oh God, You do not have to accept this."

For some reason my lamentation had an effect on the driver. Suddenly he said, "No problem. I will give you fifteen dinar—more than half." We accepted it and asked him to take us back to the hotel. He said that it was too late. We begged and said we were scared to take a taxi to the hotel because we had heard of people being robbed late at night. He still refused.

Finally he gave us directions back to the hotel, and we had to walk. Mohsin was shaking like someone who was freezing. I was bent and limping along as though I was 100 years old.

I said to Mohsin, "Your friend sure found us a good job."

"It was our fault," he replied. "We took a job that he refused."

I said, "We did this job like Egyptians—we worked for half price. Maybe your friend will be mad at us. But he may say that the first time he tried to help us we undercut his price."

"No," said Mohsin. "He has been my friend for a long time. Tomorrow I will explain to him why we took this job, and that we will promise after this to stay with him. We just needed some money so we could pay for our hotel and food. But it still doesn't look like we will be able to save any money for school."

I held Mohsin's hand and said, "God will provide for us."

Young Sheikh

In 1984, when I was fourteen, I went back to Hashazini for Eid, the concluding celebration of Ramadan. When I arrived at the house I could see that my father was very upset. I said *Salaam* to him and kissed his hand, but he did not give me a response. I gave my mother a hug and asked if she were OK. She said that Dad was not upset with her but with my cousin Ismaeel, the village Imam. I asked my father what the problem was.

"He left," my father said. "I don't know why. He does not want to lead the Eid prayers tomorrow in the mosque. Tomorrow people will come from all the other villages for the big prayer, and we have no one to lead them. What can we do? My father's last wish was that prayer would take place in the mosque five times each day. In all my life, I do not remember a single week that we missed one Friday prayer or one Eid prayer. Tomorrow will be the first time."

"God will do something," I told him.

Dad smiled. "Nevertheless, we should do something too," he said.

I told Dad the story that he used to tell me all the time about whether God was greater than Sultan Mahmood. He was an unjust ruler who sent notice to a man that he intended to hang that man the next morning. The victim sent word back to Sultan Mahmood asking if it were not true that God was greater than Mahmood, since only God knew what would happen the next day. The next morning the victim arose, and on hearing that an announcement was being made outside, went out of his house expecting to hear that he was to be hung that very day. Instead, he heard that Sultan Mahmood had died during the night, and the supposed victim was to prepare a grave for him. The victim thanked God for sparing his life.

Dad smiled again, but he could not shake the worry that he would fail his father's last wish and that nobody would lead Eid prayers tomorrow. Suddenly he remembered a person in another village some three hours away who might lead prayers, and said he would go and fetch him. He took the horse and left. I knew that he would not be home until very late that night.

The next morning I was happy to see that Dad had returned, but he was still mad. Someone had taken the man to the city, he said, and the man was not at home when he arrived.

We went to the mosque and gave morning prayer. People asked us who would lead the big Eid prayer later in the day. Dad said he did not know, and that maybe someone should tell the people that Eid prayer had been cancelled so they didn't have to come. But people were coming from other villages, and some had already started on their journey. Dad said he did not know what to do, and that we all should start praying and crying.

"Daddy, you can do it," I said.

He looked at me like he wanted to slap me in the face.

"Why not, Daddy?" I said. "You've done it hundreds of times. You know how."

"I'm not an Imam."

"You don't have to be. If you only know the prayers it will be sufficient!"

"So why don't you do it?" he said to me, like he was making fun of me.

"If you let me..."

Father looked at me in surprise, as though he did not know what to say, but our neighbor immediately said, "Yassin can do it. He can read the Qur'an. He knows it."

"He's just a kid," said my father.

"So what?"

"People don't like to pray behind a kid."

"So tell the people that's all we have. If they don't want to pray, they don't have to pray."

Eventually my father agreed, and an announcement was made at the mosque that we would have Eid prayers.

The Eid prayer ends with a sermon. When I stood up to preach, the people were shocked. I was too young, I had no beard, and I did not even have a turban. Any one of those things would have made people uncomfortable, but all three were unthinkable for an Imam who was going to deliver a sermon on a major religious day.

"Where is your turban?" somebody asked.

"I don't have one," I said. A turban was found and put on my head.

"An Imam without a beard?" somebody else asked in surprise.

"I can't grow a beard yet," I said. I realized that as long as they continued to ask questions, I would have a problem, so I decided to face the issue directly. Raising my voice, I addressed the crowd, and everyone remained silent.

"All Kurds follow Imam Shaafeyi's school of thought on Islam," I said, "so I want to talk to you about this school of thought and prove to you that our great Imam Shaafeyi himself was leading prayers before he grew a beard. According to the histories, Imam Shaafeyi finished memorizing the Qur'an when he was eight years old, and soon afterwards he was leading prayer. So great was his mastery of the Qur'an that some scholars said that they went and prayed behind the 'kid' so that they might be led to cry during the prayer and their hearts might be softened. So the very Imam that we now revere used to lead scholars in prayer when he was no more than ten or eleven years old. Do any of you believe that he had a beard at that age?"

Nobody gave me an answer, but the people all opened their eyes and listened quietly, and after that I heard no more questions. I went ahead with the sermon. I told the people that we must separate culture from religion. "We do many things because we think it is part of our faith," I said, "but in reality they are just customs and totally against Islam. Our great Imam Shaafeyi used to say, 'What sky will shade me and what earth will hide me if I say something is a matter of faith, and the Prophet Mohammad never said anything about it?'

"Imam Shaafeyi also said, 'If my preaching is the opposite of the Prophet's word, throw my word against the wall, and take the Prophet's word to learn in school.' It is easy enough to add many things to the faith that were never there to begin with. Religion should be simple, clear, and easy. Let us keep it simple, clear, and easy, and not make it hard on ourselves. God wants us to be thankful for what we have been given; helpful to our brothers and sisters; respectful to our neighbors; generous to the poor; merciful to the children; soft to our wives; clean of heart; and always truthful. God loves you. This is the faith that we should teach our children and take for ourselves as well."

When I finished, people stood in line to shake my hand and wish me happy Eid. They all called me Sheikh and tried to kiss my hand. It took hours until we were done.

I believe this was the happiest day of my father's life—to see his son as the Imam. This had always been his only hope and wish, that he could see his children leading prayer. At the time I was very excited and nervous and thought that I could not continue, but God made it easy for me. It was my first attempt at public preaching, and the villagers still talk about it and are happy that they saw it.

Art Show

1984 was my last year of middle school (ninth grade) in Chamchamal, and our school had a Student Day for Art. Every student was to prepare a work of art, and the school would choose the best fifty or sixty of them for an art show. I was not good in art at all. Instead, the art teacher chose three of us to clean and prepare a hall in the city government center and hang the artworks for the show there. When we were finished doing this, the principal said that a government delegation would come the next day to formally open the show. We roped off the door, prepared a tray of flowers and put a pair of scissors on it, and arranged to have some small girls in Kurdish clothes carry the tray to the government delegation.

The students began to assemble the next morning before 8 a.m., but they could not enter the show until the rope was officially cut by the government delegation. Around 9 a.m. I saw the principal acting very worried, and asked what was wrong. He said that the art teacher was sick and could not come.

"Couldn't he just come to open the show with the government delegation?" I asked.

"He has laryngitis and can't speak a word," the principal said.

"I have a friend who knows a lot about art."

"No, this is a student activity and it must be done by someone at the school."

"What about another teacher?"

"They don't know anything about art!"

"So what should we do? The government delegation will be coming in just forty minutes."

"The art teacher told me that *you* should welcome the government delegation and explain all of the artworks to them and answer their questions."

"ME!"

"He said that you could do it better than he could."

"He was joking."

"No, he was serious. Can you do it?"

"If you want me to. I will do my best."

The principal hesitated for a moment, and then said, "You have to be very careful. We have all kinds of guests coming from the government."

I nodded to indicate I knew what he meant. He did not have to give me a detailed explanation of the problem. Like poetry, all art is potentially political and therefore dangerous.

We agreed that I would be the guide for the government delegation. As usual, I was wearing an old, ugly jacket, and my shoes were ripped in several places, but the principal did not suggest that I change or borrow clothes from someone else. I took my place with the little girls carrying the tray of flowers and waited with a hundred other students for the government delegation to arrive.

And now here came two, three, five, ten, fifteen cars with police and guards. The principal was shaking. We welcomed the delegation to our show. We brought the mayor to the rope, he took the scissors from the tray and cut the rope, everybody clapped, and the show officially began.

Now it was my turn. I walked next to the mayor with a government official trailing behind us and a video cameraman walking in front of us, filming us. I suddenly realized that my shabby coat and ripped shoes would be broadcast all across Iraq that night.

When we came to the first picture, I explained what it represented and my ideas about it, and we continued past all of the works of art in this way. I talked about the color, and darkness and light, and symbolism. The mayor was actually an educated man and knew about art too. Sometimes he asked me a technical question, and I gave him a confident answer, as though I had grown up with Van Gogh and Picasso.

After about forty-five minutes, we finished viewing the exhibition and the mayor went to write something in the memory book as the government's representative. We took the delegation back to their cars and thanked everybody for coming. The mayor shook the principal's hand, kissed me, said "Great job," and the visit was over. The principal was excited and delighted. He hugged me and said, "Excellent! Excellent!"

After this, the show stayed open for three days, and every art lover in the city came to see it. Repressed people are often excited about art in a way that free people are not, because you can speak with images in a way you cannot always safely put into words. Every line and shade in a painting is analyzed for its hidden meaning, and everyone wants to know what influential and educated people think about the art, as a way to determine what else they may be thinking but cannot say. As the guide, I had to answer their questions, and so I was really busy. It was a wonderful opportunity for me to meet the most important and influential people in Chamchamal, and I came away from the art show with a large number of addresses and new friends.

On the third day my art teacher came to the show. "How is it going?" he asked.

"Very well, I believe," I said.

"That is what I've heard. Many people came to visit me and they all told me how successful the show has been."

"How much greater the show would have been if you had been here to give your explanations."

"You did it better."

I told him to stop joking.

"Where is the memory book?" he asked me.

"On the table."

After he read the memory book, my teacher said that it was wonderful how many people had come, but they were not commenting on the art. They were instead commenting on all the things that I had talked about.

"Stop joking," I said.

"Read for yourself," he replied.

After I had read a few entries, I said, "What would happen if all these people knew that I cannot draw a single line that looks like anything? Even my handwriting is so bad that sometimes I can't read what I wrote! What kind of artist can I be?"

My teacher just smiled.

Three days after the show closed, the principal called me to his office and gave me a letter from the mayor saying that we had done a great job, that he was proud of our school, and that he was not going to forget Yassin's explanations. Then the principal gave me a package that he said was a gift from the mayor. I told him to keep it for the school. But the principal said that the mayor's gardener had said it was specifically for Yassin. I did not want to take it, but the principal insisted. When I got home, I opened it and found a new jacket and a pair of shoes. *Thank you, Mr. Mayor,* I said to myself. *I got the message.*

Guns Rule

That year when school was over, one of my friends told me that the government was going to open a three-month summer camp for farmers' children in Arbat to teach them how to drive tractors and combines.

"That's good," I said. "You should come too."

"I can't, because my father is not a farmer," my friend explained. "But my uncle knows the people who manage the camp, and I will have him give you special approval if you want to go."

"Yes, that will be excellent," I said.

When the time came, I went to the camp. I was really excited to learn how to drive. But that summer was the middle of the Iran-Iraq war, and Arbat was only about fifty miles from the Iranian border. Every day we heard the sound of rockets exploding. In the fifth week of camp Iranian forces occupied Penjween City, only thirty miles from Arbat, and refugees began to pour in from the city. The refugee families filled the mosque and the government buildings, yet there were still many people in the streets.

Suddenly five or six cars came to our building, and men got out dressed in Kurdish uniforms and carrying weapons—these were the border guards, or *Jash*. The *Jash* ordered the camp management to empty the camp buildings in two hours to make room for them. The manager, Tarq Ali, explained that they were running a summer camp and the children came from all over; they could not just kick the students out.

One of the *Jash* leaders, Rasha Bahri, got mad and yelled at the manager, "School, school! It is not time for school. It is not time for class."

"But why do you need this building?" Tarq Ali said. "Who gave it to you? Do you have an order to take the building? You have to bring an order from the mayor."

Rasha Bahri said, "I am the mayor and I have an order from my gun. Now empty the building."

Tarq Ali refused to leave the building. Rasha Bahri became very angry and said he would beat him, and the building now had to be empty in twenty minutes rather than two hours. Tarq Ali said that he was still responsible for the students, and he could not kick them out without an order. But the *Jash* just pushed past Tarq Ali and took over the building. When he tried to stop them, they beat him with the butts of their guns until his face was covered in blood. Some of the students ran away, but I stayed with Tarq Ali and argued with the *Jash*, saying, "Please stop! Please stop!" They beat me a couple of times with their rifle butts. They began to throw our personal things out of the building. They would not even let Tarq Ali make a call, and just told us to take our things and leave. So we did.

We spent the night in the bus station. The next morning Tarq Ali came and said that he could not do anything, and he gave us all bus fare home. Eventually the Iraqi army recaptured Penjween City.

This was the situation in my country. There was no time for class, there was no time for school. The *Jash* were the mayor and everything else because they had guns, and guns ruled, and that is why life was all about suffering. We all hoped that after the removal of Saddam and the downfall of his regime, the rule of the gun would be over and the law and schools would return, and Baghdad would become like London or New York. But none of this happened, and now things are even worse. Hundreds of college professors have been killed, and thousands more have left the country. There is no basic security for civilians. The same old militia leaders are ruling the country—with guns. Baghdad has become Mogadishu or Kabul, rather than London or New York.

I Don't Want to Join

In middle and high school, we were not beaten as often as when we were younger, but society and the government began to put a lot more pressure on us. We were told that if we did not volunteer to serve in the army during summer vacation, we could not continue in school. Sometimes the teachers tried to force us to join the Baath party, and if we refused they accused us of supporting either the Kurdish *peshmerga* or the Iranian regime, or else of not loving our country.

When I was in ninth grade, I was the only student in the class who refused to join the Baath party. Every Thursday party meetings were held at school, and I was always taken to the person in charge of students so I would be persuaded to join. Teachers and government agents constantly questioned me about why I refused to join.

"Do you love your country?"

"Yes, of course."

"Don't you want to serve your country?"

"Yes. I think that I am already serving."

"If you want to serve, why don't you join the Baath party?"

"I am serving my country by learning."

"You can do both."

"I want to be independent. I don't like politics."

On many Thursdays, I refused to go to school so that I would not have to endure the questioning. But then I became afraid that I would be kicked out of school, and if that happened I would have to serve in the army for at least two years. So I decided at the end of the year to go to night school, which put less pressure on me to join the Baath party and also allowed me to work and earn money during the day.

It was better in night school, but with all the pressure most of the students did join the party, with only four or five of us in the entire school refusing to join. It was especially hard for me because my village was in a *peshmerga* area, and my family and I were being watched all the time. It was impossible for students who did not join the Baath party to obtain government jobs or to work in the army, or a hospital, or a factory, or a school, or a bank, or an electric company, or a phone company, or the post office, or almost anywhere.

How could I have ever joined the Baath party that every day killed so many Kurds and scared thousands more? But my answers to their questions were truthful—I did not like any other parties or politicians better. In my experience, politics has completely destroyed the Middle East, and most Muslims are victims of corrupt politicians. Most political groups switch affiliation every few years, from Communist to Nationalist to Liberal to Socialist to Sunni to Shiite. One day they work for Russia, and the next day they work for America. They switch and then they fight one another, even though they are all under the same leadership. All of them claim they believe in democracy, but none of them have elected rulers and all claim to be the party of the majority. These corrupt, ineffectual, squabbling parties have cost us our liberty and our dignity, our childhoods and our education, our economy and our jobs, our brotherhood and our human relations, our health and our futures, our lives and our blood.

Some students who were not so smart and got more than their share of beatings began to avoid school and hide from their parents as they became older, and when they were fifteen or so they ran off and joined the *peshmerga*. They would be given a weapon, shown how to use it, and the next day they might be in a battle without any training at all. I used to tell my friends that if they really wanted to free Kurdistan and serve the Kurds, they should be patient and steady, finish college, and get a degree. Become a doctor or an engineer—and *then* join the *peshmerga*. Some of them said it would be too late then. I replied with the Kurdish expression, "It will take so long that our children and grandchildren can participate."

Once a friend made me angry by saying that I was preventing people from joining the *peshmerga* by telling them to finish school first, and so I was helping the government. I said that I encouraged everyone to join the *peshmerga*, but middle and high school students must study first before they join. That was the way to our future. It was the Iraqi government that tried to get Kurds to leave school because they wanted us to remain ignorant. They didn't want us to have a future. Many times I told *peshmerga* leaders, "Don't accept students under twenty. Let them finish school first."

One day I was talking with one of the *peshmerga* commanders, Sheikh Worya, about that, and he told me I was absolutely right, and he quoted Napoleon Bonaparte, saying that "I am not afraid of 100 men with guns, but I am afraid of one man armed with a pen." Since then, I have always looked at my pen as my weapon. I consider myself a *peshmerga*, but I fight my battles with a pen.

There is an expression that "the Kurds eat themselves," and it is true—we have a long history of fighting each other, and we have paid a high price for it. Our ignorance has made our problems, our suffering, and our poverty. The government's policy has always been to encourage the Kurds to attack each other, and we oblige them continually. *Peshmerga* killing each other; Turkish Kurds killing Iraqi Kurds; Iraqi Kurds killing Iranian Kurds; PUK killing KDP; *Jash* killing *peshmerga*; and so on. All of this killing has been done with the goal of achieving a Kurdish state. We say in Kurdish, "It doesn't matter if it is raining or windy—the snow is going to decrease," and it is exactly true. It doesn't matter if the Iraqi Kurds or the PUK or the *Jash* or the *peshmerga* are winning or losing. All are Kurds, and Kurds are going to decrease. No one can win. All will be losers.

Chapter Five ❧
Teenage Years

Like millions of children in the Middle East, I did not have a normal life, and I lost my childhood. So what about the most important time in a young person's life, the teenage years, the cornerstone for the future? It's the time when a person builds his personality and shapes himself for the future. It's also the best time for having fun, before taking on all the responsibilities that will come later in life.

My teenage years were the second part of my life. They were not better in any way than my childhood. Because I happened to grow up in a particular time (the 1980s) and place (Kurdistan), I could get only suffering from life. I never had any of the dreams that teenagers have in the West. My only concern was getting food to survive and making sure I was safe—but I dreamed of freedom for myself, my family, and my nation. I saw daily what should not have been happening: fear, poverty, violence, humiliation, bloodshed. It made my blood boil, it hurt my heart, it disturbed my mind greatly. I knew I had to do something. What was it all about? Why was it a crime to be a Kurd? Why couldn't we have our country? Why were Kurds so poor and uneducated? Why should we have to live like that? Why...why...why...the whys didn't allow me to enjoy anything. I couldn't sleep, I found no rest in discussing our situation with my friends or searching for a solution. First I had to understand our history, what the bigger problems were, what was at the root of them.

I began to read a lot, especially about Kurdish history. I did it to find myself, as well as to find some answers. I found that the time I lived in was really the golden age of the Kurdish revolution for freedom. The *peshmerga* were growing, ideas were flowing. I read as much as I could from the publications that came out of the revolution. I memorized hundreds of patriotic poems, I began to write my own poems, and I started to speak out, using any opportunity I had to meet with people and talk with them. Art and poetry were the most effective ways to do this, and I used them. I started reading my poems and participating in many seminars and art activities. Western teenagers find excitement in sports or drugs or sex, but in Kurdistan writing a poem could get you killed, and this provided more than enough excitement for me. People responded to poetry because they were so repressed and had so little opportunity to express what they believed in their hearts: that they were hungry for words that affirmed their deepest desire to be free. I also tried in every way I could to support the *peshmerga* and to resist the Kurdish genocide that was going on all around me. But it was very dangerous to say anything about the government's policies or about Kurdish suffering.

There was a sort of thrill in living close to the edge. Often I had to hide myself for days until the danger passed. As youth, we didn't care that much about danger—we challenged the government policies proudly, and we believed that we would lose nothing if we died, because our lives were meaningless otherwise. Many times my friends would say that being in the grave was better than living like this. Youth never think the way older, more experienced people do! Anything can make a teenager emotional and cause him to want to give away his life, but because I was reading so much I knew two things: that I couldn't afford to get too emotional, and that I must also prevent my friends from making emotional statements or taking actions based on their emotions. That would certainly get us nowhere, and do us no good.

During the 1980s in Kurdistan, it was really hard and dangerous for young people to come together. We were afraid to walk on the street together or go to any public place and gather. The authorities would accuse us of supporting the *peshmerga*, and to pick us up they wouldn't have to prove anything or get any court order. Most of the time, when they would take someone, he would never come back. We knew that, and we also knew that reading poems, or even using the words "Kurd" or "Kurdistan," was more than enough to cause us to "disappear."

Life was eternal vigilance. I had to always look for food, or a way to make some money to help support the family, but I also had to be alert for danger, and danger could come in many ways. It might come suddenly, like a jet out of the sky strafing the village, or it might come with a quiet word to flee to the mountains. People you could trust were more important even than gold, but people who betrayed you were more deadly than poison. I had to know the difference. One wrong guess and I could be dead, or my family destroyed. But if I did not take chances, the same things could happen. There were no simple or easy answers. Under these conditions, it was often impossible to think just of oneself. I knew that not only did my family need me, but so did my friends and community. I could not abandon them. But life pressed down so intensely upon me that I struggled to carry the weight of responsibility.

Fun, joy, and love (for women)—my friends and I didn't have these things in our teenage years. College, clubs, the mall, cell phones, the Internet, films—those were things we didn't even know existed. If we hadn't had poems by which to express ourselves, we would have ignored how life was supposed to be, since we were completely isolated from the outside world. But because of our isolation, we were able to keep our minds focused above all on the great joy and pride of refusing injustice. We knew and believed in what we stood for. Resistance became our life—to stand for justice, speak for our rights, struggle to survive. It gave us a different test in life, which was the only test I knew as a teenager. It gave me energy—sometimes too much energy—and made me really strong.

Eat bread, sleep on the floor, work hard, wear old clothes, sing for life, shout "Death to dictators!", keep my head high, face death bravely—those were the principles of my life then. I believe there is no way for Western teenagers to understand it now. Maybe it looks foolish to them, but this is because we lived in a completely different world. One day someone asked me in surprise, "I know you are very peaceful, so why do you support the *peshmerga*, since you know they use violence?" I replied simply, "Because I live in Iraq, not Norway." I have no doubt he understood my answer.

Terror Forces

During the day, government forces patrolled the cities. Daily we saw security officers walking on the street or setting up checkpoints, but they brought no peace or security at all. They were everywhere. They stopped people, asked them questions, searched them, made fun of them. Sometimes people were let go, and sometimes the officers arrested people for no apparent reason. There was never a clear pattern. If you walked fast they would stop you, but if you walked slowly they would ask you why. If you looked at them you would be in trouble, but if you avoided them they would pick you up. If they asked for your identification and you forgot it, then you were certainly going to disappear. In this way, daily life was a constant state of fear. And that, of course, was their purpose—to instill fear. By humiliating people and searching them anytime they wanted to, without any reason, the government's forces were sending the message that they had the power to do anything they wanted to and that nobody could stand against them. They would pick some person on the street and beat him until he cried for mercy, for no reason except to make an example of him. They would go into a store and take what they liked without paying for it, or they could close the store and nobody could enter, and if anyone objected they would beat that person up. They could make false accusations against someone, or they could stand in the street and hold up traffic for hours for no other reason than to show they could scare and humiliate people.

If the army decided that you were helping the *peshmerga*, or even had a relative in the *peshmerga*, they would come and arrest you. If the *peshmerga* killed a soldier or attacked the government, then the army would move in and arrest anyone they could find and torture them to get information. Thousands of Kurdish youth died under torture during the 1970s and 1980s. At school we used to joke about it by saying, "See you tomorrow, if they don't pick me up tonight." If you did not admit guilt under torture, they often tortured you until you died, but if you admitted guilt under torture, even if you had done nothing, they often took you before a special court and gave you the death penalty. Many young people were hanged by order of this secret court, in which there were neither lawyers nor even evidence other than a confession obtained by torture. So every day you had to be prepared to accept that this would be your last day alive.

One of my friends once said to me that all Kurds were *peshmerga*. I was surprised at his statement, and I asked if he was trying to justify the genocide against the Kurds, but he explained to me that the word *peshmerga* literally means "the one who faces death." He said all Kurds were facing death, not just every day, but every minute.

The worst problem for the Kurds was the government's policy of turning them into spies against their own people. Some Kurds became spies for money, others as a result of torture or threats against their families. Whatever the reason, thousands of Kurds reported regularly to government officials about all that they saw and heard. Often they made things up. We reached the point that no one could trust anyone else. You could not even trust your closest friends, or neighbors, or your own brothers or sisters. One wrong or misunderstood word could cost you your life, and you did not know who might report you. Kurds used to say, "Hold your mouth and save your life," which simply means, "Be dumb, blind, and deaf, and live like death." It was the theory of the foolish: have no feelings, care about nothing, accept humiliation to save your life.

This constant fear of betrayal made us hate life. You came to fear anyone you met. If for any reason a person did not like you, he could denounce you to the authorities and you would be gone. We had no Bill of Rights, no basic liberties, no freedom of speech. There was no arrest warrant, no appearance before a judge. There was no court at all. One day you would just be taken away and tortured until you either died or they released you.

Fear and intimidation were everywhere in Iraq, especially in Kurdistan. In 1983, while we students were playing soccer in the Chamchamal stadium, in front of some 300 people the security forces suddenly came in, moved us all to the sidelines, and brought in two prisoners wearing handcuffs and blindfolds. The security forces tied the men to the goalposts and said, "This is the government's answer to the *peshmerga*." Then they shot the men dead in front of everyone. In 1984, the security forces brought into town some dead bodies that they claimed were *peshmerga*. They tied the bodies by their feet to the back of a truck and dragged them around the city until they were just unrecognizable lumps of flesh that stained the streets red with their blood as the truck speakers blared, "Let everyone see! This is the result of supporting the *peshmerga*." In 1988, security forces came into our classroom and arrested our teacher right in front of us. We did not hear anything more about him for seven months. When we were finally allowed to see him again, we could hardly recognize him. He had been starved to the bone and there were gross signs of torture all over him, even on his face. I heard and read thousands of stories about people being tortured, and I knew hundreds of people who were actually tortured or lost some part of their bodies. Sometimes the security forces would even gather a group of people together and demonstrate how to cut off someone's nose, or ear, or tongue, just to frighten them.

Research

In 1987 our school was chosen to participate in a national research essay contest, and I decided to write about AIDS, which I had read about in a magazine. When I told my teacher he was surprised, and asked what AIDS was. I showed him the magazine article and he was interested, but doubted that I could find any information about AIDS in Kurdistan. I did not know Arabic very well at that time and we had no computers, so it was difficult to learn about something really new like AIDS.

I read the magazine article so many times I had it almost memorized. I asked my friends for information about AIDS, but nobody had ever heard of it. I tried to locate the author of the article, Dr. Zanoon Piryadi, but nobody knew anything about him except that he might live in Baghdad. Then I went to two doctors I knew, Dr. Moosa and Dr. Iyad, and they said they could get some information for me. Eventually they found five or six magazine articles on AIDS, two in Arabic and the rest in English. I explained that I did not know either Arabic or English and I needed something in Kurdish. Dr. Moosa said there were no articles in Kurdish. He wanted to help me, but these were all he could find.

I said that I had a friend who could translate the Arabic articles for me, but I asked Dr. Moosa to translate the English articles. He said he did not have time. I asked him to just give me the main ideas and the most important information. He reluctantly agreed.

I told my friend that I had a really great job for him—not a job that would help him earn money to support his family, but a job learning about AIDS. He just looked at me and said, "Whatever you need, Yassin, even if it is my life, I will gladly give it to you." I told him that God would reward him. He did the Arabic translations into Kurdish, and I found that they led me to ask Dr. Moosa even more questions when I went back to him. Dr. Moosa then did the English translations for me into Kurdish. Every day and night for one week I met and talked with him about all sorts of medical questions related to AIDS. Finally he began to call me Dr. Yassin. I told him not to make fun of me. He said, "We have five doctors in the only hospital in Chamchamal, and not one of them knows as much about AIDS as you will."

I finished my research and turned in my essay. The school selected ten essays and scheduled a debate on each one, after which they would select the best three to send to the national competition. My essay was selected as one of the ten best, and I prepared to participate in a debate about it before the whole school and the community.

During the debate, people asked me a lot of questions about the disease: when it was discovered, how many people died from it, what treatment was possible. Dr. Moosa even came from the hospital and asked me some questions about it. I felt like a professor. Then the principal praised me and asked the doctor what he thought of my presentation. The doctor said that he himself had learned a great deal from my research. That did it: the principal selected my research essay as the best, and said all students should be like me.

Because I won the city competition, my essay was selected as one of the fifty best in Sulaimaniya State, and I was asked to go to Sulaimaniya City for another debate that would determine the ten best for the national final in Baghdad. On the day of the debate, however, my teacher and I had no car at the school, so the principal and the school gave us bus fare and the address of the debate. The bus was supposed to reach Sulaimaniya at 10:30 a.m., and the debate was scheduled for 11. But when we arrived in Sulaimaniya, we received so much conflicting information about where the debate would be held that we finally decided to take a taxi to get there, since we only had ten minutes left. After driving around the city for twenty minutes, the taxi left us off at a building that seemed right and we ran inside, but nobody knew anything about the debate. Finally we found someone who made some phone calls and gave us another address. By now it was almost noon. We eventually found another taxi, which brought us to the debate around 1 p.m. But it was over. We were told it had started at 9 a.m., even though we had been told earlier that it would start at 11 a.m. My teacher was really angry and sad. He thought my essay would have been in the top ten in the country.

I heard in 2001 that AIDS was discovered in Sulaimaniya for the first time, but the local government denied it. I hope and pray that AIDS never spreads in Kurdistan or anywhere else, but I still want people to educate themselves about it, especially now that Kurdistan is open and many foreigners visit there.

It Is Our Sin and Not God's Pen

One day when I was in tenth grade I was walking home from school with Kak Nawzar, my best friend, when another friend, Baba Ali, called to me.

"How are you, Yassin?" he asked.

"No complaint," I said.

"I want to speak with you."

"In private?"

"No. Kak Nawzar can hear too."

"Good. So what do you want to say?"

"Do you know Omar Khayyam?"

"The Persian poet?"

"Yes."

"I have read about him, and memorized some of his verses," I said.

"So what do you think about him?" asked Baba Ali.

"What do you mean?"

"How do you judge his work?"

"I am not in a position to judge him," I said. "He is a great and famous poet. But to be honest, many things that he says I don't believe in."

Baba Ali then began to recite one of Omar Khayyam's poems:

> Oh God, Science is perplexed by your deeds
> You create sweetness, and say don't taste
> You made beautiful things, and say don't look.
> With a full cup we must lay down without spilling it

"I don't believe what he says," I said.

"But you just said that you are not going to judge him," Nawzar said.

"I'm not," I said, "but if I hear or read something that I disagree with, it is my right to say so. It doesn't matter who said it."

"You believe that Khayyam's philosophy is wrong?" Baba Ali asked.

"For me, yes," I said.

"Why?"

"Well," I replied, "look what he says. In the first line he claims that God confuses science. I believe that knowledge brings peace of mind and tranquility to the heart. Scientists have knowledge and wisdom that we don't have. If someone increases his knowledge so that he understands more about creation, he will find more signs of God's power, and he will not be confused because he will understand God's natural laws, unlike a person who lacks knowledge.

"As to the second line, God never said that we should not taste the sweetness that He created. It is just the opposite. God wants us to taste the sweetness. He told us to enjoy honey, but don't taste other people's honey. Don't steal from married people and don't commit adultery. If you don't enjoy other people's honey you will enjoy the honey that was given you. But when you try out other honey, you will never be satisfied with what you have been given, especially if the other honey is sweeter than your own.

"As to the third line, God never said not to look at the beauty He created. God only wants us to lower our gaze and not transgress.

"As to the fourth line, the example that Khayyam gives is not fair. It is impossible. If you have a full cup, there is no way that you can lie down without spilling it. But God doesn't want us to have to perform difficult or impossible tasks just to taste our own honey and to look at the beauty we were given. He just wants us to leave other people's property alone. Where did you get the poems from?" I asked Baba Ali.

"Someone gave me a cassette and a book of Khayyam's poems."

"Do you understand Persian?"

"No," said Baba Ali. "The poems are in Kurdish."

"Is it Hazar's translation?" I asked.

"Yes."

"I tried to get that," I said, "but I couldn't find it. So let me have the cassette and I'll listen to it tonight and tomorrow we can discuss it more."

"What about me?" asked Nawzar.

"You can have the book," said Baba Ali.

I told Ali that he should keep the book so that he could review it, but Ali said that he had all but memorized the book. So he gave it to Nawzar. We agreed to meet at the library the next day to discuss the poetry.

That night I listened to the cassette several times and really enjoyed hearing Hazar's reading. The next morning Nawzar asked me what I thought of it. I told him to save it for the library. Nawzar said that he hadn't been able to sleep after reading the book.

"Did you memorize the poems?" I asked.

"First I wrote them all down for myself, and then I memorized some of them," he said.

After school, Baba Ali invited us to his home rather than the library because all of his family had gone off to visit a brother, and so we had the house to ourselves.

"Kak Nawzar, what do you think about Khayyam now?" I asked.

"Don't ask me," he said. "He really intoxicated me all night and I could not sleep."

Baba Ali said, "Since I got the poems last week, I've felt like I am insane. I stay up late at night; I talk to myself; I move my hands in a silent dialogue until my mother wants to know who I am pretending to talk to. She believes I have fallen in love, and she wants me to tell her the truth or she will tell my father. When I deny that I have fallen in love, she does tell my father. He says, "My dear son, only the insane or the poets speak to themselves. Which one of them are you?" I tell him that I am trying to become a poet. He smiles at me and leaves me alone."

"What makes you like the poems so much?" I asked.

Both Nawzar and Baba Ali began to explain that the poetry was completely new to them. It gave them a different meaning of life and a different means to attain it. They said that Khayyam shows us that life is just a drama. We are the actors and God is the producer. What we do and say is not our own choice, and things are going to happen whether we like it or not. Instead of struggling against this role that we have been given in the drama, it is better to just enjoy the role and take advantage of the short life we have. Get your share of enjoyment, and leave the rest to God. Forget about thinking or trying to change anything. According to Khayyam, they said, there is no way to enjoy life until you lose your mind in wine, and the best things to enjoy are beautiful women.

"So," I said, "we should not work, or have a Kurdish revolution, or take responsibility, or even think? Life and everything in it is just a game?"

"God already wrote everything, and we have no choice," said Nawzar.

"If we cry or laugh, wake or sleep, worry or not—it really doesn't matter," said Baba Ali. "It is all just a drama."

I began to get emotional. "So what the whole Iraqi army was unable to do, a simple cassette of Khayyam's poetry accomplished? Why do we blame Saddam for what he did, if it was not his choice and he was just a drunk actor who had to do what God told him to do?"

Nawzar just shook his head and said nothing. Baba Ali said, "I told you before. Sit down, don't worry. There is nothing we can do—the game is over. Just start laughing."

"Kak Nawzar," I said. "Do you remember last month when we talked about Jean Paul Sartre's theory of existentialism? You were really mad and told me it made no sense, because human beings should find wisdom and reason for existence in their relationship to God and the universe."

"I remember," he said

"So Khayyam's idea is no better than Sartre's," I said. "Why do you say Sartre's theory is meaningless, and now you don't know what you think about essentially the same theory from Khayyam?"

Nawzar was silent for a minute. Then he said, "I'm really confused. Khayyam is a big scholar."

Baba Ali began reciting some more of Khayyam's verses:

> Before the phantom of False morning died
> Methought a Voice within the Tavern cried,
> When all the Temple is prepared within
> Why nods the drowsy Worshiper outside?

> And as the Cock crew those who stood before
> The Tavern shouted—"Open then the Door
> You know how little while we have to stay
> And once departed may return no more."

> Come, fill the Cup and in the fire of Spring
> Your Winter garment of Repentance fling
> The Bird of Time has but a little way
> To flutter—and the Bird is on the Wing.

> And lately by the Tavern Door agape
> Came shining through the Dusk an Angel Shape
> Bearing a Vessel on his shoulder; and
> He bid me taste of it; and 'twas—the grape.

A Book of Verses underneath the Bough
A jug of Wine, a Loaf of Bread—and Thou
Beside me singing in the Wilderness—
Oh, Wilderness were Paradise enow!

He laughed and said that when his mother came home, he was going to tell her that he had found real alcohol and drugs, and to prove it he would show her the cassette and book of Khayyam.

I agreed that Khayyam was exactly like a drug.

Nawzar said, "Yassin, you say that the most beautiful poem written by a famous Muslim philosopher is a drug?"

"As art," I said, "it appears to be an excellent, beautiful and powerful poem, but it is against reality. What have we learned from this poem that we can apply to our lives? Who gets the benefit if young people stop thinking and working, and their goals become a cup of wine and a woman to dance with? That is what we are talking about."

"But these poems are very deep," said Nawzar. "We should make sure we understand them. I have read many scholars who say that each word of these poems is metaphorical."

"Good," I said. "You've already told me that art for art's sake is over. We need art for life. You blame Sufis for their interpretation of the Qur'an, and now you do the same here?"

"I mean that we may be wrong to say that Khayyam is telling us to go to a regular bar and get drunk on regular alcohol and avoid all responsibility for life. Perhaps he means something else."

I said, "This is the real problem. All the fighting and hate occurs because humans cannot agree on the interpretation of texts. Many things that Muslims do or believe are not in the Qur'an. It is all interpretation. They add culture and custom when they explain the text. The same is true for other religious followers. If we all go back to the text and we keep it simple and easy to understand, it will be much easier for us all to get along together."

"But when Khayyam refers to 'wine' and 'cup bearer' and 'bar', he is not necessarily referring to the literal meaning of the word, but to something else," said Nawzar.

"Do you want me to believe that 'bar' means a temple, and 'wine' means God's love, and 'cup-bearer' means an angel, like some people claim?" I asked.

"Why not?" said Nawzar. "How can someone like Khayyam call people to drink alcohol and not be referring to life itself?"

"That's my point," I said. "I believe that if you want to understand anything, you should take the text from the original language, use a dictionary, and interpret it yourself, and not accept any other explanation that is not based on the words in the original text. This should be our basic procedure if we are really going to find the truth. Wine should mean wine, bar should mean bar, cup-bearer should mean cup-bearer. I don't believe in outer and inner and hidden meanings of normal words."

Baba Ali laughed, and interrupted us to read another of Khayyam's poems:

> We are no other than a moving row
> Of Magic Shadow-shapes that come and go
> Round with the sun-illuminated Lantern held
> In Midnight by the Master of the Show
>
> But helpless Pieces of the Game He plays
> Upon this Checker-board of Nights and Days;
> Hither and thither moves, and checks, and slays,
> And one by one back in the Closet lays.
>
> The Moving Finger writes; and having writ,
> Moves on: nor all your Piety and Wit,
> Shall lure it back to cancel half a Line
> Nor all your Tears wash out a Word of it.
>
> And that inverted Bowl they call the Sky
> Whereunder crawling cooped we live and die
> Lift not your hands to *It* for help—for it
> As impotently moves as you or I.

I became annoyed and said to Baba Ali, "Listen. You brought us here because you had a question about Khayyam. You should participate in this discussion. I am not here just to argue with Kak Nawzar."

Baba Ali laughed and said, "Everything is written and is over. What are we fighting for?"

"So what do you make of Khayyam's poems?" Nawzar said to me.

"I believe his poems are really dangerous and they should be the last thing that Kurdish youth ever see," I said. "We need young people to be serious and work hard and build the country—not to lose their minds and be as careless as Khayyam is telling them to be."

"So why did Hazar translate these poems into Kurdish? He was with the *peshmerga*, you know," said Baba Ali.

"We need to know Khayyam's poems, and his ideas, and we need to know something about other cultures. But this does not mean that students and youth like us should take this book and learn to drink wine and behave irresponsibly because 'it is written and is over'," I said.

"You don't think that youth should read these poems?" Nawzar asked.

"We should not confuse them," I said. "I believe that if students read these poems by themselves they are going to learn what they don't need, instead of what they do need."

"It is good that you're not the propaganda minister if you're not going to let poems be published," laughed Nawzar.

"I don't believe that it is right to suppress ideas that will save people. But if we are going to educate people about ideas like Khayyam's, we need to explain the dangers to them—especially the teenagers—until they understand and can avoid the problems."

"If teenagers read Khayyam's poems, they are going to leave work and spend their time with wine and women," said Baba Ali. "There is no way you can change that. It is written. If this is not a drug, what else could a drug be?" Then he read another poem:

Indeed the Idols I have loved so long
Have done my credit in the World much wrong;
Have drowned my Glory in a shallow Cup
And sold my reputation for a Song.

Indeed, indeed, Repentance oft before
I swore—but was I sober when I swore?
And then, and then came Spring and Rose-in-hand
My thread-bare Penitence apieces tore.

And much as Wine has played the Infidel
And robbed me of my Robe of Honor—Well
I often wonder what the Vintners buy
One half so precious as the stuff they sell

Ah Love! Could you and I with Him conspire
To grasp this sorry Scheme of Things entire
Would not we shatter it to bits—and then
Remold it nearer to the Heart's desire.

Baba Ali laughed and said, "So you see, don't worry. What is written
for them is going to happen, whether you direct them or not."

"Khayyam really misguided you," I said.

"You do not believe that fate is decreed by God?" asked Nawzar
with surprise.

"Yes, I believe that," I said.

"So is everything already written or not?"

"I believe it is written."

"So that is exactly what Khayyam is saying."

"No, what he is saying is that we have no choice. Whatever we do
is not by our own will—and this is totally wrong."

"Why?"

"If I commit a sin—say I killed someone—is God going to punish
me or not?" I asked.

"Yes, He will punish you," Nawzar said.

"But if I had no choice—if I am just an actor in God's drama—why should God punish me?"

"That is a problem," admitted Nawzar. "It would be completely unjust if God forced me to do something and then punished me for it, even though I had no choice."

"So how do we have a choice?" asked Baba Ali.

"We can make our own decisions to do something or not do something," I said. "We can pray or we can not pray. We can help people or we can harm them. We can obey God or we can refuse. God gave us a mind, sent us light, and we must choose. But God knows before we choose what we will do."

"So it is written?" asked Nawzar.

"Yes, but we don't know *what* is written," I said. "We know what God ordered us to do, and what we are supposed to avoid. In the time of Caliph Umar, people drank alcohol, which was not allowed in Islam. When Umar asked why they drank alcohol, they said, 'God wanted us to do it. Since we drink alcohol, it must have been written.' Umar became really angry and asked Ali, the Prophet's son-in-law, what he should do about it. Ali said that he should double the punishment—one punishment for drinking alcohol, and one punishment for telling the lie that God decreed that they should drink it, when they knew that God did not permit it. It is the same with Khayyam. He is trying to blame God for the choices that humans make. It is unfair and dangerous to say that God must have wanted me to do something wrong just because I did it. Show me when and how God told you to do that, when God's book tells you to do the opposite. This idea is going to distract young people and make them destroy their futures, and this is all our enemies need."

Baba Ali read another poem:

> Ah my Beloved, fill the Cup that clears
> To-day of past Regret and future Fears;
> Tomorrow!—Why tomorrow I may be
> Myself with Yesterday's Seven thousand Years

For some we loved, the loveliest and the best
That from his Vintage rolling Time hath pressed
Have drunk their Cup a Round or two before
And one by one crept silently to rest.

Ah, make the most of what we yet may spend
Before we too into the Dust descend;
Dust into Dust and under Dust to lie
Sans Wine, *sans* Song, *sans* Singer and—*sans* End!

Again Ali said, with a sigh, "Everything is written; it is over."

I saw that he was joking and just wanted to provoke more discussion, so I said to Nawzar, "Listen, Baba Ali is still saying everything is written and we don't have a choice. Go get a stick and beat him as hard as you can. If he asks why, say God wrote that he must be beaten. We have no choice."

Nawzar started laughing. I continued, "They say that two people were arguing about this—one said that we have a choice, and the other denied it. The one who claimed we have a choice suddenly slapped his friend in the face. His friend was angry and said, 'Why did you do that? Are you crazy?' And the first person said, "It was not me. God did it. I had no choice.'"

We all started laughing.

It was close to midnight, and I asked Baba Ali where our dinner was. "Aren't we your guests?"

"It was not written," Baba Ali replied.

Nawzar said, "Don't lie. You don't know what is written for us, but you know that you should serve your guests. So go bring us our dinner!"

"I thought Khayyam was going to save me from giving you dinner tonight," Baba Ali said.

"We don't believe that," Nawzar and I both said.

Baba Ali stood up to get us some food, and as he did he read one more poem:

They tell of a paradise full of beautiful women,
Pure wine and the sweetest honey.
But I need something here and now
Why should I await that distant time?

Nawzar said, "Oh, Ali! Still intoxicated!"

I said, "This is the problem. Look what Khayyam does. First he says, 'They tell,' as though he is not sure. Second, who is telling him that he will never get Paradise here—that you have to wait until you get there? Our Sheikhs used to say that we should make our lives here to be like Paradise. After that, God will give us Paradise there. It is just ignorance. God did not want us to live in fear on this earth without joy until we can get to Paradise in heaven. We should build Paradise here."

Baba Ali brought food and said, "It is written," and began to laugh again.

I said, "We don't know what is written. But we should try to get what we need."

"It is really a crime to do something wrong and after that excuse yourself and accuse God of forcing you to do it," Nawzar said.

I was really happy when I heard this, and I said to them both, "All night this is what I was trying to tell you, but now Kak Nawzar has made it clear."

Baba Ali said, "I know you are not drinking wine, but I wish we had some grapes, at least." We began the meal, and I said that at least it was decreed that we would eat this food tonight.

Going to Basra

The weather in Kurdistan is very different from middle and southern Iraq. In the north, winter is very cold with heavy snow, especially in the high mountains. But in the south, they never see snow. In summer Kurdistan is cool and mild, but in the middle and southern parts of the country it gets really hot. In my father's lifetime, people used to move their cattle and sheep from Kurdistan to the south in the winter, where there were milder conditions, and Arab farmers would bring their cattle to Kurdistan in the summer to avoid the heat on the plains. In my lifetime, however, fewer and fewer people in the north were shepherds, and this annual livestock migration dwindled away because the tensions between the Arab south and the Kurdish north made travel unsafe. Instead, another migration began. Kurdish people started going south to look for work because the government built industries only in the south, and that was where the jobs were. Kurdistan was completely neglected. At the same time, Arabs came north to Kurdistan to do government jobs, which were open just to them in order to change the demographics of our country, especially in Kirkuk Province.

When I was fifteen years old, I left school to support my family. Later I went to night school for high school so I could keep working during the day. But before I left school, for several summers I went to southern Iraq to work for my cousin Arif Gull, who worked as a contractor for an Italian company, SAI, which built electrical towers. I worked on towers 100 feet high with a group of Filipinos. I did the same job they did, but they received $15 an hour and I received twenty-five cents an hour. They worked for the company directly, but I worked for my cousin. The Filipinos received their pay in dollars, but I received mine in dinars, the Iraqi currency.

In the summer of 1989, I went to work for Arif in Basra, in the southernmost part of Iraq close to the Kuwait border. Winter in Basra was warmer than summer in Kurdistan, but summer in Basra was impossible. The temperature was normally over 100 degrees, and could reach 130 degrees. To get there, I took the bus from Kirkuk to Baghdad, which I reached in the evening. I called Arif, who told me that I had to stay in Baghdad and wait for the rest of the crew to arrive the next morning for our trip to Basra. I asked him where I should stay, and he told me to go to a hotel.

I had to ask people for directions to a cheap hotel. This was difficult for me because I did not speak Arabic well, and it was hard to identify people who spoke Kurdish. Kurds in Baghdad normally did not wear Kurdish clothing. I had to follow Kurdish-looking people around until they spoke, and I could tell by their accent whether or not they were Kurdish. Eventually I was directed to a Kurdish area of Baghdad, where all the hotels and restaurants were Kurdish. The Kurds in Baghdad were like the Egyptians in the Middle East—they did all of the cleaning and unskilled labor jobs for minimum wage.

It was almost sunset. I went to several hotels but I was told that all of them were full. Finally I found a hotel that seemed to have some space available.

"Do you want a room or a bed?" the manager asked.

"What's the difference?" I asked.

"A room means that you take the whole room for yourself," the manager said. "A bed means that you have a whole bed for yourself, but you share the room with other people."

"What is the price for each?"

"A whole room is five dinar. Sharing a room with one person is three dinar. Sharing a room with two people is two dinar."

I was really uncertain what to do. I did not like the idea of sharing a room with a stranger because that did not seem safe. But five dinar was too expensive, and I could not afford it. I asked the manager whom I would have to share with. How could I be sure that he was not dangerous? The manager seemed like a nice person who wanted to help me.

"I know just what your concern is," he said.

"So can you help me?" I asked hopefully.

"Listen. We just had a real Kurdish gentleman take a bed in one of our rooms. He is educated and asked for a quiet place. I did not want to send anyone to his room as long as I had an empty bed somewhere else. But I will send you to his room. Please keep the room quiet for his sake."

"That's great," I told him.

"Give me your identity card, please." The manager took all my information and my three dinar. "Take the stairs to the second floor and go to the fifth door on your right, number fifteen," he said.

I carried my bag up the stairs. Eleven…twelve…fifteen. This was my room. I knocked on the door quietly so as not to disturb the gentleman, and he opened the door.

"Good evening," I said.

"Good evening," he replied.

"They sent me to this room for the night," I said apologetically.

"Of course," he said. "There are two beds in this room and I only paid for one of them. Please come in."

"Thank you very much," I told him. "Which bed is mine?"

"They are the same," he said. But I saw that he had put his bag on one of them, so I took the other.

The man, who looked to be in his forties, went to his bed and began to read a newspaper. I saw a couple of books on the table next to him. I did not want to interrupt his reading, so I went to my bed, opened my bag, took out two books, chose one of them, and started reading. But secretly I kept glancing at the gentleman to try and read the titles of the books he had with him. Perhaps he became aware of my curiosity, because after a time he put down his paper and said, "What is your name?"

"Yassin," I told him.

"Where do you come from?"

"Chamchamal," I said.

"Oh, you are Kurdish," he said.

"*Bale* (Yes)," I answered. To my great relief, we began speaking in Kurdish.

"Are you studying in Baghdad?" he asked me.

"No."

"Just here for a visit?"

"No, I am going to Basra tomorrow," I said.

"Basra?" he asked, surprised. "Are you studying there?"

"No, my cousin is a contractor and I am going to work for him," I said.

"What does he do?"

"He builds electrical towers."

"Good. Good." The gentleman smiled and returned to his newspaper.

I started reading my book again. I did not want to ask him about his reason for being here, because the manager had told me to keep the room quiet. But I hoped that he might put down the paper again and resume our conversation. After about five minutes he asked me, "What are you reading?"

"A book of poems," I said.

"What is the book?"

"*A Kind Word Is a Flower* by Latif Halmat."

"Oh yes. It is beautiful," said the gentleman.

"Have you seen this book before?" I asked.

The gentleman laughed. "He is my friend."

"You know him?" I asked, amazed.

"We are very close," the gentleman said. "What about you? How do you know him?"

"We are both from the same family—Barzingi," I said. "His cousin Ishmail married my sister Aisha, but I have met him only a couple of times. I love his poems, though, especially this book."

"Good," said the gentleman. "Are all of your books poems?"

"Yes," I said. "Do you like poetry too?"

The gentleman smiled and said, "Yes."

"Which poets do you like?"

"Kamaran Mukri," he said.

I was suddenly suspicious. How could he say the name Kamaran Mukri in Baghdad? Mukri's poems were all about Kurdish freedom and *peshmerga*. To even mention his name would have brought suspicion upon him from the government. Perhaps this was a test for me, by a government agent?

The gentleman apparently read my mind from the stunned look on my face. "Did you know Mukri?" he asked me.

"I have heard about him and I have read some of his poems," I answered cautiously.

"Do you like his poems?"

"I read whatever I can, and I love his poems."

Then the gentleman recited one of Mukri's poems:

For you, a castle, gold, and joy

For me, the hard way of struggling
You live for yourself and you die for yourself
But I live for the Kurds, and I will die for Kurdistan*

"Yes, that is one of Mukri's poems," I said. I was very nervous.
He recited another one:

Many tyrants by genocide
Try to erase the Kurds from memory
But their failure in these mountains
Has become an example for history.
This land is Kurdistan,
Cemetery of invaders!*

I was really scared. I didn't know how this man could read this poem
in Baghdad. I did not want to acknowledge the poem, so all I said was, "I
don't know this poem, but it's certainly written in Mukri's style."

The gentleman seemed very happy that I knew so much about poetry.
He opened his bag and took out a book of poetry by Ahmed Aref.

I said, "I bought that book when it was first published. I've memorized many of the poems."

"What about the author, where does he live?" asked the gentleman.

"I don't know, but I heard that he lives in the mountains—
maybe."

The gentleman laughed. "You mean with the *peshmerga*?"

I was shocked. You could not say something like that in Baghdad.
This had to be a trick. "Please," I said. "This is Baghdad! What are you
talking about? I just heard that he is living in the mountains. I don't
know what he does."

"He writes poems," said the gentleman.

"Exactly," I said. "He just writes poems."

"He also writes a great deal about the Kurds," said the gentleman.

"That does not mean that he is *peshmerga*," I told him. "Look, Halmat

*Note: these poems have been translated from Kurdish to English from memory by
the author.

wrote all those poems about freedom and he is still living in Sulaimaniya. When one of the *peshmerga* found out that Halmat was still living in the city, the *peshmerga* said that was not fair. The only reason he had gone to the mountains to join the *peshmerga* was because of Halmat's poems, and now he finds the poet himself sitting in the city."

The gentleman laughed. "That is what poetry will do to you," he said. He wrote something on the book of poetry that he had just taken out of his bag, and then he handed it to me. The note said, "To Kak Yassin, as my gift. Ahmed."

"Thank you very much," I said. "By the way, what is your last name?"

"It is on the book," he said.

"What!" I exclaimed in surprise. "This is your book? You are Ahmed Aref?"

"Yes, Kak Yassin," he smiled. And it is nice to meet you." I must have looked so confused that he took out his ID and showed it to me.

"I'm sorry," I spluttered. "I heard you were in the mountains?"

"Just so," Ahmed said. "And now I am back."

We spent the whole night talking about various leaders and policies and differences, as though we were in the high mountains of Qandeel instead of in Baghdad. We talked openly about the revolution and we read patriotic poems; I argued with him about the revolution, and asked him many things about poetry. Finally I showed him some of my poems, to see what he would say about them. He made some very important notes in my poem notebook and told me to focus on two things: one, read as many poems as possible. He said I should read at least a thousand poems before I tried to write one myself. Two, I should paint word pictures with poetry.

I asked him if he thought I needed to read more poetry before I tried to write another poem.

"No, no," he said. "Some of your poems are beautiful, but don't try to write a poem. Rather, let the poem find you by itself. How long does it take for a woman to deliver a baby?"

"I don't know," I said. "Maybe five to ten hours?"

"Sometimes it takes me five to ten days to write a poem," Ahmed said. "And all the time I am having labor pains similar to childbirth until the poem is delivered. And when it is finally finished, I am as happy as if God had blessed me with a new child. I look at my poems and my children in the same way. Both are God's gift to me, and I love them in the same way."

"*Mamosta* (Teacher)," I said, "if you tell me that I need more time to read and learn before I write, I will not feel bad. I want your sincere advice."

"Again, I am not saying that you should not write," Ahmed said. "Some of your poems are really beautiful and you have ability, but keep in mind that knowledge is not like food in the stomach. If you eat too much food you will feel sick, but you can never get too much knowledge, and the more you get the hungrier you are for it. My mind never gets full. It is a big empty space. 'Read'—that was the first word that God sent to Mohammad, and it is the first order for all humanity."

I was so excited by what he was telling me that I forgot my dinner, and I did not even look at a clock until 2 a.m. I apologized for not letting him sleep. I said it would soon be dawn, and he had to leave at 6 a.m....

Ahmed said, "No apology is necessary. I was very glad to have talked with you. Just be careful and keep reading." He gave me a friend's address, and said that he did not have an address just then but that I could find him through his friend. I asked him to wake me up before he left because I also had to get to the bus station early. He shook my hand and said that he wanted to see my book of poetry published one day. I have not seen Kak Ahmed since then, but I pray that he is well and still writing poems.

The next morning I went to the bus station and met my cousin Arif and seven or eight other workers. It was about 7 a.m. Arif told me to put my bag on a particular bus and said that he would be coming later. After several more workers arrived, the bus left for Basra.

The Baghdad-to-Basra highway is the longest and biggest in Iraq. The road is so straight through the desert that the driver could fall asleep for half an hour and just let the bus drive itself. There is nothing to hit. I sat in the back and tried to sleep, but the others were singing and having fun and they kept waking me up. Plus it was hot. Buses do not use air conditioning because it causes the engine to overheat. Instead, passengers open the windows to get some air and to smoke a cigarette.

We reached Basra about 2 p.m. It was the first time I had ever seen the city, and I thought I must have landed on another planet. It felt like a place on the sun rather than the earth, because the heat was so intense. We had to close our eyes when we climbed out of the bus because the glare was overpowering. We immediately put our bags on top of our heads to keep our brains from boiling in the sun.

"How can we work and stay here?" my friend Ahmad asked me.

"The same way three million other people live here, I guess."

"But we can't live like them," Ahmad said. "Look, look! That man is walking without any shoes on. What keeps his feet from burning?"

I was shocked when I saw the barefoot man.

"God doesn't have to send people into hellfire. He can just send them to Basra," Ahmad said.

We went to the house where we were to stay. "So this is it," I said glumly. "Sit down, why don't you, and have a glass of water."

"In this oven?" Ahmad said. "Before we die we get to go to hell, and we can drink *Zanqabuti* water." (The water that increases thirst, given to a person in the midst of hell's fire.)

"Stop it, Ahmad."

"Really, I mean it," he said. "Who can drink this water?"

He was right. It was very salty and tasted like oil. After you drank it you were thirstier than before.

"I'm going back home," said Ahmad. "Who wants to come with me?"

"Sit and wait for the contractor to come, and then talk to him," I said.

"He is not coming. He will stay cool in the Meridian Hotel in Baghdad."

"No, he said he would be here. What can we do for work if he does not come?" I did not let Ahmad go home, and late that night Arif Gull arrived.

Ahmad confronted Arif about the working conditions. "You said you had jobs for us. You did not say you had hellfire for us."

"We will start tomorrow," Arif said.

"No way," said Ahmad. "I am going back home."

"Just go and see what it's like," said Arif. "Take two or three days to acclimatize yourself. After that, this will all seem normal."

So early the next morning, as soon as the sun was up, we worked until 9 a.m. After that, the metal electrical towers were too hot to touch, and the workers were so dehydrated that some of them vomited. We stopped work around 10 a.m. and went back to our boarding house, which Ahmad now called "Hellfire." That same day, Ahmad and four other workers went home. They could not tolerate the heat another minute.

Now we had only ten workers. Arif agreed that we only had to work from five to nine a.m. and five to ten p.m. each day. We tried to work on this schedule for several days, but everyone got sick with diarrhea from the water. Arif brought in five workers from Basra to encourage us, and they worked in a very normal way, drank the water that made us sick, and did not even cover their heads or faces from the sun like we had to. We tried to imitate them, but it was impossible. We told Arif that we were going home also, that we couldn't work in these conditions. He tried to persuade us to stay, but we said no, we couldn't do it.

Arif said that he would not pay us anything if we left. We all said that we didn't need anything from him, but I told him that it was his responsibility to get a bus to take us home. What would he say to the workers' families if any of them got lost or died? He agreed to rent a bus for us, and we agreed not to ask for any wages for the hours that we had already worked. Some of us did not even have money for food.

But the workers from Basra who were with us took pity on us. They went home and brought us back a lot of food for our journey home, including many bags of dates (for which Basra is famous), so we would not need to buy anything in the restaurants when the bus stopped. They showed us a great deal of love and respect—and they also made a lot of jokes about us. Such as: "We know that Kurds are strong, hard-working, patient, and live simply...so you don't seem like you are Kurds."

We told them in return, "We can climb a mountain and we can live in the snow, but we don't like hellfire and we can't drink this water with its oily taste."

Everyone was laughing. They shook our hands and gave us hugs, saying *"Ma'Assalamah, Kaka* (goodbye with peace and safety, respected brothers.")

The trip home seemed to take forever. Some people said they would tell their families that they had just returned from Africa. Others intended to say that they had visited the sun, or that they had escaped from hellfire.

Now, after all the changes that have taken place in Iraq in the name of liberation and democracy, these same people—honest, hard workers from Basra—are no longer our dear brothers. Now if any *Kaka* from Kurdistan goes to Basra, he will not get food and dates, he will not see love and respect. He will certainly disappear, because he is Kurdish, and if any Shiite from the south goes west into Sunni Iraq, he will be killed simply because he is Shiite. The same is true for people from the south, the Arabs. If they go to Kurdistan, they will be in danger of disappearing. In those days we were still Kurds, Shiites, and Sunnis—but we were dear brothers to each other then. Millions of Iraqis like me today wish for those good old days when we were all still brothers, and ask, "Where are those days now?" People should look forward, but in the Middle East, we are looking backward.

Time for Revolution

One day in 1989 I was walking with Kak Nawzar. He was a very smart and kind person, but also a very simple person who wanted nothing but books and bread to keep himself alive. I liked to talk with him for several hours each day because he knew so much from all that he had read. At that time in Kurdistan there was no Green Party, there were no peace activists or human rights organizations, but Nawzar represented all of these ideas. There were hundreds of others like him in Chamchamal, but because of governmental repression these people could not join together to establish an organization.

Nawzar and I had an agreement that whenever one of us bought or borrowed a book, as soon as he finished reading it he had to give it to the other to read in three days, even if it was 300 pages. After that we would discuss the book. On this particular day, Nawzar told me about a book he had just finished on women's rights in Islam. He was so angry and emotional about it that I decided to discuss it with him, even though I had not read it yet.

"Why are you upset about this book?" I asked him.

"Yassin, I read it and compared what it says to what people are doing. It is like sky and earth."

"Don't be an idealist."

"I'm not! But how is it that people say they are Muslims, and they pray every day, and then they do all of these bad things?"

"What things?"

"Everything! We have to change the way we treat women, from A to Z. In our culture women are like slaves, and yet we say we are Muslims. How can slavery of Muslims exist in Islam? It is forbidden."

"Maybe the writer is exaggerating."

"No, he did not make any point except to quote the Qur'an or the Prophet's sayings. It is written that Mohammad's wife said that Mohammad never struck her, or any one of his wives, or his children, or even his servants. Yet we are expected to beat women to prove we are men. It is written that Mohammad used to come home from the mosque and help his wife with the housework. Yet we see it as a shame to do any housework to ease the women's burden. Our marriage and divorce laws are completely opposite of what Mohammad directed. People are acting toward women totally differently from what Islam requires. Look what the Prophet said. One: 'The best of you, he is the best for his wife, and I am the best of you for my wife.' Two: 'Women are similar to the men.' Three: 'Women are like soft glass. If you are not kind to them, they will break.'"

I laughed. "So is it time for a revolution? Will you stand up and lead the charge?"

"Yes," Nawzar said. "We have to educate people about what Islam really stands for. What are all the Imams teaching?"

"What can we do?" I asked.

"You know what we should do? We should cut down on our spending and save the money to buy copies of this book, and give a copy to each of the Imams in the city. We will ask them to read it and to use these ideas in their preaching."

"Great idea," I told him, and we agreed we would do it. "Which Imam will you give it to first?"

"My father," Nawzar said. "It is he who must read this book *first*!"

As we talked more about the book and its ideas, I saw a very young girl with a severe physical handicap coming toward us. Her spine was twisted, and she walked only with great difficulty.

"Nawzar, look, look at her," I said.

"Oh...I am so sorry," Nawzar gasped.

"What do you say about that?"

"It will be hard for her. All her life she will have to suffer alone."

"Alone?" I asked him in surprise.

"No one will marry her. She cannot walk, she can't work, she can't cook, she probably can't even get pregnant."

"But she is still a human being. She has the same need of someone to love her that everyone has. She has the same need of someone to live with her and be her partner."

"But no one will accept her."

"Even you?" I asked him.

"What?"

"Are you saying that you would not marry her, or someone in her condition?"

Nawzar thought for a moment. "No, I would not."

"So what has happened to all your philosophy and your beautiful book about women's rights?" I said. "If you can't sacrifice and accept a woman like her to be your partner, who is going to do it? What is the benefit of talking about mercy and women's rights if we ourselves are not willing to help and serve a sick woman like her?"

"But this is not practical. It would not be a normal life, and it would be very hard."

"But still it is possible."

"So would *you* accept her as a wife?" Nawzar asked.

"Don't turn things around," I told him. "This is my question, and I want to know what you have to say."

"I can't say I would marry her," he said.

"So go burn your book and don't talk any more about women's rights. What is the benefit if we just talk about it, but we don't act on it?"

"But this is different."

"No, it is not. She is a human being but she is handicapped and she is suffering. She needs help and support. She has the same feelings as any other human being. What is her sin? Why should she remain without any partner all her life?" I was becoming very emotional.

Nawzar started crying "Enough! Just go ask her or her father, and if she agrees, I will marry her."

"Thank you," I told him. "We should be practical about what we are saying, and we should try to set a living example. I know you and your situation, and I know that you cannot marry right now. But I wanted to see what you would say. For now, perhaps all we can do is try to understand her and people in her condition, and pray for them and help them, and at least keep open the possibility of marrying such a person if it is God's will."

Nawzar was crying like a baby. I felt bad that I had made him feel so emotional. Later he told me that he could not sleep at all that night, and for two days he ate nothing and only prayed, so strongly had this conversation challenged him to think about the life of a crippled woman in a new and different way—how such people suffered not only from their handicap but from the rejection of society, and how important it was to make his personal beliefs consistent with the message he wanted to urge on others. At that time there were tens of thousands of crippled civilians from the war, mostly women, who would have to live the rest of their lives with pain and rejection through no fault of their own. In the whole of Kurdistan, there was no special school or nursing home for the handicapped. Many of them didn't even have wheelchairs and were forced to crawl on the street. For a person like Nawzar, who possessed compassion and a sense of justice, even thinking of the problem was agonizing. Truly it was easier to remain ignorant, but we had gone too far to do that.

In the end, we saved some money and bought copies of the book, which we gave to others and to two of the Imams in the city, Imam Asuad and Imam Gareeb. In their Friday sermons, both of the Imams talked approvingly about the ideas in the book, with which they both agreed. Later I talked with Imam Gareeb about his sermon. He said he had become very emotional at one point, and he had held the book up and said, "I want every one of you to buy this book and read it. Fast for the first two or three days, and don't buy any food. Save your money, because this book is the only food you will need." I was very excited, and when I saw Kak Nawzar I told him what Imam Gareeb had said. Nawzar said that Imam Asuad had said that if you want to know Islam, you should read this book.

These two Imams were loved by everyone in Chamchamal and were very outspoken, not only about women's rights but on many other topics. I had many good debates with them. During the Anfal campaign in 1988, the government published an edict that anyone who sheltered a refugee from one of the destroyed villages would also be executed. Both Imam Gareeb and Imam Asuad immediately denounced the edict, and said to the people that when refugees came to their homes, they should take them in and shelter them because they were our brothers and sisters; they were not *peshmerga* but innocent people. We in the mosque used to sit and tremble at what the Imams said, because we were sure they would be picked up and would disappear. But the government left them alone because of their popularity and because of concern there would be a local uprising if they were arrested. It was really a miracle that they survived.

Kak Nawzar was the only person I felt free enough to talk with about love and women and marriage. In the village, a person would not talk about such things, and especially in our culture people would not joke about these things. But Kak Nawzar and I were really close. One day I was walking with him when one of our friends came by and asked for my advice.

"About what?"

"Marriage."

"Kak Nawzar knows more than I do," I said. "Let's ask him." I turned to him. "You know Kak Sirwan here. He wants to marry. What do you say about it?"

"Kak *Gian* (Dear Brother)," Nawzar said to me. "This is your job. You are a *Mala* (Imam), not me. I cannot give such advice."

I saw the look on Sirwan's face; he did not like the way we were talking. However, I also knew that I could not ask for details about the woman he wanted to marry because that would have made him even more uncomfortable. In our culture it is difficult for men to talk about such things, especially in public. So to end it, I told him a story.

I said to him, "Kak Sirwan, they say that one day a student told Aristotle that he wanted to marry. The student asked what his teacher thought about the idea. Aristotle replied, without any hesitation, 'Go right ahead—just do it.'

"The student said, 'Teacher, you never gave an answer like this before. Usually you reason your way to an answer, but this time you just gave an answer without any explanation.'

"Aristotle replied, 'If you marry, one of two things will happen. Your wife might be a good woman who obeys and respects you, and then you will become a happy person. Or your wife might be a difficult woman who argues with you all the time, and then you will become a philosopher like me.' "

Kak Nawzar started laughing and said to Sirwan, "So go ahead. Go ahead. We need more philosophers." For months after that, whenever I saw Kak Nawzar he would start laughing and say to me, "Do you want to become a philosopher?"

Chapter Six &
The Anfal Operation

Memory

Not only me,
But all my fellow stateless ones
In our unknown country—
We say proudly
That whoever wants to know
Our bitter history,
Let them search—
It will not be fun.
All they will see
Is a dramatic tragedy,
A tear-filled calamity,
Of a homeless life's memory.
(1989)

Halabja

This is the nature of the human being: maybe someone has almost daily tragedy in his life, but when things are over he will mention only some of the worst memories. The same with the good times: if he tries to count them, maybe he can remember only a few of them. As a Kurd who lived in Iraq under a dictatorship, I saw real tragedies almost daily. These were not stories or fictions. I went through many difficulties myself, but when I came to mention some of them, I was able to remember only a few incidents…or I am not capable of describing the others. This is the same with any nation.

In Iraq today, when we Kurds speak about our suffering or sacrifices for freedom, first we talk about Halabja, and second about Anfal. Both of these took place in 1988. Decades before them, and up until the present, we move to distance ourselves from them, and the drama continues.

No doubt these two tragedies were the bloodiest incidents in the twentieth century for Kurds. There is no Kurd in Iraq who does not have only bitter memories about them. I am no exception, although I lived through Anfal. I lost my village completely. At least seventy-five people in Hashazini died in Anfal; a tenth of my relatives, hundreds of my friends, and thousands more whom I knew died among its victims. Each of them could have been the basis of a Hollywood drama or film, if they had been from the West—but we are an unknown people. We live alone, we suffer alone, and we die alone, and nothing is as stressful for human beings like loneliness, because it is against our nature.

Just about two months before the Anfal attack, my father's cousin Sheikh Yahya was appointed the mayor of Halabja, and he moved there from Chamchamal. In Iraq at that time, the government appointed the mayor and all other governmental representatives; nothing was by the people's choice. Soon after Sheikh Yahya went to Halabja and began his job, the city fell into the Iranian army's hands, and Kurdish *peshmerga* came back to the city. The Iraqi government used that as an excuse for its crime of poisoning the city with gas and chemical weapons—but it was not to get rid of the *peshmerga* or the Iranian army. Rather, it was to exterminate everything that existed there, even the animals and trees. This was done in front of the world's eyes, in violation of all human conventions, including the Geneva Conventions and the UN.

This remarkable crime took place on March 15 and 16, 1988. Halabja was a beautiful city; it was the county center and the biggest city in the Hawraman region of Sulaimaniya Province. It was almost completely destroyed. At least 5,000 innocent people were murdered and many more than that were seriously injured, most of them women and children. They are always the victims in today's wars. Even Arabs, in their ignorant early times, used to make an agreement during wartime that no one was allowed to kill women and children, and 1,400 years of Islam completely prohibited this, but in modern times the number of innocent people who are victims of war has risen to more than 90%, and the number of victims who are children is even higher. They are the real victims because if they survive, war terrorizes them and makes them grow

up as orphans. And women, if they survive, will be left to suffer fear and
stress and to struggle alone all their lives. I have no doubt that the life of
every single person in Iraq who lived in the second half of the twentieth
century—especially the lives of the Kurds and particularly the survivors
of Halajba and Anfal—could be a novel or drama.

Identity

Halajba—The running stream of tears
That flows like springs from Kurdish eyes
And cascades down our cheeks.

Halabja—Tells the history
Of how we faced the enemy
And how much Kurds have sacrificed
For dignity and freedom.

Bloody Halabja—The unhealed wound
Deep in the soul of Kurdish people
The Kurdish sign of national identity.
(1988)

One of my friends whom I met at college, Loqman Hassan, told me
that he had lost fifteen members of his family in the Halabja attack, and
the rest were seriously injured. He told me that after the gas caused people
to run out of the city toward the mountains to hide, airplanes came and
bombed the survivors. The gas clouds were so thick they looked like fog.
People were falling everywhere, but others kept on walking toward the
mountains through the bombs until they lost their eyesight from the gas
and collapsed. The Iranian army and other Kurds associated with the *peshmerga* later found them and took them to Iran to hospitals. Many people
died before that help came, but God was good to Loqman's family; they
reached the mountains before they collapsed, and the trees blocked much
of the gas, so they were not as badly affected as other people.

Loqman told me that after two or three days, when his family
members were able to open their eyes and become aware of their sur-

roundings, they realized that their baby sister, who was only about two and a half years old, was not with them. They searched everywhere for her in the hospitals, and then city by city and village by village. Many Iranian Kurds took in children who were found wandering around after the attack, and eventually some of these children were brought to government orphanages.

Loqman's family looked everywhere they could think of, and even put announcements in the paper, but they were unable to find any record of their sister. Eventually Loqman accepted the fact that she had died in the attack like hundreds of other children, but his parents never accepted this and always kept looking for her. In particular, Loqman's mother kept insisting that she had seen her daughter in a dream and that she was alive. Loqman told his mother to keep on dreaming. She responded, "Oh God, I need you to bring my dream to life."

For ten years, from March 1988 until 1998, Loqman's parents continued to look for their daughter. Whenever his mother left the city, she would even look under rocks and trees for signs of a body. After all these years, the only sign that their daughter was alive was her mother's persistent attempts to find her.

In 1998, after the Kurdish KDP set up a government in Iraqi Kurdistan, the Iranian government felt comfortable enough about the safety of Kurdish orphans to return some of the children who had been lost during the Halabja attack and had been raised in Iranian orphanages. Most of them were now teenagers. The KDP opened a special home for them in Arbil, and even started a special girls' school for Halabja orphans. Kak Loqman's other sister was a student in Arbil at the time and knew some of the teachers at the school. She asked the teachers if any of the students bore the name of her lost sister, and was told that two of the girls had the same name. She asked their ages, if they knew the names of their mother and father, or the names of their brothers and sisters, or anything else about their background. But she was told that infants and small children up to about three years old who had been lost generally did not remember enough information to help in their identification.

But the school investigated further, and replied that one of the two girls was two and a half years old at the time of the attack. She also still knew her mother's name, knew that at the time she had two brothers and one sister, and still remembered her sister's name. Both the mother's and sister's names matched Loqman's family names.

The family was permitted to visit the girl at the school. When they arrived, they were taken out to a playground where some forty to fifty students were at recess. Suddenly Loqman's mother pointed. "There!" she said. "There she is!" It was the same girl who remembered her mother's and sister's names.

The family met with the girl and became convinced that they had found their missing child. But the girl was nervous about what to do, and asked for time to think. She wanted to be sure that they really were her family. For her, the situation could have been difficult, or even dangerous. She was a teenager, and many people were interested in taking in younger "daughters" to work for them or to marry them off to distant or elderly relatives. All her friends were in the orphanage, and she was not ready to leave them right then in exchange for an unknown future over which she might have little control. She wanted to get some advice from her teachers and friends, and she wanted to make sure that she would be safe and treated well, and her best guarantee of that was to get some hard evidence that she really was the lost daughter from Loqman's family. Her experience made her very cautious. But she couldn't know all that the family had done to try and find her for the last ten years, or how hard her mother had cried for her, or how much time and money her father had spent looking for her. I hope by now that DNA tests are available in Kurdistan, so Loqman's family and hundred of others like them can be reunited with their loved ones in a real family.

When I came to America, I was shaken to hear an advertisement on the radio that said, "If you don't know who the father of your child is, call this number for a DNA test." I was amazed that a woman would not know who the father of her child was. Thank God we don't have such things in Kurdistan. But many children were lost in the war and adopted by other families, and still do not know who their parents are. What kind of life will such children have? In the East, children are victims of war. In the West, children are victims of drugs and adultery. But the result is the same: children suffering, and a growing number of orphans.

Sacrifice

In all this world
I only own
My mind and heart
My soul and poetry
I want to sacrifice them all
For Halabja's bitter memory.
(1988)

Genocide

Later in 1988, the government decided that my area was so full of *peshmerga* that the only way to eliminate this threat to the government was to destroy all the villages and to declare the area an open-fire zone on anyone who remained behind. In early 1989, the government's army came and completely destroyed Hashazini as part of the Anfal campaign of genocide against the Kurds. Our family fled before the army arrived, so we survived, but we lost our home and farm. Altogether, some 1,200 villages were destroyed and over 180,000 innocent people were murdered.

When Anfal began, all of us had to move into one room of a house in Chamchamal owned by my father's friend, Haji Raza. It was very dangerous because the government had ordered that anyone who sheltered someone from a demolished village would be executed. It was even harder because my brother Ibrahim was a *peshmerga*, and if the government's intelligence discovered that we were related to Ibrahim, they would arrest us all for being the family of a *peshmerga*. But Haji Raza was not afraid, and agreed to shelter us no matter what happened. He had a deep love and respect for my father and his family. He also felt relatively safe because his son had joined the Iraqi army and had been captured in Iran, so the government was not looking in his home.

The house itself was really small, with only two rooms for Haji Raza and his daughter-in-law and her five children. But they all agreed to move into one room so that my brother Mohsin, my sister Aaisha, our sick father, and I could have the other room. We all shared one bath, one toilet, and one kitchen. We thought we would only have to stay for a few days or weeks until we could rent something else, but Haji Raza would not hear of us leaving because he did not believe any other place would be safe for us, and he knew that we could not afford any other place to live. So for almost two years we lived in this one room, as my father's health became worse and worse.

A friend told me about a man who went crazy after Anfal and began wandering around his city crying, "They are alive. I am not burying them." Nobody knew what he meant. Finally someone found out about his history and realized what he was saying. During Anfal, he had been assigned to a bulldozer and told to dig deep trenches. Then dump trucks arrived filled with refugees from the villages that had been destroyed. The villagers had been told that if they got into the dump trucks they would be evacuated to another region—but instead they were dumped into the trenches and the man was told to bury them alive with the bulldozer. If he had refused, he would have been thrown into the trenches along with the villagers and buried alive by some other person.

These mass graves are now being uncovered, and the truth is finally being discovered by the world. But the sad truth is that when hundreds of thousands of Kurds were being killed during the Anfal campaign, the world was silent. The Arab countries said that the Kurds had always exaggerated and caused trouble. But when Iraq turned on the Arab state of Kuwait and killed a few hundred Kuwaitis, the whole world rose up in outrage and overthrew the Iraqi army.

I am not blaming the world for freeing Kuwait: I support Kuwaiti freedom. I am not justifying the loss of even one Kuwaiti life; what was done to them was a crime, and I pray to never see such a disaster again. But my question is, why does the world have a double standard for justice, peace, and human life? Kuwait should be free, but so should Kurdistan. Kuwaitis must be safe in their own land, but so should

Palestinians. I want to ask the world: isn't a Kurdish life, or a Palestinian life, worth as much as a Kuwaiti life? For over fifty years Kurdish blood has been running like a river, and the same is true of Palestine. So where was the intervention of the superpowers? Where was the UN? Where was NATO? Where were the seekers of peace and justice?

After I came to America, and the government accused me of having radical ideas and of being a terrorist, the best evidence it brought to court to support this was to say that terrorists blame America for many problems in the Middle East, and Yassin does the same: he blames America for Kurdish suffering and the Iraqi situation. So Yassin and terrorists have the same ideas—therefore Yassin is a terrorist!

Meaning

When I hear about
A garden high and fertile,
For me it means: a high mountain,
Tall trees, mild weather,
Cold, sweet, running water,
Birds with many songs.

When I hear about
A desert,
Surely I expect to see:
A flat, wide, plain land,
Hot, dry, with tornadoes
Bringing dust and mirages.

But when I hear Anfal
I lose my mind with sadness,
Too much pain,
Because today Anfal
Means the genocide
Of 180,000 innocent Kurds.
An unknown nation,
A stateless people.
(1992)

During Anfal, anyone that the army found in the villages—mostly children, women, the sick, and the elderly—were put into trucks, taken south, and killed in mass executions. Every day we saw trucks driving by filled with these victims. Everybody was furious about what was happening, even the *Jash*, who normally obeyed the government. All of them had friends and family in the villages.

My blood was boiling with anger. I used to say to my friends, "It is like we are all dead. We do nothing."

They would reply, "What can anyone do?"

"Go and die!" I would say. "What's the point of living like this? It is better to have a real death than live a fake life like this." I was crazy. I ran from one place to another trying to persuade people to do something. I went to the Imams in the mosque, to the students in schools, to the players on the soccer fields, and even to the shop owners. Each time I said, "Let's do something to stop them. They are taking the victims south and will kill them. We have to do something."

Some people cried, some prayed, but everybody responded, "But what can we do?" Nobody had any idea what to do.

One day I was talking to Kak Nawzar, and my friend Bebak came along. Bebak was a young poet of our age. Some people called him insane because he talked so much and could not keep his tongue under control. He was perhaps the only person who could criticize the government openly, simply because he said so much and had so few inhibitions. He wanted to read a new poem to us, criticizing the government, but I stopped him. "We are tired of hearing all these words," I snapped. "We need to see some action."

"Well, I am ready," Bebak said. "I will do whatever you want me to do. If you jump into the fire, I will jump with you."

Nawzar gave me a look with his eyes that said, *Be careful*, but I did not acknowledge him because I was so upset and angry.

"Look what is going on!" I said. "Why are they taking all the people from the villages?"

"To kill them. It is genocide," Bebak said.

"So how can we accept that?"

"Because we are not human beings. We have no feelings."

"So why do you write poems?" I asked Bebak.

"I want to open people's eyes. I want other nations to see what we have become, and to feel our shame that we live like this."

"Stop your philosophy," I told him. "I want you to do something."

"I told you," Bebak said, "I'm ready. LET'S GO!" He said the last part loudly enough so others could hear. "We will go and demonstrate! We will close the road so the trucks have to stop!"

Nawzar tried to get me to leave, but I said no because I too wanted to do something, though I thought that demonstrating was not a good idea because they would just come and arrest all of us. Instead I said, "Listen. We'll go and wait until a truck with victims comes down the road, and then we'll go to the middle of the road and pretend to cross so the truck has to either stop or kill us. Then the villagers in the back can jump out and escape. When the government comes, they won't find a demonstration, just a group of students crossing the street."

We went to the road and stood in the middle, but the next truck that came along only honked its horn, made a big slow turn around us, and did not come to a complete stop. "Tell them to jump!" I yelled to Nawzar, and a few did, but most of the victims in the back—the old and the sick—were not ready or able to jump, and the children naturally wanted to stay with their families above all. The victims mostly believed that the government was going to move them to the cities and give them houses, as they had been promised.

I felt really good about what we were doing, but Nawzar said that only one person had escaped to safety.

"So what?" I said. "If you save one life, you've saved humanity. Do your books so affect your judgment that one life matters nothing for you?"

"No, I don't mean to say that," said Nawzar. "What I meant was that we are not doing *enough*."

"So next time yell at them to jump down, because they are being taken for execution, not resettlement!" I went over to one of my friends who was selling merchandise from the back of his cart. "I need your cart right now," I said.

"For what?"

"To roll it under the truck."

"To do what?" he asked, surprised.

I explained to him what we were trying to do. He agreed to give me the cart, and said, "If you want to throw my body under the truck, I am willing."

I told him to help me push the cart into the next refugee truck that came down the road. We waited. Finally a truck was coming…coming…coming. We went to the middle of the road and pushed the cart directly toward the truck. The truck blew its horn to no avail, and slammed on its brakes. The sound of the brakes brought many people out into the road to surround the truck. The driver was angry and told us to move the cart, but we refused. The driver climbed down to move the cart and was immediately surrounded by people; others went to the back of the truck and brought out all of the victims inside—almost fifty people. After this, those who had surrounded the driver let him go.

Nawzar laughed. "Now *this* is what I meant. Now we are doing well."

For the rest of the week, we continually stopped trucks on the road and brought the victims out to safety. Sometimes five or ten people would stand in the middle of the roadway. Sometimes we would push a cart in front of the trucks. Once a friend brought three cows, which we used to block the road. In this way, we freed several hundred people.

But soon enough the government found out what we were doing and brought in a special force from the army, and also some *Jash*, to prevent us from crossing the road or throwing things at the trucks. With the soldiers there we could not stop the trucks anymore. The government also made an announcement that they were going to search the city, and anyone who was found to have hidden a villager in his home would have his home destroyed and be arrested. They even forced some Imams to say in the mosques that it was not permitted to hide a villager.

I went to Mala Gareeb, who was the biggest and best Imam in Chamchamal, and also to Mala Asuad, and told them they should say in their mosques that it was our duty to protect our brothers and sisters who were from the villages, and to feed them and shelter them. That even at the cost of our own lives, we may not sacrifice them. That our lives were not better than their lives, and our blood was not more important than theirs. That we could sacrifice our lives to save them, but not the other way around. Both Imams preached this message, and many people were saved as a result.

Later I said to Bebak that he had proven he was honest and willing, and had put his poems into action. "This was really your idea," I said to Bebak. "And because of it, hundreds of innocent people were saved."

After the Anfal campaign ended, my family was truly homeless. My father was sick and old. There were no nursing homes in Kurdistan, and there was no way to properly care for him. My brother Issa took Father and Aaisha to live with him in Sulaimaniya. But there was no medicine available anywhere. We could not have any tests done on him, or even have his blood pressure checked. Nobody had even heard of cholesterol or diabetes. People were dying every day, and we could only suffer in silence.

Question

I don't want to open those wounds,
I am not singing that old song,
But there is the Fact.
I will ask for all time—
Anfal's victims,
A hundred and eighty thousand
Innocent Kurds—
Where are they?
(1989)

Hama Rash

The Garmian region where we had lived was the center of *peshmerga* activity because it was near Kirkuk, where ethnic cleansing was focused on killing Kurds. It was not easy for *peshmerga* to hide in

Garmian, because unlike other parts of Kurdistan the mountains were smaller and there were fewer trees. After the Anfal campaign, the areas around the destroyed villages were declared to be free-fire zones. Since all the villagers had been removed from the area and killed, anyone still living there was presumed to be a *peshmerga* and was subject to attack whenever he was seen.

Without villagers, it would have seemed impossible for any *peshmerga* to hide and survive in the free-fire areas of the Garmian district—but the government did not count on Hama Rash, one of the most famous of the *peshmerga* commanders. *Hama* is the Kurdish way of saying Mohammad, and *Rash* means "black." So he was the Black Mohammad, because his skin was in fact slightly darker than normal Kurdish skin. In some ways he looked like an Arab from the South.

Hama Rash was actually the commander of an even more famous *peshmerga* general, Mama Risha (which means "uncle with a beard"). The government and the *Jash* were scared to death of Mama Risha, and even people in southern Iraq had heard of his exploits. Mama Risha was just an illiterate villager, tall and skinny, who had no ideas about Marxism or capitalism or any other kind of ism. Many times I saw him praying. He always carried an amulet that he believed prevented the enemy from killing him. He was very social, and he used to joke with the villagers all the time and talk to them as though he was one of them. He used to call me *Shehka Gian*, which means "dear small Sheikh." Hama Rash, on the other hand, seldom smiled or joked with the villagers, and he seldom allowed himself to be seen. But he was educated and literate.

I saw them both hundreds of times in my village. They loved Hashazini because it was a little bit better than the surrounding villages; it even had two small grocery stores and some educated people who had gone to school in the city. I used to bring supplies for Hama Rash when I came home from Chamchamal. He had a friend there who often gave me things to bring back to Hashazini that Hama needed— watches, pens, shirts, sneakers, sweat pants, things like that.

One day after I gave Hama some supplies, he started preaching to me and some other young men about Arab fashion. I said to one of my friends that I would make him mad.

"For heaven's sake," my friend said, "we want someone to make him smile, not make him mad. He looks angry all the time." In fact, his dark skin, an injured lip, and his habit of scowling as he thought, did make him look angry and frightening.

But I told my friend to wait for a minute, and watch. "Kak Hama," I said. "You should not talk about 'Arab fashion.' Our problem is with the government, not with the Arabs."

Hama looked at me sharply, as if warning me not to go too far.

I persisted. "I'm serious. Many Arabs don't like Saddam."

"Yeah," he said. "But too many of them are supporting him."

"It still does not mean that we should hate them all."

"Are you supporting ASH?" he grunted. ASH was a small group that had separated from the PUK. It had been founded and was headed by an individual named Mala Bakhtiar (who is now a member of the politboro of PUK and supervisor of its foreign office). ASH was talking about Iraqi liberation, not just Kurdish liberation. They did not want an independent Kurdistan—they wanted an independent Iraq, and they were Communist, not nationalist.

"I'm not supporting them," I said.

Hama began talking about how the government was trying to change all Kurdish names in Iraq, and how most other Arab countries supported Saddam. He became very hot and emotional.

I winked at my friend, and then I said, "Kak Hama, stop talking about 'Kurd this' and 'Kurd that.' You don't even look like a Kurd. If anyone saw you, he would think you are an Arab." I was showing off.

The group fell completely silent. Hama rose up on his legs and glared at me so intensely that more than one of my friends thought he was going to shoot me. Then he growled, "You live in the city. The city has corrupted your mind." And then he laughed, and everyone else laughed with relief and surprise. They had not seen Hama laugh before.

Before we left, Hama told me that he wanted to give me something. He had written a letter to his friend in the city, and now he gave it to me to deliver. "I'm sorry," he said. "I was emotional. I know we are fighting against the government, not Arabs. Follow your path." I smiled at him, and he gave me a hug. "Be safe," he said.

During Anfal, when the army was destroying all of the villages and small towns in Garmian, many of the *peshmerga* were killed. Some joined the *Jash*, and the remainder mostly fled to Iran or the high Qandeel Mountains. But Hama Rash refused to run; he was the only *peshmerga* to stay in Garmian between 1988 and 1991, when the Kurdish uprising began, with about ten of his personal guards.

It is really hard to imagine how Hama survived during those years, since no villages or people remained to give him food or a place to hide. Helicopters searched the land daily, and if they saw anything move they attacked, because whatever it was, it was not a villager or a farmer. Since the area was a free-fire zone, no one was allowed to go back to see his village or farm. At night, if the government saw any light, it would attack with helicopters and rockets. It was common knowledge that Hama Rash was still in Garmian, because the army and the *Jash* searched constantly for him, but where was he? And how could he survive for so long with the whole country's armed forces looking for him in a free-fire zone? We all thought he must have been killed.

One day when we woke up, about ten helicopters flew over Chamchamal toward our village area and attacked something. We could hear the sound of rockets exploding. Then for the rest of the day, thousands of *Jash* and army soldiers rushed into the area and there were more sounds of rockets, as though a big battle was going on. Rumors spread that they had found Hama Rash. I was really sad and prayed that it was not true, but there was no way to know for sure. I kept my eye out for any of my *Jash* friends so I could ask them what was going on.

Two days later, I was able to ask one of the *Jash* what had happened. "Did you find Hama Rash?"

"No, but we killed seven of his commandos."

"What? You killed them all?"

"Seven of them."

"So how many *peshmerga* does he have?" I asked. I thought to myself that this seemed strange, that Hama Rash might not even have seven people with him.

"We did not kill any *peshmerga*, and we did not find any," said the *Jash*, and then he began to laugh. "But we did kill seven of Hama Rash's commandos."

"What do you mean, 'Hama Rash's commandos'?"

The *Jash* just laughed harder and harder.

"What's so funny?" I asked.

The *Jash* said, "For two days, more than 15,000 soldiers with ten helicopters fought their way through the village area. And we killed four baby donkeys and three cats."

"What are you talking about?"

"Cats—donkeys—you know. Small animals. That is what we were fighting."

"You are making me crazy. What happened?"

"Hama Rash put small mirrors on pieces of cloth and tied them around baby donkeys and cats, like shirts. When the sun reflected off the mirrors, the army thought that someone was moving on the ground and the helicopters started bombing them. The cats ran and hid themselves in the village ruins. The army was called in to find them. We found hats on the ends of rakes and clothes hung on woodpiles in five district villages. The army commanders gave us directions and they pointed to the places we were to go, and we found nothing. In one village we saw cats running, and when we killed them we found the shirts with the mirrors on them. In other villages we found donkeys with the same mirrors. Then finally we knew what was going on. After we killed four donkeys and three cats, the army also understood what was going on, but they still insisted that this was Hama Rash's joke and that we should find him. We searched under every rock and tree, and we searched demolished houses in every village for two days, but we did not find even one footprint of a human being."

"Are you joking?"

"No, by God." The *Jash* laughed. "This was Hama Rash's new commando force, and we slaughtered them wherever we found them."

I couldn't hold back my laughter any more.

About a month later, Hama Rash's friend, who used to send supplies for him, invited me to his house. "How are you, Yassin?" he asked.

"Good, thank you."

"You know the situation?"

"How is Kak Hama?"

"He is strong. He is OK."

"Where did he get his idea for this new strategy?"

"What strategy?"

"Cat commandos. Donkey forces."

"I don't know."

"Oh come on. You glued the mirrors on the shirts for him."

"No. Not me."

"When he got the mirrors, how did he stick them to the cloth?"

"There was plenty of sewing material left in the villages when they were destroyed."

"So what is next?"

"I don't know."

I felt that he was being very careful and not telling me everything. Then he said, "Listen, Yassin. What does the word 'flashlight' mean?"

"Flashlight? It is a small hand light that turns on and off."

"No, I mean, what is it used for?"

"Nighttime."

"Yassin! You know what I mean!"

"No, I don't."

"Do they use it for sending a code?" he asked.

"Who?"

"*Peshmerga.*"

"Maybe. I don't know. Why?"

"You mean you don't know if *peshmerga* use flashlights for something other than just light?"

"I don't."

"Read this." He handed me a letter.

After I had read the letter, which was unsigned, he asked me,

"What do you understand from it?"

"Well, someone is asking you to buy flashlights for him."

"But what is 'flashlight'?"

"You still don't know what a flashlight is?"

"I don't believe that he means that."

"Who wrote the letter?"

"Hama Rash."

"Are you sure?" I asked.

"Yes."

"So send him some flashlights."

"What does he need them for?"

"To use at night, of course," I said.

"No way. If the army sees any light at night, they'll attack that place because there should not be any signs of life in that area."

"But they could use the lights in caves or underground holes when they can't burn wood because of the smoke."

"Oh," he said. "Of course. You are right. So this must mean he really needs flashlights."

"I believe so."

"Good, Yassin. This is all I need to know."

"How will you send them to him?"

"That is another story."

I did not ask any more. I didn't even want to know. I told him to just give Hama my *salaam*. But then I said, "I was really sad that day when I thought the army had killed or arrested him. Is it true that he was not in the area at all? And what about the cats and donkeys? Where did they come from?"

My friend laughed. "Hama Rash left the cats in the village at night with food, and then he withdrew from the area for at least seven hours. When daylight came, the donkey mirrors started shining."

"But how could he walk? His footsteps would show the government where he was hiding. Walking in Garmian in the summer is like walking in snow, because footsteps show in the dust."

My friend looked wise. "Kak Hama told me that his footstep is five feet long and two feet wide."

"What are you talking about?"

"He ties a piece of wood under his shoes so they don't make any imprint in the dust."

It was my turn to laugh. "Now he can really be called 'Gorilla,' "I said. "So what does he need? Why doesn't he go to the Qandeel?"

"He doesn't want to go," my friend said. "He promised that he would not leave Garmian."

"But he can't do anything here."

"What he can do is let the government and the *Jash* know that the *peshmerga* still exist. If he just makes them scared, he has done something. From time to time he gives them a sign to prove he is still here. Look what he did just by using cats and donkeys. He forced the government to use thousands of troops and helicopters, and to keep a force ready to chase him the next time he leaves a sign. Think of the expense. How long can they keep it up? And the Kurds know that the *peshmerga* are nearby, and it gives them hope so they will never give up."

"Good," I told him. "Tell Kak Hama to be safe." And I left.

About two weeks later, a heavy rocket attack started one night in the village area. Even helicopters came, which was unusual at night. I went to the roof, and it looked like people were living on the mountainside. Little lights were everywhere—some of them flashing, as though they were sending signals. For two or three hours the helicopters bombed the area, but afterwards some of the lights were still on. The next morning they sent the *Jash* up the mountain to search. Soon the news came that they had found nothing except—flashlights. There were no *peshmerga* in the area. Finally I understood what was going on, and I laughed to myself, wondering what Hama's next move was going to be.

In 1991, after the Chamchamal uprising, Hama Rash came back to the city. People welcomed him like a hero. Unfortunately, he did not see many days of freedom. When the *peshmerga* tried to free Kirkuk, he was sent south to cut the road between Kirkuk and Baghdad so the government could not send reinforcements, the criminals couldn't escape, and *peshmerga* from the north could enter the city. In a town called Laylan,

Hama Rash was killed in heavy fighting.

He had been with the *peshmerga* for almost fifteen years, for three years he was alone in Garmian facing at least 10,000 army troops, and still he stayed alive. Now, just before all of Kurdistan was liberated, he was dead, and could not enjoy the fruit of our liberation. He left us, but his name will remain in Kurdish history forever. No one can deny that he was a real hero, a Kurdish freedom fighter struggling against the Iraqi regime and Saddam's dictatorship.

After his death in 1991, I wrote a poem about him.

Hama Rash

Half of your life
You gave to the mountains
Under the snow
In the cold and the frost

Half in Garmain
With the tornado
Hot winds around you
You slept in the dirt

Rocks were your pillow
The sky was your blanket
You took nothing yourself
But gave all to the Kurds.

This was what my life was like as a teenager in Kurdistan after Anfal. I studied at night school; I worked during the day; I refused to join the Baath party; I hid myself from government interrogation; I wrote poems; I supported the *peshmerga*; I waited for news of my brother Ibrahim, who had joined them; and I tried to help my sister, brother, and sick father. Finally I finished high school, but there was no way for me to go to college at that time or under those circumstances.

Chapter Seven ✑
Kurdish Uprising

In 1991, international events suddenly had a dramatic impact on our lives. After Iraq lost the Gulf War, it was forced to pull many of its troops out of Kurdistan to put down an uprising in the south. The confidence of the troops that remained in Kurdistan was shaken. You could just feel it in the air. They kept out of sight and did not try to intimidate people the way they used to. The *peshmerga* attacks became stronger and forced the government's army into the cities. For the first time, we felt that the army troops were more afraid than we were.

On March 7, 1991, while I was living in Chamchamal, I woke up one morning and told my brother Mohsin that I was going to start today.

"Start what?" he asked.

"A demonstration like the one in Rania." This was a town close to the Iranian border in Sulaimaniya Province, and on March 5 the people had staged demonstrations and freed their city from the government's forces. We called the city *Darwazay Raparin* (Gates of Uprising).

"How can you do that? Who will be with you? What weapons will you have?" asked Mohsin. He disapproved of my idea.

I told him that we didn't need anyone because the people were ready to revolt. "Even the government officials left the city yesterday because they knew they couldn't stop the people. Even the army is not going to fight," I said.

Mohsin did not believe me. But I told him that I didn't have time to argue. "Just come and do not worry. Everything will be OK."

Mohsin said, "Please, Yassin, don't be crazy."

I smiled at him and left him home. I went to get some of my friends instead. Of us, one was a Communist, one was Kurdish, one was an Iraqi nationalist, and I was religious. Mohsin joined us later. None of us knew anything about democracy except for the name, but we were friends and came together for one goal—to free Chamchamal from the government's troops.

That day we had nothing in our hands and not even a clear plan of what we wanted to do. But we all believed this was the right moment, and that people would support us if we stood up and shouted "Baath finished!" One of my friends, Qurbani, brought his father's gun, and he fired it in the air so people would believe that we were sincere. We hoped the government would be afraid that the *peshmerga* were coming.

A policeman came up to us. I asked him questions while my friend Nahro grabbed his gun. We then threatened the policeman with it and forced him to come with us. "Don't be scared," I told him. "Nobody is going to hurt you, but we cannot let you tell the government what we are doing."

After awhile I told him, "It's OK. You can go home if you don't want to help us."

"Who are you?" he asked.

"We are the *peshmerga*," I told him. I wanted him to leave and tell the government that the *peshmerga* had taken his weapon so the government would believe that *peshmerga* forces were in the city, and the people would believe that the *peshmerga* would protect them and so would come out to support us. Now we had two weapons to share between five students.

My friend Juma said we should target some big government officials now that we had weapons. I told him we should not shed blood, because if we killed anyone the government forces would stay to fight us, and we just wanted them to go and leave Chamchamal. We should only scare them. The others agreed with me.

We decided that I would go to the mosque and use the loudspeaker that called people to prayer to urge city residents to come out and support the revolution, and to tell the police and the army not to fight if they wanted to be safe. When I was finished, the others were to walk down the street firing their weapons into the air, but under no circumstances was anyone to be shot.

I went to the mosque and began: "In the name of God and on behalf of the Kurdish front, I want to tell you that we, the *peshmerga*, are here on the streets and we want you to come out of your houses and come with us. It is time to shout 'Death to dictators and their bloody regimes! Long live freedom! Long live Kurdistan! Long live the *peshmerga*!' "

Can you imagine that I was the first one ever to say such things openly in broad daylight in our city? I said it as loudly as possible on the loudspeaker, so the whole city would hear.

I continued: "To our respected soldiers in the army, to our beloved brothers in the police force, to our respected government workers: it has been decided that whoever today helps the *peshmerga*, or even sits at home and does not fight us, will not be asked about his past. The past is over! We are all Kurds now, and we are all brothers, and we are all *peshmerga*. Come help us and prove today that you are a Kurd and that you are a *peshmerga*. You all want freedom. You don't want another Halabja or another Anfal! It has been decided. No revenge is going to take place in Kurdistan. Long live the Kurds! Long live Kurdistan! Long live freedom!"

When I finished and went back to my friends, the city suddenly seemed to explode. Gunfire sounded everywhere, Kurdish nationalist songs were lifting on the air, and people came out of their houses singing and clapping.

I told my friends, "Now we have hundreds of allies. Keep singing and firing in the air."

"What should we do if the government comes?" one of my friends asked. "Maybe they will come to arrest us."

"They are finished," said my other friend.

"This is all we can do," I said. "We can only give courage to the people to rise up. Everything belongs to them and they will take what they need. Our job is done."

A crowd tore down the statue of Saddam and surrounded the police station. The crowd became bigger and bigger. But after about two or three hours, the government realized that we were not *peshmerga*, just students, and they brought in their special forces and began firing on us.

My brother Mohsin was shot in the leg. Some people took him and hid him in a nearby home. The rest of our small group ran away and hid; Mohsin and I stayed underground in a basement, and I took care of him because he lost so much blood.

"Why did you do this?" Mohsin asked me.

"Why did you come?" I asked him in return.

"I wanted to save you," Mohsin said.

On March 9, after forty hours of hiding, we tried again to rouse the city. This time the *peshmerga* really did come, and in a few hours Chamchamal was completely free.

"Come out!" I told Mohsin. "No more hiding ourselves, no more fear. Now it is our city. We are free!"

He did not believe me. We took him to the hospital.

The liberation of Chamchamal was the most wonderful moment of my life. It was hard to believe how fast a criminal, bloody regime could collapse and disappear. There was a smile on every face. People everywhere congratulated us. Kurdish nationalist songs were sung so loudly the city was shaking. Now we could test freedom. Now we had our own city. Long live freedom!

I wrote two poems about the liberation of Chamchamal on March 9, 1991:

Freeing the City

Never will I forget the day
When all of us joined together
And by singing and clapping
Freed ourselves and our city
From the grip of our enemy.

Real Spring

This is our birthday
The beginning of new life and new history.
Joyfully we welcome you
With all our beloved *peshmerga*
Back to your homes in our city.

Look at the smiling *nergz* [lilies]
Sending us the glad tidings
Nawroz is coming! Nawroz is coming!
Now it is the real spring.

Your face has the look of fear.
Forget the past. It is over.
Our people—our nation,
Black and white, rich and poor
All are coming together.

Give me your hand
We must go back to the mountains
To find uncle's grave
Raise the flag above his head
Let him and all his murderers know
That now we are free
And this is the fruit of their blood.

Freedom Lost

A few months later, the government's forces regrouped and attacked Kurdistan again, including Chamchamal. There was no way to stop them, and they killed and destroyed everything in their path like an avenging plague. No one in Chamchamal even tried to stop them. As we say in Kurdistan, some things that you get easy, you lose easy.

People were so terrified that they dropped whatever they were doing and fled to the Kurdish mountains along the border with Iran, where they huddled in caves and improvised tents against the cold and hunger—over three million people without protection against the army or the weather, and without food. Before they fled, they grabbed whatever food they could carry, but even at best they could not carry enough to last for more than a week. Some people escaped in cars, and there were massive traffic jams. Sometimes drivers tried to get around the traffic jams by driving off the roads, and their cars were wrecked. Eventually all of the cars ran out of gas or came to the end of the road, and the drivers had to take to the mountain footpaths like everyone else.

When I saw that the army was coming, I had taken my father and my sister Aaisha from my sister Nathifa's house in Chamchamal, where they were guests, to another city, Bazyan, that I thought was safer. I left them there with a cousin. I had come back to Chamchamal to watch over our houses and to encourage people to protect the city. Now I wanted to return to Bazyan to get my family, but I was blocked because the army had cut the road.

So another cousin and three of my friends and I could do no more than watch in disbelief as the crowds fled from Chamchamal. Were these the same people who, just a few months earlier, had run into the streets firing their weapons in celebration of achieving freedom? We started shouting at them, "Shame! Shame! Don't run! Stay and defend the city!" We jumped from one roof to another shouting the same words that we had shouted before, but nobody listened to us. They just kept running.

We saw one of the leaders of the *peshmerga* running away. We shouted at him to stay and defend Chamchamal. He looked embarrassed and said that he was just leaving to join his troops outside of town, and that soon they would come back in and destroy the army. But then he ran off in another direction from the way he had pointed, and we knew he was lying.

We saw three or four helicopters, and ran into a building to hide. The helicopters attacked the city. Rockets began exploding around us. Then tanks began to push toward us through the streets, with the army right behind. But both tanks and army stayed on the highways, no soldiers came out of the tanks, and nobody searched any of the houses. They just kept moving through the city and out the other side and did not bother any of the residents. However, when we looked around, it seemed as though we were the only people still left in Chamchamal. We knew that if we moved or ran, the helicopters would shoot at us, and in any event the army had cut the road out of town.

We collected as much food as we could and made ready to flee at night, since Chamchamal had obviously been lost without even a defensive shot being fired.

"We should split up and go in different directions," I said.

"Do you know any safe way out of here?" my cousin Nash asked.

"No, I don't," I said. "I think we should just go east, toward Iran."

"Suppose we walk a long way and we're trapped by a river or a dead end, and the army comes and we get caught in an ambush?"

"Listen," I said. "All this talk is not helping. We should just head for the mountains, and tomorrow I am sure we will find plenty of people who know the way."

Soon after sundown, we started walking east. It was very dark and we could not see what was in front of us. But we did hear the sound of rocket fire. Sometimes the army sent up flares that illuminated everything for a few minutes, but we could not safely take advantage of the light and had to lie down in the mud to hide. I told my friends that despite what I had said earlier, we should promise in any situation to stay together, so that we all succeeded together or died together, and that we should not eat any of our food until it was absolutely necessary because we did not know how long it would have to last.

We walked fifteen hours a day for the next nine days and nights, most of the time in the rain, until we reached the Iranian border. It was the longest, hardest journey I ever had to make. We were young and unencumbered by family or possessions, but we passed thousands of families struggling along the road crying for help, begging for food, asking for directions or news of their relatives. We helped when we could, and shared what we had, but it was overwhelming; and in the end we had to save ourselves from the advancing army because they would certainly have killed young men like us first.

Why Is God Punishing Us?

It is almost impossible to describe the scenes of chaos and devastation. It was like the flood in New Orleans except that the planes flying overhead were shooting at us rather than trying to help, and we were climbing through wild mountains rather than struggling through a city. At one point we saw a woman in complete despair take her baby and throw it over a cliff. One of my friends climbed down the cliff to try and save the baby, but when he returned he said that it was dead.

Sometimes we carried children who could not keep up with their families. Sometimes we gave them food. Sometimes we tried to reassure people who were too frightened to think clearly. Sometimes we tried to give people directions. One day while we were climbing a mountain trail, we saw an old man who had been left behind. He called to us, "Son, son, please help." I looked back at him, and I was shaken to see that he looked just like my sick father. It gave me such pain to think that I did not know whether he and my family had fled Bazyan, or anything at all about what was happening to them.

I stopped and went back to the old man, thinking about my dad, and my eyes filled with tears. I took his hand and started helping him climb the mountain trail.

"Thank you very much," he told me.

"Thank God, not me," I replied.

He looked at me strangely and said, "You're a *Mala* (Imam)?"

"No, I am not."

"No matter," he said. "Just please explain to me, why is God punishing us?"

I said, "This, Saddam is doing for us—not God."

"I know that Saddam is doing this," he said. "I am talking about the rain. Does God not see all the women and children who have no shelter? Why doesn't He stop the rain?"

"But it is not as cold as it usually is in the mountains," I told him.

"You are right, but I was talking about the rain. Since we left our home it has not stopped raining."

"My dad used to tell me all the time that rain is a blessing."

"But not now. It is a punishment."

"I don't believe so," I told him.

"What? You don't see all these people under the rain day and night? Look at these woman and children. Is this not punishment?"

"No. I believe this is protection for us."

"How?" He looked at me in great surprise.

"This weather prevented the government from using the air force against us. If it wasn't for the rain, the helicopters would have picked us off one by one and then attacked the survivors."

He just looked at me for awhile, thinking about what I had said.

"*Mala*, I swear by God you are right. Never did I think about that. Just pray that it keeps on raining. God's water is much better than Saddam's fire."

"God's water drowns Saddam's fire," I said.

A little farther up the trail someone called to me. "Kak Yassin! Kak Yassin! Come here and bring your father!" When I came up to him, he told me that seven students had found a big cave in the side of the mountain and had fixed it up as a kind of rest house for the sick and elderly. One of the students was a nurse.

"I don't know where my father is," I said. "I left him in Bazyan last week."

"This is not your father?"

"No, I am just helping him to the top. But he is like my father—there is not any difference. I want you to take him instead of my father."

The old man looked at me and said, "Imam, I am sixty-five years old and I have never seen someone like you."

"We were going in the same direction, and so I just walked with you," I said.

"But I begged many people before you, and no one answered me. Even my own people left me behind. You don't know me, and yet you say I am like your dad. It is best when, like you, people fear God and help others for God's sake." When he reached the cave he went in to rest. He did not know that I had left my own father behind.

I turned to the student who had called me. "I'm sorry, I don't know you."

"But I know you," he said.

"When did you see me? How do you know me?"

"I am from Chamchamal too, and I have heard you many times in the mosque and at City Hall and in the poetry seminars."

"What is your name?"

"Soran."

"It is good to meet you, Kak Soran. How did you find this cave?"

"We were some of the first to come here and we saw this cave, so we decided to stop here and help those who could not walk any further."

"This is a great thing," I said. "God bless you. Give all your friends my *salaam* and thank them for what they are doing. I hope to see you back in Chamchamal soon. And don't forget—the old man is like my dad. So please take care of him as though he is my dad."

When we reached the top of the mountain, we could see across the border into Iran, at the point near Sardasht, but the sight made us cold with fear: tens of thousands of refugees, like a disrupted ant's nest, were swarming over the hills below, right up to the river that separated Iran from Iraq. It seemed as though not just the 50,000 inhabitants of Chamchamal but the whole Kurdish nation was here, fleeing from the government and the army. It was like the scene that the Imams describe about the Day of Judgment, when God will collect all of humanity in fear and with praying to confront the hereafter.

Everybody looked to save himself. Friends left their friends behind; relatives left their relatives; brothers left their brothers; fathers left their sons. Everyone was waiting in fear—for death, or for something to happen so they could cross the border to safety. Some people made small tents with their blankets to keep off the rain. Other just sat in the mud. Eventually the Iranian government provided some tents, but they were not enough for even twenty percent of us.

The river that separated Iran from Iraq was in flood because of all the rain. Thousands of people were crowded on the Iraqi bank, but there was no bridge or boat or any other way to cross the swollen water. And the Iranian police on the other side were giving only a few people permission to cross. So we just sat down in the mud and waited, with the thousands of other refugees. There was nowhere else to go.

Bro Pain

As we were approaching Iran, my friend saw a flag and said, "Oh, *this* must be the border. See, it is an Iranian flag." Thousands of people were crowded together near the flag seeking permission to cross. I was puzzled about this. How could this flag be the border, since both sides of the flag were Kurdistan? It was the same land, the same nation, the same culture, the same language, and we were Kurds, but we were not allowed to cross some imaginary line. Well, the Iranian border guards did look different. They had beards. In Iraq, everyone in uniform had to be clean-shaven.

The border guards kept pushing people back. From time to time they would let only one or two people cross, and then two or three hundred people would surge forward trying to cross also, and the guards would beat them back. When a little food was brought by the Iranians, thousands of refugees would run for it. Again the guards would beat them back. All the time the guards were shouting, *"Bro pain! Bro pain!"*, which means "go back" in Persian. These were the first Iranian words we learned. But go back to where? To the army? To be killed? Or to Iraq to "disappear"? Or to the mountains to die with no food and no shelter? We had no "back." Our "back" was broken, and nobody was backing the Kurds.

Since then, the phrase *Bro pain* has become our joke. If you ask any Kurd to do you a favor or do anything for you, he will smile and say, *"Bro pain."* When children ask a question, they are told *"Bro pain,"* which in context means "Keep quiet." When I finally found my sister and cousin and her family after two months, I asked my niece, who was then three years old, whether she had seen Iran. She said, "No. All they said was *'Bro pain,' 'Bro pain,'* and they did not let us in."

Respect the Bread

While we waited to cross the border, we tried to organize people so that they could be fed. Nothing is harder than to organize hungry people, especially if there is not enough food to feed even five percent of them. People were fighting, running, shouting, crying for a piece of bread.

In the Middle East and all other poor countries, the person who can provide bread to his family is the hero. Many people in third world countries look for anything to eat that will keep them alive. They do not have the option of a restaurant or fast food, and they cannot pick and choose what they want to eat. Just to survive, especially in a time of war or during an embargo, they must take whatever they can get. It is hard for people in Western countries to understand this unless they are homeless. When I was a child, my father was most angry at me for saying that I did not like the food I was given. He would say, "If you saw what I saw during the year of starvation, you would thank God and eat whatever you are given." And then he would tell me about *Salani Nabooni*, the year of starvation.

Salani Nabooni occurred around the time of World War II, between 1940 and 1944. At that time in Kurdistan most people were illiterate, and they did not know how to write history as it happened. But they told stories about past disasters, such as earthquakes, floods, and war, and about famous people, and they might start a story by saying, "Ten years before the big earthquake...", or "Fifteen years after the death of the Great Imam...". So "Once during *Salani Nabooni*..." was how my father usually began his stories of hunger. He said that during this time, like many other people he often ate grass. When I read a story by the poet Hazar called "Respecting Bread," in which he described being in the mountains with the *peshmerga* and many times he had to eat leaves or grass to survive, it reminded me of what my father had said. It also made me understand why my mother, whenever she saw a tiny piece of bread on the floor, would quickly pick it up and say, "*Astaghfirullah*," which means "I ask God's forgiveness for this impiety." Then she would kiss the crumb of bread and eat it.

In my culture, and especially in Hashazini and in my house, there was no way for food to go into the garbage. Even when I left some food on my plate, Dad would force me to eat it. No food was allowed to be wasted. Many times my dad used to say, "I pray that God never shows you the hard days like I saw"—but God did show me the hard days on at least two occasions.

Between 1989 and 1994, because of the events in Kurdistan—the uprising and separation—it became really hard to get bread. Of course, when you cannot get bread, which is the cheapest thing to eat, you are not going to get any other food, such as rice or meat; that is food for a king. In 1989, Kak Uthman, one of my neighbors who had six children,

told me that in order to share what little food they h[...]
and three of his children would eat a meal, and the [...]
and the other three children would eat a meal. But th[...]
only if Kak Uthman was able to get a job and earned [...]
buy some bread and milk. Many days when he was not able to get a job,
he used to take his son and me hunting for small birds or pigeons. If we
caught two or three of them, there was a celebration. Kak Uthman used
to tell me, "Yassin *Gian*, hunger makes humans wild and dangerous."

One day while we were trying to organize people on the Iranian border,
I received some food to give away. Immediately many people started to
push to get it. I told them to please wait. A couple of people shouted at me,
"Wait for what? For our children to die?" Others swore that they had not
tasted food in three days and had only had something to drink.

One of my friends told me once about people in Europe who are
homeless and live on garbage. I have never understood how someone
can eat from the garbage—not because it is nasty, but because I cannot
understand how food could get into the garbage in the first place. Why
wasn't it eaten? After I came to the United States, I saw people throwing everything into the garbage—nice clothes, furniture, TVs, telephones,
and all kinds of food. You would never see this in any third world country. Many times I have heard from people in Kurdistan that whatever
food the people in America throw into the garbage is enough to feed all
of the people of Africa. I thought this was just Communist propaganda
against capitalism. But after I came here, I saw that there was some reality
to it, and that a great deal of food goes to waste in this country that could
save lives in other places. We should not think that people starve to death
just because of drugs and alcohol addiction. Many poor people want to
work but are victims of war and corruption, and the food we throw away
could save their lives. So I say: be grateful for what you have, and throw
no food into the garbage. I hope that you will not see the hard days like
my father saw, and I pray that God will never bring hard days upon
people, and I beg you and every human being to respect the bread.

Soon the refugee Kurds in the mountains were, like Hazar, reduced
to eating grass and leaves to survive. Fortunately, the people on the

Iranian side of the river were also Kurds, and they responded to our misery. They managed to throw ropes across the river, and with these we were able to pull across bags of food and materials for shelter that they had brought for us. Slowly a series of shantytowns and tent cities sprang up all along the border as people built shelters from the rain and constructed areas where they could cook food. We assumed the whole border was like this, but we could only see our own small area. We would have starved but for the compassion of the Iranian Kurds.

Many young volunteers began to bring supplies across the border to the people stranded along the mountain roads in Iraq who were too weak or too sick to help themselves. Because of their efforts, millions of people were saved from starvation. Other Kurds slaughtered their animals and brought the meat to the refugees so they would not starve. In the midst of the disaster, there was extraordinary compassion and sacrifice shown by ordinary people.

We tried to organize the refugees into camps, in groups of ten with one representative for each camp, so that when we distributed the food we only had to give it to one person in order to feed ten, and to ten people to feed a hundred. We also tried to help relatives and villagers find each other so that they could support each other and would not feel so alone. Day after day, small miracles occurred as more and more people reached out to help each other and our organization efforts expanded. I did not expect to see such compassion and sharing. People would even share their bread with strangers.

Refugees in Iran

After two weeks we were given permission to cross the border into Iran. A bucket large enough for three people was suspended from a rope over the river, like a breeches buoy rescuing sailors from a sinking ship, and people were pulled across from one side to the other. Crossing into Iran was thrilling because we were still in Kurdistan, and the people on the other side of the border spoke our language and kept our customs. They were excited to see us and very hospitable, but there was also a deep sense of sadness on both our parts because of what had happened to us.

Later I wrote a poem about what I said to people in Iran when they asked where I was from:

Homeless

Please don't ask from where I come
It hurts and makes all my wounds bleed
I'm a stranger since they took my home
I have no land and no country
I have no state, I have no flag.
My nation now lies anywhere
In all the world I choose to be
But still I am not living free
Nor do I carry an identity
That's truly representing me.

But once I was in Iranian Kurdistan, I was very eager to know everything about it—the name of every mountain and river and village and city, and the country's history as well. Many Kurdish leaders, artists, writers, and entertainers were from this part of Kurdistan, especially the most famous singers and the most popular songs. Everywhere I went I came across reminders that our country in Iraq, and this country in Iran, were part of the same culture and tradition. The people also proved that they were our brothers and sisters. They opened the mosques, the schools, the parks, and even their homes to give shelter to the refugees. They kept us supplied with food for several months. Never in all my life did I see such generosity and sacrifice.

My four friends and I walked from village to village so that we could see as much as possible. When we arrived in the city of Mahabat I decided to stay for awhile. Mahabat was the first capital of Kurdistan, where Qazi Mohammad established the free Kurdish state in 1942 with Russian support. Unfortunately, soon after that Russia made an agreement with Iran and sold them the Kurdish state like it was a piece of meat. Many now believe that after Azerbaijan declared its freedom from Russia, Iran made an agreement with Russia that if Iran stopped its support for Azerbaijan, Russia would stop its support for Kurdistan. Whatever the reason, Qazi and three other Kurdish leaders were hanged in the middle of the city, in a square called Chwar Chra, which means "four lamps." In fact, Qazi's hanging extinguished the Kurdish lamp of freedom; they were four sons of Kurdistan, not four lamps. I wanted to see Chwar Chra, and to see the graves of Qazi and his lieutenants—I wanted to see any sign of that free Kurdish state. I asked old people about it all, and I wrote down what they said and what they saw. I collected as much information as I could, but I never got a real answer as to what happened, nor why the State of Kurdistan, that began with so much promise in 1942, was all but forgotten by the outside world in just a few years.

My friends told me that we should be moving on so we could find our families. "My family is here," I told them.

"How do you know?" they demanded.

"History told me," I said.

They did not understand. "The mosques here are packed with refugees," they said. "Let us keep looking."

In the last mosque we visited, we found a small corner where we could stay. We were each given a blanket and a daily food ration brought in by people outside the mosque. I introduced myself to the man whom the refugees called *Mamosta* (teacher), and he said he was Abdul Raqeeb.

"Abdul Raqeeb Yousef?" I asked in amazement.

"Yes."

I hugged him and said, "I am so glad to meet you."

"But how do you know me?" he asked.

"Is there anyone in Kurdistan who does not know you?"

He smiled when I said that, and held onto my hand. He saw that I knew him because of his books and articles, which were famous. He took me to a small room in the mosque and we talked for two or three hours about his articles. I had hundreds of questions for him. I stayed in Mahabat for five days and spent most of the time with him.

Rumors had begun to circulate that the refugees from Iraq were going home. The Iraqi government had promised to forgive them and not arrest any of them if they returned. So people came to Abdul Raqeeb Yousef for advice on what they should do, and he spent a great deal of time dealing with each individual situation. Many people said that the army had looted anything valuable, and that the refugees would be returning to ruins. But the Iranian government wanted to send the refugees back. *Mamosta* Abdul said that for himself, he did not care about valuables, but he had three years of research papers at home for which he had no copies, and he could not afford to lose them. I told him robbers didn't want papers.

Eventually we heard through the grapevine that our families were in Mariwan, Iran. We immediately set out, and when we arrived there we were told that they had gone back to Penjween, on the Iraqi side of the border.

In Penjween I finally found my brother Mohsin. He said that everyone was afraid I had died defending Chamchamal, and he was very glad to see that I was still alive. The rest of the family was safe, he said, but nobody knew what had happened to Dad, our sister Aaisha, and our cousin and her family in Bazyan. Mohsin and I stayed in Penjween until we were sure that the UN would keep the Iraqi army south of the 36th parallel (the no-fly zone). Then we returned home to Chamchamal, and found our sister Aaisha. But the news was terrible.

Aaisha said that when the army had finally come to Bazyan, she and our cousin and her family had also fled to the mountains—but they had no way to bring my father with them. He was so old and sick that a flight to the mountains would have killed him, and they hoped that the army would not harm a sick old man who could not even walk. Besides, they had told themselves, the army would quickly leave, and they would be back in Bazyan soon.

As it turned out, none of them could get back to Bazyan for forty days; like me, they had been refugees on the Iranian border. When Aaisha and my cousin were finally able to return home, they found my father dead in the house. I never found out when or how he died, but he was all alone when it happened, with no one to comfort him in his suffering. If perhaps the army killed him, that would have been merciful, because otherwise he must have died of dehydration or starvation without any care at all, even to clean himself.

I still feel guilty today for what happened to my father. In all the land at that time there were thousands of deaths, and each death was a tragedy, but this was my father and I owed him a special responsibility to protect him, as he had always protected me. Instead, I failed him.

I Lost My Friend

One of my friends, Taha Khorshid, worked with me every summer and was like a brother to me. He was amazingly vigorous. After working for ten hours, he would come home and run straight to the soccer field for a game, which he played very well. Everybody loved him. He was a hard worker and someone you could trust.

In 1991, after he had been driven into the mountains like everyone else by the Iraqi army and had to live for months in the cold without adequate shelter, Taha became sick. He told me that his bones felt as though they had broken inside him. Finally he could not walk, and in 2002 he called me and said that he wanted to go to Baghdad for some x-rays and other tests. His father did not have enough money to send him, so I sent him $150 for his treatment. Two months later he said he needed another $100 so he could go back and get more treatments. Five months after that, he told me that the medicine was not working and that he needed to go back to Baghdad for surgery. He said the surgery would cost between $500 and $700.

"I don't have that much," I told him.

"That's OK," Taha said. "I am actually feeling a little better."

I said, "Give me some time and I will try to save some money for you."

But he never called me back. Several months later I received a call from his brother, Tahir, who said that Taha had died. He had asked his brother to call me and tell me that no matter what happened, he would never forget me.

"But he told me that he was feeling better!" I said. I couldn't believe he was dead.

"He did not want you to worry," his brother said.

"I am so sorry," was all I could say.

To this day I cannot forget what happened, and I feel guilty for Taha's death. Maybe I did not have $500 then, but I could have borrowed it. I did not understand his situation and the seriousness of his illness, and my ignorance cost me one of my closest friends. Taha, I am truly sorry. Please forgive me. I should have understood how sick you were. God knows how much I loved you and how sad I became when you left us. This is the curse of holding onto money. God forbid that someone you love should die while you hold onto money that would have saved him. You can always get money to replace the money you spent, but friends and loved ones—there is no way to get them back.

Kurdistan in Ruins

When we returned home in 1991 from Iran, we found much of Kurdistan in ruins. But Kurdish political parties moved in to fill the governmental vacuum left by the army's departure, and it appeared that we were finally going to be ruled by our own people—Kurdistan would be self-governing. We were all so happy with this prospect that everyone began to help each other rebuild the country. Schools were cleaned up, houses were repaired, fields were planted, and people began to return to normal—or at least what should have been normal if we had not been in the middle of a war all the time.

I wrote two poems about the liberation of Kurdistan, after the government's army finally left:

Imagine

O fascism, never try
To occupy this land again.
You must now know
That slavery's done
And life has changed.

Not only children
And not just women

But even rocks and trees
Are all *peshmerga*
Against you.

This Is the Second Part of Imagine

You thought a Kurd
Was like the snow on a mountain
Which your hot rain would melt.
You did not think
About the anger in the wind.
When it starts it will break down
The black cloud of your time,
And blow it away.

In Chamchamal, a group of us headed by *Mamosta* Nori Rahim decided to help reopen the schools. We had to do it quickly before the teachers became discouraged and left to find jobs somewhere else. Five teachers, Imam Gareeb, and I worked with hundreds of student volunteers to collect enough money from citizens to repair the broken windows and equipment in the schools. We went door to door and store to store to ask for donations and materials so we could make repairs and actually start to pay the teachers—if not a salary, then at least their expenses. We did a great job. Within a relatively short time, eighty percent of the schools were reopened, and most of the teachers came back voluntarily and were willing to work without salary.

Elections were held to select a new Kurdish government, and two parties emerged as the dominant political organizations, the KDP (Kurdistan Democratic Party) and the PUK (Patriotic Union of Kurdistan). But instead of working together to rebuild the country, the two parties began to disagree and finally started fighting. Everything collapsed. All our sacrifices for the last fifty years seemed to be in vain. Instead of rebuilding from Halabja and Anfal, instead of living together in freedom, Kurds began to kill Kurds once again.

As soon as we showed our weaknesses, our neighbors moved in to

take advantage of them. The Iraqi government withdrew all government services and put a complete embargo on Kurdistan. Iran began
to fund PUK, Turkey began to fund KDP, and each one fought with the
other to benefit the interests of Iran and Turkey. Money quickly ran out.
Hospitals and post offices closed, and many schools did too because
there were no funds to pay the teachers. Electricity stopped because
workers at the power plants were not being paid their salaries. The
courts and legal processes came to a halt. The rule of the gun returned.
Militias funded by different political parties fought so intensely that
some people began to wish that the Iraqi government would return to
restore order—at least under their rule we had food, fuel, schools, and
electricity. Now we had nothing, not even freedom.

More and more people began to believe that there was no future in
education, since most educated people were jobless and poor. Political
parties spent their money on their militias, not on schools or hospitals.
Children had to work instead of go to school. Students already in school
began to drop out, take up guns, and fight with their party's militia.
Young people were just waiting for the chance to escape Kurdistan and
go to Europe or America. It was hard to stop people from leaving. There
was no sign that the future would improve. I used to argue all the time
with people about this situation. I said, "It is because our parents are illiterate. If we do not study, our children's lives will never get better." They
would respond, "Who cares about the future? We just want enough bread
to keep us alive today." I really did not have a good response to that.

Illegal Immigration

Starting in 1992, I became involved in activities to discourage illegal
immigration, which was almost as big a curse as the fighting between
the Kurdish groups. People began to believe that the only way to survive was to send a family member abroad to earn money and to spon-
sor other family members later. Young people would force their parents to sell the family house and give the money to smugglers, in order
to send the young person to Europe. Of course the young person was
expected to send money back home, but how often did this happen?

Young people in Europe couldn't even take care of themselves; how could they repay the family sacrifice that sent them to Europe to save the family? Borrowed money was often not repaid. Fathers left their wives and children without any support while they tried to get to Europe to earn money. They all believed that they would quickly find a job, learn the language, earn plenty of money, and be able to send back enough for the family to live well. But often the father's life ended in tragedy and left the family with nothing.

People saw other friends and neighbors returning from Europe with money and possessions, and they believed they were missing out on a golden opportunity. People went to Europe and took cleaning jobs, but when they returned they looked like kings: they could buy houses and stores and cars and anything else they wanted. It all looked so easy. But in fact, for every one who returned rich, others lost everything, went bankrupt, impoverished their families, and often ended up dead.

Many people who tried to illegally immigrate to Europe were killed by the Turkish border guards when they tried to cross the border into Turkey. Many more died in the mountain snows while trying to cross from Turkey into Greece. Others were drowned in small, unseaworthy boats trying to get from Greece to Italy across the rough Adriatic Sea. Many others who did get through stayed in Europe for years and were never given legal status or permitted to work. And in the despair of dreams shattered and opportunities lost, many turned to gambling and alcohol. Many contracted HIV and AIDS because they never learned how to protect themselves. And meanwhile, back home, wives, families, and children were waiting, waiting, waiting for some news, for some money, for some hope, which never appeared. It was a disaster.

It was not easy to stop people from illegal immigration. Whenever we tried to talk people out of going abroad, they responded, "Sure. Find me a job so I can buy bread for my family, and I won't go." What can you say to that? My best argument was that we should think first of the nation of Kurdistan, not just of individuals. We Kurds needed to sacrifice for the collective good. We should rebuild the country. Rather than fleeing to Sweden, we should make Kurdistan comparable with

Sweden. I was accused of being an unrealistic dreamer; people said that Kurdistan was a militia jungle, no place for an educated person. They may have been right. Even a superpower like America has spent hundreds of billions of dollars in Iraq, and still the situation is getting worse, not better. To be honest, I am not very optimistic about the future of Kurdistan. I keep thinking about what my brother Issa said: that we have all been created to suffer.

At the time, I had many friends who "escaped" to Europe and who now wanted to send money back to me to live on. But I did not want to accept help from abroad when my message was that we Kurds must be giving rather than taking, and must serve rather than being served. The whole point of what I was saying was that we Kurds must stay at home, become self-sufficient by studying and working, and rebuild the country. We should not be living on handouts from Europe, and I had to set an example if I were going to urge others not to accept handouts.

How Do You Sign?

One of the problems in many Middle Eastern countries is that government officials do not follow the law. You have to know someone influential to help you obtain even routine documents from the government. If you just submit an application, you never receive a response. In 1992 I tried to get permission to go to Syria to register at college, but no one would give me permission. I needed someone who was rich and famous, or who was a great Imam or leader, to write a letter for me asking the officials in charge of the permit office to give me a travel permit according to what the law required.

One day I was at my cousin Sheikh Raza's home in Arbil, and he suggested that I talk with his friend who was head of the state's education department: maybe he would know someone who could help me? So I went to see Kak Raza's friend. He said that he would do anything he could to help me, but to get to Damascus it would be necessary for one of the political groups to help me. Kak Raza suggested that we go to the PUK office because he knew someone there. He wanted his brother Samad to go with us.

The friend at the PUK office said that permission could only be gotten from the Syrian government, since it was not possible to get permission in Kurdistan. The friend took my name and Samad's, and started to write a letter for me.

While he was writing, Kak Raza told him the story of Kurdistan's first king in 1922, King Mahmood. When the king wrote a letter, he would use three different names. He said that he did this because people were always asking him for favors, and if he refused, the people would get mad at him, since there was no way to give all of them jobs. So the king told all of his officials that if they received a letter from him signed as King Mahmood, they were to do whatever he instructed because that was his order as king. If he signed the letter as Sheikh Mahmood, it meant that the officials were free to do it or not, as they thought best. But if the king signed it only Khola—which is the Kurdish version of Mahmood, without any "respect" attached—then it meant that the officials should *not* do what he asked, because he had only signed the letter to get rid of the person.

So Sheikh Raza asked the PUK official how he had signed his letter. The official laughed and said that he had only one way to sign, and that he wanted to do this to help us out. Unfortunately, after he sent the letter, we never received any response. I told Kak Raza that it looked like his friend had just signed as Khola, to get rid of us. "Well," he replied, "what can you expect from a politician?"

Don't Give Away Your Daughter

One day in 1992 while I was praying at the mosque in Chamchamal, the man next to me was crying very hard. At first I though he was crying because of his fear of God, but then I decided something besides the fear of God was causing his tears. I remembered my Sheikh, Abo Saeed, telling me that the tears you drop for God should leave no sound—indeed, beware of any sound, for it may be only for show. And I thought to myself that perhaps the man really had such a big problem that he could not control himself, and that was why he was crying so hard. So after prayers, I waited until other people had left, intending to talk to him. But as I started to stand up, he said, "Sheikh Yassin, I come to you. The Imam sent me to you."

"I am not a Sheikh," I said. "But let us sit, and please feel free to tell me what you want to say. How can I help you?"

"My wife died last year and I have three daughters," the man said. "One of them is fourteen years old. As God is my witness, I have sold everything in my home to feed my children. After three days without food I do not know what to do. My fourteen-year-old is very nice and religious. You can ask anyone about her."

I began to get the message that he wanted to give me his daughter, and it really made me sad. I knew that some people looked for an opportunity like this to buy a nice girl, even if they were older than her father. I was scared that if something wasn't done, the man would lose all of his daughters.

"What work did you do before?" I asked him.

"I had a cart and sold vegetables."

"So what happened?"

"Day by day, whatever money I made selling vegetables I used to buy bread for my children, until one day I had no money left to buy vegetables to sell. Finally I had to sell my cart to buy bread."

"Does the Imam know your situation?"

"Yes, he knows."

"Will he be a witness for you if I ask him?"

"Go and ask him."

I believed that he was not making the story up. I told him to wait there. I did not have even one penny at that time, but I knew that many people trusted me and would be glad to help. I went to one of my friends who owned a store.

"Peace be upon you," I said to my friend.

"You are welcome. How are you?"

"Not good at all," I told him.

"What is wrong?"

"I need your help."

"Take whatever you need," my friend told me.

"I want enough food for four people for a week." He looked at me, shocked. "I am not joking," I said.

"What kind of food?"

"Anything that keeps people alive. Even if it is just bread."

"When do you need it?"

"Right now."

"Watch my store," my friend said, and left.

In about twenty minutes he returned with another man pulling a cart, which was piled high with all kinds of wonderful things: flowers, greens, rice, bread. "*Salaam,*" he smiled at me. "Tell this man where you want him to go with the cart. I have paid him already for the delivery."

"God will reward you, my friend."

I told the man with the cart to wait five minutes, and I would come back for him. I went back to the mosque and brought the man to the store with me. On our way, I told him that I had found some food for him to take home that would last about a week. I told him I would do something else for him, but first I needed to know the price of a cart. He said about fifteen dollars.

When we arrived at the store, I told the man that the store owner had brought all of this food for him, and had even paid to deliver the food on the cart. The man started crying because he could not believe that all the food was going to be his. He shook our hands and said, "God bless you."

After he left, my friend told me that he knew the man and that he was a really good person. I was relieved to hear my friend vouch for his good character, but I remembered that the man had been about to give away his daughter, and I said in my heart, *No, you don't really know him.*

I was very affected by what had happened. I felt I had to do something to save children from being sold. If a really good man was forced to give his children away to keep from starving, many children must be at risk, and I must find a way for this man to feed his children. All that night I kept thinking and praying, *God, please do something.*

The next day another friend came to see me. "Yassin!" he said. "Let's go!"

"To where?"

"Your friend Dawood has come home from Germany."

"When did he get back?"

"The day before yesterday."

"Is this a good time to visit him, or should we let him rest a little?"

"Oh, many people have visited him already. Better to go now and welcome him back before he has to come to you."

When we arrived at Dawood's house I greeted him warmly.

"I missed you too much," Dawood said.

"Don't joke with me," I told him. "Would someone in Berlin remember anyone in Kurdistan?"

"By God," he said, "it is much better here than in Berlin. You have everything in Germany, but you never have a good feeling. The loneliness can kill you."

"Everyone who comes back from Europe says the same thing," I responded. "If this is true, why do they go back to Europe?"

"It is like a drug," he said. "You can't quit it, but that doesn't mean you are happy."

I smiled and said, "If you missed us so much, you can always stay with us."

Dawood said we should eat dinner together. I told him to take his time with his family, and I would meet him tomorrow at the mosque for noon prayer.

The next day, Dawood was already at the mosque when I arrived. We joked, and then we prayed, and then we walked down the street and talked. He told me about life in Germany. It seemed to me to be a place on another planet. I told him it was our duty to make Chamchamal like Berlin, and to make Kurdistan like Germany, that it was not the land but the people. Dawood looked at me and said, "We have a long way to go, but if the people will throw away their guns and take up their pens and leave hatred behind, and love each other, and respect the law, it is possible."

I said, "Centuries ago in the Dark Ages, Europe went through what we are going through now. But we have not learned from their experience. We have not even learned from our own history in the East."

"Kak Yassin, in Germany life is totally different. God has blessed them with everything," Dawood said.

I said, "God has made natural laws, and whoever obeys them will succeed. But if you do not obey them, God is not going to change them for you, no matter how holy you are. There are proper ways to achieve everything, but we are not using them. Suppose I want children, but I don't want to marry, so I pray to God to bless me to have children, like a woman…it is not going to happen. God can do it, but He is not going to change natural laws just because I want to do it my way. God wants people to follow the laws of nature that He put in the universe."

Dawood said, "The Germans work hard, they have a beautiful system, they respect and follow the law, but many of them do not have peace in their minds or tranquility in their hearts."

"That's the problem in the West," I said. "People worry about life, and many of them forget about God. Their bodies are strong, but their hearts are not. In the East people have strong spirits, but their lives are trouble and misery. Both of them need a balance. We are humans with both body and soul. Neglecting either one is a big mistake."

"Kak Yassin," said Dawood. "Don't get me wrong or get mad."

"You know me," I said "We are friends. Feel free to say whatever you want."

"Do you promise not to get mad, and do for me whatever I need?"

"Anything that is permitted and I can do, I will gladly do for you," I said.

Dawood brought out an envelope from his pocket and handed it to me.

"What is this?" I asked him.

"Please just take it."

"Tell me what it is first."

"A small gift."

"For whom?"

"For you."

"Can you tell me what it is, please?"

"I know it is nothing, but believe me, I had too many responsibilities for family and many other friends."

"I know it is money," I told him. "I am OK. You should give it to someone who is in need."

"No, this is not a need gift. This is a friendship gift. It is hard to bring things back from Europe with all the checking and dragging bags around. So take this money and get something that you like. Please don't reject it. It is not charity. You know that in Islam, a gift may not be rejected."

"No no," I said. "I am not rejecting it. I accept it. Thank you. But just please keep it for me until tomorrow, and I will take it from you then." We agreed to meet the next day at the library building.

I went immediately to see the man with the fourteen-year-old daughter. "How are you today?" I asked.

"Very well," he said. "Please come in and see my children."

"No, I must go. But I need you to meet me tomorrow just before ten o'clock in front of the library building. Don't forget. It's important." He agreed.

The next day, a little before ten, I went to the library and met up with him. I told him that I was waiting for my old friend Dawood. When Dawood arrived, I asked him whether he had my envelope with him. He was surprised that I would ask this in front of someone else, and he did not want to give it to me, but I insisted. Inside the envelope was $100. "Let's go," I told them both.

I took them to a place where we changed the money into 2,500 Iraqi dinars.

"Now, where do they sell carts?" I asked the man with the daughter. He took us to a seller that he knew. "Choose the best cart," I told him, and he did.

The seller told us the cart was 350 dinar, or about $14. We bargained, and he gave it to me for 300 dinar, or about $12. He told me he would have given it to me for less, but it was not his store alone and he had to share the money with his partners. I asked his name and he laughed. "I know you, but you don't know me," he said. "I am Ali. Never will I forget the day long ago when you explained to me all about art at the student art show here."

I asked Dawood to be patient, and I asked the man with the daughter what he wanted to sell, now that he had a cart again. He said that he could be a porter and use the cart like a taxi for people who wanted to transport things to their homes.

"But you told me that you used to sell vegetables."

"Yes, but the market now is very slow for vegetables. I could sell candy and other things, and whenever I see people who need a cart to bring items home I can act as a porter."

So we bought candy and other merchandise, and at the end I had spent about $48—$12 for the cart and $36 for the merchandise. I could see that it was not going to be easy to spend the whole $100. Dawood couldn't understand what I was doing, and the man with the daughter could not believe his eyes. This was his dream.

I remembered that he said he had already sold all of his furniture. "Let's go," I said again.

We bought four mattresses, each of which cost 25 dinar ($1), and four blankets, each of which cost 40 dinar ($1.50). The man swore that he did not need anything more. "I will be OK forever," he said. "I can sell the candy and items you have bought for me, and I can use the cart like a taxi, and I can take care of my children, and I will not be poor anymore."

Dawood just stared at me. I told him to be patient and to keep quiet. Altogether, I had spent about $70, and I still had $30 left. "What else do you need?" I asked the man.

"No more! No more!" he said. "I will be OK."

"That's good," I told him. But I still had too much money left. So I gave him 300 dinar (about $12) to buy new clothes for all three of his daughters. "I want to see your daughters going to school next week," I told him, "and I want them all to be wearing new clothes, and wearing shoes and carrying book bags, and I want you to get some new clothes too."

The man started crying hard, like when I saw him the first time at the mosque. "I don't know how to thank you," he said.

"This was Dawood's money," I told him. "Thank God and him, not me."

The man tried to kiss Dawood's hand, but Dawood gave me an exasperated look and took his hand away.

"Listen," I told the man. "I want you to promise me and Dawood one thing."

He said, "My life and my three daughters are yours."

"God owns your life," I told him. "But still I want your promise."

"Ask me whatever you need and I will promise."

I said, "I want you to promise to let your daughters go back to school, and don't give any of them to anyone until after they finish high school, and then only with their complete consent."

The man promised. "God knows that poverty forced me to try to give away my oldest daughter because I could not feed her. Now we will be OK, because those problems are over." We shook hands, and he took his new cart and his merchandise back to his children.

I was elated. I remembered my Sheikh (my teacher) telling me that you got more happiness from giving than from receiving, and I was sure that he was right. However happy the poor man felt, I felt much happier. Indeed, I felt joy. I do not believe that I could have possibly spent the money in any other way that would have given me such pleasure.

I started walking with Dawood and explained to him the man's problem and his desperate choice so he could survive. Dawood said, "Give me back the rest of the money," which was about $18.

I knew that he wanted to take back the $18 and give me another $100. I told him, "I am more in need of reward than you."

He gave me another exasperated look and said, "Less than $100 here saved a whole family, whereas in Germany many times we went shopping and spent $100 for unnecessary things. If I just stopped unnecessary shopping, how many families could I save?" There were tears in his eyes, and I could see that he was very affected by what had happened. I have no doubt that he did not waste his money, and that he helped many poor families.

My Leg Is Burned

In 1993, Iraq was under an international embargo, and Kurdistan was included in it. Food, fuel, electricity, medicine, telephones—everything was embargoed. People were forced to start cutting down trees for fuel in order to survive, and whole mountainsides were completely denuded. When complaints were made about the ecological damage this was doing to the country, people responded, "What is more important—our lives, or the beauty of the mountains?" So how could we say that trees were more important than children? If it were not for the wood, children would have frozen to death in their own homes.

People began to smuggle food and fuel from Iran and from Kirkuk. One day we heard that five tanker trucks of gasoline would be coming to Chamchamal and that the gas would be for sale. Everybody got a sixty-gallon steel drum and went to the marketplace to wait for the trucks.

Around 2 p.m., Mohsin took our barrel and went to wait in line with all the others. It was a very cold day. By 8 p.m., my sister Aaisha told me to go and get him and send him back to eat his dinner.

Once I got to the market, I saw the long line. Mohsin was shaking from the cold and was really angry. "Why didn't you come earlier?"

"I did not know the line would be so long. And why is this taking so long?"

"There are people with weapons who break into the line, and if people try to stop them, they fight. They've used their weapons two or three times already."

"Who are these people?"

"*Jash.*"

"OK. Go home and eat your dinner."

"I don't think I should leave you here," he said, "because it's not safe."

"So what difference will it make if I am here or you are here?"

"I know how to deal with these people."

"Listen, you'll get sick," I said. "Look how you are shaking. I will be OK. There are not many people in front of us now."

Finally Mohsin agreed to go home for awhile. I stayed in the line.

It was crazy. Here we were, forty miles from Kirkuk, one of the largest centers of the oil industry in the world, and we had to wait for hours in line to buy smuggled gasoline. It was our oil, but the government would not even sell it to us.

It was really cold and raining lightly. People argued about who was first, and pushed each other, and got into fights, and complained about others breaking into line. I just stood and watched them. About 11 p.m. Mohsin came back.

"Yassin, what is happening?"

"See for yourself. There are still people in front of me."

"Go home," he said. "I will stay here. I've eaten and changed into some dry clothes."

"You were already here for six hours. I've only been here for three."

Eventually Mohsin agreed to go home, since it looked like I would get to the head of the line in less than an hour. By 2 a.m., my turn finally came. I filled my drum and someone helped me to roll it to the side of the road. Now what to do? The drum weighed several hundred pounds. Usually there were donkey carts or cars that would help you bring the drums home, but not at 2 a.m. on a rainy night. And I could not leave the drum by the side of the road and go for help, because somebody was likely to steal it. I would have to wait until Mohsin came back in the morning.

By 2:30 a.m. I was wet and freezing. About a hundred feet from where I was standing, some people had built a fire and were warming themselves. I went over to them and stood so I could keep an eye on my drum.

"*Assalamu-Alaikum* (May peace be upon you)," I said to the men. "Can I warm myself?"

"Of course," they said.

I raised my right foot to the top of the fire for awhile. Then I raised my left foot over it. But some gasoline must have spilled onto the side of the drum, and when I rolled the drum to the side of the road, some of it must have soaked into my pants, because I saw my pants suddenly burst into flame. Immediately the flames roared up over my body.

I started running and shouting "HELP! HELP!" People ran toward me, shouting at me to lie down, but I was too scared and just ran faster and faster until I fell down. They dumped water on me and put mud all over me, and the flames finally went out. I saw one of my friends looking at me in shock.

"Oh Yassin! You are not all right!" He quickly sent someone to bring a car and take me to the hospital.

I remember chanting, "O Allah, O Allah," and then I passed out. When I opened my eyes again, I was in Ibrahim's house, and my sister's hand was on my forehead.

"How are you, dear brother?" Aaisha said anxiously.

"Thank God I am alive," I said. But I have never experienced such pain. From my toes to my belly, everything was burned. I cried out, and my sister told me to be patient.

"What time is it?" I groaned.

"Six o'clock," Aaisha said.

"How did I get here?"

"Your friend brought you to the hospital, and after that he came and told us what had happened. After the doctors were finished treating you, Ibrahim and Mohsin and I brought you here. Thank God your face is not burned. You will be OK."

"Can I have some water?"

"I must ask Ibrahim."

Ibrahim came into the room. "Yassin is awake!" he called. Mohsin came running in, and Ibrahim asked me gently, "How are you feeling?"

"Thank God I seem to be OK."

"I am so sorry this happened to you."

"You don't have to be sorry. This is life. Can I have water?" I asked again.

My sister turned to Ibrahim. "Can he?"

"He can have water and breakfast and anything else he wants."

Most of my leg was covered with third-degree burns. It was very painful and took almost five months to heal. I was lucky because Ibrahim was a nurse and got some medicine and took very good care of me; otherwise I probably would have lost the use of my leg. For a long time, the skin on the front of my leg was not growing out to cover the burns on the back of it. The doctors wanted to take a skin graft from my other leg, but I refused, and as a result I had to stay longer in bed. Because of this, my leg stiffened, and when I tried to straighten it the pain was almost unbearable. Ibrahim was mad at me because I would not exercise enough to straighten my leg, and Aaisha had to keep reminding me that he was mad only because he loved me and wanted my leg to heal completely. So I would bite my lip and try again to straighten it.

The first time I left my bed was to go to a poetry seminar. I read a poem about Halabja. Ibrahim was furious when he found out that I had left the house without his permission, because he was afraid it would cause the wounds to open again and become infected, which is exactly what happened. We fought about it. Finally I told Aaisha that I was going to move out and go to my friend's house. She started crying and said, "You can't! Ibrahim did not mean for you to go. He just wants you to heal!" But I was still so angry that I told Ibrahim I was leaving.

He immediately apologized. "Yassin, God knows I never meant to hurt you. This is not my home—it is your home. If you want I will move out. I just want you to be OK and it should not take too much longer. Look, you have been suffering for five months and you still can't walk." He started hugging and kissing me.

But I was still angry, and I told him I would go to my friend's house. I was also feeling somewhat guilty because I was taking so much of Ibrahim's time, and even his nights were disturbed because all my friends came to visit me. Ibrahim told me he would swear by God that if I left his house, he himself would never return to the house, he would abandon it and never go back. Then I did feel bad, and I promised that I would not leave, but I still felt uncomfortable that so many of my friends came each day at all hours to visit me. My sister had to serve tea to all of them, as is our custom, and their visits gave Ibrahim no privacy.

Of course, it was wonderful that so many people showed me love, and joked with me, and brought me news of the world, but my concern during this five-month period was that Ibrahim and his wife Wajiha, and Mohsin and Aaisha, should not have to care for my guests as well as for me. One day when one of my cousins came, so many people were already there to see me that there was no place for him, and he had to stand outside and wait until I was free. When he finally got in, he whispered in my ear that Ibrahim was right when he said that all 50,000 people in Chamchamal knew Yassin and visited him here.

Going to College

From 1992 until 1994, life in Kurdistan became almost unbearable. 90% of the people were unemployed. There were no jobs anywhere. Everyone tried to find a way to escape Kurdistan and go somewhere else. Thousands went to Iran to find jobs. And if anyone had any money, he went to Turkey and tried to find a way to get to Europe.

I did not know what to do. I did not believe in escaping to Europe and leaving my people to suffer and the country being destroyed. I did not want to go to Iran to get a job, and in any event it would have been very difficult for me to get permission from the government to go. In Chamchamal, there were some things that people did to make money, but because these things were not permitted in Islam or by my tribal custom, I could not do them.

I had nothing. I lived in Ibrahim's home and I had to depend on him for everything, including pocket money. Sometimes for two or three months at a time I did not have even one penny. Whenever Ibrahim asked if I needed anything, I had no ready answer. Ibrahim knew that I would never say yes, so many times he gave money to my sister Aaisha to give to me. It was really tough to live that way. It was not freedom. I constantly thought that I had not fulfilled my promise to Mom and Dad to finish college and get married. This caused me a great deal of personal stress, just as the situation of Kurdistan was heavy in my thoughts.

At the suggestion of one of my friends, I submitted applications to colleges in Saudi Arabia and Syria. I began praying that I would be accepted at the college in Saudi Arabia, because then I could make pilgrimage (*Hajj*), I could work and make some money, and I could study and get my degree. I was not accepted in Saudi Arabia, but in 1992 I was accepted in Syria.

Now I had to find some way to get enough money to travel to Syria and support myself while I studied at the university. But the problem was how to get a job, and how much money I could save both before and after I went. People who came back from Europe said that Syria was really cheap. They would stay in a hotel for about $3 and go to the best restaurants for $2. But for someone like me to save $2 in Iraq, I would have to work hard for at least a month. I could work hard all day, and by the end of it I would not have earned even five cents. Iraqi money was just colored paper with nothing to support it; even if I could save some dinars, once I changed it into Syrian currency its value was almost nothing. For me, Syria was the most expensive country I could imagine.

It really made people mad that they had to work all day for five cents, since, if they could just get a relative or friend to send them $2 from Europe every month, that was worth far more than a month's work in Iraq. People stopped looking for jobs in Kurdistan. Farmers did not even use tractors, because the money they made would not pay for the gas. Why bother working? Just figure out a way to get a friend or relative to Europe, so he could send back some money.

I had many friends in Europe at that time, and I knew they would have very happy to help me and send me money. They even asked me if I needed anything. But I could not accept such money when there was so much poverty around me. I did not want to live by handouts. My philosophy was that we should make money, not take money, and that we should eat only from whatever we could make.

Finally I remembered the poor father with the cart whom I had helped, and I said to myself that maybe I could work as a porter (*Hamali*) to make money for college in Syria. I realized that I could not do this in Chamchamal, because no one in Chamchamal would allow me to carry bags for him like a servant. People knew my family background and our relationship to the House of the Prophet, may peace be upon him, and they would not let me serve them as a porter because it was the lowest job in Kurdish culture. I would have been proud to do it, but I knew that my two brothers would see this as a shame on the family. In fact, many times when people saw me carrying my own bags, they tried to carry them for me, to show respect for someone from the House of the Prophet. I always refused, and sometimes if they were insistent I had to joke with them about it by saying, "No, please! This bag is mine, not yours." So I decided to go to Sulaimaniya, the big city where I knew fewer people, and work as a porter there. I told my brothers that I was going to Syria, and left for Sulaimaniya.

Before I went, my brother Mohsin asked me to show him the money I had saved so he could be sure that I had enough to get to Syria, but no matter how hard he tried, I always refused to discuss it with him. I told him I needed nothing, but he did not believe me. Eventually he forced me to accept about 2,000 dinar ($80). I told him I would give it back to him in three or four months.

Hamali

I went to Sulaimaniya, bought a cart, rented a room in a hotel, and started working. I kept my face covered in case I met someone from Chamchamal. One day while I was working, I saw my cousin calling to me—or, rather, calling for a porter: "*Hamali! Hamali!*" He had two big bags of flour that he wanted a porter to carry to his house. I pretended that I did not hear him, but he ran after me and grabbed my hand. Fortunately, my face was covered like a woman's, so he did not recognize me. I pointed out another Hamali and indicated to my cousin that he should ask him. The other Hamali was delighted to get the order and ran right over, thus saving me from discovery.

It was so hard to get petrol during this time that most taxi drivers had stopped driving their taxis, and so the only affordable way to get goods to and from the market was by cart. There was a big demand for porters, but it was hard for me to make any money because I had to pay for both a hotel room and a garage for the cart to keep it from being stolen while I slept. I was also worried about what would happen if

Issa should learn that I was working as a porter in Sulaimaniya, where he lived. He would be furious that I was not staying at his house. But how could I stay at his house without his finding out what I was doing? And I was certain that I did not want him to know what I was doing.

I spent most of 1993 and 1994 working as a porter in Sulaimaniya, while my family believed that I was studying in Syria. In fact, I did go to Syria on several occasions for a few weeks, so that I could then go back to Chamchamal from Syria and people would believe I had been there and I would not be lying.

In 1994, while I was pushing my cart piled high with a customer's things along the street, a cameraman on the other side of the street was filming a documentary about life in Kurdistan. The cameraman followed me with his camera for about two or three minutes, although I was unaware of what was happening. But when I returned for a visit to Chamchamal, people congratulated me for being an actor in a television drama. I had no idea what they were talking about. They told me that I had played the role of a *Hamali* very well. I sent one of my friends to the art center to ask if they had a copy of the film, but the center did not have it. So I just laughed whenever I was asked about my role as a film star and did not answer any of their questions—because what, truthfully, could I say?

I especially had to laugh at Mohsin and Ibrahim. Both of them used to look down on *Hamalis*, saying that porters did shameful work, but now they were so proud that their brother had played the role of a *Hamali* on television. Ibrahim told me that my three-minute appearance, in which I had conveyed all of the pain of a *Hamali* without ever saying a word, was the most beautiful part of the whole drama: "The way you pulled the cart, it looked like you had been a *Hamali* all your life. Everybody tells me that you acted out the reality of Kurdish life in the most convincing way." I just smiled and said thank you, for in fact it was true.

I'm Still a Villager

I never cared much about the way I looked. I used to wear ripped clothes and shoes, and sometimes I would not even comb my hair for days. Once when I had come back from Syria with two of my friends, we visited one of the PUK leaders, Imad Ahmad, who had become the new health minister. My friends were both dressed as though they were going to a wedding, complete with tie and shined shoes. But I was dressed like an old villager.

It was my first time visiting Mr. Ahmad on a personal basis. When we entered his office, one friend, who was also named Yassin, said, "Mr. Ahmad, this is Kak Yassin." I smiled, because in Kurdistan, when two people have the same name, the joke is that they should not sit together because they will make a "short" (an electrical short-circuit).

Mr. Ahmad looked at me, and it was obvious that he could not believe what he was seeing. I was dressed like a poor villager, and yet they told him I had come from a big city like Damascus, the capital of Syria, and was a college student.

"Well, do you know Kak Dana?" he asked with a little bit of suspicion. Kak Dana was the PUK's representative in Damascus.

"Yes," I said.

Mr. Ahmad then asked me a lot of questions about the situation in Syria. But I could see in his face that he was really puzzled by me, and did not understand how I could know so many people in Damascus and still be dressed so poorly. To explain, I told him this story:

A farmer sent his son to study in the city. After two or three years when the son came home, he was acting very strangely. He could not sit on the floor anymore like the other villagers. He could not work in the fields because he might rumple his clothes. He was afraid to eat by hand because of possible bacteria. He refused to even ride a horse because he was afraid that he might fall off. At night he was scared of every sound. His father became angry and started beating him, saying, "If this is all the knowledge you learned, I'm not sending you to school again."

So I told Mr. Ahmad that I was not working in an office, and that I was still living like a *peshmerga*. In response, he hugged me and said that was what we all needed to be, because there was nothing more beautiful than simplicity. We wished him success in his new job, and he assured us that he would do his best to rebuild the hospitals according to the new plan of the Kurdish Health Ministry. As we left, he said to me, "Stay as *peshmerga*. Nothing can overcome you."

I grinned and said, "I need the example to follow!"

Time to Marry

In Kurdistan, at the beginning of every new year we say that we wish for the previous one. During my life there, this was certainly true. We would finish a year of suffering and look forward to a new year, and by the time the new year came we would wish that we had the old one back. Hundreds of times I heard my father and brothers say that if we waited until the situation got better, we would never be able to do anything. At that time, when people were asked when they would marry, it was common for them to make excuses like, "I want to wait until the war is over," or "The economy needs to improve," or "When I get a job." We would tell them, "Go dream about it," or "Wait for the next life in the hereafter."

In 1994, after I had started college in Syria, one of my friends pushed me very hard to get married. I knew that if I made any excuses, he was going to make fun of them and say that conditions were always going to be bad in Kurdistan, so what relevance does that have to marriage? If everybody waited until things improved, there would be no new generation of Kurds. So instead I joked with him by saying, "Find someone for me." To my great surprise, he said he had found someone for me. Now I had to face reality and not dream about the hereafter.

At that time, things were particularly bad in Kurdistan. The PUK and the KDP were fighting each other, and there was no government. Kurdistan was under two separate embargos—one from the UN against Iraq, and one by the Iraqi government against Kurdistan. I was a just a student, and I still pushed carts daily to make some money to live on. But I remembered my mother's wish that I marry and give her grandchildren, so I decided to say yes to marrying.

When I went back to Chamchamal, Mohsin was very surprised to see me, because he thought I was in Syria.

"Why did you come back?" he asked.

"To get married."

Mohsin did not like this answer and thought I was making fun of him. "Yassin. Please. This is not the time for a joke."

"No, I am not joking," I said. "I want to get married."

"How can you marry?" he spluttered. "How many pennies do you have? What is your job? Where is your house?"

"Don't be afraid," I said. "I am not going to ask you for help."

"Yassin, please!! Why do you speak to me like this?"

"Mohsin, why don't you want me to marry? Is it because in our custom you can't marry if you have a bigger brother or sister who is not married yet? Is that what you are worried about—that I should wait for you to marry first?"

Mohsin rolled his eyes. "What is wrong with you?"

"Nothing. I am serious, but you don't believe me. What can I do?"

"You want me to believe that you are not joking."

"No, I am *not* joking," I said. "Have I ever joked with you about marriage before?"

"So who are you going to marry?"

"Kak Latif's sister," I told him.

"Who?"

"You know, Kak Latif, who lives down the block from Ibrahim's house. I want to marry his sister."

Mohsin just stared at me, speechless. I believed that he would not have any objection to the family. "Are you sure, Yassin?" he finally said.

"Yes, I am positive."

"So what do you want me to do?"

"Nothing. Just don't prevent me."

"Did you speak to the family?"

"No, not yet. I still have to do that."

It is our custom that the female relatives of the potential groom go to the girl's family first to see the girl, and maybe even speak to her—indirectly, of course—and also to her mother, to determine what is in their minds and whether they would agree to a marriage. Since my mother was dead, we sent Ibrahim's wife, Wajiha, to make the inquiries.

Wajiha came back laughing. *"Mubarak! Mubarak,* Yassin! (Congratulations! Congratulations, Yassin!)" She continued to laugh.

"What happened? Did you see her?" asked Mohsin. "Did you speak to them?"

"Oh yes. Latif has two sisters, Zuhur, the older one, and Nigar, the younger one, who are very smart, nice, beautiful, and educated. Yassin is certainly lucky," she said.

"But what did you tell them?" asked Mohsin.

Wajiha started laughing again. "It seemed to me that they knew about it already. Yassin seems to have done everything secretly beforehand."

Mohsin started laughing. *"Khosh Mala, Khosh Mala* (Good Imam, Good Imam)," he said. "But Imam and love? Something is not right here."

Now they were both laughing. Wajiha said, "By God, Yassin is free to proceed, but in fact it seems that he has already arrived."

I was annoyed and told them to stop.

Wajiha said, "Latif has two sisters. Which one are you asking for, the older one or the younger one?"

"I don't know," I said. I remembered a joke by Kak Nawzar that he did not care what his future wife looked like; he would be satisfied if she had just one patch of hair on her head. "What should I do next?" I asked.

They both started laughing again. "Oh Imam, you have no more patience."

I was getting really annoyed at this point. "No, I don't have any patience. You have one hundred 'trouble' (tribal) rules, and I want to know what is next."

Wajiha said, "It seems everything is ready. All that is necessary is for Mohsin and Ibrahim and a few more people to go and talk to them directly."

"Before I see her?" I asked.

Wajiha laughed. "I know you saw her before. They knew everything."

Mohsin started in again. "Imam, Imam, can't be trusted!"

"No, by God!" I said. "I did not know them, and never did I see her before."

Wajiha just stood there shaking her head like she did not believe me. Mohsin was laughing behind her.

"Good," I said, pretending to be angry. "I don't want to see her. I am like Nawzar. If she has only one patch of hair on her head, she is acceptable. Just go and finish what you need to do."

"Mala, how can you marry someone before you see her, or she sees you?" asked Mohsin. "In Islam, are not both required to see each other and agree? If not, then the marriage is invalid."

"So what do you want me to do?" I said. "You two are just making fun of me. Please, enough."

Mohsin said to Wajiha, "Go back and tell them to let Yassin and the girl see each other, and if Yassin and Zuhur agree, we are going to do it."

"Good," I said. And then I started laughing and harassing Wajiha by saying as she left, "Hurry…hurry…hurry!"

Wajiha said, "I wish Ibrahim was here to see this. This is the first time we have ever heard Yassin talk like this."

"It is a sign of the hereafter," said Mohsin, "when Imams start to act like this. Wajiha, go and tell that to the family, before Yassin loses his patience or goes insane."

✎ ✎

"How did you accomplish this?" Mohsin asked, after Wajiha had left.

"God did everything," I said.

Mohsin shook his head, as though he did not like my answer. "I know you well enough," he said.

"Then you should believe what I say."

"I told you...I told you...I told you!" Wajiha said when she came back.

"What happened this time?" asked Mohsin.

"Yassin is just doing a drama," she said. "Everything was already arranged."

"Yassin! You did it already!" said Mohsin in surprise.

"I did not. I want to do it now," I said.

Wajiha giggled and said, "Kak *Gian* (Dear Brother), go ahead. They are waiting for you."

I went to Kak Latif's house and spoke with everyone. Kak Latif, his mother, and his sister Zuhur, who was to be my wife, were all there, and God made everything perfect for us. I was very happy, and the family accepted me.

According to our tradition, twenty or thirty of my family members, with an Imam present, then must go to the girl's family and talk to them. After that, if they still agree to the marriage, the Imam will perform a religious wedding ceremony. Mala Gareeb, the Imam in the biggest and most famous mosque in the city, went with us and witnessed the agreement. After that, Zuhur was my wife, and I could talk to her, see her, and go out with her, but we still had to do three more things before we began to live together: I had to give her a gift (a dowry) of gold and clothes; we had to register with the court as husband and wife; and we had to have a ceremony and party.

In fact, I was not ready to do any of those things at that time. Although Mohsin said that he would pay all of the expenses for me, and Ibrahim said he would make sure that we had furniture and whatever else a house would need, and both of them wanted me to go ahead and finish the requirements, I told them that I had to go back to Syria first to continue with college, and that when I came back we would finish the wedding. They tried to pressure me to complete what I had started, but I would not listen to them.

I went back to Syria, thinking it would take me a couple of weeks to get ready, but six or seven months went by before I returned to complete the ceremony. Once I went back, life was very different from before. Not only was I away from my country, my family, and my friends, but I was separated from my love partner. During that time, I read many romantic novels about this period of a youth's life, which in my culture is the most beautiful time. It is permitted when "engaged" to love someone—to see her, talk to her, explain your love for her, even go out in public with her. When this period of time is extended, a man can become poetic. I even started singing for the first time in my life. I have heard people say that after completing their marriage ceremony that they wished they had waited longer in this romantic, poetic period where dreams are real and reality is far away. But for me, it was more difficult because I was far away from Zuhur, and it was really hard to communicate. Being permitted to see someone and talk with her is not so romantic if you are too far away to actually do it.

My college friends realized my problem and joked with me about it. "Where is your heart, Yassin?" Kak Anas said. "Don't think so much and you will be OK," Kak Ali advised. "You will be home soon," Kak Abdul Jabar reassured me. They told me hundreds of stories about famous lovers of the past. Finally they collected some money among themselves and forced me to go back to Chamchamal and complete the marriage. Kak Anas said, "We don't want to see him on the street with children calling him 'Insane Yassin.'" Kak Ali laughed and said, "This alone is the time for lovers in the East." Kak Abdul Jabar said, "No. Keep him here. We want to hear some more poems." They all wished me a happy marriage.

So I went back to Iraq, but the situation in Kurdistan was even worse than the year before. It was really difficult to enjoy this opportunity that God had given me because so many people were suffering from the war and joblessness and poverty. Zuhur and I went to the court—the first time in my life I had ever seen a courtroom—and we married in front of a judge so we could get a marriage certificate. And we had a small party. In my culture, they say that marriage is half of faith. And that you cannot be a man until you are married. And that you can't be a great man if you don't have a great woman backing you up.

My time of youth was over. I could no longer indulge my emotions as though I was completely independent. I had to change. I had to think differently than before. I needed a place to live; I needed a plan for raising future children; I needed a job to support my family. When you are alone, you don't care about such things as much.

Zuhur and I discussed the situation. Kurdistan was getting worse, not better. There was no way for me to continue my education unless I left. Neither of us wanted our children to grow up the way we had grown up, and yet how was it possible now to raise children safely in Kurdistan? I was opposed to immigration from the country, but I felt as though I was being forced out, with no real alternative. As the saying goes, "When you have been forced, your philosophy will be invalid." I persuaded myself that I was not really doing what I objected to with immigration. I was not going far away—just to Syria. I was not fleeing my country—I was going to study. I was not running away—I intended to return as soon as I received my degree. I was not leaving my wife—I was taking her with me. I was not immigrating illegally—I had permission from the authorities. Yet with all these excuses, I was still not comfortable leaving Kurdistan when it was so beaten down. But it was the only way for me to stay independent.

I wanted to be free from the economic pressure of being unemployed, from having to depend on my brothers for a living, from having to join one militia group or another to support my family. Both of my brothers were now working for political groups and had a salary from the politicians, but I was a student and had nothing. I wanted to be independent from all the "trouble" (tribal) rules and cultural walls that numb and fool your mind if you follow them, and that shock and disturb people if you break them.

And so I took my wife's hand, and we left Kurdistan. I thought we left the country and its people with all their troubles far behind. Now I realize I left them behind physically, but in reality they never left me. They are still with me in my heart and in my mind.

Time for Flight

I strongly believed that it was wrong to run away from your country, leaving your people to suffer and face hardship while you looked elsewhere for a better future for yourself. For years I urged people not to leave, but to stay and rebuild Kurdistan. I tried to stop my friends from going to the West. We should not think about ourselves only, I said, but also think about our nation. I argued that we should take responsibility for the country, be patient, rebuild what had been destroyed, and remake our society so that it was as good as Sweden's or Norway's, or even better.

I never believed that I would flee my own country under any circumstances. But there is no force stronger than hunger. People will face an army, bombs, rockets, and torture with bare hands. But we cannot face hunger for more than a couple of days before we are ready to give up. My teacher used to tell me all the time that human beings change constantly. We change our minds, our actions, and our habits, and it is normal as we get older to adjust our thinking to reflect new knowledge or new circumstances or a new reality. My dad used to say that a person cannot think and act as a real man until he has married. Before that, he is just an emotional youth, and he doesn't understand what responsibility means. This is exactly true. In Kurdish culture, marriage is the biggest change in any person's life, and the most common way to prove that you are a man is by providing for a wife and family. I had wanted to get married, but still I never thought that anything—including marriage—would force me to leave my country.

I used to say, "What is the worst consequence for me—to die? Then I will be happy to die. Better than to flee Kurdistan." But reality is different than theory. Our patience, our knowledge, our power, and our abilities are all limited. In the end, maybe it is better to acknowledge your defeat than to stay arrogant and deny your reality…

This is hard for me to write, because I am still not sure how I came to change my mind and leave Kurdistan. But I changed it soon after I married. I said that I was only going to Syria to study, which I had to do if I was going to serve my people and my country. I remembered what the

Prophet said, may peace be upon him, when he left Mecca. He turned his face to it and said, "By God, you are the most beloved place in my heart, and if people had not forced me to go, I never would have left you."

When I left Kurdistan, I was not able to withhold my tears. I did not so much leave my country as hold it in my heart; I did not so much leave my people as carry them in my mind. I am still carrying all of their problems with me, and I am still searching for ways to change the situation in Kurdistan, to rebuild the country, to bring peace to the people.

As a Kurdish poet wrote:

> I swear by mountains
> I will move the entirety of Kurdistan whole
> To my tiny room
> In the foreign land*

But for me, I am allowed to swear only by God, and I swear by Him that I have the whole of Kurdistan and all of my people with me in my tiny cell in the jail. Pashew, the Kurdish poet, said, "Every single night I see you in my dreams." And my cousin Marf Gul said, "If not for the dream, I would lose my mind!" Not only do I see the people every night, but every day I talk to them, especially since I have started to write about my life. I am like the poet Hemin Mukriyani; I say

> Oh friends, whom I will never forget—
> I am a wanderer now, if you recognize me, if you see me!*

All that happened to my friends was expected, because it was Kurdistan. But how can I now believe everything that has happened to me in a free land?

My wife Zuhur was busy packing all of our clothes and things for our journey to Syria—and I was packing my mind and heart with the entire country of Kurdistan. I saw three or four big bags, and I asked her what they were for. She said they were only what we needed for

* *Note*: These poems have been translated from Kurdish to English from memory by the author.

the journey. Then my niece, Kwestan, who was about five, came to me crying and said that she wanted to come with us.

"Sorry, Kwestan," I said. "We can't take you with us."

"Why not?" she said.

"Because you don't have a permit, and your name is not on a list at the border."

"You can put me in one of these big bags," she said. "I promise I won't move."

"But they are going to open each of the bags and check them," I said.

She started crying harder and hugged me. "Uncle, please don't leave us," she said.

"We will be back soon," I told her.

Then everyone started crying as we put our bags in the taxi. "I will be back soon, Kwestan," I told her again. But her words are still ringing in my ears—"Uncle, please don't leave us."

Traveling

Traveling should be a beautiful part of life. It is an important way to encounter people and their cultures and to see the beauty of nature in this universe. Western people are blessed with many opportunities to travel, but in the East traveling is very difficult, especially in the Middle East.

When I was in Iraq, most Kurds were never able to get a passport. Many people never saw anyplace other than their home state in their whole life, not because they didn't want to travel but because they could not. They could not take a vacation from their jobs, and they could not save enough money to travel abroad—and even if they could, they would have a hundred more pressing needs for the money than traveling abroad. They could not travel because it was—and is—not always safe to go to a neighboring country in the Middle East. Security is bad, and wherever you are a stranger you are treated with suspicion.

In addition, travel in the Middle East is not really fun; it is more a form of punishment. Most people don't have their own cars, and even if they do, gas is expensive. Although we live over a sea of oil, we often have to wait in line five to ten hours at a gas station in order to fill our tanks. Travel by bus is also very slow. You go to a bus station, buy a ticket, and you wait until the bus fills up with passengers— sometimes it takes three to five hours for the bus to be full. When it starts moving, you encounter checkpoints at many cities and villages, where all the travelers have to get out of the bus and have their papers examined. There are hundreds of cars waiting, and the checking takes hours. There may be fifty miles between two cities, but it may take at least three hours to make the journey because of all the checkpoints.

In the bus, people talk loudly to be heard over the roar of the engine; they open the windows onto the dusty roads and smoke cigarettes. Most of the buses are old and smell of burning gas. The roads are rutted and broken. In Kurdistan we joke that after eating a good meal, the best way to burn off the calories is to take a drive. Sitting in a car is like riding a horse. By the time you get to your destination, you are sick and tired—and sore. Some people prefer to walk instead of using the bus. And even then, when you get to your destination there may not be any hotels or parks or museums or anything for you to visit.

Chamchamal, with a population of about 50,000, is now the county center of Garmian Province in Sulaimaniya State, but when I lived there not one hotel or public park or museum existed. There was only a small library, with two small rooms for the managers and one large room for all of the books. There were no other cultural activities going on in the city. There were no computers, and no Internet connection was available anywhere. In Kurdistan there are many waterfalls and places of great scenic beauty that could be centers for a tourist industry, but the Iraqi government has prevented development of such an industry.

The first time I went to Syria was in 1993, and it was the first time I had to pass through Badinan Province. About 70% of all Kurds speak the dialect of Badini, from which the province gets its name. The rest speak the Sorani dialect, which is the dialect of my home province, Sulaimaniya (there are some other local dialects, like Hawrami and Khanaqini). From Chamchamal to Badinan Province, the main highway goes through Kirkuk, and then to Mosul. But at that time, both of those cities were under the control of the Iraqi government, and so we Kurds were not permitted to enter them.

There were other, longer ways to get to Badinan Province—through the mountains, over a single road packed with traffic—so when my wife and I left Kurdistan for Syria in 1995, we took these routes, which the Kurds had been using since the 1991 uprising. We enjoyed the trip because of the beautiful areas we passed through. It was the first time Zuhur had ever seen such places. I knew the names of many of them, and I had a great time explaining to her about each area and its history. There is nothing that makes a man prouder than to be a teacher to his wife, and he really enjoys it when he knows she is listening! The best way to make that happen is to know interesting things that she doesn't know. I was truly the husband in our traveling—I knew the area because I had seen it before.

First we crossed the Qandeel River and saw the Qandeel Mountains, which have been the "castle of the *peshmerga*" throughout history. After that, we came to Barzans Province, the land of Sheikh Ahmad Barzani and the place where the new Kurdish revolution had been declared by Mala Mustafa Barzani. Each mountain and city and village and rock is part of that history. In this valley, famous poets, writers, artists, and leaders were born and struggled and won victories.

Gate of Kurdistan

Finally we arrived at Dhok, which is the biggest city in Badinan Province and the provincial capital. About fifty miles to the west was Syria, and fifty miles to the north was Turkey. We headed west and eventually came to the Tigris River, at the place where the Tigris enters Iraq and separates Iraq from Syria by about 500 feet of water. This place is called Fish Khabor, and it was here that hundreds of people returning from Europe or going abroad passed over the Tigris every day. It was the only gate into Kurdistan. At that time, Turkish Kurdistan was about a quarter of a mile to the north, Syrian Kurdistan was 500 feet to the west, and the Iraqi army was about half a mile from us to the south. Three different flags; three different governments; three different laws; three different currencies; and yet it was all part of Kurdistan. There was no bridge across the Tigris, and no way to take a car across the river. There were only two small boats for transportation, each of which held about five people.

So my wife and I waved to our friends and family who had come with us to Fish Khabor, said a final goodbye to them and to Iraq, crossed the Tigris in the small boat, and got out on the other side—still in Kurdistan, but in Syria this time, where we set our faces and hopes for a new life in a foreign country.

226

Yassin with two of his brothers, Issa and Mohsin; the rest of the men are cousins.
Yassin is seated, smiling, second from right; in front of him is his nephew, Issa's
son. Issa is standing, second from right. Mohsin is seated on the far left.
Family photo.

Yassin's brother Ibrahim (standing, second from left) and sister Nathifa (standing, second from right). Ibrahim's arm is around his wife, Wajiha. Next to her is one of Nathifa's daughters. The others are members of Ibrahim's and Nathifa's families.
Family photo.

Yassin's sister Nathifa and her son in the mountains near Hashazini.
Family photo.

Yassin's brother Issa in The Netherlands.
Family photo.

230

Hashazini village, April 22, 1989, after the Anfal operation. Omar Gull preaches for
the people and speaks about the destruction. Omar Gull is Marf, Yassin's cousin.
Family photo courtesy of Arif Gull.

Yassin in Syria in the mid-1990s.
Family photo.

232

The Muslim Solidarity Committee organized a rally, march, and vigil on August 15, 2007 to mark the third anniversary (August 4, 2004) of the arrests of Yassin Aref and Mohammed Hossain in the FBI "sting" operation. The rally began in front of Masjid As-Salam at 278 Central Avenue in Albany, which was raided and ransacked by the FBI on that day and where Yassin was imam. Pictured near the masjid are, from left: Kotcher (Azzam) Muhiddin, Raiber (Salah) Muhiddin, and Steve Downs.

Photo by Katherine Hughes.

August 15, 2007. From left: May Saffar, Alaa Muhiddin, and Cathy Callan. May and Cathy are the co-founders of the Muslim Solidarity Committee.
Photo by Jeanne Finley.

Kathy Manley, one of Yassin's appeal lawyers from the Albany firm Kindlon Shanks and Associates, addresses the August 15 rally outside the masjid. At right are Steve Downs and Raiber Muhiddin.
Photo by Jeanne Finley.

The banner over the front door of Masjid As-Salam.
Photo by Steve Jacobs. Courtesy of Albany Times Union.

Shamshad Ahmad, founder and president of Masjid As-Salam, speaks to the media in front of the mosque at the August 15 rally. At left is Steve Trimm, a member of the Muslim Solidarity Committee.
Photo by Jeanne Finley.

Raiber holds his sister Dilnia.
Photo by Dave Capone.

PART TWO:
SYRIA

Yassin Aref at the villa where he was employed as a
nator (gardener), Qudsaya, Syria, mid-1990s.
Family photo.

Chapter Eight ☪
Immigrants

Crossing the Border

After we had crossed the Tigris into Syria, we first passed through an area called Rumailan, where you could see oil wells spread across the landscape. "Look," I told my wife. "They are taking Kurdistan's blood."

"What do you mean?" she asked.

"Don't we have blood in our bodies?" I said. "So the land has blood too."

"Oh. You mean water."

"Water runs above the land, but under the land is oil. That oil is Kurdistan's blood, and they are taking it."

"Well, at least here they are just taking oil," she said. "In Kurdistan they were taking our oil and our real blood as well."

She was right.

For hundred of years, tens of thousands of Kurds have lost their land and homes and shops and have been deported from both the city and province of Kirkuk. Thousands of other Kurds have been killed or have "disappeared." It all has to do with oil. Oil has brought no good to Kurdistan. We never received enough of it to even heat our houses or fill our cars. Even now, in Kirkuk people still have to wait in line between five and ten hours at a gas station to fill their cars, while they are sitting on a huge underground lake of oil. Only by smuggling oil in from Iran can the Kurds get even a fraction of what they need.

One day I heard on the BBC that in the last ten years the oil fields in Nigeria have been exploited, the Nigerian economy has become much worse, and people are really suffering in what is potentially one of the richest countries in the world. If that is true of Nigeria, what about Iraq? How many wars have been caused by oil? How many Iraqis have lost their lives? Why is the Iraqi economy so bad, and getting worse? Iraqis should be some of the richest people in the Middle East rather than some of the poorest, without even enough bread to eat.

Most of the Kurdish problems in Kurdistan started with oil. The Iraqi government tried to drive all the Kurds out of Kirkuk and repopulate the province with Arabs so they could take control of the oil. If it were not for the oil, the Baghdad government would have gladly left Kirkuk with the Kurds. So for us, oil was a curse. All the wars that followed, all the millions of victims, all the poverty, started with oil. A friend of mine used to say that the only thing we ever got from our oil was black smoke covering our cities and destroying our health and fresh air. The government sucked the land dry, and then left the Kurds to die on it.

Barzani, the head and founder of KDP, said that Kirkuk was the heart of Kurdistan. I believe it's true because a heart pumps blood and Kirkuk pumps oil, the Kurdistani blood. And just to show that his group was as patriotic as the KDP, Talabani, the head and founder of PUK, said, "*Kirkuk Qadsi Kurdistana*," which means, "Kirkuk is Kurdistan's Jerusalem," or "Kirkuk is Kurdistan's holy city." Of course, people love politicians when they make statements like this, but I do not believe that Kurdistan will ever recover Kirkuk. It is lost forever. The politicians sold it.

In 1994, I wrote two poems about this time—when the KDP and the PUK, both claiming that they were trying to recover Kirkuk from the Iraqi government so it could be Kurdistan's capital, began to fight with each other instead of working together to free Kirkuk and rebuild the country.

Let the People Enjoy Independence

When they say
"Kirkuk is Kurdistan's Jerusalem"
They lie.
If not a lie, why did they not rise
Like Palestine's children with rocks
To free Kirkuk for the Kurds?

It is enough. Shout no more.
Kirkuk is Kurdistan's heart.
All Kurds know that,
For your own benefit,
You sold not only Kirkuk
But the rest of Kurdistan too.

Untitled

Pashew* spoke out loudly against them
Crying and calling like a hawk,
"Our flag has become just an old piece of cloth."
I joined my voice with his:
"Shame on you. Shame on you."
We recovered a little piece of our land
But you separated it into two.

As Kirmangim

We arrived in Qamishly, a very old city compared to other big cities in Syria. It is the biggest Kurdish city in Syria, but there were no signs to show that it was part of Kurdistan. Most Kurds in Syria do not wear Kurdish clothing, and the Kurdish language is not spoken in schools or government offices. Qamishly looked very poor; a great deal of construction needed to be done. It was like Chamchamal: in winter it was all mud, and in the summer it was covered with dust. If you went shopping in the winter it looked as though you were coming out of a flood, and if you went shopping in the summer you looked like a soldier in the desert.

I had a number of friends from college who lived there, so I went to visit one of them, Abdul Bari, and stayed with him until late at night. His family was very excited to see us and thirsty to hear about Kurdish freedom and the political situation in Kurdistan and Iraq. Krmang, Abdul Bari's six-year-old brother, showed me a picture of a man.

"Who is this?" I asked him.

*Abdulla Pashew, Kurdish poet

"Our father, our leader," he said.

"Is he your father?" I asked.

"He is everyone's Kurdish father," Krmang said.

"What is his name?"

"You don't know him?"

"Well, tell me who he is," I encouraged him.

"*Heza Baraznia* (Honorable Barzani)." He was showing me a picture of Mala Mustafa Barzani, the founder of the KDP and the Kurdish revolution after World War II.

"Do you like him?" I asked.

"I love him," Krmang said. "His is the crown of the Kurdish head."

"Are you Kurdish?"

"Yes. *As Kirmangim*." (Which means, "I am Kurdish.")

"So why don't you speak Kurdish?"

"Because I can't speak Sorani."

"So that means you are not Kurdish," I joked with him.

"*As Kirmangim*, but I don't know Sorani," Krmang said.

"If you are really Kurdish, you should know the language," I said.

"So can you speak Kirmangi?" he asked me.

"I can't," I told him, and I joked that he was Kirmangi, not Kurdish.

He started crying in frustration. "Yes I am Kurdish! Yes I am…we are Kurds!" he shouted.

Kirmangi is the largest dialect of the Kurdish language. All Kurds in Syria and Turkey and in the Badinan Province of Iraq speak Kirmangi. The rest of Iraq and Iranian Kurds speak Sorani (this is what I speak). Because people did not move easily between different parts of Kurdistan, and because the Kurdish language was not taught in any schools, it was very difficult for Kirmangi Kurds to understand Sorani Kurds, and vice versa. But after the 1991 uprising in Kurdistan, both dialects were spoken. Kurdish professors are now planning to unite the Kurdish language by mixing both dialects. If this works, I hope that our children will one day be able to easily understand each other.

Abdul Bari and his family made every effort to serve us, showered us with hospitality, cooked special Kurdish food for us, and gave us cheese and honey to take with us on our journey. They gave my wife a wedding gift. They even tried to cancel our bus ticket so we could stay a few days longer with them.

Krmang begged his father to keep us from going. At the bus station I joked with Krmang by asking, "What is your name?" And he shot right back at me, "I told you, *As Kirmangim!*" I told him that I knew he was Kurdish, but what was his *name*? His father laughed and explained that his real name was Kirmang (with an i), which is a common name among Kirmangi-speaking Kurds. I asked the father why he had nicknamed his son Krmang (without an i), and he said that Krmang meant "Poor Kurd." His answer really shook me because it was so true. They lived in a rich country and they struggled hard to survive, and still a majority of the Kurds were very poor.

Damascus by Bus

The next evening Zuhur and I went by bus to Damascus, which was about a nine- or ten-hour drive. The bus had an air conditioner, a luxury like something out of Europe and something I never saw in Kurdistan, so it was a comfortable place to sleep at night, and it would be good to wake up to Damascus in it in the morning. We left about 10 p.m. I knew that the bus would go through many beautiful areas and some big cities, but because it was night there was no way to see outside in the darkness, so I put my wife's seat back and told her that she should just catch some sleep. The bus was really comfortable. Nobody smoked, and you could not open the windows. It even had a TV and screens over the windows.

Soon the bus left Syrian Kurdistan, and it looked like we were going into another country. Going from a Kurdish city like Qamishly to Damascus was like going from Africa to Europe, or from a backward village to a modern city. We drove ten hours without anyone stopping us; in Kurdistan over the same distance, we would have had to stop at numerous checkpoints. Zuhur and I talked until sleep finally took us.

We arrived in Damascus around 8 a.m. I uncovered the window of the bus and started showing my wife the sights of the city as we passed.

Even though we had slept for a few hours, we were really tired when we got off the bus. I brought our bags out to a corner where there were many porters and taxi drivers. All of them wanted to carry our stuff, but having been a porter myself I knew what we needed and told them to leave us alone. I told my wife to watch the bags while I made a phone call.

"Who are you going to call?"

"One of my friends."

"Why?"

"We can go to his house and rest," I said. "After that, I can leave you and our bags there and find a place for us to rent."

"No no!" she said emphatically. "Please don't go to anyone's home!"

"We have to," I said. "We can't search for a place to rent with all these bags. Suppose we search for hours and we don't find anything today—where will we sleep? We are already tired from the journey."

"That is not a problem," my wife said. "I will wait here with the bags while you find a place to stay."

"It's at least an hour or two before the rental offices will even open," I said.

"I can wait."

"What is wrong with you?" I said. "Why don't you want to go to my friend's house? He is Kurdish, from Iraq. They speak Sorani, not Krmangi. Look at Abdul Bari and his family, how happy they were to serve us. That is why it is good to have friends."

My wife still did not want to go to my friend's house, and I could not understand why. This was the first time that I had had a woman in my life. I knew nothing about the way a woman thought. I was just a villager, and this kind of relationship with a woman was completely new to me. This was my honeymoon, but I couldn't even rent a room in a hotel for one night, or take my wife to a restaurant, until I could find a place to rent—just as my father used to live in the village.

Later I found out that as happy as I was for all the hospitality shown to us by Abdul Bari and his family—the food, the gifts, the sharing, the respect—that same hospitality made my wife very uncomfortable. I remembered that at Abdul Bari's house she had refused to join in the conversation and had refused to eat much, and had not even changed her clothes, but at the time I had not paid much attention to it. We were traveling, and I thought maybe she was just tired. But I learned that she was a very shy person, and all the hospitality embarrassed her. Also she believed that it was a shame to accept presents from my friends, such as the cheese and honey—she thought that proved our poverty, and at least for her it meant we had no dignity. She did not want me to take her to the home of another friend, where she was afraid that the embarrassment and shame would just be repeated. I told her that my friend was just like my brother and it was a special occasion because we had just been married. There was nothing wrong with that, I told her. But still she would not agree. I did not want to argue with her because it was too early in our marriage for that, so I told her, "Good. If you do not want to go to my friend's house, we will go to an office where Kurds go for changing money, renting houses, making phone calls, and so on. I know two or three of them, and they will find us a place to stay."

I called a taxi and put our bags in. In our tradition, men always sit in the front seat, and women sit in the back. But to show my wife that I was a modern man, I sat with her in the back seat.

"Ahhhh." She took a deep breath and put her hand over her mouth and cheeks as a sign of surprise and shock. "Aeeb!" she said, which means "shame."

I just laughed and pretended not to hear her. "Masakin Barza," I said to the driver, which was the name of the Kurdish area in Damascus. Then I leaned back in my seat like an important politician and said to my wife, "I am a modern Imam!"

She covered her face with her scarf and began laughing under it.

"I'm not joking," I said firmly. "I sit in the back so I can sit with my wife! I go to college. I live in the capital of Syria. I wear pants. I don't cover my head."

She did not like it one bit. She must have thought this was a sign of the coming of the Hereafter. Or at least that her husband had a strong personality.

When we arrived, I took all of our bags out of the taxi, but the office had not yet opened for business, so we waited outside until my friend Ibrahim came to open up.

"Oh, Kak Yassin," he said. "Welcome back to Damascus!"

"Thank you," I said. "This is my wife."

"*Mubarak* (Congratulations)," he said. "How are you, sister?" he said to Zuhur.

She was too shy to answer, and I could not hear any words from her mouth, but I could see her lips moving.

"Kak Ibrahim," I said, "I need a small house to rent."

"Well, first let me take your wife to my home," said Kak Ibrahim. "She can rest there while we look for a place."

"No thank you," I told him firmly, without daring a look at my wife. "It is better to just find us a house."

Kak Ibrahim shrugged, as though he was surprised that a reasonable offer of hospitality was being rejected. But he said, "There are about five houses available now but all of them are big, with three or four bedrooms."

"I only want a one-bedroom house," I said.

"How much can you afford?"

"Not more than $100."

"All the houses available are over $200," he said. "You will need either a one-bedroom house, or to share a three-bedroom house with another family."

Without looking at my wife I said, "Please, one bedroom."

Kak Ibrahim sighed. "Let me call the other offices for you," he said. He made many phone calls, but I saw no sign of hope in his face. Finally he said, "The cheapest I can find is a two-bedroom house in a bad area for $150."

I refused. I only had $120, and I figured I would keep $20 for food while I looked for a job. The rent had to be under $100.

We waited until almost noon, with my wife sitting outside on the bags without any hope. I felt bad. This was our honeymoon in Damascus and we were traveling Kurdish style. Western travelers, arriving in the Damascus bus station, would simply have taken a taxi to a five-star hotel, ordered food at a fancy restaurant, gotten maps and information at the tourist center, visited beautiful and interesting places, and lived like kings for $200 a week on the best that Damascus had to offer. But I did not have that kind of money to spend on my honeymoon. Zuhur was so tired she could hardly hold her head up. Suddenly I felt very guilty and afraid. This was no way to treat a wife. I remembered Mohsin's words to me: *How can you marry? How much money have you saved? What is your job?* Fears began to crowd my mind. What had I done? I was so upset I even forgot where I was.

Suddenly I became aware that someone was calling my name. I turned to look, and it was my friend from college, Kak Ali. He gave me a big hug and held my hand in friendship. "You did not bring your wife?" he asked.

"Yes. Here she is," and I introduced him to her.

After Kak Ali welcomed Zuhur, he said, "What are you waiting for? Why are you here?"

"Kak Ibrahim is trying to find us a house to rent," I said.

"I will move out and go to my friend's house," Ali said. "You can have my room." He was single and lived by himself.

"No," I told him. "We need a house."

"Good," he said. "Use my room until you find a house."

"Well...we need one right now."

"What is wrong with you?"

"Nothing," I said. "But it is better to move only one time. Look at all the bags."

"So what does Kak Ibrahim say?"

"All he has now are big houses. I need a small one."

"Oh, I know one," said Kak Ali. "Just this morning a Kurdish family left for Sweden. Their house is good."

"How much is it?"

"$80. It's a...small house."

"That is all we need."

"Give me ten minutes," Kak Ali said, and started running.

In fifteen minutes he came back with a car and we climbed in, bags and all. The house in fact was really small, but it was sufficient for two people and that was enough for us. While my wife went inside, I spoke to the owner and gave him $80 for one month's rent. We wrote out an agreement, Kak Ali witnessed it, and then he left.

Suddenly all my fears went away.

About an hour later, the doorbell rang. I was surprised. Who knew that I was here? Should I answer or not? But when I opened the door it was Kak Ali, bringing lunch for us from a restaurant. I did not know what to say, except to smile and stutter that all this kindness was not necessary. My wife was sleeping and I was not hungry, but Kak Ali insisted that I take the food for later. "I am going to leave you now," he said. "Get some rest."

"Listen," I said. "Don't tell anyone that I am back, and don't give anyone this address."

Kak Ali started laughing. "Of course. You are married. You don't need any guests."

I rolled my eyes. "No, not that. We are half-dead and we need some rest. We've been driving for two days."

Kak Ali continued to smirk. "I understand. No friends anymore. You are married."

"See you later, Kak Ali," I said.

Honeymoon

Damascus is a very old and beautiful city. People still believe that Adam's two sons, Cain and Abel, lived there. The weather is very nice, not too cold in winter and mild in summer. Many Western people visit Damascus because it is inexpensive and there is a lot to see. Many Arabs also visit because they can come without a visa, and in the summer they can escape the heat. As a result, Damascus has a good tourist industry, but still a large portion of the population is impoverished. They do not have enough income to even cover their rent, much less the cost of their food, and many people have to work two jobs at low wages just to survive. Office workers, for example, often drive a taxi as a second job. Many people eventually go to the Gulf countries (Saudi Arabia, Bahrain, Kuwait, Qatar, United Arab Emirates) to work.

In summer, many Syrian families rent their furnished houses to people from the Gulf countries and move into tiny summer houses on Qasuon Mountain so they can save money for the winter. Syrians can rent their houses for $300 to $400 while paying rent in their small mountain houses of $30 to $50. Some Syrians also let their daughters stay behind in their furnished homes as servants to clean and cook for the foreigners. Tragedies have resulted from this.

Syrian women have a European look, and many men from the Gulf countries want to marry them because their color is different from the darker Arab countries. Some rich men from the Gulf have also developed the bad habit of marrying girls twenty or thirty years younger than they are, in exchange for giving a large amount of money to the girl's family. (The money is a large amount in Syria, but not in the Gulf states.) Then after a few years, the man divorces the girl and marries another—and the pattern continues. I have heard many stories of such relationships, and I have seen some of these "marriages" with my own eyes. In most of the cases, the women are victims. Even though they are technically married, these women work as servants. They are married to men older than their fathers who are foreign to them and may not even speak their language. In a few years they will be divorced, and there will be no future for them. In our culture, it is very hard for divorced women to remarry. People believe that the woman was divorced because she was bad. And men who marry for the first time will accept only a virgin.

The exploitation of women is the same in many third world countries. I have heard similar stories from people in the Middle East, Asia, and Africa, from Morocco to the Philippines. People are selling their daughters to get money or the opportunity to go to a Western country or a Gulf country. Some are driven to do this by need. But I have no doubt that in many cases it is just greed. All this is going on in Muslim countries, even though Islam requires that any girl who is to be married must freely consent to the marriage, and if she does not, the marriage is not valid. Maybe some of the girls are pressured into consenting as a sacrifice to lift their families out of poverty, but I wish they could understand that they have the right to say no and that they can find other ways to help their families. As for the men who enter these marriages, I will only say, fear God. Don't buy human beings; don't play with religion. Your marriage is invalid if at the start you intend to divorce your wife in two or three years. At the time you marry, you must have the intention to stay married all your life. Otherwise the marriage is invalid.

I did not enjoy the beauty of Damascus and my honeymoon because I was consumed with the need to find a job within the month. What would happen to us if I failed? Daily I went out looking for work, and found—nothing. It was difficult to look for work in Damascus because there was no classified section of the newspaper, no Internet listings, no government office for employment. Because I was a student and a foreigner, I was not allowed to work at any government job, and most of the jobs were with the government. I had to find a private job in a store or on a construction site. I asked all my college friends for leads and advice. I talked to imams, I went to stores, but I found nothing.

Finally I had only a day left before I had to make the next rent payment, and I had no money left. I was really scared, and Mohsin's words kept ringing in my ears: *How can you marry? What is your job? Where is your house?*

I tried to hide my feelings from my wife, but she knew already. She always said, "Don't worry. God will help us. I will sleep on the street if necessary. We will be all right." But tomorrow I would have to pay another $80 or move out. I tried to ask Zuhur what she thought about moving into the home of one of my friends, but I knew that she did not want that. I did not know what to say.

She seemed to understand. She smiled and said, "I have rent." I stared at her. She reached into her bag and took out some money. In our culture, when people marry, men will give gifts of clothing or blankets or furniture or plates, but women sometimes give gifts of cash, and the wives of my friends must have given her the money as a wedding present. I knew Zuhur did not know anything about Syrian currency or how much her money was worth in Syria, but here she was, offering it all to me. I thought it was too early for me to start taking her money, but it was certainly better than having to move out. I told her that I would accept it as a loan. She smiled and said that between us we did not have separate accounts. That same day I paid the landlord the $80 rent, and now I had another month to find a job.

I kept looking. I talked to more people, and the problem became clearer. Even if I found a job in a store, I would not earn enough to pay the rent, and so I would have to find a second job. But even if I could find a second job, this would not leave me any time to study. Someone suggested to me that I should look for a job as a gardener (*nator*), because gardeners in the big villas in the hills around Damascus usually had tiny servant's quarters where they could live so they did not have to pay rent. Gardeners did not make much money, but since they could live rent-free the money went a long way. Many rich people in Damascus had such villas, which they used full-time only for a few months in the summer. At other times the family might come once a month for a barbeque. For most of the year, the gardener was essentially a caretaker to prevent theft and to take care of the plants and trees. It sounded like a solution to my problem, but I visited a number of places and still I did not find anything. For any other kind of work I would have to find two jobs to survive, and this was especially difficult because there were few night jobs in Damascus. If I found a job that was a long way from my house, I would have to go to and from work by taxi, and this would eat up so much money that it would be better not to work at all. And of course, I did not want to quit college in order to work two jobs, because college was my dream and my Mom's wish for me.

My wife was having her difficulties as well. She did not feel safe in Damascus as a foreigner, especially at night. But if I worked a night job, she would be left all alone in the house. I was really in trouble. Mohsin's words kept echoing in my head. I feared he was right. But what about my father's words? "If we wait until the situation gets better," he would say, "we will never be able to do anything." If I had waited until I had a house and job and saved some money, I would never have been able to marry. So Father was also right. How could both of them be right?

Sometimes when we are not ready or prepared for something, we trick ourselves by saying, "I put my trust in God." We know that it is just an excuse, because it is unacceptable to hold up our lack of preparation to God as His problem. Once a person asked Mohammad, may peace be upon him, if he should tie up his camel, or if he should trust God that the untied camel would not wander away. The Prophet said to *first* tie up the camel, and *then* put your trust in God. I knew this teaching. I knew that it was not right to wait for a miracle unless you did your absolute best to solve the problem by using your mind and ability and all means available according to natural law. God is not going to change natural law for my convenience, and I will suffer the consequences if I do not understand God's laws and obey them. Praying for a miracle rather than obeying natural law actually means that I don't trust God and his laws.

So what should I do? My wife knew how concerned I was, but she always told me that God would help us. She told me to be patient and to keep on searching. We only had seven days until the next rent payment was due. I tried to talk to her about it.

"Don't worry," she said.

"I must worry," I said.

"Listen," she said. "Take all of my metal and sell it in the market. I don't need this metal. Pay the rent with that."

I felt as though the sky was falling on me. I could not take care of my wife. I hated myself. Anyone who would sell his wife's wedding gold, her dowry, was not a man. Instead of giving her gifts and money, I had taken her money. Now did I have to take her dowry as well? She tried to make it easier for me by calling it "metal," but I could not accept this and have any self-respect left.

In our culture, when people cannot take care of themselves the first thing they do is sell their wife's gold. After that, they sell their furniture and property. In order to satisfy the tradition of a dowry for the bride, some of my friends who were getting married made agreements with other married friends to borrow their wives' wedding gold for a few weeks until after the wedding was over, and then return it. But I could not take my wife's gold. I tried to explain this to her, but she told me that she would be happier if I did. So I took it. It was like fire in my hand, like a curse on me, it was telling me *Shame, Yassin. What kind of man are you to take your wife's gold?* I began to think that the grave was better than this shame. This was not the life I was seeking. I had not brought my wife to Damascus for this.

I kept blaming myself for what was happening until I reached my friend Kak Mateen's house and asked him to help me sell the gold. I could not tell real gold from fake gold, and I did not know what a fair price might be. In Syria, if you are a foreigner the sellers will often inflate the prices by as much as ten times. There are no laws to govern the marketplace, and merchants look for opportunities to make a good bargain, especially from foreigners and Westerners. When you buy something worth $1 with foreign money, they will tell you that you must pay $10. When you refuse, they will say $7. When you walk away, they will say $3, and then they will run along behind you shouting $2. You finally buy it for $2—and still you paid double the fair price. So I wanted Kak Mateen to go with me to sell my wife's gold so I would not be cheated.

Mateen was Turkish, with German citizenship, staying in Syria on a German passport and attending the same college that I attended. We could only communicate in broken Arabic. He had told me before that he had bought gold in Syria and had taken it back to Germany, where he sold it at a profit. So I knew that he was familiar with gold and its quality, size, price—and with the tricks of the trade.

"Peace be with you," I said.

"You are welcome, Kak Yassin. Please come in."

After we talked and told some jokes, I explained that I needed his help.

"I told you before," he said. "In Kurdistan they say we are brothers but we have different pockets. But this does not apply to me and you. Between us we are brothers and we have only one wallet."

"Well, brother, look at this," I said, and I showed him my wife's gold.

"Beautiful! Very nice. Where did you get it?"

"In Iraq."

"What carat is it?"

"I don't know. That's what I was hoping you could tell me."

Mateen checked the bottom and said, "Oh, good. It is twenty-one carat. That is excellent."

"I want to sell it," I said.

"Why?"

"My wife told me to."

"She doesn't like it?"

"We need to sell it."

Mahteen said, "This is nice gold. It is much better to save gold right now, not money. Every day, money loses its value. But gold is gaining in value."

"But we don't need it," I said.

"How much do you want for it?"

"I don't know what the price is. If you need it for yourself, give me fifteen percent less than the market price."

"How much did you pay for it?"

"My brother gave it to my wife when we got married," I said. "I have the receipt for it, so we can check on the price. I think it was about $190."

"You should never sell this," Mahteen said. "It is quality gold."

"But we need the money," I said.

"What do you need the money for?"

"To pay the rent."

Kak Mateen's face went dark, and for a moment I thought he was having a heart attack. "Yassin! You were just married, and now you want to sell your wife's gold to pay your rent?" He was shaking.

"So what can I do? I cannot find a job."

"So why do you bother to call me your brother?"

"It is our tradition. We are Muslim and you are one of my best friends."

"Is that how you see it?"

"Please don't take me wrong."

"How many times have I tried to help you, and each time you refused? You promised me that when you needed something, you would tell me."

"But we are OK," I said. "What do we need gold for? It is just metal."

"This is not yours, it is my sister's," Mahteen said.

"But she wanted me to sell it," I said.

"Listen. How much is your rent?"

"Please just take it to the market and sell it for me."

"Good. I will buy it myself."

"I don't want to sell it to you." I knew what he was going to do.

"Good. I am not giving it back."

"Keep it, then," I told him. "*Mubarak* (Congratulations)."

"Kak Yassin, you really disappoint me," Mahteen said.

"What did I do?" I said. "I came to you because you know about gold and how to sell it on the market. If I go by myself, they will cheat me, especially because my language is not good enough."

"But why didn't you tell me that you needed some money?"

"I asked you, and all my other friends, to help find me a job. I have been searching for two months, but I cannot find any jobs except for a few that will not even pay the rent."

"Listen," Kak Mateen said. "I bought this gold from you and now it is mine. Take this $200 for it—and give this gold as a gift to your wife."

"She will not accept that," I said. "She told me this is just metal. Why do I need it?"

"I will have my wife bring the gold to your wife. She will feel differently when she gets it from a woman. Women think differently than we do. Don't tell her how it happened. Just say someone sent it back to her."

"I can't do that."

"Yassin! Stop talking to me like that! I thought you accepted me as your brother."

"We are brothers."

"So why did you allow your brother Mohsin to buy this gold as a gift for your wife, and you will not allow me to do the same? How are you treating me like a brother?"

I did not know what to say. I just told him that it was not under my control, and that my wife didn't like to accept gifts.

Kak Mateen said, "Just tell her that nobody wanted to buy her gold, and you found somebody who would pay the rent." He gave me the gold back and put $200 in my pocket.

"Let me take only $100 as a loan," I said. "My rent is only $80."

We argued some more, but eventually I took $100 as a loan. I told him I'd see him later and went home to Zuhur.

"What took you so long?" she wanted to know.

"I was not able to sell your gold," I said.

"Why?"

"I don't know. I offered it to somebody, and he told me not to sell it."

"But we have no choice," Zuhur said. "You should have lowered the price until you could sell it."

"It's OK," I said. "Someone gave me $100. We can pay the rent and buy food for another month."

"Who gave you the money?"

"One of my friends."

"You take from your friends," Zuhur said, "but you won't take from me. Am I not your friend too?"

I said in my heart, *Oh God, must I fight her too?* I told Zuhur, "You are not my friend. You are my heart—you are my life. Please stop fighting me. Just pray for me that I get a job as a gardener."

Nator (The Gardener in the Garden)

Two weeks later, a friend said that he had found a job for me, and took me to a suburb of Damascus called Qudsaya, about twenty miles from where Zuhur and I were living. My friend stopped at a huge garden with a villa in the middle that looked like Saddam's palace.

The owner came out. He introduced himself as Mazn Shaqrah, understood that I was applying for the job of gardener, and then asked me, "Do you have residency papers, Yassin?"

"Yes," I said, and I produced them.

"Can you work in a garden?"

"What exactly must I do?"

"In autumn and winter you have little to do in the garden except to keep your eyes open and make sure that no children break the windows and that no one tries to steal anything. In late spring and summer, you have to water the trees and clean up the leaves and branches that have fallen." .

"That is easy," I said. "But I have one problem. I am a student every day from 2 to 7 or 8 p.m., except in the summer when school is closed."

"You are married, are you not?" said Mazn Shaqrah.

"Yes."

"So when you go to school, your wife will stay here and keep an eye on the place, no?"

"Yes, of course," I said.

"Then that is all we need," he said. "The biggest part of the job is in the summer when you don't have school. Our neighbors are good people and they will never cause trouble."

"How much do you pay?" I asked.

"The same as I paid Yahya," Mazn Shaqrah said. "$100 a month, and if you do well I will increase it during the summer." Yahya was a student from Sudan who had held the job before me. He had finished his studies and was going back to Sudan.

"What about a place to stay?" I asked.

"That room in the corner of the garden is the gardener's place," Mazn Shaqrah said. He showed us the room and it looked good to me, so we wrote an agreement and my friend witnessed it. I said I would start tomorrow. Mazn Shaqrah gave me the keys and his card, and said if I needed anything to call him.

I was really happy. I did not need to sell my wife's gold now, and I could recover some of my dignity. I did not need to ask people for handouts anymore. I was a man again.

When I got home, my wife could tell by the glow on my face what had happened. She laughed.

"Why are you laughing?" I asked innocently, but then I could not contain myself and began laughing too.

"I can read your face," she said. "You found a job."

"Thank God," I told her.

I told the landlord that I would move tomorrow. "But you have fifteen more days till the end of the month," he said. "You've already paid."

"I have a job and I have to start tomorrow," I said.

"I thought you were going to Europe," he said.

"No. I will be living here."

"All the Kurds that rent from me are coming from or going to Europe."

"Not me."

"What kind of a job did you find?" asked the landlord.

"I will become a gardener," I said.

"Anything as long as you can take care of your family," he said.

"Exactly. Take care of them without begging."

"God help you," he said.

"Can you give me back $40, because we used only half a month's rent?" I asked him.

"Sorry," he said. "If you like, you can keep the key until the end of the month—or you can stay. But if you leave, I can't give you your money back."

"I don't want to lose this job," I said

"So keep the key till the end of the month," the landlord said. "Even if you bring one of your friends to live here, I have no problem. I just can't give you your money back."

I gave him his keys back and told him to keep the money and to pray for me. He looked at me as though pondering something in his mind. Then he said, "Since you have been here, I have not had any problems. Many Kurds make frequent requests and complain about everything, but you don't. I wish you would stay longer. Wait a minute." He went inside to his home, came back, and handed me $20. "This is for one week," he said. "If I rent the house quickly, I will give you the other $20 back."

"I told you it is OK if you keep it," I said.

"But I'm not OK about it," he said. "I don't feel good about taking your money while you are working as a gardener to support your family. You are not like the ones coming from Europe. For them $20 is nothing, but for us it is a lot."

"Thank you," I told him.

"Visit me sometime, *insha-Allah* (by God's will)," the landlord said. He hugged me and wished me good luck.

The next morning I hired a taxi and my wife and I went see our new place. I had the key for the gates. The road from Damascus to Qudsaya was very beautiful, with running streams, mountains, and trees. It was really very similar to Kurdistan except for all the signs for hotels and restaurants. When I opened the gate, my wife was shocked. In all of Iraq, she said, she had never seen such a house and garden, except on TV when Saddam showed off his palace. I whispered to her that this was Saddam's palace.

From the gate to the house was a drive of about 1,500 feet, lined on both sides with flowerbeds and trees. We paid for the taxi and carried our bags into the gardener's house. It was a single room, about fifteen feet by twelve feet, plus a kitchen that was about six feet by four feet and a shower that was five feet by five feet. This empty room would be our living room, dining room, and bedroom. Suddenly I saw that the ceiling was dripping moisture, which meant that it leaked in the rain. And I suddenly remembered that the cave in Hashazini where we used to hide from helicopter attacks was much bigger and better than this room. I did not know what to say to Zuhur, and so I just joked with her that it looked like the Sheraton Hotel.

She looked at me and said, "I did not come to this country to live in a palace. I came to live with you. Wherever we go and live is good with me—even if we live in a cave."

I had no words to answer this, so I just hugged her. "I'm sorry," I told her. "I believe that life is like climbing a mountain. You cannot run to the top, and you have to walk slowly or even crawl sometimes, but if you are patient and keep walking you will certainly reach the top one day." I looked at her and was surprised to see that she looked happy.

"Happiness should be in our hearts," she said. "Happiness comes from loving and respecting each other. People who live in the Sheraton Hotel may not really be happy and may be searching for a little peace for their minds and tranquility for their hearts. Their house can help, but it can't give happiness by itself."

I was excited and surprised to hear this. It seemed to me that my wife was a better poet than I was, and she left me no chance to proclaim any more philosophy.

Men in the East depend more on their women than people of the West—we survive because of the strong, unquestioning support of our wives. They hide themselves with us when the army follows us. They fast with us when we run out of food. They live with us in caves. They work with us on the farms. They do not ask for gold or cars or castles or furniture. They cook food when we can't order it. They bake bread when we don't have any to buy. They take care of the children when we don't have a babysitter. They wash our clothes when we don't do the laundry. We are nothing without them. Thousands of men like me sold their wives' gold to survive, and when they did their wives supported them. If not for their love and support, how can we take all of the pressure of the hard work we have to do? Still, despite all of this, we men in the East are often very ungrateful to our women, and many of us yell at them and drive them like they are our slaves, or at least our servants.

It turned out that we were indeed happy in that tiny little room in the big garden. We had each other. We spent about three years living there, even after we had two children. No matter how small it was, I felt like it was my castle and that I was king. We did not care so much about the room, because during the day we could sit in the garden or on the balcony of the villa like a king and queen and fill our senses with the trees and flowers and birds. And love, honesty, and respect between a wife and husband make their life together as happy as though they are in Paradise, even if they live in a cave and don't get enough food to fill their stomachs. By the same token, no matter how huge the house or how beautiful the car or how wonderful the food, a couple can never be happy without love, respect, and honesty.

Chapter Nine ☪
Breaking the Iron Wall

Residency Permit

After I found the job as a gardener, I was able to get food for my wife and our daughter, who was born after we moved in. Then my concern turned to security and protection from the dangers around us. I had a residency permit, but it was no real protection at all. On the back it stated: *The government that has provided you with this residency permit has the right at any time to cancel the permit without any reason.* You might think that this meant the government could someday decide to cancel my permit and request that I leave the country within a certain period of time—but I took a more sinister meaning from the phrase. To me, the notice was telling me to be ready at any time for the Syrian government to arrest me and give me back to the Iraqi government.

Iraq and Syria at that time were in the process of improving their relations. The countries had exchanged diplomats after more than twenty years of official silence between them. Almost all of the Iraqis who lived in Syria were helping one of the Iraqi opposition parties, and the Iraqi government wanted to capture these opposition leaders. So what better way to make friends with the Iraqi government then to have the Syrians cancel the residency permits of the Iraqis and send them home to the waiting arms of the Iraqi security forces? The Iraqi government needed no evidence to execute anyone it did not like. In fact, merely being in Syria was by itself a crime, since an Iraqi passport specifically prohibited anyone from going to either Israel or Syria.

The problem is illustrated by what happened to Abdullah Ocalan, the head and founder of the PKK (Kurdish Workers Party) in Turkish Kurdistan. Ocalan had to flee Turkey because of the activities of his party, and he lived for decades in Syria. But when Syria developed a better relationship with Turkey, and when the U.S. put the PKK on the terrorist list in exchange for Turkish support of the U.S. invasion of Iraq, Syria told Ocalan that he had to leave. He went to Greece because no other European nation would accept him, but in Greece he got no refugee status and no right to stay, so he went to Kenya—where the CIA helped Turkish intelligence track him down and arrest him, and he was brought back to Turkey.

There are no friendships or good relations in politics today. Friends today are enemies tomorrow, and yesterday's enemies are today's friends, especially in the Middle East. I cannot defend Ocalan and his party. They are Communists and I am religious, but I can't understand why Turkish Kurds are terrorists but Iraqi Kurds are freedom fighters. Both are Kurds; both are seeking to establish a Kurdish state; both countries have a history of violence. Just because America has a close relationship with Turkey is no reason to label Kurdish freedom-seekers from Turkey as terrorists, while Kurdish freedom-seekers from Iraq are labeled freedom fighters or democracy builders or liberal thinkers just because they agree with America's goal of removing Saddam from power. The labels have no relationship to reality on the ground.

Ironically, both Iraq and Syria were ruled at the time I was there by the same political movement—the Baath party—and I heard the same slogan everywhere: "Arabs are one nation and carry one message: unity, freedom, and Socialism." I saw this propaganda a hundred times a day. But like so many other things in the Middle East, the practice was just the reverse of the ideology. *Peace, independence, freedom, Socialism, human rights, unity, patriotism*—the words were plastered on every wall, but they were just words with no meaning or true reality.

The same was true of the law. Iraqi law after the American invasion sounds much like Swedish law:

No arrest without a warrant—but every day in Iraq hundreds of dead bodies are found, and most of them have been killed by the police and security forces.

No detention of persons for more than forty-eight hours without a charge—but at least 20,000 Iraqis have been held in jail without charges for years.

Freedom of speech—but if you say one critical word about any of the warlords who are running the Iraqi government, you will certainly disappear and never be seen again.

Iraqi unity—but if you are Sunni and go to a Shiite area you will likely lose your head, even if you have a passport and visa. And if you are a Kurd who goes west into an Arab area, you stand a good chance of never coming back.

So I read the notice on the back of my Syrian residency permit with these bitter thoughts in mind—but what could I do? At least I was in a better position than hundreds of thousands of other refugees who did not even have a piece of paper. My three oldest children were born in Syria, but they have no papers, and to this day they are not citizens of any country on earth. They were never registered in Iraq, they do not have Syrian citizenship, they have been raised in the U.S. for seven years, but they do not even have green cards. They speak only English; they know only American culture; none of them know Kurdish, nor do they know anything about their extended family, their aunts and uncles and cousins. But even so, they are real Kurds: they have no citizenship anywhere; they live in fear and poverty; they may be targeted by the U.S. government for deportation at any time; and their only crime is having been born to Kurdish parents.

Even in Syria, if they had been born there to parents who were Arabs from an Arabian country, they would have been given Syrian citizenship, but they were not allowed to be Syrian citizens only because their parents were Kurds. There are about half a million Kurdish immigrants from Turkey in Syria who arrived after World Wars I and II, but they still do not have Syrian citizenship and they are not allowed to own property. And in the U.S., if a person comes as a refugee and stays for five years, he is entitled to citizenship—but my wife and three oldest children have not been given U.S. citizenship, although we have all lived here for more than seven years. My children are victims of a crime that neither they nor their parents committed. We are paying for being Muslims and Kurds. This, and nothing else.

Going to the UN

The notice on the back of my residency card, my experience with Iraqi politics, and my concern about the safety of my wife and daughter caused me a lot of concern for the future. The joy of finding a job—the lowest job in Syrian society, but a job nevertheless—soon faded as I had daily discussions with my friends in college and elsewhere about the right course to follow. The problem was not a personal one, since neither my wife nor I had done anything wrong, but in the Middle East you do not have to do something wrong to be arrested, tortured, and executed. So it was a daily concern to plan how to avoid these kinds of troubles. That was the reality of our lives.

Many people advised me to apply as a refugee to the UN office in Damascus, but I was doubtful about it because I did not want to go the West. One day I said to my friend Anas Abdullah that I did not want to apply to the UN refugee program because I was afraid they would send me to Europe. He started laughing.

"Kak Yassin," he said. "Thousand of families are refugees under the UN program, and some of them have been waiting more than five years and still have not had a chance to follow their dream to Europe. Do you think that if you apply today, by tomorrow they will come and take you to the airport and fly you off to Europe?"

"Maybe not," I said. "But one day it will happen."

"Maybe," said Kak Anas. "And maybe it will happen for your children and not for you."

"So why should I apply?" I asked.

"You get two benefits," said Kak Anas. "First, you will be under UN protection, so if the Syrian government cancels your residency permit they cannot send you right back to Iraq. And second, the UN will help you financially, especially with medicine and the possibility of traveling."

"So you think I should apply."

"Why not? You should use any opportunity to help your family and make your life easier."

"But I don't want to go to the West, and I don't want to live on handouts."

"It is our right. Do you think that the people who presently get help from the UN are more worthy than we are? Do you know how much they take every year from Iraqi oil to help Iraqi refugees?"

"What about you?" I asked.

"I applied, but they denied my request," Kak Anas said. "I applied again, and they denied me again."

"So why would they accept me?" I said. "You are from Kirkuk and I am not." In 1995 Kirkuk was still under the control of the Iraqi government, but the rest of Kurdistan was under *peshmerga* control. Kurds living in Kirkuk could get refugee status because they had to flee from Saddam. But in the rest of Kurdistan the Kurds were self-governing, so they were not given refugee status.

"Just apply and see what happens," said Kak Anas. "Hundreds of families have been denied, but you never know what is in God's plan."

So I went to the UN office, asked for an application, and paid someone to help me to fill it out, as is the custom when one doesn't know the language required on the application. I submitted it and they gave me an appointment for an interview—in two months.

For that interview, however, I received a great deal of advice from my friends: "The UN will ask about your background and why you came here. What problems caused you to leave your country? They will ask about your job, your health, your family, and many other things. You have to be prepared with detailed answers." I told them what my father had always said: "The truth speaks for itself. If you speak the truth, you don't have to worry that a lie will catch up with you." I knew many people who were so desperate to get to Europe as refugees that they made up stories claiming they were Communists and the Islamists had threatened to execute them, or they were in love with a girl and under tribal rules their family would have to kill them, or they were Kurds living in Kirkuk or Baghdad and had to flee from Saddam. What could I say, except what was true?

Two months later, on our way to the interview, my wife asked what we should say. I told her to just answer the questions.

"But they will ask us about everything," she said.

"Then you just tell them the answer to everything," I said.

"But they will interview us separately."

"The truth is one and the same. If we don't lie, there will be no contradiction."

My wife just smiled and shook her head. "I know you want them to deny our application," she said. "Everyone has told me to prepare my answers in concert with my husband, and to practice them over and over before the interview."

So we went without any preparation.

After the interviewer obtained the basic information about our family and background, he said to me, "Kurdistan is free. What is your problem?"

I said, "My problem is the freedom."

"What do you mean?" he said, surprised.

"Look what has happened," I said. "Freedom has closed all our schools. Freedom has closed all the hospitals. Freedom has turned off all our electricity. There is no fuel, no phone, no mail. Freedom has made ninety percent of us jobless. Freedom has forced eighty percent of us to carry a gun. Freedom has made seventy-five new political groups appear. Each group has its own state, and we cannot go from one city to another without asking permission. In the time of the dictator, people could not criticize the president or his group, but now we have hundreds of presidents and groups who fight all the time. Formerly people used to disappear in the night. Now people disappear in the middle of the day. Now we are free to kill each other and destroy our own land. But we can't criticize any warlord, or they are likely to kill us. Freedom closed all of the courtrooms. Freedom has cancelled the law. People have the right to carry guns and kill you, but without the law and without the police there is no protection. I am fleeing from freedom!"

The interviewer laughed and said, "Do you want Saddam back?"

"This is the problem," I said. "They give you the choice of a dictator or a civil war—choose one. I want neither of those choices." I was starting to get mad. "I want my family to be safe and my children to go to college. I want that choice."

The interviewer looked at me for awhile and did not ask any more questions. He shook my hand and told me to come back in three weeks for the result. I thanked him and tried to smile.

As we came out of the interview, my wife said, "I know that you did not want to be accepted."

"Oh, stop," I told her. "We need it."

"So why did you talk crazy like that?" she said

"What was I supposed to say?" I retorted. "He said, 'Now Kurds are free, so why are you asking to become a refugee?' and I answered him."

My wife shook her head as a sign of disapproval. "There is no medicine for you," she said. "You just can never control your mouth!"

"The one who conceals the truth is a dumb Satan," I told her.

"The one who tells the truth will always be poor, jobless, and attacked," she replied.

I laughed and asked her which one she wanted me to choose. She smiled back at me. "There is no cure for you."

After three weeks I went back to the UN office. A big crowd had gathered and many of them were cursing. It was like a demonstration. Someone told me that the people cursing had just learned they'd been denied.

"How can I find my name?" I asked. I was told there was an alphabetical list of names on the wall of those who had been approved. Before I could reach the list, one of my friends found me and congratulated me. He took me to the wall and put his finger below my name: Yassin Muhiddin Aref—APPROVED.

Remembering what Zuhur had said, I started laughing. I was not sure whether to say *Thank you, God, for this approval*, or *Sorry, God, for this approval*, but I thought I should always thank God regardless of what is given, because God always knows what is behind it. So I just said, *Thank you, God*. I did not want to go, but the acceptance was so unexpected that it was hard not to think that God was behind it. There must be some purpose to this approval.

I was still laughing when I came home and Zuhur asked what had happened. When I said that we had been accepted, she did not believe me. I told her about all the people who were really mad because they had been denied, and I told her that tomorrow I would take her to see our name on the wall, which I did. I told her again, "The truth speaks for itself. You do not need training if you do not make up a story."

Breaking the Iron Wall

After I was accepted into the UN refugee program I felt as though I could relax a little and enjoy Sham. Sham in ancient times was the land in what is now Syria, Lebanon, Palestine, and Jordan, but now when people refer to Sham they are referring to Damascus. I remembered a line of a poem written by Jigarkhwin, one of the famous Syrian Kurdish poets: "Sham is sugar, but my land is even sweeter." I found Sham to be very very sweet, and believed that it also was my land as a Muslim because part of my history was there. In a huge area of Damascus called the Kurdish Zone, many places have Kurdish names; hundred of families have Kurdish backgrounds (except that they have long since forgotten the language); and Salahuddin (known to the West as Saladin, the conqueror of the Crusaders) is buried in Damascus, along with hundreds of other famous Kurdish leaders, poets, and scholars.

I felt as though a new life was beginning for me. It was true that Syria was a poor country and did not have real freedom or democracy, but it was so much better than Iraq that I felt it was the gateway to the world. In Iraq we lived behind an "iron wall" that kept us isolated from the world and allowed us to see only what the government wanted us to see. You just cannot see things correctly if you are viewing them through twisted, darkened glass. Your knowledge and thinking will be very limited if you have no access to the world and no contact with other cultures, because you never hear a different point of view or compare your culture with others. I was really thirsty for knowledge, and life in Damascus made all of this possible for me.

Ninety percent of the students at Abu Noor University, which I was attending, were foreigners who came from over fifty different counties. Every kind of book was available, and there were many publishers in Damascus and Lebanon to keep the latest ideas flowing. Damascus was the most popular gateway to Kurdistan, so many Kurds returning from Europe came through Damascus with the latest information. There were also many Westerners in Damascus, as well as Arabs from different countries. All this made life very exciting, and learning was easy in such a diverse and intellectual atmosphere. In Kurdistan we used to look at other nations and their people as fundamentally different from us—especially Arab nations. But when I saw all these foreigners each day and talked with them, listened to them, and exchanged ideas with them, I began to see them as individuals, struggling like I was to escape from the limitations that culture had placed on them.

After I was jailed in Albany on terrorism charges, one day an inmate asked me if I were a terrorist. I smiled at him and asked him why he thought that.

"Because you look like a terrorist," he said. "You have a beard."

I said, "What answer would you like—yes or no?"

He was surprised at my answer and repeated his question. "Are you a terrorist?"

"If I were really a terrorist, do you think I would tell you? And if I say I am not a terrorist, you will not believe me."

He looked even more surprised. But I liked his sympathy, and so I smiled at him. When two people come from very different traditions and cultures, sometimes understanding starts with a smile and some sympathy.

My family was from the house of the Prophet, and people believed that because of our genealogy we had special holy powers. Whenever my uncle or grandfather or even my illiterate dad walked on the street, people ran to them to get a blessing. I do not believe that you can get a special blessing just from touching someone's clothes, but I do think you can get a blessing from religious scholars by learning from them and following their advice and imitating their character and manners. Now when I walk in the prison, people do not come close to get a blessing— they often avoid me. Perhaps they are afraid that I might blow myself up. This fear is the fruit of ignorance, and ignorance is the result of not using our minds. Many people never use their minds, but rather see through other eyes, and hear through other ears, and think what others have told them to think. Such people can never find the truth. There is so much propaganda now in the West that portrays religious people of Islam as wild and dangerous radicals instead of holy men, teachers and helpers of others, and this misconception really bothers me. In Islam, God sent the Prophet to mankind as an act of mercy, so that if we follow God we must always show mercy to all mankind.

When I was growing up, I was taught that I should show my love of my country by how much I hated other countries—especially Arab countries. If I were a real Kurd, I must hate Arab countries. If I wanted to build Kurdistan, I must destroy Turkey. The same iron wall of isolation is not built around the West, yet most Westerners do not seem to know much of what happens outside their countries. They only see and hear what the media broadcasts, and they believe that what the media tells them is the correct interpretation. Why don't we try to learn and think on our own, and keep an open mind? It is not just a question of trusting the media or the government to tell us the truth. The point is to activate our tools—our eyes and ears, hearts and minds—and use them to improve our ability to think and make intelligent decisions.

If we could all leave our prejudices behind, we would solve half of our problems. When I was growing up in Iraq, everything that I learned about America was from two sources: the Iraqi media, which was owned by the government, and the Kurdish revolution. Day and night they repeated the propaganda that America was the imperialist, colonialist enemy of freedom for all countries and the greedy exploiter of oil. Even the Kurdish revolution propaganda described America as the capitalist enemy of freedom and blood-shedder of other nations. There was no other point of view, no satellite TV, no Internet, no foreign visitors to turn our minds in a different direction. So whether we wanted it or not, the media shaped us—unless, of course, an individual decided not to believe the media and kept an open mind until he could check the information for himself. When you can do that, you are really free and you can become yourself. And if you reject that, then you give your mind and heart over to someone else to control, and your existence is reduced to a body instead of a being.

This was the most important thing that I learned in Syria. My Sheikh (teacher) had told me repeatedly that the shortest and easiest way to knowledge was to ask a single question: "Why?" It doesn't matter how much you trust and believe in someone—when he tells you to do this or not to do that, ask him why, and see what he says. In my culture, children were never allowed to ask why; many times when my father beat me, I did not understand why and could not ask. Even the government had a policy that required all citizens to obey an order first, and only later ask why. But God gave everyone a mind, not just the rulers. Why do all of us have eyes? It is our individual responsibility to find the truth and to speak it. In Syria I found, for example, that it was not true that Arabs were our enemies. They were actually very kind, simple people, they loved Kurds, they respected Kurdish scholars, and they felt sorry for what the Kurds had gone through.

Later when I came to America, I discovered that many things I had heard about this country were just not true. One day in jail, Mr. Steve asked me why, in a November 1994 speech in Chamchamal for a Kurdish Islamic group (which the government used at my trial), I had said that President Clinton was Jewish.

"Because he is a Jew," I said. It seemed self-evident.

"What??" said Mr. Steve.

"President Clinton is Jewish," I said. "Everyone knows that."

Mr. Steve started to laugh and told me that he was definitely not Jewish. But I swear by God that was my information at the time.

The same was true about one of my diary entries in 1999, in which I wrote that America was "religion-less." At that time, I did not know that wherever you went in America, you always found churches. I did not know that a majority of Americans went to church every Sunday. I did not know that there were hundreds of charities in America, or that many people gave up to ten percent of their incomes to charity, or that people asked others to pray for them, or that when they sneezed someone would always say "God bless you."

Now I know it is simply not true to say that America is "religion-less."

For me and for millions like me, especially in poor nations like Kurdistan, we have only the excuse that we never had a chance to educate ourselves, or to travel, or to find ways to search for answers. But how can I excuse people who are educated and can travel easily, and who have the latest innovations to search for answers, and still do not make the effort to learn? How can we be proud of our diversity and our open-mindedness while at the same time we are afraid of a person with a beard and believe this to be a sign that he is about to blow himself up? I hope everyone who reads this book will be more open-minded as a result, and will promise not to blindly follow people until it is clear that the person is speaking the truth. The key is always to ask why, and to do nothing until you are sure that you understand why you are doing something, and that it is right to do it. I wrote a poem about this.

Why?

If you claim to be independent and free
Never be shy.
Before you obey any order that's given
Always ask why.

Don't imitate others, or copy someone
Or believe in a lie.
Try to understand first if it really is true
If not, then deny.

Jamei Abi Noor (Abu Noor University)

Some Westerners have described Damascus as the city of minarets. Others have said that in Damascus, next to every mosque is another mosque, and between each of these mosques there are yet other mosques. Each mosque has at least one minaret from which the call to prayer is sounded five times a day, so that at the hour of prayer the whole city vibrates like a violin from the joyous chants. In 1997, a group of citizens asked the government to stop the call to prayer over the loudspeakers, especially in the early morning, and they used as an excuse the hardship that the noise gave to patients in the hospital. A group of Imams opposed the idea, and it was decided to interview the patients in the hospital to see what they thought. It turned out that ninety-three percent of them said they loved the sound, and five out of six Christian patients who were interviewed said they liked to hear the call and were not bothered by it.

One of the mosques was called Abu Noor, and was part of the university that I attended and from which I graduated. Abu Noor was a big complex, with a huge eight-story building that included four colleges, two institutes, and one high school. In addition, there was a summer camp and a special training facility for converts to Islam. Abu Noor was the main center in the world for Sufism, which is one of the many different schools of thought in Islam. There are many different schools of thought within Sufism as well, but in general all Sufis believe in avoiding politics and violence of any kind; self-purification; *jihad* directed at fighting your own desires and learning to control them; rejection of sensual pleasure; isolation from the world in order to concentrate on God; and punishing the body to strengthen the soul. Sufis are focused on the Prophet's love, and they proclaim that love without necessarily worrying too much about knowledge and science. They are focused on their preparation for the next life, and tend to neglect the present worldly life and its joys.

The founder and leader of Abu Noor at that time was Sheikh Ahmad Kaftaro. He was Kurdish but he did not speak the language, and he was regarded as the world head of the Naqshbandis Sufi movement. At least 25,000 people attended his Friday services each week, and his words were simultaneously translated into more than ten languages because of his great knowledge and the respect that people had for him. The Syrian government appointed him as head of religious scholars, and he represented Syria in hundreds of international conferences. In 1986, Sheikh Kaftaro was chosen as the head of all interfaith activity. In the West he was called the Muslim Pope, and he met the Christian Pope in the Vatican many times, as well as most of the political and religious leaders of the world, including Americans. His son, Dr. Salah Kaftaro, was the head of the college. At that time, it was impossible for any Iraqi to study in a Syrian university, but Abu Noor was an exception because it wasn't run by the Syrian government. It accepted Iraqis because of Sheikh Kaftaro, and the college was supported by Libya, not Syria. Still, there was only a small handful of Iraqi Kurds like me studying there.

The university was known for its courses in comparative religion, which were enriched by the interfaith activity of Sheikh Kaftaro, and he had students from all over the world. I followed a course in Islamic studies, and after four years I graduated and enrolled in a master's degree program. I finished the first year of the program, but in the middle of the second year I was approved by the UN for resettlement in the United States. I came to America hoping to finish my master's degree and Ph.D., but I didn't have the chance because I had to take care of my family and education was too expensive. Instead I had to comfort myself with what my father used to tell me: "Life is the real school. You can learn best from experience." I hope that my children will progress in school and get the master's and Ph.D. degrees that so far have eluded me.

Two Kurds

Wherever I go, I find that people who are in the minority in society have better relationships with one another than with the majority, especially when other factors bring them together. One of my neighbors in Qudsaya was Abu Suhaib. He was Kurdish, although he could not speak the language. His grandfather had immigrated to Kurdistan from Turkey after the First World War. After he found out that I was Kurdish, he visited me and we became friends. We were both poor. We prayed together and faced the same problems together, and it made our relationship stronger.

Abu Suhaib represented the life of most people in Syria, especially those who worked in government offices and received a monthly salary. In the Middle East, there are very few private companies. Everything belongs to the government—schools, hospitals, banks, electricity, phones—so all the people who work in these fields work for the government. But it was well known that a monthly salary would not provide for such workers for even half a month, and usually the last ten days of every month they had to take out a loan to buy food. There was no way that their income would cover their expenses, especially for those who paid rent.

Abu Suhaib did not have to pay rent because his father had died and left him a small house, but still his income was not enough because he had to feed his mother, his sick brother, and his wife, as well as his four daughters and one son. All of them depended on him. He was an electrician who worked in a hospital. Every day he needed to take two or three buses to get to work. He told me that when his father had first moved to Qudsaya, it was a small village with only a couple of families living there. Land was almost free, but his father did not buy any, even though he could have bought a big farm, because he was waiting to go back to Kurdistan. He was Sufi, and all he wanted was "bread for today"; he did not care about tomorrow, and yesterday was over. Like most immigrants, year by year he waited to go back...and like most immigrants, he continued to wait, generation after generation.

Like most Syrians, Abu was always looking for a second job. People were always calling him to do something in their homes, to fix a refrigerator or take care of other electrical problems. Many people told me that Abu did not take money for these small jobs. One day I asked him if this were true.

He said, "Most of the people know me because we were among the first residents in this city, and it does not make sense for me to charge my friends and neighbors for calling me to change a light bulb. If it is an hour's job, let me get paid, but for simple stuff it is not worth it."

"But it is not just one person and not just one time," I said. "And your economic situation is not so good."

"Kak Yassin," he said, "that is not the way I grew up. My father's pleasure was in helping people."

"But now the times are changing."

"Humans may be changing," Abu said. "But the pleasure is still the same."

One day I went to a friend's store to buy some vegetables, and I found Abu Suhaib taking care of the store. "Are you working here?" I said.

"Not right now," he said. "The owner went to pray and he told me to watch his store. Usually I work every day stacking items and cleaning the store, and I get some fruit and vegetables for it."

Just then the owner, Abo Rami, came back. With a big smile, he said *"Ahlan wa Sahlan,"* which means "welcome, please feel relaxed." After some talk and some jokes, Abu Suhaib left. Abo Rami asked me if I knew Abu Suhaib.

"Yes," I said.

"He is a good man. I try to help him. Look, I put up a sign for him in case someone needs an electrical repair job. If they do, I call him. Many times I have told him to fix up the store so that I can give him some income. He thinks I don't care about him because I will not hire him full-time. But in the mornings he goes to the hospital, and in the evenings I am here, so how can I hire him? Besides, I don't have that much in the store to do."

Abo Rami was an engineer, but now he sold vegetables. Not only him—there were thousands like him. After government workers finished their daily work, they needed a second job like this. I knew this, but still I asked Abo Rami why he sold vegetables even though he was an engineer.

He looked at me and smiled. "I have to sell vegetables because no one in this country uses maps, especially your Kurdish people who live in Syria. Their buildings are all like caves. There is no way for a car to get there. There is no way to collect trash. They build by themselves without government approval. The government uses that as the reason for not giving them any services, and tomorrow the government will demolish the buildings because they were not built in a civilized way. Even those that the government has approved are just some buildings that a small contractor built in the same way that his grandfather built them a hundred years ago. So there is no need for engineers in our country."

"So why did you study engineering in college?" I asked him. "You would have done better to go to a farm college."

"It was my father's mistake," he said. "My father told me that life can change, and that an engineer can rebuild the country in a modern way. But Father was wrong. We don't need to change houses to palaces. We need to change the people who are living in palaces, so they will put those who live in simple houses first. Practically, I work like a Kurd, and I am emotional like a Kurd, and I would be proud to be one of you," he said.

"Thank you very much," I said.

Before I left the store, I told him that if he promised to accept the money, I would take some tomatoes, but if not I would buy them from another store. I knew that if I took anything, he would not let me pay for it. In our culture, many sellers will not take money from people whom they know well.

"Be a good brother," he said. "Don't separate our accounts."

"You are my big brother," I said. "But running a store is different." I started to leave, but he told me to take the tomatoes. So I told him a story.

A Kurdish student in Damascus did not speak much Arabic. He went to a store to buy tomatoes, but he wanted to make sure that he could select the tomatoes by touch. In Syria, sellers do not want you to touch the vegetables, so they will select them for you. But the student did not know how to say in Arabic that he wanted to select his own tomatoes. After awhile, he remembered the Arabic word for "voting" (*tasweet*), which he thought was similar to the Arabic word that means "choosing" (and can also mean "electing" or "election"—*intikhab*). So he asked the store owner, "Uncle, do you have voting for your tomatoes?"

And the owner said, "No. There is no democracy here for the vegetables."

It was a crime that Abo Rami had to sell vegetables. That was what prevented real change from happening in the Middle East. If he were living in the West, he would have been a professor because he was a talented, thoughtful person. Or he might have had a job with a big construction company. But this is life in the East: we struggle to death to finish college, and after that we must look for a village job as a gardener, or push a cart, or drive a taxi, or sell vegetables. I do not say that these are low jobs, and I have full respect for anyone who does them. It is an honor to work hard, and I did my share of such jobs. But shouldn't people have a chance to work in the profession for which they are trained? It is wrong for an engineer to drive a taxi and for a professor to sell vegetables to feed his family. And it is wrong for illiterate people to run the country.

I told Abo Rami that I enjoyed working as a gardener because my dad was a farmer and I had lived in a village. He laughed and said, "But I am not Kurdish. Why should I live like one?" I joked that for centuries they had been trying to change Kurdish nationality—so now we would welcome him as a Kurdish citizen. Abo Rami laughed and said, pointing at the tomatoes, "You cannot touch them. I will feel them for you."

"I am not Iraqi anymore," I told him.

"Yeeeeh," he said. "We are all the same in the *Iier*." (Which means we are all facing the same problems and looking for solutions).

I took some tomatoes and I left the store. Whenever I would see him after that, I would joke with him and ask, "Uncle, do you have voting tomatoes?"

And he would reply, "No. We do not believe in democracy."

Amazing Rawand

In 1997, on the ninth anniversary of the Halabja massacre, a photography and video show was presented in Damascus on the tragedy. Like thousands of other Iraqis in Damascus, I went to the show, which ran for three days. Each day I met with many different people and talked to them about the situation in Iraq. One day I had an opportunity to talk with two Kurdish artists: Ashti Mahdi, who was a sculptor in stone, and Kak Showony, who did drawings and photographs. We talked about the importance of photographs in today's society and the problem of reality. How do you know whether the photograph, which appears to record actual events, actually does so? How do we, as Kurds, confirm the thousands of tragic events throughout our history when no photographs were available and often no contemporaneous written records were made?

Kak Ashti remarked that in the West, people often prefer a picture or a caricature, since many of them don't have the time for reading. They read in cars, buses, and trains, where it is difficult to concentrate for long on serious subjects, and so they like pictures with short captions that get the point across in one small, easily grasped unit. Westerners also like cartoons, especially on serious subjects, spiced with jokes or irony. In the Middle East, artists do not generally caricature those in power in a funny or disrespectful way, and for obvious reasons do not openly oppose their policies.

I told the artists that when I was growing up, there was a sign on the door of my school that read, "If the President Said It, Then All Iraqis Say It." One day I told a friend that the sign was right. He looked at me in shock that I would say such a thing.

"What happened?" he said. "They bought you too?"

"No," I said. "I did not get any money from them."

"Have you lost your mind?"

"I don't believe so."

"So how can you say that the sign is true?"

"What do you take the sign to mean?" I asked him.

"That all Iraqis are behind the president and support him in whatever he says and does."

"I don't believe so," I said. "I think the sign means, 'All Iraqis are forbidden to oppose. If the president says something, no one can have another word.'"

My friend laughed and agreed with me. In fact, in most Middle Eastern countries—not just Iraq—the situation is the same. When it comes to speaking the truth, people are like the dead: they say nothing. Instead they have to dance and sing praises to the leader. No one can oppose the dictator.

Kak Ashti also agreed with my story and said, "In this regard we are far behind Western countries."

"Whatever the West has," I said, "was not gotten by a miracle. They got it by struggle. They struggled to get out of the Dark Ages and they paid a high price for it. But they were able to change the basis of their culture from nonsense stories to scientific knowledge and rational thinking. We are still stuck in the past. We worship at the graves of religious figures and dead presidents and hope to get medical cures or fulfill our dreams."

Kak Showony said, "Kak Yassin, you are the first Mala I have ever heard talk like this!"

During our conversation, a handsome young boy who knew Kak Ashti and Kak Showony came over to us and was introduced to me as Kak Rawand. He said he had heard about me and wanted to talk to me. I was surprised. The youth looked like someone who pretended to be Western and who spent his time getting high and searching for girlfriends. What could he want with me?

But it was Kak Rawand's name that got my attention. It was the first time I had ever met a person with that name, and I liked it immediately. We Kurds use names to explain what we are or what we need. The most popular names show what we dream about: Rizgar means "free"; Azad means "independent"; Nabaz means "undefeated"; Chalak means "active"; Sarbarz means "the one who stands proud"; Khabat means "struggling." My own children's names reflect these values. Alaa, my oldest daughter's name, means "flag"—as in national flag, our Kurdish dream. Raiber, my oldest son's name, means "guide"—one who shows the right way. Kotcher, my youngest son's name, means "immigrant," because we were coming to America when he was born. Dilnia, my baby daughter's name, means "certain"—she was born after I was arrested, and I wanted my wife and family to be certain that everything would be OK.

Rawand means "wanderer"—one without a residence, homeless, forever a traveler. It is a male name, otherwise I might have used it for my first child (my daughter). The boy Rawand held my hand in the Middle Eastern custom and said, "I'm really glad I found you today."

"I was not lost," I smiled back.

Rawand said, "I want to test all of you and see what kind of artists you are."

"I'm not an artist," I said.

"I'm referring to these other two gentlemen," Rawand said. Turning to them, he said, "In your opinion, what is the most beautiful picture in the show?"

The two artists looked around for a moment, and then Kak Ashti pointed to one picture, and Kak Showony pointed to another.

"You should go back to school," Rawand said, laughing. "I don't know how you got your degrees."

I was shocked by this kid. How could he speak with such disrespect to people much older and more accomplished than he was? They were professional artists, and Rawand looked like a lost youth. But would he speak like this if he did not know about art?

"Let me show you a real Mona Lisa," Rawand said, and pointed to another picture.

The picture was of a sitting girl, two or three years old, looking at the sky. There was deep fear in her face. Her eyes were open and red from chemical gas, and they were full of tears.

"Why is this your favorite picture?" I said to Rawand, to test what he knew about art.

"Because this picture tells you the whole story of Halabja," he said.

"How?"

"The dead bodies surrounding her in the background tell us that she lost all of her family. The red in her eyes tells us that she was in a gas attack. The tears tell us of the pain she was in. She was looking up for help, but no help came. Her eyes were open because she still had hope for survival and for her future. Her eyes were complaining to God, but she is no longer living, and in death she is frozen in time. This is not some sentimental tableau by a romantic artist. It is a photograph."

I could not believe that this boy could say all that about a picture. As he talked, he reminded me of how I explained the art show for the mayor in Chamchamal when I was fourteen years old. Rawand said that if this picture were exhibited in Sweden, it would be seen all over the world and would win medals.

"So send it to your mom," Kak Showony said.

"Oh, your mom is in Sweden?" I asked.

"Yes," said Rawand.

Kak Ashti said, "Kak Yassin, be careful. He has had no problem on other occasions speaking for ten hours straight. Don't get him started."

"What did he say?" I asked.

"Oh, everything," said Kak Ashti. "Whatever he can think of—art, history, patriotism, sports."

"I must go," said Kak Showony.

We all decided to go with him, but outside we split up. Rawand went with me.

"Where do you live?" I asked.

"I'm homeless," he said.

I assumed that he meant this in a poetic way—that we Kurds have no land—so I told him to stop philosophizing.

"No," he said. "I really am homeless."

"Do you mean that you have no place to stay?"

"Last night I slept in the mosque," he said. "But they woke me up and put me out the door, so I had to walk around on the street all night. When they opened the mosque in the early morning, I went back and slept in a corner. No one saw me, and when they came for noon prayers they woke me up."

I said to myself, *So I am right. He's a lost youth.* Aloud I asked him, "What about your family?"

"My mom lives in Stockholm," he said. "She brought us here, and we are waiting for our papers."

"Who else is with you?"

"My dad. Two other brothers and my little sister."

"So where are they?"

"They live in Doomar."

"Oh, that is just ten minutes from where I live," I said. "Why aren't you living with your family?"

"The day before yesterday I got into a fight with my dad and brother and I left them."

"So what are you going to do?"

"I don't know. But someone told me to speak to you." Rawand smiled. "You are Mala Yassin, are you not?"

I smiled back and said that my name was just Yassin, and that it was my dad who wanted me to be a Mala—but I was not.

"But people do call you Mala Yassin." I knew that he wanted to make sure he had come to the right person.

"Yes," I said. "Some people."

"I was looking for you for a long time," he said. "Now I've found you, but unfortunately I am in this situation."

"I am sorry for you," I said. "But I have only one small room where I live with my wife and daughter. If I had two rooms…"

"Kak Yassin, I was not looking for you to put me up. I heard a lot about you. I just wanted to meet you. I am sure I can learn a lot from you."

"Perhaps the opposite is true," I said. "Maybe I can learn from you."

"Well, I will let you go back to your family," he said. "But please keep in touch with me. I need to talk more with you."

"And where will you go?"

"I don't know. Maybe I can find someplace."

"Let's go," I said.

"No," Rawand said. "You have only one room."

"I have three friends who live by themselves. I will take you to one of them and you can stay there at least until tomorrow."

I took Rawand to my friend Kak Ali's house and introduced him. He agreed to let him stay the night, and then I went home. But there was something about Rawand that would not let me go. Here was this handsome boy who looked like he was from Norway, with a completely European outlook. How dangerous it was to let a youth dressed like that wander around the streets at night. What about his parents? How could his father sleep without knowing where his son was? Suppose he fell into the hands of bad people? What if the security police picked him up? Thousands of questions came to mind. And I was still in shock that he could be so smart, and know so much about so many things, and be so confident in talking with adults. He was no more than fifteen years old, and this must have been the first time he was ever homeless. Of course, all Kurds are homeless, but this was literal. It was not like the U.S. or Europe, where you can stay on the street the whole night or sleep in a bus station or a park. In the Middle East everything closes before midnight, and if the police or security forces find you outside after midnight, they will certainly stop you or even arrest you.

Early the next morning I went to bring Kak Rawand to my home. He was still sleeping, and Ali and I had to wake him up.

"Good morning, Kak Yassin," he said. "I am very sorry. Just give me one minute and I will be ready." He sounded as though he was in a rush to leave.

"We have plenty of time," I said.

He thanked Kak Ali and we left and headed to my house. I asked Rawand how his night was.

"Kak Ali did not let me sleep until 3 a.m.," he said.

"I told him to let you rest," I said. "And I told you not to start telling him your story."

"I did not talk about myself," he said. "We talked about other things."

"Art or politics?"

"Your friend is very nationalistic."

"And what about you?"

"I try to be bigger that that," Rawand said. "We should open our minds to the universe—it is much wider than we can imagine."

"What is wrong with loving your country?" I said. I was testing him to see what he would say.

"It is not a problem to love our land and people, but we should not believe we are better than other nations and be proud of our nationality only. How is it the fault of other people that they were born to a different culture?"

"Oh, you're a Communist?" I asked, still testing him.

"Are you repeating their propaganda that whoever is not an arrogant nationalist is certainly a Communist?" Rawand asked. "If I say my nation is not better than other nations, and that I am not different from other humans, that doesn't make me a Communist."

"So where did you get this idea from?"

"From Islam. Islam tells me that all humans are from Adam, and Adam is from the dust. Arabs are not better than non-Arabs, nor are non-Arabs better than Arabs, nor are whites better than blacks, nor are blacks better than whites. These are Mohammad's words, are they not?"

"Yes," I said. "Those are his words."

"So would you say that Mohammad was a Communist?"

"*Astaghfirullah!*" I said (meaning, "I ask God's forgiveness for this impiety.")

Rawand said, "I believe we should not look at ourselves as though we are more special in God's eyes than other people, and our love for our country should not require that we hate or destroy other people's countries."

I was very pleased with what Rawand said, and I thought that his mind was developed like that of someone twice his age. But why was a kid so young talking like this? We arrived at the villa and the garden where I lived. When Rawand saw the villa, he was surprised, and asked if I lived in this palace.

"You think that I cannot pass as the proletariat?"

"You live here—so that must be why you don't like Communists," he said.

"Actually I am the gardener," I said. "I live behind the villa in that little red house in the corner of the garden. I have just one room, and that is why I took you to Kak Ali's house yesterday."

Rawand and I talked all day. Indeed, as Kak Ashti predicted, he was an impressive talker and left no subject untouched. We talked about his family, why he was in Syria, what problems he had, politics, philosophy, and many other matters. He was smart, articulate, emotional, and very kind. He knew about history, sports, geography, and philosophy. I was surprised that although he looked like a lost kid, he really wasn't.

Finally I said to him, "Kak Rawand, I would like one thing from you."

"Whatever you want I will be glad to do it."

"I would like you to go back to your home," I said. "I will come with you."

"Kak Yassin," he said, "I will do anything else, but please, not that."

"But you just told me that you would be glad to do anything I asked. Now the first thing I ask from you, you refuse."

"I told you. What happened is too much. I cannot go back."

"Nothing is too much. Whatever we do is never enough to repay our parents for what they have done for us."

"But it concerns my brother. My father supports only him."

"He is your big brother. Too bad that you cannot support him also, simply because of your father."

"Kak Yassin," he said. "I know that you don't have a place for me, but I would be glad to sleep outside here under a tree. I would be happier here than to go back."

"Of course we can find places for you to stay," I said. "But it would not be right, because if you want to be religious, you have to prove it by being patient with your parents and serving them. Do you understand that God will never be pleased with you if your parents are not? Tomorrow they will say, 'Where is our son? Yassin took him from us!' Nobody will ever respect you if they know that you fled from your home. In our culture, disrespecting your parents is the biggest sign that a person is not a good man."

"Do you want me to lose my mind?"

"Follow the Kurdish way," I said. "The punishment of the parents makes the child grow up faster. As to your brother, as the Kurds say, 'He can cut your flesh, but he will never break your bones.'"

"Why should I give my parents even my flesh?" Rawand joked.

"Because we owe them," I said. "And they never want something bad for us. But the problem is that we see things differently because we live in different times and have different ideas. It is not easy for them to understand these new views. They want us to deal with them in the same way that they dealt with their own parents half a century ago."

Rawand laughed. "I wish they understood that."

"Imam Ali used to say, 'Let your children be children in their time. Don't try to make them be children in your time, which is over.'"

"Why don't Imams preach such things today?" Rawand asked.

"Some of them do."

"Culture and ignorant nationalism hold us down and keep us from changing," he said.

"Listen," I said. "We've talked the whole day, it's 5 p.m., and I know you well enough by now to believe that you could continue talking all night. We have no more time, and I can't promise you a new age. Let's go to your parents. I don't want you to say no again. For the moment, I am the dictator, and I want you to do this for me."

"I escaped from Iraq and ran away from dictators," he said, laughing.

I took his hand and we went to his home. I rang the bell. His brother opened the door. I greeted him and asked if he would call his father. After a moment, his father appeared. "Peace be upon you," he said. "You are welcome here. Please come in."

"No, Uncle," I said. "I brought Rawand back to you. He promised me that he would do his best to help you and obey you. But please, watch his brother, and don't let him bother Rawand."

"Who are you?" the father asked in surprise.

"I am Yassin, Rawand's friend."

"Are you a Mala?"

"Some people call me that," I said. "But my name is Yassin only."

"Please, please come in," he said.

"Next time," I replied. "But please help Rawand to help you."

"We need nothing from him," said the father. "All I need is that he is willing to stay with us."

"He will, and he will do every possible thing for you," I said. "Really, you should be proud of Rawand. He is a very kind and brilliant person."

"Thank you," said the father.

"Kak Rawand," I said. "I will see you later. Don't argue with your brother and don't disrespect your father. You have no right to do that."

Rawand began crying. His father hugged him and said, "I'm sorry. It was not your fault."

I felt very good when I heard that, and I turned to leave. The father called after me, "Mala! I want you to bless our home."

I looked at them all. "God bless you," I said. And then I turned back and started walking down the street.

After that, Rawand came to see me almost daily. He helped me work in the garden and helped babysit my daughter. I thought that God had given my dead baby brother Jalal back to me, because Rawand was so much like Jalal. Later in 1997, Rawand was approved to go to Sweden with his family. He said that he did not want to go to Sweden, and wanted to stay with me. When I met the family again, his mom was crying and his dad was arguing with him, but Rawand kept saying that he did not want to go and he was going to stay in Damascus. I tried to persuade him, but nothing worked. For the second time I became a dictator, and I played the traditional role of big brother, ordering him to go without making any further objections.

"Why? Why?"

"Because you have no future here. If I could be sure that you could study in college here, and get a master's degree, and find a good job, and a place to live, and a wife—of course I would suggest that you stay. But you are likely to get none of these things if you stay here. Go build yourself up abroad, and after your career is a success come back, buy this villa, and I will be happy to be your gardener."

Eventually Rawand went with his family to Sweden, but after he arrived there he again left his family. Since he was under eighteen, he could not get a house by himself. He called me and said that he had been sleeping in the park or on the metro, until one night an old lady saw him and took him back to her home. The lady was rich and he was the only foreigner in the area. I told him to study hard and maybe he would become the next king, or at least the prime minister of Sweden.

In 1999, after he turned eighteen and obtained his emancipation papers, Rawand came back to Syria. He had grown up and was a tall, strong man. Now I looked like his little brother. I was very happy to see him and asked if he were going to buy the villa. He said, "Not yet. Actually I want to buy one in Lebanon. It is much better there than here."

"Why, is Lebanon closer to Sweden?" I chuckled.

"In Beirut there is more freedom, a better chance for an education, better business opportunities, more contacts with the West."

"I have never seen Lebanon," I said. "But they call Beirut the 'Eastern Paris.'"

Eventually Rawand went to Kurdistan, and then back to Sweden. Later I heard that the PUK appointed him chief of the Kurdish student organization there. I still don't know if he bought the villa—but surely I am still looking for a job as a gardener.

Chapter Ten ☪
Refugees

Refugee Camp

Most people in third world countries never travel because it is very expensive and difficult for them to get visas. Most of them do not even travel extensively inside their own countries. If they do, it is not for vacation or fun but for visiting family members or in connection with work. Usually they do not use hotels. Many people take years to save enough money for just one trip inside their own country.

After we learned that Kak Tarq, one of my wife's cousins, lived in Syria, we searched for him so we could visit him. We were told that he lived in an Iraqi refugee camp in Hasaka, which is the city center for Syrian-ruled Kurdistan. Hasaka is not an old city and not as large as Qamishly, the biggest Kurdish city in Syria, but it was made the provincial capital because it is not a purely Kurdish city like Qamishly. We had to cut back on many of our expenses until I was able to save some money, which unfortunately was just enough to cover our expenses for the journey, with nothing left to buy gifts for the family.

We made the nine-hour trip from Damascus to Hasaka by bus, and asked for the Iraqi refugee camp. No one had any idea where it was. After asking around for quite awhile, we found someone who told us that it was about an hour and a half from Hasaka. The man even knew Kak Tarq. To confirm that he knew the right Tarq, the man told us the name of Tarq's oldest son, Chalak. He also said that the camp was in Hasaka Province, but not in the city itself.

"Where can we find a bus for travel to the camp?" we asked.

"No bus goes there," he said. "Sometimes UN cars go, and sometimes a tractor from a nearby village goes."

"So how can we get there?"

"You have to walk, or you can take a taxi."

"How long will it take to walk?"

"About five hours—depending on how fast you walk, of course."

"What about a taxi?"

"It costs about three or four hundred lirah ($6–8)."

Oh my God, I said to myself, and took a deep breath. I asked my wife what she thought. She said, "Let us go back to Damascus. We cannot afford that."

"But we have come all this way," I said. "How can we go back without seeing them?"

"We cannot walk five hours through the desert, and we cannot afford a taxi," said Zuhur. "So what can we do?"

The man was Kurdish and was sympathetic to our problem. He said, "Wait right here. I am going to bring my nephew, and he will take you to the camp for half price—$4."

We thanked him. After about twenty minutes he came with a taxi that looked to be at least forty or fifty years old, which made us very nervous. We put in our bags, climbed in after them, and I said, "*Chaway Saida?*", which means "How are you, sir?" in Badinic Kurdish. Immediately the driver began to talk, but it was like Chinese to me; I understood only a few words because he spoke in the Badini dialect (or Kirmangi; I speak Sorani).

Soon we left the city and entered a dirt road. I felt as though I was going back to Hashazini. As we drove deeper into the desert on tiny dirt paths, we became scared and I asked the driver in Arabic where he was taking us.

"To the Iraqi camp," he answered.

"But what do people do in this desert?" I asked him. "No one can live on this land."

The man laughed and said, "The Syrian government is smart. This area cannot be used for anything. Nothing will grow here. So they rented it to the UN, and every month they get a million dollars for useless land."

"But how do people live here?" I asked. "How can they get food or clothing or shelter?"

"They are in a UN food program," he said. "Once a month they give them enough to last for another month—rice, sugar, flour, oil."

After two hours, we were covered in dust as though we were soldiers who had come from a desert battle. Finally we saw something in the distance. Our driver said, "There's the camp."

"Is it a camp or a prison?"

"What's the difference?" he said. "They cannot leave the camp except with a permit."

When we finally arrived, I thought we were in Uganda. I saw children—never have I seen such children, except in the news about Somalia. But when we got out of the car, I heard them speaking Kurdish. My wife was crying.

I gave the driver 200 lirah and thanked him for his help. I told him that if I had 2,000 lirah I would give it to him, and still it would not be enough for what he did.

He smiled. "Kurds are Kurds," he said. "I don't know why God created us."

"Please just wait one minute," I said. "Let me ask if Kak Tarq lives here."

I called one of the children over and asked if she knew of Kak Tarq. The child replied, "He is my dad." Immediately I called my wife over, and Zuhur asked the child what her mother's name was. "Awaz," the girl said. At this, Zuhur started crying hard, and the girl kissed her and showed her the house where the family was staying. I signaled to the driver that he should leave.

We were shocked to see these children, many of whom were not wearing any shoes and had on only old, ripped clothing. Flies covered their faces. I thought that I must have been taken to Africa or Darfur, but how was it that they were all speaking Kurdish? What had brought these Kurds to live in this desert without any means of support except "charity" from the UN? Could this jail possibly be better than the worst situation in Iraq? How could anyone be reduced any lower than this, or suffer more? I was speechless.

We entered what was called a house, but it was really a toilet with mud walls built around it. "*Assalamu-Alaikum* (May peace be upon you)," we said as we entered. Awaz hugged Zuhur and started crying. Tarq laughed loudly and told me that women's business was crying, but he shook my hand and hugged me too. "You must be Kak Yassin, Zuhur's husband," he said. He hugged me again. "I am glad to meet you." Then, laughing, Tarq said to his wife, "For God's sake, stop crying. Why do you make my cousin so sad? She came all this way to visit us." Then he turned to Zuhur. "Please don't imitate Awaz," he said. "She is always like this. She only knows how to cry."

We sat down and I said, "I'm sorry. I had no idea that you were living in these conditions."

Tarq began to curse the UN. "It was all my fault," he said. "Ask Awaz. I used to have a castle in Kirkuk. I had a restaurant, I drove a new car all the time. But we left everything in order to live free. They jailed us here, which is worse than Abu Ghraib. Every month they tell us that next month we will go to Europe. Month by month they delay us, and now after four years we are still here in this prison camp. Look at my children. They look like gorilla babies."

"But why did they put you here in the desert?" I asked.

"It is all business," Tarq said. "Maybe the UN people get $400 every month for rent, and $200 for electricity, and $500 for food, plus some medicine, all of which they're supposed to spend on us, but they don't spend even $50 on us. They all drive nice cars and live in five-star hotels, but they don't care anything for us."

"So why don't you leave?"

"Because every month we expect that we'll go to Europe," he said. "Besides, where can I go? I don't have any permit to live here in Syria. They won't let me work. I have no money because I sold everything I had in Iraq to pay for the travel to get here."

"I'm very sorry," I said. My eyes were full of tears.

Kak Tarq laughed and said, "Kak Yassin. Don't let the women affect you and get you crying too."

"You think men don't have hearts?" I said. "Why should men not feel any mercy?"

"Men should use their minds, not their emotions," Tarq said. "Every day when Awaz starts to cry, I start singing and laughing. Most of the people in the camp know when Awaz is crying, because they can hear me singing and laughing."

Awaz had been Tarq's brother's wife. When his brother died, Tarq married her to take care of her, even though she was ten years older than he was. In Kurdish culture, it is common that if a man dies, his brother will marry the widow, especially if he left small children, so they will be provided for. Kak Tarq was very young and a cultured Kurdish man. But sometimes he seemed like a villager—joking all the time, raising his voice, cursing at his children, ordering them to do things, and after that laughing and making fun of them when they failed to do it.

Tarq called each child by a different country's name. One was Somali, one was Ugandi, one was Filipino, and so on. He joked that he was like the UN Secretary General because he had brought all of Africa and Asia into his camp. Awaz told him to stop making jokes, he had guests to think of.

"Who are my guests?" he asked. "You?"

"Look," she replied. "Kak Yassin and Zuhur are here. Do you see them?"

"No," he answered. "These are not my guests. This is my brother and this is my sister. There are no foreigners here. Only you."

I changed the subject and asked him where Kak Chalak, his oldest son, was. Tarq said that he did not know. He thought that Chalak had a girlfriend in Hasaka, that he visited her once a week, and that he should be back before morning. Awaz got mad and said, "Tarq! That's not funny." (In our culture, a young man is not permitted to have a girlfriend.)

Tarq laughed and said, "No, I am joking. He is a construction worker building a house, and at night he stays there as a gardener-watchman. So he is a hard worker twenty-four hours a day, and if it were not for his pay we would all have been dead of hunger a long time ago."

That night many people in the camp came and visited us. The next day we visited many more. Each of them had a very sad story to tell and they asked me for advice, but I was helpless too. I hated myself when I saw them, and they told me they had been living there for four or five years on fake promises. They could not even get medicine for their children. They all said, "We are prisoners here, and our only crime was to flee Iraq for our families' future and a free life."

I was really upset. There was no way that the UN should be taking care of refugees in this manner. Even if they were in a war zone they would receive better treatment than this. I asked them to write a letter and give it to the UN manager. They laughed. They said many times they had requested an investigation and signed letters and petitions, and all they had ever received were empty promises.

On our second night there, Kak Chalak came back to the camp. He looked like Amazing Rawand, only he was twice the size—he was built like a boxer and had muscles like Mohammad Ali. It looked like God had created him for hard work. When he came into the house, Kak Tarq laughed. "The commando has come back. Look at his muscles from the construction job. The whole day he has to carry cinder blocks and concrete. He looks like Tarzan!"

I shook Kak Chalak's hand, hugged him, and introduced myself. He knew my name but we had never met before.

Chalak was about fifteen, but he looked like a real man and a hard worker who took care of the family. He had an air of both strength and humility. The only thing he appeared to lack in his life was joy. He was living a real Kurdish life of a teenager who had to take responsibility for supporting his family, without having any fun. Awaz said that for the last two years they had been depending on him alone. He reminded me of myself at that age, when I had to work at construction jobs in Kirkuk, but I had not been in the physical shape he was.

I told him to be strong. I told him that it wasn't just him, and it wasn't just the Kurds, but it was the way youth live in the third world. They leave school to help their parents survive, or they flee from war, and when they go back they find that their homes and school do not exist anymore. After that, they must join a militia and carry weapons to earn their daily bread. Why should they be blamed for violence? When they finally get some peace and love, then they will be able to give it back to others. There is no way to end the insurgency or the violence in the Middle East until children are allowed to grow up like children in America and get the food and love and security that children here generally get. When children grow up in fear and hunger doing hard work, when they have no medical care, when they wake up at night to the sounds of rockets and see bloodshed and death, how can we expect them to grow up kind and peaceful and loving?

Let us be honest and ask ourselves what we have done to end the violence against children around the world. Let us ask what we have done to help the people of the Middle East find freedom and lives of dignity. War has destroyed Iraq, even while America claims it wants to free Iraq. In the process, hundreds of thousands of innocent people have been killed; those are lives we can never bring back. And rather than improving Iraq for the living, the war has cut off electricity, running water, and fuel for millions and has destroyed the economy for millions more. Instead of improving education, the war has driven thousands of intellectuals, professors, and philosophers out of Iraq and the Middle East. Instead of bringing the rule of law, the war has improved on age-old techniques of torture. Rival warlords are now armed against each other, destroying any hope for peace. Instead of bringing civil rights to the people, huge jails have been built. The new Iraq pays twice as much for Special Forces and army soldiers as it does for intellectuals and Ph.D.s, and yet it claims it wants to modernize the society. If we walk in the wrong direction, we will never get to the right place no matter how long we walk. If the first steps are not right, we will never get a good result.

We left Tarq and his family and their camp the next day, but we brought with us all of the suffering and hardship they had to endure. And when we arrived back in Hasaka, we found that we did not have enough money to buy bus tickets back to Damascus. In the camp I had seen the children, and I did not have even one small piece of candy for them. I had felt so guilty that I gave them some money to buy candy and forgot how much money I needed to get home. Zuhur probably also had some money when we got there, but she had probably felt as guilty as I did and gave it to someone at the camp. Aziz Nesin, the Turkish writer, wrote in one of his novels that whenever you travel, you should not put all your money in one pocket, because if you are robbed you will lose everything. Instead you should keep your money in at least three different places—some in your wallet, some in your pocket, and some in your baggage. I used to do that all the time, but the sight of the children in the camp made me take it all out.

I asked Zuhur if she had any money with her, and she said that she was penniless. I did not know what to do. I knew some of my college friends lived in the city, but I did not know how I could find them. My wife was really tired and still in shock over what she had seen in the camp. I asked her what we should do.

"Good," she said. "You ask me now, when you are out of money, what I plan to do about it. Before that you did not bother to ask me. Why do you always do that?"

I laughed and said, "Because I am a real Kurdish villager from the Middle East, and we only ask women for help when we are really in trouble."

"I don't know whether to laugh or cry."

"Would you like to walk back to Damascus?" I suggested. "It is only about a thousand miles."

"Have some fun yourself," she said.

"Yes, this was always my father's advice," I said. "When something bad happened, he used to always say *Okhay*, which meant, 'I like it.' It did not matter what had happened. All the villagers believed that if they laughed when they were in trouble, God would fix their problem."

"What happened to your religious studies?" she said. "Are you now going back to your village faith?"

I could see in her face how tired and sad she was, and I realized that more joking was not going to help the situation. All of a sudden I remembered something. "I found the way!" I said.

"Wonderful Sheikh," Zuhur said. "I know you perform miracles all the time." She tried to laugh, but she was so tired she could not.

I felt that something was wrong, because she did not normally speak to me this way. "I'm not joking," I said.

"So what did you just find?" she said

"I just remembered that a friend told me that the train is much cheaper than the bus if you take third-class," I said. "We are going back to Damascus by train, so before we die we will have ridden in a train too."

"How much is it?" she asked. But she looked happier.

"I don't know," I said. "But he said the train was *much* cheaper. If it is just ten percent cheaper, that's enough, because we are only just short of that amount for the bus."

"Let's go," she said.

The problem, though, was that if we took a taxi to the train station, we might not have enough money left over to buy tickets. "We should walk to the train station to make sure we have enough money for the tickets," I told her.

We started walking and asking directions to the station. "We are Kurds," I said. "We should live like *peshmerga* all the time. They never use cars."

"Yes," said Zuhur. "But we left our country to live like real human beings."

I reminded her of the Kurdish proverb: *A donkey goes to Baghdad, but it never becomes a horse.* Which means, a fool will remain a fool wherever he goes. "I think you've already applied that to me," I said. She just looked at me, still too tired to laugh.

>᷿᷿᷿ ᷿᷿᷿<

It took us two hours to walk to the train station. By then it was noon. We asked the price of a ticket to Damascus.

"What class do you want?" the ticket agent said. "We have three classes: supper class with a bedroom, normal class where you can sit or sleep on a seat, like on a bus, and third-class, which is cheaper than the other two."

"What is the price for each class?" I asked.

"100 lirah for supper class, 70 lirah for normal class, and 40 lirah for third-class."

"When does the train leave?"

"Once a day at 6 p.m., and it arrives in Damascus at 10 a.m. the next day."

"We have to wait for six hours?"

"You don't have to wait here," the agent said. "You can go home and wait, but be back at least forty minutes before the train leaves. In fact, it is better to be here by 5 p.m."

"Good," I said. "Give us two third-class tickets." While he was checking our identification, I thought, *He's right. We should go back home, sleep, and return by 5 p.m. But which home should we go to, and how can we go and come back? We are half-dead already.*

We had six hours to wait. What should we do? There was no park, no library, no public place to spend time. Hasaka was a provincial center but it looked like a village. The bus to Damascus left almost every half-hour, so there was never a long delay like this. Plus the bus trip took only nine hours, and the train trip took sixteen hours. I looked at Zuhur's face and felt guilty. I was supposed to take care of her better than this. I should not have brought her here to suffer. Her family believed that she was living the high life in Damascus. Most Kurds believe that *Kharig*—meaning anywhere outside Iraq—is Paradise, perhaps because in Islam we believe that there is one Hell (and of course, Iraq is that Hell), so if we escape Hell we must be in Paradise. But this did not feel like Paradise to me today.

I told my wife that we would open a second refugee camp in the train station. We would stay here until 6 p.m. on the floor. At least the floor was made of concrete, unlike the floor in Tarq's camp, which was made of dirt. We put our bags in a corner and sat on them.

"Zuhur," I said. "Would you like breakfast?'

"It is afternoon, and you ask me about breakfast?" she said. "But I know why you ask me about breakfast instead of lunch. You want to buy eggs." (Eggs are the cheapest fast food in the Middle East.)

"All I have left is 30 lirah (about sixty cents)," I said. "It has to take us through the next twenty-four hours of traveling."

"What about a taxi from the Damascus train station to home?"

Oh my God. I never even thought about that. "It doesn't matter," I said aloud, "because we don't have enough for a taxi."

"So go buy some *kabab* for our lunch, then," she said. She was making fun of me because *kababs* are one of the best and most expensive foods in the Middle East, especially in Iraq. I told her to stay where she was and I would be right back.

What can I do? I asked myself. *Sixteen hours in a train, and how many times will it stop? How can I buy food?* I was really starting to feel ashamed of the kind of man I had become. The best solution to the food problem I could find was to buy two loaves of bread and some water. It was my dad's theory that as long as you had bread and water, you would survive, and if you also had your health then you were a king.

I brought the bread and water back to Zuhur. She was half-awake and almost asleep at the same time. I laughed at the sight of her, and I told her I had brought her the food of kings! I put the two loaves of bread and the bottle of water in front of her. She just stared at me through half-opened eyes.

"You told me that if all your life you had only bread to eat, you would be content," I said.

"Good," she said. "I am not saying anything more. But just don't eat too much bread, unless you want to genocide everyone on the train with a gas attack like at Halabja." Then she dissolved in laughter. (The bread sometimes makes people pass gas.)

"Finally you laughed," I said

We sat next to each other and covered our mouths as we ate the bread little by little, because we did not want people to see what humble food we were eating. I told Zuhur that many times in the village, I ate only bread with my father, but he ate it proudly and now we hid it from people. She said, "So make a call to prayer and announce to the people that you are eating bread. Just don't gas innocent people on the train."

It doesn't really matter how hard things are and how much trouble

⌐ ı are in. Time still passes. Of course, it may seem to pass very slowly when you are oppressed, and maybe it passes very fast when you are having fun. But when it is over, it is over. What do you remember of those hours? Life is like this. Your most precious and valuable possession is your time. You will not live forever, and you have to decide how you want to spend it. We calculate closely how to spend our money, but do we calculate as closely how we want to spend our time? Do we say that we want to spend so much time worrying, so much time rushing, so much time resting, so much time enjoying the family, or so much time building houses—or so much time making money, and saving money, and making more money, which we cannot use when we die? Do we calculate what we will do with our time? If not, we may not have enough time to spend with our wives or our children, or enough time to maintain our health. And we spend too much time running, running, running to make more and more and more money, without getting any benefit from it. You will get sick and old and face death. You cannot get your youth and your health back. Nothing is as beautiful in this life as living a simple family life, full of love, respect, and fun.

About 5:30 we boarded the train. I thought we could sleep once we were on our way because we would certainly spend enough time on it. This was my first time riding a train; in the whole of Kurdistan, there were no trains at all. Even in Iraq, the trains in the south were mostly freight trains, and very few people used them for travel.

But riding on a tractor over a dirt road in Hashazini was much more comfortable than riding that train. It was really slow, made a lot of noise, and smelled very bad. It stopped in every single village and city it passed through. The passengers were fighting and arguing and smoking cigarettes, shouting at each other and threatening violence. It was more like an old-fashioned tea shop. Zuhur and I were scared to close our eyes for even five minutes, for fear the shouting would escalate and we would be beaten. I complained to the officer, who just sighed. "This is third-class. Next time don't take it."

The trip reminded me of 1991, when we fled to the mountains to escape the army and had to walk for nine days straight eating nothing but bread and afraid that the army would catch us. I don't think I was any more scared in the mountains than I was on this train. But eventually the sixteen-hour ride was over, although it felt like sixteen days. We reached Damascus about 10 a.m. with Zuhur about ninety percent dead and me only a little better. I forced myself to open my eyes, but I walked as though I was intoxicated. I talked as though I was dreaming; I did not even know what I said.

I poured water on my head to improve my thinking and went to look for a taxi. I told the driver to take us to Qudsaya. The trip took forty minutes, but it felt like forty seconds because I must have fallen asleep. The next thing I knew, the driver was shaking me awake as though he thought I might be dead. He said he had been shaking me for five minutes. "Sorry," I said.

"This is Qudsaya."

"But we just got in the taxi."

"That was half an hour ago," he said.

"I live just one block from here," I said, and gave him the directions to the villa.

Then I woke Zuhur up. I told the driver that I did not have any Syrian money and I would have to go to my neighbor's house to borrow some. The driver said the fare would be 50 lirah ($1).

I went to my neighbor's house, but he was not home. I came back and told this to the driver, but I was so sleep-deprived that I was not sure what I was doing or saying. The driver said he could not understand me, and asked if I was drunk. "Sir," I said, "I never drank in my life. We did not have enough money to take the bus from Hasaka and so we took the train, and we have been traveling for many days without sleep and are almost dead."

"You live in this castle and you don't have 50 lirah?"

"No, sir, I don't live in this castle. I live in that tiny house in the corner of the garden."

"Oh! This is not yours?"

"No, sir, I am just the gardener here."

"Good," the driver said. "I don't want any money. Goodbye."

"No, sir, wait! You can't go, I must pay you first. Let me think…"

But the driver said that he had been a gardener for seven years before he became a taxi driver, and he understood my situation. He did not want anything. I gave him my radio from my bag and told him to keep it, and that if he came back tomorrow I would pay him, and pay for him coming back as well. He said that he did not want anything and forgave me. I asked for his address so I could pay later. He still refused.

"Then just give me your address and we can be friends," I said.

"No, you are not going to be my friend," he said.

"Why?" I said. "Because I am a gardener?"

"No. I told you, I was a gardener for seven years."

"So why can't I be your friend?"

"Because you are my brother," he said. "We are both Muslims and both gardeners. We are both poor and hard workers."

I hugged him and said, "Thank you for your Communist theory that all poor workers should be brothers."

He laughed. "No, Islam said this. We are all from Adam, rich and poor, and we are all brothers. The Communists got it from us."

"How can I see you again?" I asked.

"I live in Qudsaya too," he said. "If you come to Sheikh Riath's mosque for night prayer you will see me there, because I usually pray every night."

"Good," I said. "I won't be there tonight, but I will see you tomorrow, *insha-Allah* (by God's will)."

He gave me 50 lirah and said, "Use it until you see your boss."

"No, I am OK."

"What kind of brother are you?"

I laughed and told him what my teacher, Abo Saeed, used to tell me: "Whenever someone is introduced to me as a 'brother,' I understand that this is not just a word but a responsibility. What would you do if your real brother was sick, or had no food, or needed your help? Would you help him? So we lie to ourselves when we say 'nice to meet you, brother' if we do not really look at him like a brother or worry about him like a brother."

The driver shook my hand and said, "Well, by accepting all respon-sibility, you are my brother. I must go back to my job."

I thanked him and said I would see him tomorrow night. The next day my boss came and paid the fare for me, and that night I went to the mosque and saw my new brother and we settled our account. Most taxi drivers in Damascus are like thieves, but he was different. It is true that you can find good people everywhere. (As well as bad people, too!)

For a whole week, my wife and I felt as though we had died and were slowly coming back to life—all from that travel and from what we had seen in the refugee camp and on the train. In Kurdistan we say after a hardship like this, or after any big trouble, "I pray that God will not show such a thing even to my enemy."

Mazn Shaqrah

Nothing is more beautiful than humbleness when you are rich and powerful, and nothing is uglier than to be poor and arrogant. It is easy for a servant like me to be humble and talk about justice, but it is not easy to keep from being proud and arrogant when you are a rich, strong, powerful man.

Mazn Shaqrah, the man I worked for in Damascus who owned the villa, was an amazing person. I called him Ustath Mazn (Teacher Mazn). He was a well-known businessman who traveled to Europe easier than I could go from his house to Damascus—about twenty miles. He had a big office in the heart of Damascus, a big house, a couple of cars, and this huge villa with its garden. I don't know how many other properties he had, and how much money he had in the bank. He knew many people in the government, and both his and his wife's families were powerful in Syria. Most of his children had been born in the United States, but I think he was a German citizen. Yet all of his money and power did not make him proud or arrogant. He was really a very humble person, and never ordered me to do this or that. He used to encourage me to study, and many times he told me that if I had an exam at college he would pay someone to work in my place that day. He said that when he was young he had worked very hard. After he worked in Germany, he said his life changed.

He was a liberal Socialist, but he knew that I was religious. Many times I saw him wearing a gold necklace. He knew that in Islam a man should never wear gold, and so whenever he came close to me he would hide his necklace and put it under his shirt out of respect for me. My children used to play with his children; often he gave them toys and clothing. In the same way that Martin Luther King dreamed of seeing the children of slaves play with the slave owner's children, our children were really equal. Without my asking, he raised my salary from $100 to $150 a month after the first year. Even though I was just a servant, an immigrant, a foreigner, and a Kurd, he always said to me, "I am your brother. Feel free to ask for whatever you need."

Being a gardener in Syria was the lowest job in the culture. Most people who did such work were foreigners, Kurds or Somalis, but I was very happy with my job. I liked it not because it was exciting, or it paid well, or it was easy work, but because I did not need to ask anyone for any favors. I could go to school, and my landlord/boss was very supportive. I was actually my own boss; nobody told me to do this or that, or blamed me for something I did or did not do. I knew what my duty was, and I did it to the best of my ability.

I worked as a gardener for Ustath Mazn for about three years, but it was becoming increasingly difficult for my family, since now we had two children and all four of us had to live in our one small room. On the days I went to school, I would leave at 1 p.m. and come back at 8 or 9 p.m. So it was really hard for my wife to stay alone with a new baby in a big jungle all day without anyone to talk to. Before sunset, she had to lock the door, and I told her it didn't matter what happened, they could come and steal the whole villa, but she shouldn't open that door. Many days during the winter I had to miss half of my last class so I could be home by sunset, since I had to change buses two or three times.

One night about 1 a.m. I heard someone throwing stones at the door and calling my name. I woke up and at first was completely confused until I recognized my neighbor's voice. My wife was shaking. I went out and opened the gate for him.

"Where were you, Yassin?"

"Fast asleep."

"I called you over and over and I thought you were not home—that's why I threw stones at your door. Look! Your electric generator is gone."

"What?"

"Two men stole it from the villa and were bringing it over the garden wall when I was coming from my brother's house and saw them. I ran after them and they dropped it and ran. The police captured them. This all happened about midnight."

I thanked him profusely, and he helped me bring the generator back to the villa garage. He told me to call Mazn Shaqrah.

"I will do it tomorrow," I said. "I have to get up very early."

"Better do it now," my neighbor said.

"I don't have a phone."

"There is a phone in the villa."

"Yes, but I don't have a key for the villa."

"You don't have a key?" the neighbor said, surprised. "Well, we'll call him tomorrow."

He shook my hand and I thanked him again. He smiled and said, "Don't sleep too hard."

I just laughed. Of course I slept heavily every night. I was up early every morning so I could get my work finished by noon and then leave for class. I usually only had six or seven hours at home for my family and for sleeping, so I was often very tired.

The next morning I called my boss at 7 a.m. and told him what happened. He said he would come, and about an hour later he arrived. I showed him the generator and told him what had happened.

"So what were you doing at that time?" he asked me.

"I was sleeping," I said.

"But you should watch and be careful."

"Ustath Mazn, you know it is not my job to stay up all night to watch the villa," I said. "My job is to work as a gardener in the daytime."

"I know, but you have to watch to see if people are stealing."

"But even if I were awake I couldn't do anything," I said. "How would I know what was going on in the villa? Even if I thought something was going on, I would not go out to investigate."

"Why not?"

"Suppose they have a gun and shoot me?" I said. "Or suppose they jump on me with a knife? What am I supposed to do? I don't have a gun to scare them."

"You can call me or call the police," he said.

"How can I call? I don't have a phone, and you did not give me a key to the villa so I could use your phone. I can't walk to the market at midnight to find a phone, and anyway no store would be open at that time. The police station is too far away to walk."

Kak Mazn realized then that the robbery was not my fault, and that it was not my duty to guard the villa at night. Indeed, I could not do anything even if it was my duty, and besides, if I stayed up all night to guard the villa, I would have no time to sleep at all.

"It is not your fault," he said. "It is more important that you are safe. If they destroy the villa, it is no problem." After this incident, he had a telephone installed in my house so I could call if anything happened.

After that, I was not comfortable being away from home at night. On dark or rainy nights I cut my last two classes so I could be home before dark and my wife would not be so afraid. We learned that the man who stole the generator was Kak Mazn's former driver and knew how to break in; the villa did not even have bars on the windows. We were relieved, because such a thing had never happened before.

I did not think about changing jobs because I was sure that any other work would prevent me from going to school, and if I had to pay rent I could never earn enough to support my family. And it would be hard to find a humble gentleman like Ustath Mazn. However, in the summer when they came to live in the villa, Ustath Mazn's family began to ask me to do many favors for them that were not part of my job. But because I had a great deal of respect for Kak Mazn, I did them, like washing the car and taking care of the children and shopping for them. Kak Mazn had two Filipino women who served in the home, and he also had a driver. He always told me that I did not have to do any of these extra things, because there were servants. And I used to tell him that I was happy to do anything for him.

The problem, however, was his wife. She used to call me to do this and that, and eventually it became routine for her to call and tell me I *had* to do things around the house—things that should have been done by the servants. Then she started calling my wife as well. Finally I said no, and told my wife to say no. Yet even after I refused to do anything except work related to the garden, she kept asking me to watch her children or to buy something for her in the market. I kept telling her that I had a job to do, and I could not do it if I kept having to stop and do other work.

Kak Mazn talked to his wife, but things did not get better. Finally I told him that I would have to quit in two weeks. He said he understood, and that there was nothing he could do. He asked me to help him find a young religious man whom he could trust. I introduced him to my friend, Rauf Khalaf, who was a Kurd from Syria, and he became the next gardener. He actually was a better gardener than I was, and had covered for me on other occasions when I had to take an exam.

On the day I left, Mazn Shaqrah was almost in tears. He said that human beings were weak and that sometimes small problems overtook us. And he apologized for the misunderstanding that had led me to leave. He gave me an extra $100 and told me that I had his number, and if I needed anything to just call him and nobody else. I told him that I was not jealous of all that he had, but that I was jealous for his humility. I said I prayed that God would bless him more and more and protect his children, whom I loved like my own. He assured me that he also looked at my children like his own and wished the best future for them.

Since that day long ago, I have had no contact with him. I am sure he would be happy for me if he knew that at least I was in the U.S. now, because that would mean that my children are not going to live in one small room all their lives and do gardeners' jobs in order to survive.

Jabal Qasuon (Qasuon Mountain)

After I lost my job and was unemployed again, I moved to the Kurdish Qasuon district of Damascus and renewed my Kurdish nationality by living with my wife and two children in one of the district's tiny houses in the oldest part of the city. Many of the houses were built when there was no electricity, running water, cars, or government services. In some places the buildings are so close together that it is impossible for a car to squeeze between them. Damascus spreads out over Qasuon Mountain, and some houses are built on such steep hillsides that the only way to get to them is by climbing 500 to 600 stairs. You cannot even bring a cart to the house; you have to carry everything up the stairs. It is colorful but inconvenient. One day I asked my friend Kak Ali why the Kurds lived like this, and he said that we are like fish that cannot live without water—Kurds cannot live without mountains. As long as it is high, the Kurds enjoy it!

So in 1998 I started to live the same way that my father used to live in Hashazini—only now I was in the capital of Syria. If you were not willing to live in Qasuon with all of its inconveniences, you would have to pay at least $100 a month for a one-bedroom apartment elsewhere in Damascus; if you took a rundown two- or three-bedroom apartment, it would cost $250–$350; and a modern apartment would cost $500–$700. But in Qasuon I paid just $40 for our little cave. For myself, being a real Kurd I enjoyed the climbing as though I was really living in the mountains. It strengthened my national character. I loved carrying bags on my back up the stairs, climbing mountains to my home, dreaming that I was *peshmerga*. Kak Ali told me one day that I was *peshmerga afandi* (a modern *peshmerga*), wearing pants and living in a cave. But I believe that my wife's back pain and knee problems came from this little hovel that we lived in; we had to carry the children and all of our stuff up endless stairs.

That same year, the government decided to demolish some of the houses so they could bring a road through the district and provide other services. But the Kurds took it as a threat and started a demonstration against it. One of my Syrian friends at college said, "You

Kurds are amazing. If we try to provide services for you, then you see it as a plot to destroy Kurdish houses, but if we leave you alone you say that the government is ignoring the Kurds. We are wrong whatever we do. What is to be done?"

I laughed and said, "Leave us alone. We love the mountains." But the reality was that most of the people in Qasuon could not afford any other place. I told him, "Build a complex for the Kurds that they can afford, and they will be happy to destroy their 'caves' and go live in nice houses. But don't destroy the houses and give them no other place to live. Where will they go, and what will they do? Having no road is better than having a road and no place to live."

My friend held my hand and told me that he was just joking. He knew what was going on.

Constantly being poor and jobless has given the Kurds a faith and philosophy of life that is hard for modern people to understand. When the poor people of France demonstrated because they did not have enough food, the French queen said, "Let them eat cake." She did not understand what the real life of the people was like. The rich and the poor live in two different worlds, and we have to demolish the walls between our worlds and build a bridge. Without it, there will be no way for real change to occur. I cannot accept or believe that there are any nations that dislike freedom, hate peace, want to be ruled by dictators, want their rulers chosen by someone other than themselves, or reject hospitals, schools, roads, electricity, phones, computers, universities, libraries, or bridges.

People do not reject modern life, but they reject being manipulated and lied to and having changes undermine the fragile balance by which they are able to survive. They distrust the objectives and motives of the people who urge modernization. Will modernization help them, or someone else? The poor really do not believe that "improvements" will ever help them, and their experience is that the opposite is true—they will get only more blood and poverty, and life will go backwards, not forward. Iraq and Afghanistan are two good examples. Real improvement for the poor will come only from clear plans that empower the poor with humanitarian jobs based on professional expert advice. This is the right way to bring about peace and progress, not by armies and bombing. The most important thing is that the "improvements" and the changes should not have to require people to change or give up their religion. Modernization should not mean a religion-less life. People should be able to keep their faith and have a modern life as well.

The Crying Cave

This is a typical Middle Eastern story. After a two- to four-hour hike, close to the top of Qasuon Mountain there is a cave that many people believe was the home of Qabil and Habil (Cain and Abel, the sons of Adam, the first man). Some stonemasons have "restored" the cave to make it similar to its description in the ancient writings. According to the Biblical account, after Qabil killed Habil he went back to the cave, felt guilty for what he had done, and started crying. Since then, water has been dripping from a crack in the ceiling of the cave because the cave itself is crying too. People regard this water as holy and believe it will cure all kinds of sickness. People from India in particular regularly come to the cave to take the water. Even the government-appointed guides bring their Western clients to the cave to take pictures.

In 1998, the Syrian government changed its system of official guides and appointed a new Sheikh named Safi. He did not believe in the holy water story, and to prevent the story from continuing he blocked the source of the water. He wrote a book about the cave, entitled *Forty*, because other stories said that forty messengers of God had spent their lives in the cave. In the book, Safi stated that there was no evidence that Adam's sons were ever in the cave. He thought it more likely that the sons lived in India, while acknowledging that there was no solid evidence to deny the story, either.

Stonecutters have shaped the mouth of the cave into the mouth of a lion, and the pools into which the water drips look like human eyes. But Safi proved that the cave was not crying. He wrote that people had put water into a hole on the roof of the cave and let it run down a crack so it would fall into the pools, drop by drop. He published a picture of the roof of the cave showing the hole at the top, into which water had to be placed in order to make the cave weep. Someone had to fill the hole with ten gallons of water, and it took fifteen hours for the water to run through the crack and into the pool. Safi explained that he had blocked up the hole because the stories about holy water were just nonsense.

But Safi's action made the government mad at him, because now travelers would not come to the cave to get holy water and the government would lose tourist money. Safi was fired, the government appointed a new Sheikh, the cave started crying again, and people returned to get their "medicine." Safi was accused of having mental problems, and his book disappeared from the market.

So who is in charge of fooling other human beings? Why is it against freedom to deny a foolish act in the name of religion? Why should people do things that are false, and no one can tell them they are wrong? Should you go along with foolishness that generates business, and not say anything against the culture or against tricking foreigners into buying regular water as holy water and medicine? Or should you educate people to know the difference between truth, fable, and fiction? In modern times, we say, let people be free to worship stones if they like, and if they believe that the water dripping from a cave is Qabil's tears, let them believe that also, even though the water was put into the cave's roof from a bucket fifteen hours earlier. Modern civilized people go to a doctor and a hospital when they are sick, but in third world countries they go to a cave or a grave to find a cure. So who is responsible for that?

Chapter Eleven ☪
Politics

Dirty Games

One of the most famous Turkish writers and novelists, Aziz Nesin, said that if you are out in public, in a bus or a market or a tea shop, and someone asks you what time it is, do not answer. If the person tries to start a conversation about the weather, how hot or cold it is, don't answer him. Say nothing—because all of this is just the first step to starting a dialogue with you. If you answer, the second step will be, *What is your name? How are you? Where do you live?* A formal introduction will follow. And if you take the second step, the third step will undoubtedly be political—and if you respond to the third step, you will certainly disappear. The wise man in the Middle East is the one who hides his watch, makes himself dumb, and closes his mouth to anything that leads to foolishness and trouble—and politics.

This is the nature of life in the Middle East, where you cannot live free and independent. There is no law to protect you. You can only be saved if you approve of what the government is doing, or if you are very rich and you can bribe those in power. The problem is that the governments are all unstable, and in order to survive most of the politicians must face whichever way the wind is blowing, so every day they have to face in a different direction. These politicians believe they know better, because all they read is Machiavelli's book; they deny that there are any moral principles in politics; and they proudly believe that what they are doing is in the highest political tradition. It is all intended to achieve noble goals, and so it is permissible to use any means to achieve the end, even if the steps are long, dangerous, and immoral. They don't follow the expression, "You should have the correct step for the perfect result." As the Persian poet said, "If you place the cornerstone incorrectly, the building will never be straight."

A political party is like a company that produces only cheaters, liars, and hypocrites, so you cannot be both a man of principle and a politician in the Middle East. Politicians have a sweet tongue and a nice outlook, but their deeds are completely different from their words. In the West, when a politician fails to fulfill his promises, he may not be re-elected. But in the Middle East, people pray every night that God will take their leaders back by giving them death, because there is no other way to change them. In most Middle Eastern countries, you see the same president and leaders in power for thirty or forty years, and when they die a son or a brother replaces them. And yet they claim that they are not a kingdom, and they get a lot of money from the U.S. in order to build democracy. In the West, political parties spend millions of dollars to win elections, but in the East each change of government costs thousands of lives and millions of jobs, and usually the next government is worse.

One day I was with two of my friends, Barzan and Ahmed, and Barzan said that he had seen the Syrian president, Hafez Assad, on TV. I said, "Pray God takes him back." Ahmed said, "No, no, pray God keeps him as president for the next twenty years." "Why?" I asked in surprise. "Because," said Ahmed, "for the last twenty years he has been sucking out our blood, and maybe now he is full. But if he dies and his son takes over, we will have to give twenty more years of our blood to fill him up."

Religion is the opposite of politics. In religion, which is based on principle, you must avoid things that are forbidden, you must do things that are required, and as for things that are permitted, you may do them if you like. So I (and millions like me, especially in the Middle East) am confused about what to do with regard to politics: how can you be a man of principle and also a politician? Politicians do not leave you alone or allow you to be independent. They are like George Bush, who says, "If you're not with us, you're against us." If you are not clapping for them and praising what they're doing and singing for joy, you are the enemy. To get rid of you, they don't need a court order. All it costs them is twenty-five cents—the price of a bullet around midnight.

There is no way to strike a balance between principle and politics. You have to sacrifice one or the other.

In Iraq, we paid for this dirty game more than any country in the world. Western governments and Gulf countries supported Saddam in the 1980s by sending him weapons because he was fighting Iran. In eight years, those weapons took close to one million lives. In the 1990s, after Saddam invaded Kuwait, the Western governments and Gulf countries put an embargo on imports. After ten years of the embargo, which was completely borne by the Iraqi people and not by those in power, some 2.5 million children were dead. But whenever Saddam's family or anyone in his ministers' families fell ill, they could go to a special doctor from Europe. After ten years, I heard with my own ears Tony Blair say, "The embargo was wrong"—that it did not weaken Saddam, only the people. That "wrong" by the West cost us 2.5 million children—but who is going to bring them back? Who is responsible for that?

As soon as the U.S. decided that the embargo was the wrong approach, it declared war on Iraq, supposedly because Saddam could destroy the UK with chemical weapons in less than forty minutes. America also said that Saddam threatened the U.S. with weapons of mass destruction, and if Saddam didn't use them he could always sell them to the terrorists. Then America said that the embargo was wrong because they wanted to try another plan—attacking Iraq—and after five or ten years and millions of lives, the next president will say this was also a wrong choice. As a result, 100,000 innocent Iraqi kids have already died in the fighting. Now America says that it believes Iraq had no weapons of mass destruction—but what about all those innocent people who died? Who is responsible for their lives, and how can anyone bring them back? And now there is talk about invading Iran, or Saudi Arabia, or Pakistan, or Egypt...it will be continuous. There will always be different reasons, but the result will always be the same: innocent lives lost, children's futures squandered, disease, poverty, joblessness, suffering.

This is not something I *believe* will happen. It is something I have seen with my own eyes during my lifetime. There is a Kurdish joke about this dirty game. After many broken promises and continual fighting between the PUK and the KDP, Kak Masood Barzani, the head of KDP, got very mad at Jalal Talabani, the head of PUK, and swore by God that he would never again shake his hand or sit with him. When Mam Jalal heard that, he said, "I am older than he is, and I have more experience in politics. Nothing will remain the same. He will shake my hand and sit with me again and again." And Mam Jalal was right: as soon as the U.S. invaded Iraq, circumstances forced the two leaders to come together. But when the U.S. leaves Iraq, who is going to keep them together?

Mam Jalal is the most famous Kurd who has mastered this dirty game. In the 1960s, he first obtained weapons and support from Syria to gain an independent Kurdish state. In the 1970s, he claimed he was a Communist and took weapons and support from the U.S.S.R. In the 1980s, he claimed he was a social democrat and took weapons and support from Iran for the Islamic revolution. In the 1990s, he claimed he was a liberal democrat and took weapons and support from the U.S. Now, in the 2000s, he declares that he doesn't want an independent Kurdish state because he is now president of Iraq and all Kurds should be Iraqi—yet for fifty years he has been head of the PUK, and he is still head of the PUK, which is working for an independent Kurdish state. No one ever chose him, and he never had to win elections, but we are all still supposed to believe that he will bring democracy to Kurdistan. Each time he changed his mind and the goals of his organization, 10,000 people died, all for Kurdish independence. But basically it was the same group, the same leader, the same land—just different ways to make money.

All the other political groups did the same in Iraq. If anyone blames them, they will say that this is what you must expect from politics. I believe many of them now take money and weapons in the daytime from the U.S., and at night they sell the weapons to the insurgents. If not, where are the insurgents getting the weapons from? In the daytime they are the police and the security forces; at night they are the death squads and the sectarian fighters. This is the way politics works in my country, and many people have no choice except to participate in order to escape government retribution.

A politician's salary is much higher than a university professor's. In the West you can be very rich and spend huge amounts getting elected, but in the East the only way to get rich is to become involved in politics. Scientists, professors, doctors, teachers, scholars—their salaries do not cover their rent and expenses. But a politician can buy a couple of castles, dozens of cars, big hotels, nice restaurants, and most of the cities. They even own the people in them. In the West, the only way to succeed in politics is first to be rich. In the East, this dirty game costs millions of lives. All in the name of saving the people.

My family's historical role for hundreds of years was to be religious leaders who did their traditional work by being men of principle and examples for others. The necessary qualities for religious leaders are humility and honesty—as opposed to the political leaders. I have struggled all my life in the Middle East to both keep my faith and stay alive as a principled person who avoids hypocrisy. In Kurdistan, we say of a hypocrite that he is an innocent sheep by day and a dangerous wolf at night. I chose to be simple, to live poor, and to suffer so I could keep my principles. I refused to sing for the Baath Party, and this caused me to fear for my education and to remain poor. I lived with *peshmerga* and helped them and advised them, but I opposed many things that they did, and in order to keep my principles I never joined them.

IMK

After I lost my job as a gardener, I was very concerned about my family and what would happen to them if I did not find another job. Every day I went out and asked all of my friends to help me find something, and again it was the same problem: no jobs. After four to five months of searching, I still had no employment.

A number of Kurdish political organizations had offices in Damascus because so many Kurds came from and went to Kurdistan through Syria. During this time, Kak Musheer, who was representing one of these political organizations, the Islamic Movement of Kurdistan (IMK), obtained a visa and went to London. He gave up the Syrian office and moved it to the apartment in London that his family was living in. People used to call it Musheer's tea shop. His entire home was one room, separated by a small table that held the office phone and fax machine. When he was back in Syria, he would invite one or two people to have tea and a political discussion with him.

After Musheer left the IMK, Loqman Hassan, one of my college room-mates who was from Halabja, was appointed head of the IMK office in Syria. Most of the IMK leaders were from Halabja, and the organization had been founded in part to give voice to the victims of the massacre.

One day I asked Loqman if he had found any leads on a job for me. He responded, "Kak Yassin, I need you."

"What do you need me for?" I asked.

"I just took over the IMK office in Damascus," he said, "and I don't want it to be just a tea shop any more. Nowadays thousands of Kurds are coming from Europe to visit their families in Kurdistan. I need someone to help me do the visa work. Daily I have to go to government offices, immigration offices, the airport, and hotels here and there—it is just too much for one person. Since they pay a fee for the job, we will at least have enough to take care of your expenses."

"What would my job be?" I asked.

"There are supposed to be two people in this job. I don't know if Kak Jameel Ameen is coming back or not, but even if he comes back we will need him. Ninety percent of the job is visa work. Sometimes I have to go to the airport five or ten times a day."

I told him to give me a couple of days to think about it, because I knew that the day after tomorrow I finally had an appointment with someone for another gardener's job. If I got that job, I would refuse Kak Loqman's offer. But if I didn't get hired, I would have no other choice than to work for the IMK, because I was desperate for a job.

During those few days I asked many of my friends again if they had any job leads for me, but they all said "Sorry, not yet." Even the interview for the gardener's job was cancelled because the gardener who was supposed to be quitting decided not to leave after all. After a week went by without a single new lead, Kak Loqman himself called me and said he was waiting for my response. So I agreed to work for Kak Loqman and the IMK.

After I started working, I was able to rent a house in Damascus. I brought my family down from the "cave" house on the mountain and we started living like real human beings. Every day I was introduced to ten or fifteen new people coming from Europe, the U.S.A., Canada, and Australia—all of them Kurdish refugees. Suddenly I had access to the whole world: I could read newspapers, make phone calls, see people, get addresses, and learn about the Western world from people who had just been there.

I also had to deal with Kurdish and Iraqi opposition leaders who were leaving Iraq and Kurdistan for the West, and who had the latest news on the political issues that were boiling away in Iraq. I met with most of the leaders of IMK when they came to Damascus on their way to Europe or to the *Hajj* in Saudi Arabia. Most of them seemed to like me, and they tried in different ways to make me go back to Kurdistan and work with them or to take over the office in Syria. But I used to joke with them that I was just a villager and I could not live without a farm, and that I kept looking for a farm to work on.

I worked in the IMK office for about one year, until I left Syria in October 1999. My job completely changed my life. It turned out to be a golden opportunity for me to meet and come to know thousands of educated and successful people. I exchanged opinions with hundreds of different people; I received hundreds of important books to read. I was busy ten to fifteen hours a day. Most of my time was spent helping travelers move through Damascus. My home was like a hotel; because of the different time zones between Syria and Europe, people came and went at all hours. At any time I could get a phone call from someone in Europe, or there could be a knock on the door with a request that I go to the airport to collect another traveler. My comfort and rest came only after helping these people.

My friends—and even Kak Loqman—used to tell me to take more rest. "Travelers can take a taxi every now and then so that you don't have to be up all night," they would say. But I told them that since the government demolished my village in 1989, I was ashamed to be related to my grandfather, Sheikh Aref, my Uncle SayGul, and all of my relatives who took such joy in serving guests, because I could not reciprocate. I told them what my father used to tell me: if you want to become rich, give your bread to the poor and don't eat it yourself. If you want your home to be blessed, bring guests to the house. If you get any opportunity to do something for someone, do it, because God may be giving you a test, and if you refuse you will never get that chance back. Nothing is more honorable than helping the needy. I told them that I believed this job was my test, and I didn't want to fail. My Uncle SayGul used to say: if you refuse to help people when you can, one day when you need help there will be no one to help you. But if you help them with a smiling face, God will not leave you alone but will send helpers enough to lighten your burden. In Kurdistan we say *Donia dastia wa*, which means, whenever you help, you get it back. One day you can help someone; the next day you need someone's help. I saw this come true when they arrested me and I left my wife and children with fifty cents and zero income—but God sent many people to help them.

I was very excited that God had put me in a position to help others, and my wife was a big supporter. People used to call me and come to my house twenty-four hours a day. I might drive someone to the airport, or pick up someone who had just arrived; then I would have to take him to the immigration office, then to the bus station so he could continue his journey, then help him change money, carry his bags, make a phone call for him, advise him on the quickest, easiest, or safest route to his destination, write letters for him, and so on. All of these activities were very simple, but they were a real help to the travelers. In the East, all of the procedures for traveling have not been streamlined, as in the West. Every time you cross a border, the language may be different, the money may be different, the visa and travel documents may be different, the safest means of local travel may be different, the procedure for making a phone call may be different. I was like a guide who led people through the strange new procedures that they did not understand and that otherwise nobody would have explained to them.

If you needed to change your money, certain people might give you fake money. If you took a taxi that should have cost fifty cents, some drivers might charge you $25. If you went to the immigration office, often they would not give you the documents you needed without a bribe. If you wanted to buy something, stores would usually overcharge foreigners by ten times the value. But with my contacts in Syria, I could make all of this go smoothly for travelers.

Everything in Syria was cheaper than abroad. One day I was in the office and a man named Salah came in from the U.S. He said that he had come by taxi and had given the driver $10. But the driver realized that his customer knew nothing about the local currency, and asked him for more. Salah gave him another $20—and then the driver jumped out and started shouting that this was a special express taxi service, so Salah gave him $20 more. I ran out and tried to get the number of the taxi's license plate, but it was too late. Salah mentioned the fare to me only because he thought that a $50 fare was pretty high, even by U.S. standards. I told him that for $50, he could rent the taxi for the whole week, and that the trip should have cost about twenty-five cents.

This kind of experience really bothered me. This was not a proper way to treat foreigners. How could people cheat and steal and then go to prayers? What is the point of prayer unless it stops you from cheating and stealing? Are we Muslims or wolves? Is this a Muslim community or a jungle? Should we show people the right path or mislead them? Why do we love money so much? Does our happiness and success come from the money, or from God? It is really a shame upon us to claim that we are Muslim and to tolerate such corruption. We should be the best and the highest examples of human values. What would people want to learn from us, and what benefit could they get from our culture, if we tolerate such practices?

It is said that once a non-Muslim went to Kak Ahmadi Sheikh, a very famous Imam in Sulaimaniya, and the Imam asked him if he wanted to accept Islam. The man said, "Sheikh, if by Islam you mean your Islam, I don't believe I am so advanced that I can be you and do like you do, but if you mean to be Muslim like the people, I believe that my atheism is better than their religion." I believe this is true in all the Muslim countries, and that this repels non-Muslims from joining Islam. We are the worst examples of our faith. We should close our mouths, show people our faith by actions that improve life in our countries, eliminate corruption, and educate our children. In that way, we can show people what Islam really means. In Muslim countries, human beings are slaughtered like animals. Torture and humiliation are everywhere. There is no law, and with money and bribes you can do anything. For food and medicine and all other needs, we depend on non-Muslims. And we top it all off by being proud we are Muslims, when in fact we are just ignorant beggars and dangerous cheaters. We should realize that we cannot find a cure until we locate the sickness. The Qur'an tells us that "indeed God will not change the people's situation until they change themselves."

During my job in the IMK office, I met thousands of people from all over the world who carried with them many different ideas. I had many dialogues, and each of them is a separate story. Many of these people moved me deeply. They are still living in my heart, and their words still affect me. I want to share some of these experiences with you.

Kak Loqman, my college friend who was in charge of the Damascus IMK office, was a really good person with a pure heart. He liked to help people and was not selfish. I saw so many good things in him that I stayed in touch with him for years after I left the IMK. But there were problems in the office. He was not as diplomatic as someone in charge of the office should have been. Daily he saw hundreds of people, but if he heard or saw anything that he did not like, or if he got mad even a little, it showed on his face. He would look grim and his face would grow bright red. Not only was he unable to smile, but he was even unable to talk because he would bite his lip, breathe deeply, and sweat. I used to laugh and think to myself that my illiterate father in the village was more diplomatic than he was.

It was a natural reaction, because Loqman's pure heart and simplicity were not able to act in two different ways. He was not a hypocrite. But he had a problem directing his emotions. If I was angry because I had a problem at home, why should I direct that anger at my friend at school? But if Loqman was upset with a situation at home, he was unable to go to school and joke and laugh with his friend. Since he was the head of the office and was dealing with all kinds of people, some of whom were high-level, it was important that he put aside all of his concerns while he was in the office and be cheerful with people. But he had difficulty doing this. At that time we received bad news from Kurdistan daily, and Kak Loqman's face always looked like it had been baked in an oven. People who met him did not know why he was upset, and some assumed that he was upset with them. He was from Halabja, and he had been affected by the gas attack in 1988; he tired easily, breathed only with difficulty, and sometimes had coughing fits when he was tired and overworked. This all made me believe that he was the wrong person in the wrong job at the wrong time and place.

In addition, Kak Loqman had control issues. He used to follow Jameel (who had returned after all) and me around to find out what we were doing. In his management responsibilities he was a dictator, probably because that was the only example he had ever seen growing up. He was like my father at home who ordered people around; teachers in school used to do the same. They always wanted to know what you were doing when you were not with them. Many times in school I saw teachers beating kids because someone told the teacher that the student had been somewhere that he was not supposed to be.

It really bothered me that people believed they had to watch other people and follow them. Everyone has the right to privacy. The Prophet Mohammad said that one of the best manners a person can have is to leave alone what doesn't relate to you. In America people say, "It is none of your business." But Kak Loqman could not avoid meddling. Perhaps it had to do with the mentality in the East that does not distinguish clearly between personal and business matters. If you work for someone, your employer often feels that he has the right to be involved in your personal life. For example, many times Kak Jameel used to complain that when he used the computer, Kak Loqman would check to see what websites he visited and whom he communicated with. Loqman even told me two or three times after I kept a paper I was interested in, to throw it in the trash. I was really surprised at how he tried to control us, but I said, "So let him make sure we are doing our job. After all, he is the boss." Kak Jameel did not agree with me, and said he was going to do something.

Kak Jameel began to write fake e-mails with no contents, only titles, and leave them unsent on the computer so Kak Loqman would find them and go crazy. For example, he would write an e-mail to all the IMK leaders with the title "About Our Problems," and then just leave it on the computer. He did this every day, and I could see in Kak Loqman's face that he was furious.

After about two weeks, Kak Loqman said, "Kak Yassin, I want to speak to you!" He showed me a bunch of e-mails with nothing but titles, and said, "Look at all these e-mails that Jameel sent."

"So what are the e-mails about?" I asked.

"I don't know," said Kak Loqman. "He did not save the contents."

"Where did you find these titles?"

"In the web history or the trash bin."

"Why are you checking the trash bin?"

Kak Loqman stated to get red in the face and had no answer. I started laughing.

"What are you laughing at?" he demanded.

"None of the letters were sent," I said. "He just wrote these titles because he knows that you are after him to find out what he is doing."

Loqman just stared at me while taking deep breaths, one after another.

I said, "Kak Loqman, we love you and we want to respect you as the manager we work for, but you must understand what it means to be a big brother." After that, things became much better.

At one point, I had a chance to meet with Sheikh Ali Abdul Aziz, the head of IMK, and was asked to give my sincere opinion about the Damascus office. Since it is part of my faith to always say the truth, I told Sheikh Ali that it would be better to appoint someone else to be the head of the Damascus office. When Kak Loqman learned what I had told Sheikh Ali about his problems with his emotions and with control, Loqman was furious with me and accused me of not believing in him. That was not true, because I never had any doubt that he was a good person, humble and dedicated to his job. But every person has different abilities, and each job requires different qualities. It is often very painful to tell the truth, and people will get mad at you for speaking truthfully. As a great Imam, Sufian Thawry, once said, "Truth left no friend for me." My Sheikh used to tell us to love people and make them your friends, but to love truth more than all of them.

At the time all this happened, Kak Loqman was just twenty-three years old, and this was the first time he had taken such responsibility. After he left the IMK, he finished his master's degree. Now he can lead a whole group and not just a small office, so I guess he learned a lot from his first experience. I wish him the best, and I pray for him that his lungs get cured so he can breathe normally. No one is born with knowledge. We get it only by experience and learning, as Kak Loqman did.

Don't Lose Any Opportunity

Jalal Talabani, or Mam Jalal, is the clever and pragmatic Kurdish leader who has played the biggest role in Kurdish history in the second half of the twentieth century. He will forever be seen as a giant figure in the struggle for independence, and like any other leader he has supporters who praise him as a hero, as well as detractors who accuse him of lacking principles. But nobody can deny that he has dominated the political scene and that he is a really intelligent diplomat. His critics say that he has no firm principles, that he simply looks for opportunities to obtain an advantage, and that he goes with the wind in whatever direction it is blowing. His supporters argue that this is the art of politics, and that all Talabani is trying to do with his endless maneuvering is to get something for the Kurds. He is a good speaker; he is clever at diplomacy, charming with people, and persuasive. He is always optimistic and respectful of guests in a manner very characteristic of a Kurd. After talking with him, people always come away with hope and big promises, but later they see that sometimes they have received something quite different. I often heard about peace agreements between his group, the PUK, and other groups; no one has had more experience with such

330 Son of Mountains: Syria

agreements than Kak Masood Barzani, the head of KDP and the current president of Kurdistan. Mam Jalal was famous for saying, "Give me a plain sheet of paper—I will sign it first, and afterwards you can specify all your conditions or whatever you want. I will agree to everything in advance." Unfortunately, he was equally famous for not fulfilling these agreements. And often this resulted in bitter fighting.

I met Mam Jalal at the end of 1998 when he came to Syria from Turkey. At that time, the situation was really hard in Kurdistan. The border area between Turkey, Syria, and Kurdistan was controlled by KDP, and Mam Jalal, as head of PUK, could not cross from Syria into Kurdistan because the PUK's relationship with KDP at that time was very strained. When Mam Jalal arrived in Damascus, I went with Kak Loqman to welcome him, as we did with many Iraqi citizens who were returning to Kurdistan through Damascus.

When we arrived at his house, I saw him sitting with about fifteen Iraqi and Kurdish opposition leaders, including Kaka Hamay (Mohammad) Haje Mahmood, the head and founder of PSK-1 (Socialist Party of Kurdistan)—who, because of his size, nobody could miss. Kak Dana, the PUK representative in Syria and Mam Jalal's appointment secretary, took Loqman and me to another room and welcomed us. He then brought Mam Jalal to meet us and we shook hands. As usual, Mam Jalal had a big smile; he hugged both of us and kissed our heads as though we were his sons. When we sat down, I joked that we were not female (since women were generally separated from men in different rooms, as we had been separated from everyone else). But Mam Jalal said that Kak Dana knew that we did not smoke, and that is why he had moved us to another room, away from the "tea shop" where the clouds of cigarette smoke would not offend us.

In our brief meeting he talked about three things: the importance of education (and after Kak Dana told him that we were both master's degree students, he encouraged us to also get Ph.D.s); the importance of establishing strong relationships with other people and countries and of disseminating as much information as possible about the Kurds and the genocide during Anfal and Halabja; and the importance of taking advantage of the opportunity that had been created earlier in 1998 when the U.S. Congress approved a law, the Iraq Liberation Act, that supported the Iraqi opposition's call for regime change in Iraq.

When they brought in some tea, one of the teacups was very different from the other three on the tray. Mam Jalal asked Kak Dana which cup was his. I just smiled and said that it could not be missed. Kak Dana explained that Mam Jalal was diabetic and did not want to forget which cup had no sugar in it. In Kurdish culture, people do not serve sugar separately from the tea—they are just cooked together. When we started to drink our tea, Mam Jalal reached into his pocket and brought out a small nylon bag. He said to Loqman and me, "Look, I follow the *Sunnah* better than you." *Sunnah* is an action that Prophet Mohammad performed during his life, or advised others to perform; such an act of imitation done by any Muslim is considered very honorable and is expected to be appreciated by other Muslims.

Then out of the bag Mam Jalal took a date and put it in his mouth, and said, "It is *Sunnah*." (The Prophet used to put dates in his water cup and drink the water). Then Mam Jalal drank the tea over the date, not only to put some fructose that his system could handle into the tea, but also to show us that his honoring of the Prophet was better than our putting simple sugar in our teacups.

Before we left, Kak Loqman asked him to give us one special piece of advice so that we could say afterwards that Mam Jalal told it to us as a light on our path. Mam Jalal said that both of us were young, and our lives were in front of us. "Don't lose any opportunity!" he said. We shook his hand, thanked him for his time, and wished him a long, healthy life.

America's Plan

During that meeting in 1998, I heard for the first time from Mam Jalal about "America's Plan" (the Iraq Liberation Act). Mam Jalal was very optimistic about this U.S. plan to remove Saddam Hussein from power and free Kurdistan from direct Iraqi rule. I was really excited, and wanted to find out the details of when America would start to act on it. IMK was the only *religious* Iraqi Sunni organization in Syria at the time that wanted to participate in and support America's Plan; the Syrian government opposed participation, and it was really unhappy when it heard that IMK supported the plan. As a result, the IMK office where I was working came under the scrutiny of Syrian intelligence, which wanted more information, but there were no more details about the plan available at that time.

I remembered that Mam Jalal had told us not to lose any opportunity. I don't know why, but I thought that this was the biggest opportunity yet for the Iraqi people to get rid of Saddam's regime and make big changes in Iraq. This time our dreams could come true, and we could have our freedom. I used to go daily to encourage all of the groups representing Iraqi refugees to come together and become involved in the plan. I thought it was time for the Iraqi people to be free from Hell and to change Iraq into heaven. I used to imagine how new technology would come to Iraq with America's Plan, and how Baghdad would be like New York or London. But it was really hard to show support for the plan, because Syria was so opposed to it. The government was not convinced that America's Plan was only for regime change in Iraq, and worried that it might include Syria too. No one was sure at that time just what the plan would do. But the Americans started to provide training facilities to Iraqi opposition parties, so everyone knew that something was going to happen.

In retrospect, I have never regretted anything so much as my support for America's Plan. If in 1999 I had known that Iraq would be destroyed and that things would be as they are now in 2007, I never would have supported it. In 1999, we did not think that America would eventually send its army to Iraq; we only thought that it would support the Iraqi opposition and would participate in the country's renewal. But as a result of the American invasion, Iraq has been set back 100 years, and Baghdad has become like Mogadishu rather than London. My regret today is especially ironic because of how much difficulty my support for the plan caused me in my criminal case. In 2005, the U.S. government claimed to a federal judge that I was a dangerous terrorist, and as part of its proof the government submitted portions of my 1999 diary, written in Syria, that talked about my support for America's Plan. The government twisted the truth into knots by mistranslating the phrase "America's Plan" as the "Plan in America," and then claimed that the plan I was referring to was a terrorist plan directed at America that I was discussing with various groups in Syria. If the government had presented all of the journal entries fairly, it would have been obvious that the entries referred to "America's Plan"—the Iraq Liberation Act of 1998, passed by the U.S. Congress—to overthrow Saddam in Iraq, but the government was not interested in accuracy or fairness, and so as a result of this and other misrepresentations, the judge cancelled my bail. I certainly got my reward for supporting America's Plan. The government was able to convict me of conspiracy for a terrorist plot, and to this day I have no idea what the plot actually was, nor has anyone ever been able to properly explain it to me. But this is life, and we all should learn some lessons from it. Never participate in or support something until you know all the details. If you don't know all the details, like me and like millions of Iraqi people who welcomed the American army into Iraq, you will regret it.

Federalism

There was an Iraqi center in Damascus called *Dirasat Al Iraqia* (Iraqi Research), headed by Iraqi journalist Adil Rauof. The center used to publish a magazine seasonally under the same name. One day in 1999 after I visited the center, Kak Rauof said that he wanted me to come back next week because he had scheduled a debate about federalism in Iraq: should Kurdistan and all the other regions have self-government with a weak central government in Baghdad? He wanted me to participate, and joked that he wanted me to prove that I was a Muslim more than I was a Kurd. If I supported federalism, that would mean that I was a Kurd more than a Muslim. (I do not know where he got this philosophy from.) At the time, the debate over federalism in Iraq came down to a question of whether it was more important to give regional and ethnic groups more control over their lives through self-government (an option favored by the Kurds), or whether Iraq would be stronger if ethnic divisions were suppressed and the country presented a strong, central, unified government to the rest of the world. Kak Rauof, who was opposed to federalism, must have thought that as a supporter of Islam, I would tend to favor a strong central government that emphasized the unity of all Muslims, and that being a Kurd I might persuade other Kurds that federalism was not a good idea.

On the day of the debate, the participants included Kak Dana, the PUK representative, and Sheikh Tahir, the representative of the PSK-1 (Socialist Party of Kurdistan), who were both in favor of federalism; and Adil Rauof and Sheikh Taqi Mudarisi, both of whom were opposed. I was in favor of federalism. During the debate we talked about two main points. Would federalism divide and weaken Iraq (which, after all, was surrounded by potentially hostile neighbors, and had oil coveted by the West), or would it unite and strengthen Iraq? And would a Western-style federal system be practical in Iraq, where the ethnic divisions went so deep? The two sides argued back and forth; from time to time they would make fun of me and ask what kind of a religious person I was if I were willing to divide Islam and support federalism.

I told them to give me one reason why federalism was contrary to Islam or God's will. I said, "For centuries, Kurds have been suffering in the name of Islam. Kurdish land has been taken, as well as Kurdish freedom. For centuries the Kurds have been servants, not brothers. We were not even paid for serving, but rather we were forced into slavery and received nothing but humiliation. Kurds are not even allowed to speak their own language. We have been gassed, we have no rights in the countries in which we live, we are second-class citizens. Tell me, where is that permitted in Islam? Why am I your brother in Islam if you rule over me and I serve you, but if I ask for equal rights as a brother you accuse me of not being a Muslim?"

I said that 95% of the Kurds wanted federalism. Why should I go against their will in order to prove that I am a Muslim? Are not the Kurds also Muslims? Why do we claim to be Muslim only when it is in our interest? I do not believe it is against any principle in Islam to have our own rulers to protect the interests of the people, their culture and language, and their right to enjoy the fruits of their labor and their land. I believe that God created nations each with their own diversity as a sign of His power and will. Why should we try to stop that? What did the Iraqi regime do to Kurds that is part of Islam? Did God tell Saddam to commit genocide on the Kurds? Kurds should have equal rights with the Arabs in Iraq, and the Turks in Turkey, and the Persians in Iran. We should all be brothers.

Kak Dana, the PUK representative, was very happy with what I said, and stated that he thought it was time for the Kurds to get their rights and time for the rest of Iraq to support us. Federalism did not mean that the Kurds would have a separate country. It meant that Kurds would serve in the Iraqi Army, have the same foreign policy, participate in the central government, and follow the same laws as the rest of Iraq. But each province would have its own local government.

On the other hand, Kak Rauof said that he thought I would be on his side—opposed to federalism. I told him that I was unhappy with all of the "isms"— Marxism, Darwinism, federalism. I am a villager, I told him, and all I want is for Kurds to live free with dignity, like all other nations. I did not believe that there was anything against Islam in that.

Kak Rauof said, "I am with you in wanting freedom, but which system is most likely to give it to you?"

I laughed and said, "Justice, equal rights, real brotherhood and not slavery—that system will get the Kurds what they want."

Kak Dana laughed and agreed that this was all we needed. Sheikh Tahir, the representative of the Socialist Party, also laughed and said, "It looks like everyone is becoming a Socialist and will join my party— you are all looking for equality."

And I said, "This is exactly what Islam is about."

Hajj

The *Hajj* (pilgrimage to Mecca) is one of the five pillars of Islam. Muslims believe that it is obligatory for each person—if he can, and if he has the ability—to visit the holy city of Mecca at least once in his lifetime. For millions of Muslims, it is their dream to get that opportunity—especially someone like me who grew up in a village. For people like me, travel was impossible. In Iraq at that time, usually no one could legally go outside the country unless he was at least forty years old, unless he worked for the government or knew important people within it, or unless he was very rich and could give bribes to immigration officers. None of these routes for travel had ever been available to me. I was also a Kurd—which reduced the chance of getting a legally approved Iraqi passport and exit permit even more.

But soon after I started working for IMK, Kak Loqman visited the Saudi embassy and asked for visas for Mecca. The Saudis agreed to give him two visas. He came back very excited and said, "Kak Yassin, are you ready?"

"For what?" I asked him

"For *Umrah*," he said. *Umrah* is a small pilgrimage. It can be done at any time of the year, not just during Ramadan, the fasting month for Muslims. The big pilgrimage, *Hajj*, happens only once a year, at a specific time of Ramadan, and it involves much more than just visiting Mecca.

"Are you sure?" I asked him.

"Yes, thank God," he said. "They promised me two visas."

"What about expenses?"

"All we need is to just buy the tickets."

"But what about food and hotel?" I asked.

"It will be Ramadan and we will be fasting," Kak Loqman said. "In the mosque they have food for breaking the fast. We will stay in the mosque. We will not have to rent a hotel room. We are Kurds. We should live like *peshmerga*."

"It sounds good," I said. This is the way that people from the Middle East travel. Many times we went from city to city and we did not have one extra penny. If anything had happened, we would not have had any money to buy food or get a hotel. Some people go on pilgrimage when they have enough money for a one-way ticket only, even though they do not have enough money for the return trip. They all say that they are just trusting God.

For both Kak Loqman and me, this was the first time that we had ever flown in a plane. In January 1999, we bought our tickets and were approved to fly from Damascus, although we did not exactly determine which day we would be coming back; we had a visa to stay a whole month. When we arrived in Mecca, I could hardly believe my eyes. All the places that I had been dreaming about, like the holy mosque Haram, were right there before me. I said in my heart, *Thank you, God!!* I don't know why, but immediately I remembered my mother—her biggest wish was to visit Mecca. It brought tears to my eyes. We believe that children can do the *Hajj* for their parents, and so I decided to do the *Umrah* for her. I prayed for my mother wherever I went.

The Haram mosque was huge. It is really hard to describe, and harder still to imagine. At least three million people were there during the last ten days of Ramadan, and many stayed at the mosque. But there were no bad words, no arguments, no fights, even though most of the people did not know each other. They all belonged to different groups and schools of thought, and they were from countries that were fighting each other. But there was no discord. I was very surprised. It is true what the scholars say about the *Hajj*—it is a global meeting in which everyone is equal. You see and hear many different colors and languages; you meet both rich and poor, kings and workers; and all of them are doing the same thing, wearing just a simple piece of cloth to cover their bodies. So you cannot differentiate between rich and poor because everyone looks the same—and is equal. The goal of Islam is to bring people together so that they will know each other and live as brothers in peace. And during the *Hajj*, people do it. But after they go home, the old habits start again. I said to myself, *We really do not get the benefit from the* Hajj *that we should.*

Most of the traditions we observe during the pilgrimage started with Prophet Abraham (Ibrahim in Arabic), who we believe is really the father of all the messengers of God. We believe that we are following Ibrahim and his religion, which we believe he named Islam; thus the origin of the name Islam goes back to him. We also believe that Ibrahim, with his oldest son Ishmael (Ismael in Arabic), built the Haram mosque, also known as House of God; Ibrahim was the first one to go on a pilgrimage, and he was the first one who proclaimed to the people that they should answer a call to pilgrimage (*Hajj*) to this House. Since he called, until now and forever afterwards people will be answering his call.

As part of the performance of *Hajj* rituals, we run seven times from a small hill, called Safa, to the top of another small hill, called Marwa, because Hagar, the mother of Ismael, ran back and forth seven times over these hills to look for water after Ibrahim left her with baby Ismael. She found no water, but God opened a spring for her after she sat down next to Ismael to wait for death. The spring, called Zamzam, is now inside the mosque, and people use it for holy water and even as medicine for their illnesses and their sins. The tradition of animal sacrifices began because Ibrahim was ordered by God to sacrifice Ismael as a test. But just as he was about to sacrifice Ismael, God sent an angel who told Ibrahim to sacrifice a lamb instead. Since then, people have sacrificed lambs to commemorate Ibrahim's intention to please God. Thus one can see that many of the cornerstones of Islam go back to Prophet Ibrahim and his family, and are also part of the Judeo-Christian tradition.

Loqman and I stayed in Mecca for the ten last days of Ramadan, and most of it we spent in the Haram, where we slept. But we did not confirm our return flight with the airline because it was our first flight and we did not know that we were supposed to. So we got into trouble.

The end of Ramadan is the Muslim festival of Eid. We tried to travel to the Saudi capital of Riyadh to sightsee, but we were not permitted because *Hajj* visas were not good for travel to the capital. So we decided to go back to Syria to join our families for Eid. But we could not get a return flight. Millions of pilgrims were going back home, and all the flights were booked. We went to the immigration office in Mecca, but they told us just to go to the airport and wait for a chance to grab two extra seats.

We ended up sleeping for two days in the airport without getting a flight. Then, after many phone calls, we found someone who was able to get seats for us. We were happy that we would be home on the very night of Eid. However, when we arrived at the Damascus airport, they would not let us enter the country because they said our names were not on a list for Iraqis returning to Syria. Iraqis needed special permission to get back into Syria, and someone from Syria had to bring this permission form to the airport officials. At the IMK office, we used to do this for thousands of people; we knew all the immigration officers in Syria because we went to them every day to get these same permission forms for other travelers. Since both Loqman and I were living in Syria with residency permits—not coming from Europe, but living in Damascus—we did not think that we needed special permission to re-enter the country. We tried to contact people at the IMK office to bring us the permission forms, but everybody had gone home for Eid and we were unable to get any help.

So for three days we were trapped in the Damascus airport without any way to leave, because all the offices were closed for the holy days of Eid. Once again we had to sleep on the floor. Everything in the airport was twice as expensive as outside, and they sold only fast food, so our families had to cook for us and bring the food to the airport.

One night when a friend came to see me, he brought my daughter Alaa with him. She was three years old at the time. She was sleeping, and when they woke her up she was surprised to see me and looked at me like she did not quite believe what she was seeing. Then she jumped up, ran to me, and hugged me; she would not let me put her down for a whole hour. She was holding onto me like a scared child who wants to hide herself in her parent's arms. When my friend was ready to go home, Alaa refused to go with him, and the police had to come and tell her that she couldn't stay. I told her that I would come home tomorrow, but nothing made her change her mind and let me go; the police finally had to pry her out of my arms. Until they took her out the door, I could hear her crying and shouting "Daddy! Daddy!"

Altogether, the trip to Mecca took thirteen days—eight on pilgrimage and five sleeping in airports. This is what travelers in the Middle East have to go through. It is really no fun to travel with checkpoints, police, bribes, security officers, and permits, all of which make you wish in some respects that you had stayed home.

Sheikh Uthman

The best way to know someone is to examine his actions, because human beings reveal their values in their deeds. And no one can be considered great without having a great commitment to service. How much did he give? National heroes and the great people of history have always given of themselves first. Of course, not everyone has an opportunity to be great. Many people inherit wealth from their parents, or power that allows them to become famous, or they just live at a time or in a place that allows them to develop their fame. All this is fine for people who just want to be famous. But to be a real hero and a great man, one must start from zero and live in harsh times and unstable places, then overcome it all and raise oneself up and make a difference by giving back to people and society. These are the people who really change history, the great ones. Sheikh Uthman Abdul Aziz was one of them.

Many times people respect a leader because they hope to get something from him or be protected from harm or danger, especially in the Middle East. So the strength and influence of most politicians comes to an end when they die. But for scientists, artists, and scholars it is completely different, because the love and respect of the people will outlast their deaths and remain in peoples' hearts—not only for those who knew them, but for centuries afterwards. Sheikh Uthman had no money to provide for the people, and he had no army to scare the people into following him. All he had was his profound knowledge and his commitment to serve.

In Islam, we don't have a rank for religious scholars, as the Catholic Church does (Pope, cardinal, bishop, priest). Our only rank is the person's knowledge and popularity. The good thing about this is that nobody needs to have any mediator to assist him or her in contacting God and asking for help. There is no doctrine that someone is so sinful or illiterate that he needs to ask an Imam or Sheikh to pray or intercede for him because he cannot do it himself; he *can* do it himself. We believe that God is always waiting for sincere prayers, and He is available twenty-four hours a day, everywhere. God understands all languages and knows our needs in every situation. If you sincerely call to Him, He will always respond to you.

On the other hand, because there is no rank among Imams and no religious head of Islam as there was in the time of the Prophet, there is chaos in the Muslim world with respect to religious requirements, which confuse some people and misguide others. Various Imams and scholars can issue opinions about religious questions, and they will be obeyed or not depending on whether people believe them. Only from time to time does an Imam become recognized by his great wisdom, knowledge, personality, and service as a leader among all leaders—as Sheikh Uthman was. Most of the Imams in Kurdistan looked at Sheikh Uthman as first among equals. As Sheikh Barzingi said in tribute at Sheikh Uthman's funeral, he was the Imam of Imams, and the teacher of teachers.

It is part of our tradition to visit a sheikh (Imam) and ask him to pray for you and advise you before you travel. Before I went to Syria, I went to many Imams in Chamchamal, and then I decided to seek out Sheikh Uthman and ask for his blessing. When I told him I needed his advice, he read for me this saying of the Prophet Mohammad, may peace be upon him:

> Fear God wherever you are.
> Do good deeds to wash away your sins.
> Show the People a gracious manner.
> Deal with them in the manner that you want them to deal with you.

Sheikh Uthman began to cry and said, "My son, people are looking for examples to follow. They hear a lot but they cannot see. They are surrounded by corruption, suffering, and misunderstanding wherever they go. This is because of ignorant leaders and politicians who don't protect the people but destroy them. Oh my son, our value is in our deeds. Obtain knowledge and act upon it. Put it into practice. It does not matter where you go. Everywhere is God's land, and all humans are God's people. Try to be the best example."

I kissed his hand and asked him to please pray for me. He told me, "Do not forget my daughter [meaning Zuhur, my own wife]. She will be alone and a foreigner. Don't break her heart. The women are kind and soft only if you are the same for them. You can have their heart and love. Be kind and soft."

Sheikh Uthman was the founder and head of IMK, but he had nothing to do with politics. The only reason he founded IMK was because of Saddam's gassing of Halabja and its aftermath, when the survivors had to flee to the mountains. People asked Sheikh Uthman if they were allowed to fight to protect themselves from the army that was following them. He said they were, and led the defense.

In 1995, when problems led IMK and PUK into a conflict, PUK arrested Sheikh Uthman. He went on TV and said, "I am not allowing anyone to fight and shed blood." After that, he did not lead IMK again, and his brother Sheikh Ali took his place. But Sheikh Uthman's scholarship remains. He had a great impact on the Kurds, he had many students, and his books are a source of learning. To this day, I would say that his is the best interpretation of the Qur'an.

In 1999, Sheikh Uthman came to Syria on his way to the United Arab Emirates to see a doctor. When he arrived, Kak Loqman and I went to the border to welcome him, and that night we all stayed in Qamishly in a hotel. The next day we flew from Qamishly to Damascus. This was only the second time I had ever flown in a plane (the first had been the pilgrimage to Mecca a few months earlier). It was a small plane carrying about forty-two people. I was very excited, not so much because of the flight but because I would be Sheikh Uthman's companion.

Sheikh Uthman died in Damascus. Just two days before his death, I invited him to my house with his son, Kak Abdul Rahman. Sheikh Uthman sat on the floor because I did not have any furniture. After about half an hour, while I was serving them and preparing dinner, he told me to sit down. I sat humbly in front of him. He said, "Some people don't fear God, and they say what is not true. Yassin, I had a different picture of you. But now this week, having spent the time with you, I saw everything by my own eyes, and I see that you are not what people told me. I thank God that I traveled with you, and ate with you, to make me know you by myself, and that I cleared my heart for you before I die."

After Sheik Uthman's death, we took his body back to Halabja. From the border until Halabja—about ten hours' driving time—people stood on both sides of the road crying and throwing flowers. I had never seen such a thing in my life. Thousands of cars followed when we reached any city, filled with people waiting to say goodbye to him. When his brother Sheikh Ali spoke, he said maybe politicians can bring people out to listen, but they can't make them cry. I wrote a poem, which I read at the funeral.

Sheikh Uthman

Today is the day of mourning
Kurdistan is quiet and sad
People are waiting,
Searching for the way
Looking always for news...news.
People all whisper to each other
Sheikh Uthman is on his way
Coming back from Damascus in Sham,
Coming home to Halabja.

Oh, great Guide—
Sheikh, Imam and teacher—
Open your eyes for one last time.
See how you plan has unfolded,
See what your preaching has brought

Oh Halabja, City of Peace,
Will it be poisonous gas
Or Sheikh Uthman himself
That will make you known to everyone
All across the world?

Oh Sharazur
Be proud and happy—
Tell Ibn Salah
That the great scholar Uthman

Today is coming to be his guest

Oh Halabja,
Raise your head up
Even higher than Hawramans Mountains.
It is enough for you to be proud
That you brought up for the Kurds
And all Muslims and the world
Such an Imam and scholar.

Notes: Sham is the ancient land that is now Syria. Sharazur is the area in Sulaimaniya Province in which Halabja is located. It was also an ancient city. Ibn Salah was a scholar of Sharazur Province who lived 500–600 years ago. His most famous book is *Ulom Hadith* (*Science of Hadith*), the latter being oral traditions relating to the words, deeds, and teaching of Prophet Mohammad. The Hawramans Mountains (the Avroman Range) are about thirty miles from Halabja.

IMK Delegation

Later in 1999, while I was in class one day at Abu Noor University, I was told that my principal, Dr. Ahmad Kaftaro, needed to see me in his office. When I arrived, the office was full of people with turbans. I did not recognize many of them, but I did recognize Sheikh Ali Abdul Aziz (Sheikh Uthman's brother), who was the head of IMK, and Ali Bapir, who was one of IMK's political leaders (and who subsequently founded the Islamic Group of Kurdistan, which now holds six seats in the Regional Parliament of Iraqi Kurdistan). Dr. Kaftaro smiled and said, "Welcome, Kak Yassin. I have some guests for you. Do you know them?"

"Some of them," I answered.

Abu Noor had students from fifty different countries, and because of its central location in Damascus there were daily visits by delegations from many countries. Whenever the school received a delegation from a particular country, they would call a student from that country to guide the group around and explain everything in the language of the group members. Once Dr. Kaftaro came into a class with a huge black man and introduced him as Mr. Mohammed Ali, the famous American boxer. We were really excited to see him. Mohammed Ali told us about Islam in the U.S. and how he had become a Muslim. I believe that he stayed at the university for about forty days because he was participating in a health cure (which included fasting). One of our teachers, Dr. Mahmood Barsha, was in charge of a program of health fasting, in which a person restricts his diet to water and juice for a period of ten days for five to six months. Mr. Ali said that he had gone to many doctors in different countries, but nothing had helped him like this fasting. We also had some visits to Abu Noor by members of the U.S. Congress.

The IMK delegation was on its way to a pilgrimage in Mecca, but because their visa paperwork was delayed they had to stay in Syria for ten to twelve days. It was a big opportunity for me to get to know these people better. I was with them most of the time. I took them shopping, and to mosques and museums, and anywhere else they wanted to go. We also visited some embassies and some famous Sheikhs. Then I went with them to get their visa approvals. After awhile I was like a friend to them; most of them had sons older than I was. I was really surprised at how simple and humble they were—not like big leaders and important politicians. At first I was surprised at their simplicity, but after a couple of days I came to believe that it was really part of who they were. The time I spent with them was very important to me. I also found most of them to be very religious scholars whose politics actually came second.

There were fifteen people in the group, but they all slept on the floor in the two small offices of the IMK. Each day two of them were in charge of cooking and cleaning the offices. They not only slept on the floor, they cooked by themselves, and no one was allowed to see them do this except Loqman, Jameel, and me. One day I joked with Dr. Ibrahim, a member of the delegation, and told him that people probably assumed they were living in the Sheraton Hotel and eating at five-star restaurants, when they were actually living like shepherds. Daily they met with important people; they did not have a car to drive to these meetings, so they had to go by taxi. I asked Dr. Ibrahim whether this was the political image they wanted to project, or whether it was because they really were so poor that they could not afford a hotel and restaurant. He laughed and told me that tonight, when everyone was asleep, I should check their bags and pockets and see if they had any money with them. At that time there were no credit cards or banks at all in Kurdistan; only Syrian citizens living in Syria could get or use these. Kurds were not considered residents of Syria and so could not have accounts; any money they might have would therefore be in the form of cash.

"So how are you able to lead the people?" I asked him.

"By example," he said.

"No, I mean how do you feed them and give them a salary?"

"We are in a revolutionary period," he said.

"So when are you going to pass beyond this period?" I asked.

"When we die."

I laughed. "You are a hopeless *peshmerga*."

"For us Kurds, it has taken a thousand years," Dr. Ibrahim said. "There is no reason to think that it will not take another thousand years."

Sometimes we had to wait twenty or thirty minutes for a taxi, or an hour for a bus. Once while we were waiting for a bus door to open, Sheikh Ali Abdul Aziz was the first one in line. As he started to get on the bus, someone pulled him back down and yelled at him, "You go back! Wait!" It was a security officer, who said that he had to check the bus first. After he checked the bus, he stood in the door to check our identification. I told our group that if we rented a private car, we would not have these problems.

"So why don't you rent one, rich guy?" they said.

"Because people will believe that you are all millionaires, like other politicians," I said.

They responded with a Kurdish expression: "Whatever the house owner knows about his house, if the thief also knows, he will empty the house."

Once we went out with *Mamosta* Ali Bapir and Sheikh Mohammed Barzini, who in 1999 was living in London. Sheikh Barzini was one of the founders of IMK and was head of the political wing. He went with Ali Bapir when *Mamosta* split off from IMK to begin the Islamic Group of Kurdistan, and then became a leader of that group. I asked Sheikh Barzini why he did not wear a suit like *Mamosta* Ali. He said that even in London he did not wear a suit; he always walked about on the streets with a turban and a long shirt. I asked him whether people in London thought it strange to see people walking in Middle Eastern clothing. He said that London was better than Turkey; last year, when he had gone to Turkey with some associates, everywhere they went people had taken pictures of them and followed them around as though they were from another planet. *Mamosta* Ali laughed and said, "No, they were following you because they knew you were a Neanderthal." Sheikh Barzini was from Shanidar, where Neanderthal graves have been discovered.

Us, Not Them

One day after I went to the IMK office, which had only two small rooms, I found some of the delegation having a discussion in one room. So I went to the other. When I opened the door, I found Sheikh Ali Abdul Aziz sitting alone. We exchanged greetings and I immediately apologized for interrupting him. I tried to leave, thinking that he wanted to be alone, but before I left I asked him if he needed anything. He responded, "Yes."

"What do you need?" I said.

"Some real men," he said.

I was confused about what he meant. "I'm sorry, Sheikh," I said. "Did you say 'men' or '*nan*' (bread)?"

"Men. Men!" He did not sound happy, but I could not tell what was bothering him.

"Sorry, Sheikh," I said. "I don't understand."

"Yassin," he said. "There is nothing worse than hypocrites. They say one thing and do the opposite. When they see you they praise you, and when you go away they say all sorts of bad things about you. If you give them what they want, you are the best, but if you don't, you are the worst. They push you to do something, and afterwards they blame you for doing it."

"I am very sorry, Sheikh," I said. "For the sake of God, if it is me, tell me what I did."

He smiled. "I wish I had other Yassins like you," he said.

At this point, Sheikh Ahmad Kaka Mahmood, a member of the delegation and a very famous Kurdish writer, and Dr. Ibrahim came in. I welcomed them and left them alone with Sheikh Ali. I never found out what was bothering Sheikh Ali that day or who the hypocrites were. Even the Prophet said that among the people, the worst are the two-faced (the hypocrites), who go to one group with one face and go to the other group with another face.

Most people blame their leader or president for all that he does, but in fact it is not him alone but also those around him who are responsible. Scholars keep silent. Advisers are too scared to disagree. In America we say, "We allowed them to do it." In my culture, we say, "As you are now, your leader is going to be." It is our responsibility, not theirs. Our silence kills us, not our leaders!

Peace in Islam

In 1986, Sheikh Ahmad Kaka Mahmood had published a book about freedom in Islam that focused on the issue of women's rights. The Communist Party, which had always claimed that under Islam women were treated like slaves, saw the idea of women's rights within Islam as a threat and got people to buy up all of his books and burn them. Then the party threatened him so he would stop spreading his ideas about freeing women in Islam. They could have saved themselves the trouble, because the Iraqi government would not allow a second publication of his book. In 1987, Sheikh Kaka Mahmood published another book called *Wtay zanacan bawar baxwa*, which translates as *What Scientists Say About Belief in God*. The whole book consisted of statements by Western scientists and philosophers, such as Augustine, Edison, and Galileo, about their beliefs in God. Both of these books were a slap in the face to the Communists. The Communists were very strong in Kurdistan at that time, and most political groups claimed at least to be socialist.

In the 1970s in Kurdistan, it was considered a shame if you did not pray regularly, and people would make fun of you and ostracize you if you neglected your prayers. But just ten years later everything had changed, and people made fun of you if you *did* pray. Yet books by Sheikh Kaka Mahmood, Ali Bapir, and Mohammad Sharazori really created a revolution and brought young people back to faith.

One day I went for a walk with Sheikh Kaka Mahmood, and we began talking about his last book, *Ashti La Islam* (*Peace in Islam*). To test him, I asked why, when Muslims are weak or in trouble, they ask for peace, but when they are in a position of power they give people only the sword.

The Sheikh stopped walking. He looked shocked and asked me where I had gotten that idea.

"I don't know," I said. "We have 1,400 years of history."

"The history of Hajaj*, the Tartars, the Mongols, and Saddam are not a good history of Islam," he said.

"What is the difference?" I asked.

"The difference is that these bloody leaders in Muslim history and countries do not represent Islam. Look what Prophet Mohammad, may peace be upon him, did when he achieved power. After thirteen years of suffering in Mecca, he fled to Medina. When he returned to Mecca in triumph, what did he do to those people who had driven him out of the city? He gathered them together and asked them, 'What do you think I am going to do to you?' They replied, 'You are the best and the son of the best!' And Mohammad told them, 'Go—you are free.' Those were the same people who had tortured him and his companions for thirteen years and killed many of them, and yet when he returned in triumph he forgave them and did not take revenge."

"So why do people say that Islam is spread by the sword?"

"Because people don't know Islam," he said. "There is no way to force people to have faith, because faith is in the heart. You should believe and love God, not be scared into believing. Nobody has the power to put faith into your heart by force. You can force someone to pray, but that will not make him faithful. If he doesn't believe in what you made him do, you will have no control over his mind or heart."

* Hajaj was a bloody tyrant of the Amaween Caliphate, ca. 800–1500 A.D., which included Iraq and Damascus. Hajaj was said to have killed the Prophet's grandson.

I started laughing.

"Why are you laughing?" he asked.

I told him his words reminded me of my cousin and his nephew. My cousin Sheikh Umar was an Imam, and his nephew was living with him, so he forced his nephew to pray. Just before Muslims pray, we state our intention by saying, "I want to pray such prayer for God…" One day I was standing by the nephew's side at the mosque when we started to pray, and he said to me quietly, "I want to pray for Sheikh Umar…that he will stop forcing me to pray."

Sheikh Mahmood started laughing too. "What is the benefit from such prayers?" he asked. "Do you know which is the largest Muslim country in the world today?"

I said I did not know.

"Indonesia," he said. "Think about it. What forced them to convert to Islam? Did any Muslim army ever reach there? If you force someone to do something, he really does not choose, because when the force is removed he is not going to do it. For centuries Islam remained in our country because it was never forced on us. If they had forced us, we would have rejected Islam as soon as the force was removed. Look at Saddam. He forced millions of Kurds to sign up for the Baath Party. In 1991, when the pressure to join the party was removed, millions deserted it. Today, does anyone follow Baath?"

"No."

"Why don't they teach Baath principles to their children? Because they joined the Baath Party only through force, and now there is no more force. Why has Islam remained for centuries if it was the occupier? Has any nation accepted occupation centuries after it is free?"

"So then," I said, "why do people say that Islam forced itself on others by sword and slaughter?"

"Because they do not know history," he said. "In all twenty-three years of Mohammad's life as a messenger, when he built a Muslim community or even a state made up of both Muslims and pagans, how many people were killed?"

"I don't know."

"I thought you knew history?"

"I don't know the exact number," I said.

"Read the books," Sheikh Kaka Mahmood said. "You will not find even 1,000 people who have been killed in all the battles from both sides over the twenty-three-year period in which Islam expanded across Arabia. You cannot find twenty-three innocent people who were killed—women or children or elderly. And no churches or temples were destroyed. Today just one battle will easily cause an even higher loss of life. Look at the city of Halabja. In just three hours—not twenty-three years—over 5,000 people were killed. Not one percent of them was carrying a weapon. What about the First or Second World Wars? Wars are the normal way that change takes place in history. But Islam brought about change peacefully. Its idea for bringing about change was to not force people."

I wonder what the Sheikh would say now about "democracy" in Iraq. Estimates are that 700,000 Iraqis have been killed in three years, and still there is no democracy. Before democracy can take root, perhaps more than a million people may die. And perhaps democracy will not take root at all, and we will be left with the rule of the gun. Why is nobody saying that they are trying to force conversion to democracy by the sword?

We had to start back, and the Sheikh said to me, "Let me put it to you in a few sentences. Force can affect the body and bring about physical movements, but it has no authority over the mind and heart. Real change is fruit from the mind and heart."

I told him that I agreed. I said that his books had brought back thousands of youth to believe in God after they had been abandoned by the Communist Party. "You did not force them to come back," I said.

He smiled and said, "God changed their hearts, not my books."

I said to him, "Sheikh, I would like some special advice from you, please."

"Stay independent," he said. "Parties and politics try to limit Islam. Don't limit yourself. Stay free so you can always tell the truth." Sheikh Mahmood was a big leader of the IMK, and so I was impressed that he was telling me not to join IMK, don't accept their offers, and stay independent. I took his advice sincerely.

In his book *Peace in Islam*, Sheikh Mahmood states that peace is made in three stages. Peace begins first in our own minds and hearts. Nothing gives tranquility like faith in God, because the opposite of peace—stress and doubt—come from fear. Believing in God gives you trust and removes your fears. God will always help you. You have nothing to fear. If you have lost anything—your health or business or a loved one—believe in God and accept His decree. There is wisdom in acceptance, and you will be rewarded for that. In heaven you will see everyone again. If someone believes this, he will have tranquility enough to enjoy even hard times.

Once peace takes hold in an individual, it spreads among the family members—between wife and husband, between children and siblings. Islam gives each of them special responsibilities and rights. If they follow these responsibilities, their home will be a small heaven, full of love, respect, and joy. It is really sad in today's Western life how many people lose their families. Children and parents are often separated and never get a chance to be together, whether they are eating or talking or working. Many children do not see or talk or write to their parents except for birthdays and a couple of holidays. Even the husband and wife often live separately. Many mothers and fathers have orders of protection keeping them from seeing their children, and many children do not even know who their fathers are, and have never even seen them. Even those families that stay together do not share much family time. Many families do not eat together—at mealtime someone is on the Internet, or another is watching TV. For real peace, families should spend time together before the family becomes a thing of history.

Once peace becomes established in families, peace will spread throughout society. Racism, hatred, selfishness, political trickery, isolation—all of which violate Islam—will dwindle away because these evils come from fear, and faith overcomes fear and brings peace to society. Individual peace leads to family peace, which leads to community peace, which leads to global peace. We are all tied together. As the

Arabic saying goes, "If you don't have something, you cannot spend it." If, as an individual, you don't have peace in your mind and heart, you cannot spread it to your family. Do not talk about family peace; first fix yourself. Only after you have peace in your own heart can you bring peace to your family. And if there is no peace in your family, do not try to bring peace to the community; first try to mend the broken relationships within your own family. And if you do not have peace in your community, do not try to bring peace to the world. Start first with your own community. It is a step-by-step process. If each of us were to practice this discipline, peace would be everywhere.

Chapter Twelve ☪
East to West

Unknown Future

If humans could foresee the future, no doubt there would be much less going wrong. Many times our expectations do not come to pass. We flee from something only to end up in the very situation we want to avoid. One of my friends, Kak Farhad, immigrated to Germany because he hoped it would be safer than Kurdistan and would offer him a better life. I met him in Syria before he went to Germany and I found him to be a really sincere, decent person who knew a great deal about history and religion. Since I was studying these subjects at the time, I formed a strong bond with him.

One night in 1999 in Germany, while he was walking back to his home, a group of thugs attacked Kak Farhad and beat him to death. They were neo-Nazis who were trying to stop the immigration of Muslims into Germany. There were several other similar incidents around this time. I went with another friend to the Syrian airport to receive Kak Farhad's body because he had been my friend. A gentleman came up to me at the airport and thanked me for waiting for the body since early morning. He said that he still did not have enough information about how this tragedy had happened; the first police report simply acknowledged that Kak Farhad was a victim of racism, and that the Nazi party was growing again in Germany.

I asked my friend who was accompanying me who this gentleman was. He replied, "Kak Asuad Ado."

"You mean the one who has the TV show '*Fulclar*' ('Kurdish Tradition')?" I said.

"Yes."

It was hard for me to recognize Kak Ado as the same person I used to watch each week on TV. He looked very different. On his show he was a great joker, laughing all the time, but now because of this disaster and his lengthy travel his face was dark. I asked my friend, "Why is he coming for the body?"

"He is Farhad's father-in-law."

I was surprised; I hadn't known that. I went to Kak Ado, introduced myself, took his hand, and said, "I am very sorry. God will give him Paradise."

"No one can flee from death," Kak Ado said. "It follows us always, and when our time has come, it will not miss its mark."

"Still, this was a very big crime," I said. "He was a peaceful man. It is completely unfair."

"Tell me," he said, "when and where have Kurds ever been shown fairness?"

"*Mamosta*," I said. "One of my wishes was to meet you, but I am sorry that it happened in this troubled time."

"Kak Yassin," he said. "I am glad to meet you. Be strong."

"I hope to see you again," I said, before he drove away with Kak Farhad's body.

It is really amazing how we are all looking for a future that we just cannot foresee. Thousands of people left Kurdistan to save their lives and died on their way to Europe. Thousands of people wanted to live with dignity but ended in humiliation in refugee camps, unable to get papers that would give them legal status. Thousands sought freedom and ended up in jail. All these people were finally caught by the very thing that they were fleeing from. I myself am an example of this. For twenty years in Iraq, I expected at any minute to be arrested by the security forces and thrown in jail just because I was a Kurd—but it never happened until I came to America to live free. Jail in America was the last thing I expected.

Even in Iraq, where speaking the truth was dangerous, I was able to write poems, many of which were critical of the government. I was never arrested for this. It is ironic that in 2006 in America, where people are supposed to have the right of free speech, a speech in Iraq from 1994, and also a poem from 1999, were used against me at my trial. I was shocked that a 1994 speech and a 1999 poem could be a crime in America in 2006, especially because neither the speech nor the poem said anything about killing or bombing or fighting or terrorism, or said anything that would scare people. I was simply telling the truth. I was even more amazed when I sat in my jail cell listening to the radio, and every day I heard on talk shows statements that incited hate and violence against Muslims that were a thousand times more dangerous than anything the government claimed I had said. But nobody stopped these people from speaking hatefully against Muslims, because it was their right of free speech to do that.

On the day the prosecutor showed my poem to the jury, I got back to my jail cell and turned on the radio. There was a talk show on about Iraq and about what was happening now in Fallujah, after four American contractors had been murdered and hung from a bridge in 2004. The host of the show said that it had been a mistake not to just level the city. "We should have just wiped it out," the man said. "I don't know why our government didn't do it."

Fallujah is a city of 400,000 people. The talk show host wanted a city of 400,000 people to be demolished, and to let no one escape. He wanted to incite our government to do this. So this is free speech in America.

On another program, the same host talked about the Iraqi police and how every day several dozen of them died because they were working with the Americans. The host called these men who were dying to help the American cause "savages," "monkeys," and "animals." He said, "We give them weapons, and now they kill each other." He said this about Iraqi police, and not about terrorists or insurgents.

On another occasion during my trial, the prosecutor introduced a paragraph from my diary in which I said that my friend Idris came from America and talked to me about "America and the corruption there in America." The government mistranslated the phrase as "America and its immorality" and then accused me of being anti-American. The prosecutor also mistranslated my 1994 speech to claim that I referred to President Clinton as an "immoral Jew," and then accused me of anti-Semitism. Actually the word I used referred to sexual immorality, and as to the word Jew—well, I thought he was Jewish. It was common knowledge in Kurdistan that President Clinton was Jewish. Everyone described him as being Jewish, and in 1994 I had no way of knowing anything different.

Whenever the media in America talks about my case, they describe me as a Muslim, which is OK because I am Muslim, even though Islam had nothing to do with the charges. But if, in 1994 in Kurdistan, I mistakenly thought President Clinton was Jewish, is it acceptable for the prosecutor to charge that I am an anti-Semite? (Actually we Kurds believe that we are a Semitic people—Sami is one of the most common names in Kurdistan.) Is it really true in America that people are all equal before the law? Is it true that people have freedom of speech? Is it true that the law protects everyone? Or is it true that immigrants and green card holders are considered lesser human beings? Or that Muslims are a special group to target and abuse? Certainly it would appear from the trial transcript that my only crime was being Muslim, and I was found guilty of that even though I did nothing wrong and said nothing wrong. I never said anything against the U.S. or gave any support whatsoever for terrorists or terrorism.

From East to West

One day in 1999 when I went to the Red Crescent in Damascus, they told me that I should go to the UN office. When I arrived at the UN office, they told me that my name had been approved for resettlement, most likely to the U.S. They gave me some phone numbers to call and some addresses that I had to visit with my family for different tests, such as X-rays, HIV, blood, etc.

I was not sure whether to laugh or cry. I was very happy, and also a little sad, and I was also in between: I felt emotional without knowing which emotion was dominant.

In fact, I hoped that they would delay my departure for eighteen months so I could finish my master's degree. I was working in the IMK office at that time, and my life was close to normal—it was not as it had been before, when I was working at the villa or when I was jobless. If I had to leave, I preferred to go to Europe because it was closer to the Middle East and it would be easier for my wife and me to make return visits to our families. Through my job at IMK, I had met thousands of Kurds living in Europe, and many of them had given me their addresses and asked me to visit them in their adopted countries. If I went to a European country, I would know people there, which would be nice, especially because I had three young children.

It would be easier for me to go to Europe—but there was nothing I could do about it. The UN would not delay our departure so I could complete my master's degree, and they would not switch me to Europe. We had to have all our tests and be ready whenever they called, or lose our refugee status.

It would have been very unwise for me to lose my UN refugee status at that time, even though I had a job, because our three children, all of whom were born in Syria, were not Syrian citizens. They had no citizenship in any country, not even Iraq. They had never even been to Iraq. If Syria were to send all of the Iraqi refugees back to Iraq, what would happen to our children in terms of citizenship? This was especially a concern in 1999. I talked to my wife about the problem, and she supported our going to America. But many of my friends opposed it. Some of them said they would pray that I changed my mind; some of them told me that it was not a good idea; some of them reminded me that I used to speak against immigration and against fleeing to the West, and yet now I was going myself. They read me a verse from the Qur'an: "Oh, you who believe. Why do you say that which you do not?" (Surah 61, verse 2). I would joke with them and say I was following Imam Abu Hanifa, the founder the Hanafi school of thought in Islam. He used to say, "Forget my idea. I am a human being. Today I will say one thing, and tomorrow I will change my mind." And this is really true: humans will change their minds, and there is nothing wrong with that. All progress depends on people changing their minds. You're confronted daily with new realities to deal with, and you have to be flexible, especially in the Middle East. Changing your mind in the Middle East is as common as changing your clothes—although some people actually change their minds more often. They wear some clothes for years, but they change their minds (and their groups) many times.

I began to collect information about the U.S. and about life in America. At the UN office they gave us a booklet about the U.S., which we all memorized, and they said we were going to a place called Albany. I asked everybody I met who knew something about the U.S. to tell me what they knew. Once I picked up a lady from the airport who was coming from the U.S. In the car I told her that I was going to the U.S., and she asked which state. "Albany," I said. But she had never heard of that state, and she told me that it might be some kind of a trick: maybe the UN was planning to send us to Albania, the country.

This suggestion really alarmed me. I remembered that one of my friends in college was from Albania, so I asked him if the UN ever sent refugees to Albania. He replied that the country did not have enough food for its own citizens—why would they want refugees? If they opened the border, he said, 90% of the Albanians would try to flee to western Europe. I told him that someone thought the UN might be sending us to Albania, since she had never heard of such a place in America. He laughed and said, "Go to Eritrea—it is much better."

"Why don't you want me to come to your country?" I asked.

"Oh, by all means come to Albania," he said. "Just be sure to bring your own food with you, because I'm sure you can't get any there."

"Why not?"

"Because the Communists made everybody equal, and the only way to do that was to make everyone penniless."

"Really! Nobody is richer than anyone else?" I asked.

"Only if you're in the government," he said.

"Stop."

"I'm serious," he said. Then he brought some of his friends over and introduced me to them by saying, "This is Yassin, my best friend. He is a Kurd from Iraq."

"I'm not your friend," I said.

His face got red and his friends looked at him with surprise. "What's wrong?" he said. "Why aren't you my friend?"

I pretended not to have heard his question.

"Please, Yassin. Tell me why you aren't my friend."

"Because I am your brother," I told him.

He hugged me and started laughing. "Yes, by God it is true. You are my brother."

I became very scared that the UN had lied to me and might send us to Albania. I went to the bookstore and bought an atlas with a world map and checked both North and South America, but I could not find a state in the U.S. called Albany. This made me believe even more that the woman from the U.S. was right, and that we were really going to Albania. Something was wrong. I went back to the UN and asked the representative about it, but she insisted that we were going to the U.S., to a place called Albany. I asked her where on the map I could find Albany. She tried to find it for almost one hour, going back and forth between North and South America, but the place did not exist on the map. She told me to come back next Monday when the management would be there.

Now I was sure that something was wrong. I went to another friend who spoke some English; I thought he might have been a refugee in America. But he said no, he had lived in Australia.

"Where did you learn English, then?" I asked him.

"In Australia," he answered.

"Do you speak Australian too?"

He smiled. "English is the Australian language."

"What?" I was surprised. "How can that be?"

"The Australian language is English," he said.

"Sorry," I told him. "I thought just the U.S. and the U.K. spoke English."

"Australia and Canada too," he said. That made me even more surprised.

I stopped talking about this because it just proved my ignorance about the world, but I asked him where Albany was in the U.S. He said he had never heard of it, and then he took out his cell phone and started dialing a number. He said he was calling his friend in Illinois.

"Where is that?" I asked.

"In America," he said.

"You can just call America like that, with no phone card or telephone office?"

He just smiled at my innocence and started talking in English with his friend. Of course I could not understand him. After he was done, he said that he was not sure, but he thought Albany might be in New York State. When he mentioned New York I was relieved, because I had heard of New York. I had also heard of Washington, Los Angeles, Texas, Chicago, and Florida. But these were the only names I knew in America, and I had just learned there were fifty states. I saw I still had a lot to learn.

⤙⤚

On Monday I went back to the UN office, and the representative said she had confirmed that I was going to New York.

"Are you sure?" I asked her.

"Positive," she said.

I was quite relieved, because I had learned two things about New York from the book the UN gave us: it had the Statue of Liberty, and it had skyscrapers. I said to myself, *This is good. Before I die I am going to see both.*

I was still struggling with conflicting emotions. I knew I would miss my friends, and I would feel guilty for leaving my extended family and my country, but I comforted myself by thinking that I would get a passport and make money in America and return for visits whenever I wanted. In the East, we believe that all you need to do is *get* to the West—Europe or the U.S.—and then you don't have to do anything after that to become a king. As soon as you arrive, you will be a millionaire. I did not know at the time that if you wanted to go to college in America, you had to pay for it. In Iraq and Syria, college was free. I did not know that as an immigrant in America I would start out doing the most menial cleaning jobs, and that my income would not be enough to support my wife and three children. I did not know that a single trip to the Middle East would cost around $5,000, and in five or six years I would not be able to save that amount, much less all the incidental expenses for gifts and hotels.

Gifts were a real problem for me. If, on a return trip, I had 100 friends I wanted to remember, and I bought a $10 gift for each one, it would cost me $1,000 that I did not have. And for close friends, if you are coming back from America, what is $10? The expectations do not match reality. People would think, "Oh, look at Yassin. He just came back from America, and all he had to spend on me was $10. Maybe he has forgotten our friendship. Maybe America has changed him. We were so close that we shared even the little bread that we had, and now that he is rich he is not so interested in sharing."

Before we left, the UN told me that in six months my family and I could get travel documents, that in one or two years we could get green cards, and that in three to five years we could get citizenship. But my family has been in America for over seven years, and they have never received travel documents or green cards or an opportunity for citizenship. None of my children— except Dilnia, my fourth child, who was born in the U.S. and who is a U.S. citizen—have citizenship in any country. I tell them that they are real Kurds—in the entire universe there is no place that they belong. My brother Issa was right when he said, "It looks like we Kurds just fell from the sky."

Finally we were told our exact departure date, and we were given tickets. I signed an agreement that after I started working, I would pay back the money for the tickets, which was about $2,600. In 1999 in Kurdistan, $2,600 was a huge sum of money, and if you had that much you could buy a big house. I told the UN official that if he would just give me the $2,600 I would be glad to go back to Kurdistan and buy a house. He thought I was joking and laughed. But everything changes. Now, in 2007, to buy a house in Kurdistan it costs $26,000, not $2,600. And even if I were free, it would still take me twenty-six years to save that much. So I am actually falling farther behind.

Most of my time before departure I spent with Kak Unis, one of my friends who was living in Germany. He was in Damascus waiting to get a visa for his wife so he could bring her back to Germany. When I showed him my plane ticket—from Damascus to Frankfurt to Chicago to Albany—he said, "Kak Yassin, this is great. Get off the plane in Frankfurt, and after it leaves go to the police and ask for asylum. I want you to come to Germany."

"I can't," I said. "They made me promise to go to the U.S."

"Yes, but you're allowed to ask for asylum in Germany," he said.

"I don't want to see Hitler," I joked.

"You are not going to see him in Germany," he said. "Germany is different now. It is the best place to live."

"Right," I told him. "Tell that to Kak Farhad." (He was the Kurd who only a few months earlier had been beaten to death by a neo-Nazi group in Germany because he was dark-skinned and a Muslim and a foreigner.)

"Believe me," Kak Unis said, "there are very very few racists. The majority of Germans are kind people. They respect you as a human being and they do not care about your race."

I told him that I was just joking. I had many friends who were living in Germany and all over Europe, and they had told me a lot about Europe. I wanted to go to Europe because I knew more about it, but I was being sent to the U.S., which I knew little about. But maybe America was even better.

"The U.S. is an excellent country," Kak Unis said, "especially for workers. Most refugees in Europe are not allowed to work, but in the U.S. you are allowed to work. The only problem is that it is so far away."

"So, we are not walking to the U.S.," I said. "We are flying…flying!"

Kak Unis just laughed. He saw how excited I actually was. Until he left me at the Damascus airport on our final night in the Middle East, he kept pressing me to come with him to Germany. That was the last I ever heard from him. And each time I would tell him, "I promised and agreed to go to the U.S. God chose, and God knows better."

I will never forget that emotional last night, when we left Damascus and the Middle East. During 1999, while I had my job in the IMK office, I must have brought thousands of people to and from the airport. Sometimes I went to the airport ten times a day, waiting to receive people or to say goodbye. Most of the people I came in contact with wished for me that one day I would have an opportunity to travel, and all of them wished for me to travel to the places where they lived abroad. Many times travelers used to cry. It was so hard to say goodbye, especially to someone they loved, when they did not know if they would ever see him alive again. Many times people recited the Arabic poem,

> Don't say goodbye,
> Say, see you later.
> If not on earth,
> We'll meet in heaven.

But tonight it was different, because this was the first time that people were saying goodbye to me. I was the one who was leaving. Ten or fifteen people came to the airport to say goodbye. Kak Unis, Kak Jamil, and Kak Usif brought their wives; they were all very close friends whom I had known for years. Our wives were crying, like women always do at funerals. But this time the men were also crying. I tried hard to hold my emotions in check, but when they finally called us to go past the boarding gate checkpoint, I just let all my emotions come flooding out, like a child. I hugged them and asked them to pray for me, and I promised them I would stay in touch, that as soon as I arrived at my new home I would send them my address and phone number. Kak Unis said he prayed that God would change my mind and allow me to stay in Germany, and he gave me some German money so I could buy things when we arrived at the Frankfurt airport.

This was the first flight for my wife and children, and they were all very excited. I was the only one who had flown before, but this was really a new experience for me as well because this was a large plane (Lufthansa), whereas my earlier two flights were just in small planes.

By the next morning we were in Frankfurt. The children were throwing up, and my wife and I were both tired because we had not slept much. In fact, we had not slept much the whole previous week because we were so nervous about the trip. There were about twenty or twenty-five refugee families making the trip together—some were from Somalia and the rest were from Iraq, but my family and I were the only Kurds. I found two other Iraqi families and told them, "If I fall asleep and something important happens, please wake me up so I can follow you, because we don't know the language and cannot even read the signs. We don't know when and where we should go, and it is a really huge airport."

Wherever I looked in Frankfurt, I could not believe my eyes. I had never seen such things. I remembered my friend Ahmad from Basra in southern Iraq, when we had gone there to work and it was too hot, and how he had said, "God does not need to send people to Hell—He can send them to Basra." I was thinking that if Ahmad were with us now, surely he would say, "God does not need to send people to Paradise—it would be sufficient just to send them to Germany."

Thousands of thoughts raced through my mind. In my valley in Kurdistan, one of our neighbors often used to say that after the Third World War there will be no more fuel, and cars and airplanes will become obsolete. I don't know why this strange thought came to mind just then, but it made me sad to think that if it happened, we could never cross back over the ocean and see our homeland and family again, especially since we were going all the way to the U.S. Suddenly I realized that we were really going far away. I was so tired that I felt I was dreaming, but I was afraid that if I went to sleep I might lose Zuhur and the children or my trip plan in the airport, and then what would I do? I felt as though I was going crazy.

I asked one of the Iraqis how long it took from Frankfurt to Chicago, and he said about eight hours. I looked at my children sleeping on the floor, and I thought if they went through eight more hours of this, they might all die. The Iraqi said we could just stay in Frankfurt. "Please don't make fun of me," I said. "We are going to the U.S., and I just wanted you to keep an eye on us."

"I am not going to leave you," he said.

"Thank you very much," I told him.

I must have fallen asleep, because finally the Iraqi woke me up and said, "Let's go." So I woke up my daughter Alaa and my oldest son Raiber; my younger son, Kotcher, was only a baby, two months old. I held Kotcher in one arm, put Raiber on my neck, held Alaa's hand, and tried to keep an eye on my wife. She looked to be more than half-dead, and I was scared to think what would happen if we ever lost each other, because neither of us could speak the language.

When we went to get on the plane, the flight attendants would not let us board because we did not have a boarding pass. Nobody had told us that we needed a boarding pass, at least not in any language that we understood. I started to yell at the gate attendant in Kurdish, but nobody understood me. Then I held up the bag with all my papers inside that we had been given by the UN office. Written on the outside of the bag were three big letters. I had no idea what the letters meant, and still don't,* but I was told that in any airport when people saw this sign they would come and help you. The attendant stopped us at the gate, but someone else went to get a boarding pass, and then they let us board. All this was not a serious problem, but I could not tell at the time if it was a serious problem because I had come from Kurdistan and Syria, where *everything* was a serious problem. So I felt I had to react. Perhaps I over-reacted.

I also spent far too much time and emotional energy worrying about the children. When you see people laughing in airplanes and casually pulling their bags through airports on their way to travel and adventure, you dream you could go, too. But when you are actually taking your wife and children through a maze of rules and procedures that you do not know, in a huge modern airport of the kind you have never seen before, in a language that you don't understand, and you are tired and unable to sleep from worry—it is torture. Maybe it is self-torture, but it still hurts.

I don't remember arriving in Chicago, but I do remember it was another Paradise. Everything was busy, everyone was going some-

---

* *Note:* The letters were probably "IOM," an acronym for International Organization for Migration, which works with the United Nations High Commissioner for Refugees (UNHCR) on travel arrangements for refugees, among other tasks.

where fast, and I felt as though I was standing amazed in the middle of it all, just looking. Then suddenly I felt as though we had been arrested. People took us by the shoulder and brought us to a room where we were fingerprinted. What was happening? Was this like Iraq, where you could be arrested and just disappear? The man who did the fingerprinting looked like someone from Iraqi security. I will never forget him—yelling, shouting, pulling and pushing our hands back and forth. We did not know if he was cursing us or not, but his face indicated that he was not happy. We did not know why he was so upset. Was it because we did not know what he wanted us to do? Or was it because we were from Iraq, or that he did not like my wife's headscarf, or that he was having a bad day and his girlfriend was bothering him? Why was this guy acting like that? He was really representative of the Iraqi police, not the U.S. people or even the U.S. police, because he never once smiled.

After they took our fingerprints, they took our pictures, too. Soon after that, we received a white card—the A-94 form with our prints on it. I smiled at the security officer and turned to my wife, saying, "Look! Now we are Americans." The card was in English and we could not read it, but it had our pictures on it, so we had to be Americans. My wife forced a smile and gave me her approval. The security guard apparently thought that we were making fun of him because he still did not smile back. Sociologically sick people think this way. Any gesture that they do not understand they take for a threat.

The guard took us to a hall and showed us where to sit. Each refugee family was being sent to a different place in America, and we were the only family waiting for the Albany plane. After five hours of waiting, we were finally freed from the police. Now we would really be in America. Everybody smiled at us and tried to speak to our children. We were almost dead from exhaustion, but we tried to smile back. I tried to remember some English from middle and high school in Iraq, but I couldn't.

We boarded a small plane and started flying again. They told us that this would be the last plane, and they meant "for this trip," but I thought that it looked like the last plane ever, because I doubted that I could ever save enough money to fly back to the Middle East again. And now I wonder, as a result of my conviction, whether the judge will ever let me out of jail to fly back, or whether my name will be on a no-fly list, or whether fuel prices will become so high that planes will be obsolete. I pray none of this will happen, and that finally my family can have the life that they came here to have—a life of freedom.

PART THREE:
AMERICA

Imam Yassin Aref speaks at the Islamic Center of the Capital
District to welcome the center's new imam, July 24, 2004.

Photo by Angela Bishop. Courtesy of Albany *Times Union*.

Chapter Thirteen ◀
Welcome to the U.S.A.

The New World

It was October 27, 1999, and as soon as our plane landed in Albany I experienced strong feelings of anxiety and many questions came to mind. What would happen if no one came to meet us? I did not have even one dollar with me. I could not rent a taxi or a hotel or buy food. I was penniless. I could not even communicate. I did not know English and I did not know anybody in Albany who spoke Kurdish, or even Arabic. I did not know any Kurds who were living in the area. I did not even have a telephone number or an address of a mosque in Albany where I could meet Muslims. But the UN had told us that someone would meet us at the airport. I had to trust.

We got off the plane and followed people to the exit. Some people had friends waiting for them. All of a sudden I saw a woman carrying a sign, written in broken Kurdish, that said "Welcome to America." *What is this?* I thought. *Who is this lady, and whom is she welcoming in Kurdish?* And then nearby I saw someone else with a sign written in Arabic that said "Welcome Aref Family." I smiled at this one. These people probably recognized us because Zuhur was the only woman wearing a headscarf, and we were the only family of five standing in the airport looking confused.

The people with the signs came over to us and welcomed us very warmly and showed us love, and thanked God that we had finally arrived. There were others with them. One of the men, Kassim Shaar, was Iraqi and spoke Arabic, and even knew a couple of Kurdish words, as did Nada, his wife. Later they became our friends and they visited often to translate for us.

I felt wonderful. All my fears were gone. We had been traveling for at least twenty hours in the air, or waiting in airports, and we were half-dead. But the love that we received from these people made us forget our fatigue and our fears. We took this as the first and biggest sign that we had come to the right place. They were really welcoming and gave all kinds of help. I said to my wife, "It looks like we are the president's family with all these people coming to welcome us. They are our new family." Zuhur just smiled her approval.

Feelings and ideas raced through my head. I was talking to myself. *No more security forces to scare us. No more checkpoints. No more humiliation. No more embargo. No more rockets firing every day. We are out of Iraq. We are out of the Middle East. We are free and we can have our own ideas and we can speak out. My children will never have to repeat what I went through. They will live peaceful lives. They will get toys and they will play and have fun, and they will get the best education, and they will grow up happy.*

Kassim and the others asked me if we were OK, did we need something? I told them that we needed a place to rest because we were very tired. They all laughed and said, "No more talk. Let's go to the cars." We came out from the airport to see the new world, and they took us to the home of one of the men, whose name was Paul. He was a very gentle man who made jokes and, like my dad, took pleasure in serving guests. He and his wife tried to get us to eat dinner, but we told them we just needed a place to sleep. It was almost sundown, and we did not wake up again until the next morning, when we opened our eyes to our first full day in America.

The children were very excited. They had slept well, and they woke us up early. They got out their coloring books and toys that they had been given yesterday. We tried to keep them quiet, but they were full of energy and went downstairs to where Mr. Paul's room was.

Alaa, who was four, shouted so loudly that even the neighbors heard her. I ran down and tried to discipline her. "What is wrong, Daddy?" I said. This is the way I respond to my children when they call me. If my son had called me, I would have said, "What do you need, Daddy?" I told Alaa she had to be quiet. "Ho, ho, ho, uhh, *sag*," she said, which means "dog" in Kurdish. She was pointing at the dog and she looked afraid. "No, that dog is not going to bite you," I said. "It is not like dogs in our country." I carried her back upstairs and tried to find words to tell Mr. Paul and his wife that I was sorry she had woken them up. But I did not have the right words.

After awhile, Mrs. Paul came upstairs, bringing glasses full of ice. One was for me and one was for Zuhur. I looked at the glass of ice, and I looked at Zuhur. "Zuhur," I said, "what is this?"

"*Bafra, bafra* (It's ice, it's ice)," she said, surprised.

"I know," I laughed. "But what do we do with this ice?"

"I don't know," she said. "Maybe they will bring us something to drink and we can put the ice in there."

"No, maybe they think Alaa has a fever and we have to put it on her forehead to cool her down," I said.

"Stop it," she said.

"I am not joking," I said.

Then Raiber came upstairs and said, "Daddy, I need some sugar." (In Kurdistan we have rock sugar, which we cut into small pieces like crushed ice.)

"Shh—shh—shh," I said.

"The man downstairs is eating sugar," he said.

I picked Raiber up and said to him, "Just be nice and don't touch anything. Also don't run around."

But Raiber looked over my shoulder and saw the glass of ice. "Daddy, you have sugar too?"

"No," I said. "That is ice."

Raiber jumped down as though he did not believe me and touched the ice in the glass. "But the man is eating the same thing," he said.

"What, he is eating ice?" I asked, surprised.

"Yes," Raiber said. "I thought it was sugar."

"Did he eat it with tea?"

"No. He just put it in his mouth."

"Zuhur, Zuhur," I said. "This must be our breakfast, and we must eat it."

"Stop, Yassin, please," she said. But I told her to confirm it with Raiber, and he repeated what he'd told me.

It was October 28, in the early morning, and frost covered the ground outside, but here was someone who was eating ice. I did not know what to make of it. I guessed it was just something people did in America. I remembered when it snowed in Kurdistan and I used to eat some of the snow. Whenever my father saw me doing that, he would beat me. So one day when he left the house and went to the mosque, I started eating snow—but I ate too much. The next morning when I woke up I could not speak, and no sound came out of my throat. My dad started beating me, saying "That means you ate ice." Now, in America, even old men eat ice.

Mr. Paul and his wife and their two dogs gave us a real picture of life in the U.S., which was so completely different from life in the Middle East. About 8:30 he and his wife invited us down for breakfast. My wife and I were afraid of the dogs and we kept trying to keep them away from us, although Mr. Paul kept saying that the dogs were friendly and would not bite. I'm sure he was right, but we had a bigger problem. In Islam, dogs are not "clean," and if a dog licks you or your clothing you cannot pray until you have washed or changed your clothes. And if the dogs drink from something, that also becomes "unclean." After a Muslim friend explained our problem, Mr. Paul was careful to always keep the dogs in another room with the door closed.

I was really surprised that Mr. and Mrs. Paul would keep dogs in their home. In my country, nobody would bring a dog into the living room or the bedroom. If people owned dogs, it was to guard the house, so they stayed outside. In winter the owners would make a small place for the dogs close to the outside door, where they could act as an alarm system for the house. Some people had hunting dogs in the villages, but in the city it was hard to find dogs at all. But after a couple of days, I understood why Mr. Paul had the dogs. It was for companionship. His children were living in another part of the country, and it was just him and his wife in their big house.

We stayed for one week at Mr. Paul's house. He was generous and hospitable to me and my family in a way I will never forget—not just sheltering us and feeding us, but advising us and showing us love and thoughtfulness. Every day we learned English from him. His house was the first classroom in which I learned about American life. Most Americans do not understand the blessing of the life that they live, because they have never had to live in a different way. In Kurdish we say, "Before you get hungry, you don't understand the importance of bread."

After one week, an Iraqi woman, Umm Salam (Salam's mother), took us into her home until I could find a job and a house to rent. We moved from Mr. Paul's house, but he never left us. Daily he came to visit us, and he worked hard to find us a home of our own. After that he visited us often, and we kept our relationship until they arrested me.

Umm Salam made us feel as though we were back in Iraq. We spoke Arabic and she made Iraqi food. She spared no effort to make us feel good. She did not have a dog, but she had a big cat that quickly befriended my children. We were surprised by the size of this cat, which looked like a small lamb. Umm Salam's husband, Abo Salam, used to come home on weekends. He loved my children and spent a lot of time talking and joking with them. We spent about ten days in their house, and it was the most beautiful time that we spent in this country. The Salam family made us see the beauty of life in America.

One day when we were in their home, Father Jim Kenyon came to see us. He was from St. Michael's Episcopal Church, which had sponsored us in America. He wanted to be sure that we were OK, and he told us that they had rented a house for us that was just being cleaned. As soon as it was ready, we could move in. He repeated over and over that if we needed anything to let him know, and before he left he gave us an envelope containing $500 as a gift for my children. What is more beautiful than to help someone you don't know and not expect anything in return, especially when that person has a different religion and ideas from you? As happy as I was about the life that I saw people living in America, I was sad that people in the Middle East had no chance to have such a life or even a good job. I asked myself, how can I live this way in the U.S.? I was ashamed for my dependence on the generosity of others, and daily I urged Father Jim to move us to the house that the church had rented for us and to help me find a job so I could live independently, support my family, and help people instead of taking help. I am young and healthy, I told him, and I can work.

I have not accepted much philosophy from Karl Marx, and I am not a trained economist, but I have learned from my own experience that to be economically independent it is necessary to remain who you are and to retain people's respect. As much as you have to beg or depend on other people, that is how much you lose of your dignity. My poor father used to prefer fasting to begging for food. Many times he advised me that all my life I must be the one to serve, rather than accept the service of others—to give, rather than to take. As the Prophet Mohammad said, may peace be upon him, "The higher hand is better and more loved by God than the lower hand. The higher hand is the hand that gives, and the lower hand is the one that takes."

Looking for a Job

Wherever you go, East or West, poor people are the same: looking for a job, concerned about finding food for their families. In the East, most unemployment is caused by war, corruption, illiteracy, and stagnation, while in the West most unemployment is often the result of families destroyed by alcohol, drugs, and laziness. Of course, there are some poor people in both East and West who do not have these problems and who still do not have the opportunity to find a job.

When the church people moved us to our new rented house, I started searching for a job. The refugee organization told me that I had six months to find one, and after that they would not pay my rent. I thought I would not need more than six days to get a job. This is the way that Easterners think about the West, especially the U.S.A. But I found that it was very difficult for someone like me, who was not skilled in anything, who did not have an American education, and who did not know the language, to find a job. Who was going to hire me? The situation was even more difficult because I could not work in a restaurant or store that served alcohol, which is prohibited in Islam.

Liz, a lady from the church, helped me in my job search. She also helped me apply for a Social Security number and food stamps, and she came with me to many job interviews. She was really a big help in the beginning. But after awhile, Liz became frustrated and angry with me because she apparently felt that I was "extreme" in my religious practices. As a Muslim, I believe that I may not shake a woman's hand, and I must pray five times a day in the mosque, and I have to wear a beard. These practices make it especially difficult to get a job in the West. When Westerners see a Muslim who observes these practices, they say that he is "extreme," because many other Muslims in the West do not act like this. In the Middle East, such practices are common, but when Muslims come to the West they often drop these religious practices to get along. Some Muslims even smoke cigarettes and drink alcohol, and some Muslim shop owners even sell these things, which are prohibited in Islam. These Muslims are considered "modern" Muslims in the West and not "extreme." The reality is that people like me in the West who follow the normal religious practices of Islam have nothing to do with extreme, radical, or violent philosophies. The only "extreme" thing is that we continue to follow our normal peaceful practices in the West, where people are not used to them. Once people in the West become used to our religious practices, nobody will think of them as "extreme."

One day Liz took me for a job interview. She said it was a hard job—construction—but it paid well, $10 an hour. I told her that I was young and healthy and I had done many hard jobs in my life. I had no problem with hard jobs, even if the pay was bad. I was willing to do anything; I just wanted to be able to take care of my family. On our way to the interview, I asked her what happened to my Social Security card. She said that they would not give me a card.

"Why?" I asked, surprised.

"I found you a job," she said. "But you refused to take it. So you cannot even get food stamps now. They are mad at you."

I almost lost my mind when I heard that. The job she had found for me was recycling bottles at Price Chopper. Most of the bottles were beer and wine bottles, which I am not allowed to touch in my religion. I had asked her to let them give me a job cleaning the floors or fixing shelves or anything else, but I could not deal with alcohol. I was not offered any alternative, however, and so I refused to take the bottle job.

When Liz told me that Social Security was mad at me and wouldn't help me anymore, I became emotional and told her to turn the car around and take me to the Social Security office, where I would tell them to send me back to Iraq right now and let Saddam hang us all. That would be better than having to work with alcohol, which was forbidden. I came to this country to live free and practice my faith, I said, not to be told that I had to do a job that was forbidden in my faith.

Liz took me back home and left. I never saw her again after that. But when I finally went to the Social Security office, they told me that they had never said such things, and I believe that she just made up the story. After this incident, the people of the church stopped their help without asking me what had happened or why Liz was mad at me. Only Mr. Paul, the one who first gave us shelter, kept up his relationship with me.

Even before they sent us to the U.S., the UN office in Syria told us that we had the right to practice our religion freely, so why was I being forced to do a job that clearly was against my religion? And if I said that I was sorry, but I could not do a particular job, why was I being "extreme"? It was still my first month in the country. How could I do something that I believed was wrong? How would I feel if I did it?

Ali Yaghi

After I lost Liz's help, I really needed advice to find a job. Liz had been a very big help to me, which I will never deny or forget. But I still believe that it was not my fault that we had a misunderstanding, because I told her that I was willing to do almost any job no matter how difficult or how little it paid, but I would not do work that was against my faith. In Kurdistan we have a saying that God will not close one door except to open a couple more for you. The door represented by Liz closed, but God opened another door when I was introduced to a young man named Ali Yaghi, one of the most amazing people I have ever met in the U.S.

Ali Yaghi was always joking. He had a very bad mouth and mixed his jokes with curses, yells, shouts, and outrageous statements. He was emotional and became upset easily, but at the same time he had a clear mind and a pure heart and no difficulty in apologizing if he offended someone—which was fairly often. I particularly liked him because he was simple and humble and rejected politics. His only political belief was to work hard and support his family. But he was also very generous and would give away the last penny he had. His pleasure in giving helped me a lot, because for at least one year I completely depended on him. He came with me to many places when I was looking for a job. He read letters for me that I received that were written in English. He helped me with the paperwork for everything, which seemed to be endless. He translated for me at interviews. He helped me file many job applications. And finally he got me a job at Albany Medical Center.

On two occasions he gave me a car. The first car I used for five or six months, until I had an accident while I was coming out of a parking lot. The police report said that the accident happened because I was familiar with the UK system of driving on the left side—without thinking, I drove on the left instead of on the right. That was how the accident happened—I was careless—but it was not because I was familiar with the UK system. I had never been to the UK, and did not even know that they drove on the left side. I do not know why the police officer made this excuse; maybe because I only had an international driver's license, not a New York State license, at the time.

When Ali offered me another car, I insisted on paying for it. In response, he said, "Give me $300." I thought he was joking, as usual, and that perhaps he meant $3,000, but he insisted that $300 was enough. I went to a friend of his and asked how Ali could claim that the car was worth $300. The friend said, "If you gave me $300 to take that car I wouldn't take it, and I wouldn't drive it even if you paid me $300." At that point I realized that people had different views of life. I bought the car from Ali and drove it for at least two years. I was driving a $300 car that ran as though it had cost $30,000. Once I drove my family all the way to Florida in it. Some people were surprised that an Imam would drive a car so old. I told them I drove to work, I shopped, and it was big enough so that we could go out as a family—what more did we need? I don't believe what they say in the U.S., that if you want to know about someone, look to see what he is driving. I believe it's wrong to judge people in this way.

When I started working much later with AMA Transportation as a driver, I often used to take a disabled woman to see her doctor. The lady who was her caregiver told me that she was looking for a second job. When I asked why, she said that she needed another job to make her car payments.

"How much did you pay for your car?" I asked.

"$45,000," she said.

"You have a president's car," I told her.

She told me that every year she traded in her old car for a new one and paid the difference in price. That year, her monthly payments were about $700. I did not want to criticize her, so I just told her that I did not think it was a good idea to pay so much for a car. But I said to myself, *Thank God for saving me from such a sickness.* $700 for a car payment, $1,000 for the mortgage, $500 for clothes and makeup, $500 for food and restaurants, plus utilities, taxes, and all sorts of other normal expenses. How can you cover all of this on a basic salary? You would have to take out a loan and pay interest for the next twenty years. Once when I visited one of my American friends, he told me that many people in the U.S. have already spent their money for the next twenty-five years. They cannot quit their jobs because of the amount they owe—for cars, houses, credit cards, loans, insurance, etc. It is not a problem to spend such sums if you are earning more, but if you are spending more than you earn it is suicide to keep on doing it, especially when the purchases are not necessary at all. We should be known by our manners and compassion rather than by our houses and cars.

Being around Ali always meant a lot of laughing and joking. Of course I had to accept a lot of cursing too, which I did. I fought a lot with him, and he cursed me a lot. But I knew him, and that is why his cursing never stopped me from seeing him. It was his habit, when he saw anyone he liked, to try and make them mad or emotional or incite them in some way. He knew that I was a Kurd from Iraq and that I had fled from Saddam. So whenever he saw me he would say, "Saddam is good! I like him because he finished off the Kurds. I don't know why Saddam missed you." And then he would laugh with delight.

When they arrested me, one of the FBI agents told me that Ali had said in my house that he hated two things—women and America. I told him that Ali's habit was to say outrageous things to get people mad. One time when he came over with his best friend from Sudan, Dafullah, Ali said to me, "Sheikh, Sheikh, look here. This is my nigger, my slave." I always told him, "You should clean your mouth," and I repeated the Kurdish saying, "If you close your mouth, you save your life." Even the Prophet said that the mouth will take people to Hellfire. Unfortunately, Ali did not listen to this advice, and he paid a big price for it. They deported him because of one of his outrageous "jokes," in which he said he liked what happened on 9/11. It was the same kind of statement that he would make when he said he liked what Saddam did to the Kurds. I knew him very well, and he was in no way involved with any groups or politics in his life. He just had a bad mouth, bad jokes, and an outrageous sense of humor.

Here is another example of Ali's wit. One day he said that he had bought some books, and when he got home he checked the index to see what he should read first. He saw that one of the subjects listed was *Halqat-al-dhakar*, which in Arabic means "cutting off your private parts." He was astonished, and immediately read the pages in the book referred to in the index, but the book had nothing to do with cutting off one's private parts. He said that he wanted to ask the Imam about it, but he was too shy (although knowing Ali, this was very unlikely). All week long he wondered why this subject was listed in the index when there was nothing about it in the book. Later he saw a friend and asked him about the entry for *Halqat-al-dhakar*. His friend began to laugh and said that Ali had misread the index. The actual subject was *Halqat-al-dhikr*, which means "circle of remembrance of God." I told him, "Thank God you did not take the title too seriously."

Note: This problem arises in written Arabic because typically only consonants are written; vowels are assumed from the context. So in Arabic, both these words are written and spelled exactly the same way: Hlqlthkr. In order to distinguish between them, either the reader uses the context and reads appropriately, or additional vowel-symbols are placed on the letters (but apparently not in the book Ali had purchased) so the reader can immediately see the difference. In the Qur'an, vowel-symbols are almost always used so the reader will not make mistakes.

Albany Medical Center

Through one of Ali's friends who was working at Albany Medical Center (AMC), I finally got a cleaning job at minimum wage, which was $5.25 an hour at that time. Coming from the Middle East and growing up in a poor village helped me to accept this job. I was used to hard physical labor, in which you have few tools and have to work with muscle power alone, so in my mind it was not a shame to clean toilets or serve or do any low-paying job—it was actually a shame to beg if you were healthy and you could work. And it was a shame not to support your family. Cleaning bathrooms actually made me feel good: I had learned from my humble father to live simply and to never show any arrogance, so this job, humble though it might have been, was a job that I was very grateful to get.

Whenever people asked me where I worked, I told them AMC, and they would respond, "Are you a doctor?" And I would say, "Yes. I am a bathroom doctor. If nobody takes care of the bathrooms, they will poison our lives." Some people laughed. Some people did not believe me. Some people probably felt sorry for me. But I was proud of my job. I used to clean five floors with at least ten complete units in them. I had to take out the garbage, vacuum, and clean the floors and facilities for twenty-four public bathrooms every day. I was in a big hurry to finish within eight hours. Unfortunately, what they paid me was not enough to allow me to support my family. I made less than $900 a month. How can you support a family of five on that amount? In some respects I felt that I was back in the Middle East, where you work hard at a full-time job and still you cannot earn enough money to support your family. It was difficult to believe that this was America and not a third world country. Shouldn't a full-time job at least cover the expenses necessary for survival? I'm not talking about drugs, or nightclubs, or alcohol, or gifts, or restaurants, or hotels. I am talking about reasonable rent and food only. If minimum wage for a full-time job is not enough to cover someone's basic expenses, shouldn't the minimum wage be raised? People who do not have a high school education or professional training but who are still doing hard work should be able to feed their families. This problem leads to crime, which costs the community dearly. How can someone who works full-time in the richest country in the world not be able to feed his family? If raising the minimum wage reduces crime even slightly, or allows people to support their families in dignity, would it not be worth it? And why are companies allowed to make billions of dollars a year but don't pay their employees a decent wage? Shouldn't something be done about this unacceptable fact of life in this country?

One day I was praying in the hallway of the medical center. When I prostrated myself, a lady came close to me and stopped. "Are you OK?" she asked. "Are you OK?" When we pray, we are not supposed to speak, so I raised my head to do the next part of the prayer, and when I stood up she realized that I was OK, and she left. At that time, when people would see me praying and then saw that I was a Muslim, they usually smiled or waved or sometimes talked to me—always showing love and respect. But after 9/11, things really changed. Many people gave me harsh looks. Some people openly cursed me or said something humiliating. Hundreds of times while I was walking, people would shout at me, "Osama! Osama!" just because of my beard. Now if people saw me prostrating myself, they did not come to make sure I was OK but instead called the police. Some people were really scared of us and thought we were dangerous. Other people were just unsure about us and did not know what to make of a man with a large beard or a woman with a headscarf. It was really sad to see and experience this.

After 9/11, my family and I stopped going to the mall, and we did not go much to the park or the library or other public places because we were Muslims and people were suspicious of us and we did not want to make people feel uncomfortable. I did not want to scare people and stop them from enjoying what they were doing. Nothing is more disruptive to joyful living than to look at foreigners as though they are your enemy or hate America. People with peace in their hearts who think positively about other people and want the best for them do not think this way. It all comes down to the assumptions you make about people when you see them, and after 9/11 many people changed their assumptions about us.

In Iraq, I experienced the problems that occurred when no one could trust anyone else, not even a close friend or a brother. We had to assume that everyone was an undercover government agent trying to get us or destroy our lives. We had to doubt everything and everyone. The more insincere "nice" talk everyone was forced to make, the more poison crept into the community. It made us hate life and wish for death. When I came to this country, I said to myself, *That's over*. I decided never to worry again whether someone was undercover or not because I was in a free country and I was allowed to speak freely, so why should I be scared? I know the situation in the U.S. is not as bad as in Iraq. But many people still look at Muslims with suspicion, and they do not feel safe when they hear people talking in Arabic or see a headscarf. At the same time, many Muslims look at each other with suspicion and wonder whether their fellow Muslim is a government agent who is spying on the community. This poison of suspicion will bring us all to disaster if we don't break down the barriers between our communities and overcome prejudices born of fear. Real freedom that comes from equal rights, from knowing each other, and from respecting each other's faiths and ideas is the right way to build strong communities that will reject terrorism or violence. Accusing each other of treachery and spreading negative and hateful messages like the kind we hear every day on talk radio is the wrong direction to go, and makes us all less safe. We must all recognize that Muslims are human beings too, and that like everyone else they have limited patience. For how long can we remain silent and accept all these unfair accusations? And what will happen if we lose our patience?

We live in a time of stress. Every day we start the day by hearing bad news, and we end it by getting sad news. Wherever we go, people are looking for peace of mind, a little smile, some happiness. They are tired of lies and politics. The Kurds say, "Some people fish in dirty water," and the Americans say, "Don't throw gasoline on the fire." We need to control the fire, for if we do not, none of us will be safe.

Shamshad Ahmad

One of the most important things in life is to have good friends. In Kurdistan we say, "You know your real friend in a time of trouble." Which of your friends are with you when you need them? What do they do when you ask for help? Do they stay with you and give you support when you are in trouble? Or do they disappear? If they do disappear, they are not your real friends.

I could not have survived the difficult situation that I grew up in if God had not blessed me with true friends who supported me and carried my weight on their backs. Most of my friends are like this. I was never a rich or powerful person, so people never made a friendship with me in order to gain money or influence. People came to me because they loved my ideas, accepted my character, and wanted to help me. And I needed them continuously. Since I have been in Albany, the person I have depended on most is Shamshad Ahmad.

As soon as I came to this country, I met him. He is a professor with a Ph.D. who has taught physics at the University in Albany for close to thirty years. He speaks at least five languages. He owns many houses and properties in Albany. He is a leader of the Muslim community in Albany, founder and president of the Masjid As-Salam, where I became the Imam, and has a deep religious education. But despite all these accomplishments, Shamshad is a simple man and a real example of humility. He used to sit in the back of the *masjid* like a person who had come to pray for the first time, and never came up to the front to show that he was the leader and founder of the mosque who must be placed first. If it were not for his dedicated work to improve the *masjid,* its roof would have collapsed long ago. His pleasure was only in working to fix up the *masjid* or helping people in need. He never introduced himself as "Doctor" or "Professor"; he did not hold grudges; and he was always there when I—or anyone—needed him. Many times I would argue with him and disagree with him, and most of the time after one or two days I had to go back to him for help, and whenever I would do this he acted as though we had never had any argument. I was new to this country and he barely knew me, but he put down a deposit on an old house for me that was being sold by the government and helped me fix it up through workmen he knew, so that my family and I had a place to live that was ours.

When the FBI arrested me, they found half a dollar in my wallet. That was all I had. They did not find one penny in my house, and in my bank account they did not find even $300. When I went to jail, I left my wife and three children with not even enough money for one month's rent. During the three years I have spent in jail, before and after the trial and now before sentencing, all the money that I've needed—for rent, for bail (which was eventually cancelled), for food, for clothes—has been provided by Shamshad, because my wife is in poor health and has the baby and cannot work.

One day I called Shamshad from jail and told him that my only concern was for my family. He said, "As long as I am breathing, you do not have to worry about them—they are mine." Is this not a blessing to have a true friend such as this? If not for his support, how could my family have survived on the fifty cents I left them? When the FBI told my lawyer that they had found only fifty cents on me, I said to my lawyer, "Look at this. They claim that I am representing a Kurdish organization, IMK; that I am commander of a terrorist group; that I am part of a plan to destroy New York City—and I am supposed to do all of this on fifty cents!!"

After I started working at Albany Medical Center, Shamshad began cleaning and fixing up an old building on Central Avenue that he had bought at auction. He intended it to become a mosque. Because I was working from 3 p.m. to 11 p.m., I often went to the building to help in the cleanup and repair. For one whole month, Shamshad, Ali Yaghi, and I worked on the building. Shamshad carried mud out of the building and threw himself into all kinds of construction the same way that I used to when I was a teenager working in Kirkuk. For the five or six months that we took to complete the renovation, he was the only person who worked continuously. I knew many Muslims who had nothing to do but walk the streets, but they did not bother to come and help. After I learned that Shamshad was a Ph.D., I was shocked.

When the *masjid* was finished, we opened it for prayer. Everyone chose Shamshad as the president. I was very happy and thought that this was part of his reward, but in fact he received little benefit from being president. He did not even use the title. The respect that the community had for him was much greater than just the title of president. In fact, he was not really the president but rather the servant of the community and the *masjid*, and that is the way he wanted it to be.

Shamshad began to teach me English. For almost a year I used to preach the Friday sermon in Arabic, and he would translate it into English. But he encouraged me to try preaching directly in English, and I took courage from his confidence in me. As soon as I started preaching at the *masjid* I began arguing with him, as though I had forgotten all that he had done for me. But nothing stopped me from asking him for favors and loans hundreds of times, and nothing stopped him from giving me help each and every time. What is more beautiful in a human being than to be intelligent, well educated, humble, generous, and devoted to serving others? I saw all of this in Shamshad. And most importantly, he was the person you could count on in times of trouble when trust really counted.

He was happy to work almost anonymously for the mosque until the day I was arrested and the mosque was ransacked by the FBI. Then he stood in front of the building and said, "I am the president. I am in charge. For anything that is wrong here in this *masjid*, I am fully responsible—no one else. If something is wrong, arrest me and give me the charges." Never before had he stood up and said he was the mosque's president, when he would have received praise for all that he did. He only stood up to accept the responsibility. May God bless him and reward him. And may God grant our community more such humble, quiet, peaceful people to lead and give an example to our youth.

American Imam

A *masjid* without an Imam is like a class without a teacher or a car without a driver. In the Muslim tradition and culture, the Imam plays a big role in society. Long ago, when most people were illiterate, the Imam was the most important person in the community, and people went to him for advice on everything. The Imam taught the children reading and writing; he advised the community; he counseled people on their personal problems; he judged problems that were presented to him; he led prayers (which at that time were the only medicines available); he married couples; and he performed funerals. In some Middle Eastern countries, Imams still perform these roles. If an Imam is well educated and has good training, he can make a big difference in a community. But the opposite is also true. A poorly educated Imam with a narrow view can bring disaster. Even with all of the professional advice available today, Imams are still very important to Muslims, because faith is a very important motivation in their lives.

For more than a year, Shamshad and members of the *masjid* looked for an Imam, but they were unable to find someone who could fully communicate in English and who knew American culture well. So eventually they persuaded me to become the Imam, even though my English was still very poor. I was also new to the country and did not know the culture well, and so I knew it was going to be difficult for me to do the job of Imam. But I told them I would try my best.

Even though I grew up in a religious family and knew the responsibilities of an Imam, how could a villager from a third world country like Kurdistan be a leader in American society? I told them I was a son of the mountains—which meant Kurdish culture, Iraqi mentality, seeking a Kurdish revolution—without any experience as an Imam. All my life I had had a mouth with which to speak, and now I could not even find my tongue. How on earth could I do this job? But for some reason, people supported me, and they even seemed to enjoy it when I yelled at them. Many times I tried to preach something, but in the middle of a sentence I had to stop because I did not have enough words to finish. (I would pretend to search my pockets to find the missing words that I needed.) Sometimes I would say a word in Kurdish, and people thought that because my pronunciation was so bad they had misunderstood one of my English words. In my culture, we say that if a word comes out of a person's heart it will go to other people's hearts, but if it comes from the mouth only it will never even enter their ears. I believe that my best contact with people was with the message that I could send from my eyes rather than from my tongue, and I spoke to them from my heart, not only through my words.

Through God's will, things seemed to work. People claimed that they were happy and "getting the message." Month after month the community grew, and the *masjid* began to fill up. We started Friday prayer with twenty or thirty people, but by the time they arrested me there were about 200 to 300 people present at Friday prayer. Simplicity is sometimes the best sermon. You can use your hands, your eyes, and your face to deliver the message. Charlie Chaplin made millions laugh without using a single word.

One day one of my friends in Albany returned from Turkey. I knew that he did not speak Turkish. So I asked him if people there ever spoke a second language. He said, "Yes. Almost all of them."

"What is the second language?" I asked him. I thought he would say Arabic, because of Islam.

Instead he laughed and said, "Sign language. For all my needs I had to use sign language with my hands to talk with them. And they talked back to me in the same way."

I laughed, and he asked why I was laughing. I said, "The first time I tried to use sign language, it was to talk with a deaf and dumb man in my village in Kurdistan. It ended with my being beaten by my father because I accidentally said something wrong with my hands. So much for sign language!"

Because an Imam is like an advisor, his success depends on his honesty and sincerity. As long as he is honest, says only what is true, keeps confidences, and works only to help other people achieve success, he will be a community resource. The important thing is not to use people for one's own benefit, but to give them the benefit of one's role without expecting anything in return. A good Imam should never argue with people or listen to backbiting and gossip about others. He should simply love people and think positively about them. An Imam should stay independent and not rely on one group of people against another group. He must be bigger than any group and benefit all; being involved with mosque politics destroys one's credibility. Truth should be bigger than everything else. Nothing should prevent him from speaking the truth. But it will benefit people only if he speaks the truth wisely, and he should choose the right time and the right opportunity. As Imam Ali used to say, "Not everything that you know must you say immediately. Wait for the right time, and when the right time comes you should look for the right person to tell in the right way." None of the messengers preached continuously for one or two hours. They used to speak for five or ten minutes only, and sometimes only a few words. But those few words guided people and changed their lives. Today you can sit for two or three hours at a meeting, but you do not get even three words of benefit.

As an Imam, I learned a lot about life in America. People opened their hearts to me and told me what they were going through. I heard about many problems that made me understand that wherever you go, life is life—human beings will suffer. Sometimes all they need is a big lovely smile, or a kind word, or sincere advice. It costs you nothing, but it may change their lives forever.

Senior Citizen

In my faith, seeking knowledge is obligatory, and for me it was also my illiterate parents' will—they both wanted me to educate myself and obtain an advanced degree. I believe one of our problems in the East is that we are way behind in terms of technology. I've had many arguments with my friends about what is most important to learn. Like most Easterners, I love poetry, art, and history, and we grow up immersed in politics. In Iraq, after ninth grade we had to decide whether to study humanities—art, literature, and history—or science and math. I wanted to choose humanities because of my love for poetry, but my physics teacher wanted me to go into science because he said I was good at physics and math. I refused, and we had many discussions about it.

"Yassin, we need scientists," he said.

"Yes, but history teaches us many lessons and can help us figure out how to survive as Kurds," I replied.

"We Kurds claim we are the oldest civilization, dating back to the

Neanderthals, but look—what do we have now?" he asked.

"If not for our knowledge of history, we never would have survived the genocide against us. And if not for art and poetry, they would have defeated us long ago!" I countered.

"But poems don't give us bread. History does not take us to the stars."

"Yes they do. Poetry inspires us, and history teaches us how to get our rights back."

"Yassin," he replied, "Iraq is one of the oldest nations, and many civilizations were here—Sumerian, Akkadian, Babylonian, Assyrian—but all this history did not give us a better life. Look at America. They don't have 5,000 years of history, but they went to the moon and they have all this technology—it's science that's important, not art, not history."

"Yes," I said, "they have no history, and that's why they don't know what to do with all their technology, or how to use all their science. We need both."

I never changed my mind, and I took the path of humanities, but my high school teacher's words resonated with me: "America has no history but has science, Kurds have history but no science, and look at the difference between the two."

In any case, in Iraq we did not get a chance to learn about science and technology. I left Iraq in 1995 without ever having seen a computer. In Syria there were computers, but there was no Internet. I really wanted to learn how to use a computer, and how it worked, so I took some classes in Syria. But when I came to the United States, I couldn't use what I had learned because all my knowledge of computers was in Arabic, and I didn't know English; and that meant that I didn't know the keyboard, or the instructions or processes, and I could hardly even read what I got on the screen.

I wanted to take college classes, but I had to work to feed my family and couldn't have afforded the tuition anyway. So I went to the Adult Learning Center in Albany and paid for a computer class. I could never make it to the class, though, since I was always working. After seven or eight months, I asked if I could get my money back. They said no, but that I could take a different class. I tried again, but I couldn't find the time for that class, either.

Then one day I was in the Albany Public Library and saw a sign that said "Free Computer Class for Senior Citizens." I asked the lady at the information desk about the class, and she said it would begin next month. I signed up. When the time came, I showed up for the class and was told to go to the second floor.

"Is this the computer class?" I asked, when I'd found the room.

"Yes," the teacher answered. She seemed to be looking at me strangely. "Are you a senior citizen?"

"No ma'am, I am not a citizen yet, but soon I will be," I said.

"But are you a senior?' she asked.

"Yes, I am sincere," I told her. "I signed up two weeks ago and I really want to learn about computers."

"No, no, I asked if you are a *senior*," she said.

"Ma'am, I am very serious!" I told her.

"No. No. A *senior*. A SENIOR. Are you a *senior*?" she repeated, getting rather agitated.

"What does senior mean?" I finally asked.

"It means are you fifty years old or older?" she said.

"No, I am thirty-four years."

"But you must be fifty or older to attend this class."

"But they did not tell me that when I wrote down my name."

"Sorry," she said. "Maybe they thought you were a senior."

"What?" I was surprised. "Do I look like I am fifty years old?"

"I'm sorry," she said again. "You can't take this class."

"Ma'am, I am coming from Iraq to learn—to relearn—computers. Can you let me in, please?" I pleaded.

"Sorry," she said. "I can't help you."

I gave up and went downstairs. I was not a senior or a citizen, even though I was sincere and serious, and so I could not take the class. Actually I was surprised to see many old people, some of them carrying oxygen tanks, some in wheelchairs, going to this class because they wanted to learn. I remembered my high school teacher saying, "It's science, not art, that's important." Now I understood how America went to the moon and became so powerful through technology—because four-year-olds go to pre-K, and seventy- and eighty-year-olds take computer classes! It's through work and science, not by miracles or accidents.

I took a deep breath and said to myself: *Yassin, it's not history—it's technology. It's not poetry—it's science. It's not accidental—it takes work. It's not a miracle—it's a struggle. It's not guns—it's pens. It's not missiles—it's minds. It's not politics—it's organization. It's not force or fear—it's hope and freedom. It's not racism—it's equal rights.*

I left the library, and before I got into my car I talked to myself again. I said, *Yassin, it may be too late for you, but make sure your children get an education.*

Family Man

It is not your fault if you do not know who your father is, but it is your fault if you don't know who your children are. In my culture, we do not use the term "family man," because a person without a family is not a man. People are expected to get married, have children, and live together as a family. It is our tradition. It is rare to find someone who doesn't want to get married, or is willing to get married but doesn't want to have children, or is willing to have children but does not want to live as part of a family. In our tradition, husband, wife, and children should live under one roof, and if they don't, they are not a family. I was really shocked when I came to the U.S. and found that many children had orders of protection to keep their parents from seeing them. Many children did not know who their fathers were, and if they did, they did not see their fathers or even visit with them. My brain could not comprehend that a father would rape his own children. How can this be? What kind of people would do something that even animals do not do? I want to give a warning to all Americans that they should not endanger their way of life by destroying the family through alcohol, drugs, and immoral sexual relations. This is the biggest threat to the peacefulness and richness of this country. We need to address these problems before it is too late.

As a Muslim, I have repudiated many things in my tradition which

I believe are wrong, but one of the things that I am proud of in my tradition is the strong relationship between family members based on love, respect, and responsibility. In my own house, I tried my best to keep this tradition alive and to prevent anything that would destroy us as a family. I did not see any difficulty in this because my wife agreed, and we had a similar background and tradition. We were also foreigners alone in a new country, which usually binds you closer together as a family. As they say in America, "If we have no one else, at least we have each other." So as a practical matter, I told my wife and children that if we have no family here—no uncles or aunts or cousins or nephews or nieces or grandfathers or grandmothers—at least we have each other.

I tried to be first for my family and second for my community, and to grow bigger behind it. I especially tried to keep a good friendship with my children. Daily I took them to school and picked them up afterwards. I played with them and rode bikes with them. I took them out once or twice a month to a restaurant and once a week for shopping, and we went to museums and libraries and to see waterfalls. I tried to do everything with them. I was very happy to see that they had fun and played in a way that I never could or did during my own childhood. I did not teach them what my father told me; I wanted them to be free. Whatever I was not allowed to say or do in front of my dad, I saw to it that they did it continuously in front of me.

My father was fifty-eight years old when I was born, and that may have been the reason that he did not want to play with me. Whenever I used to see children walking with their dads like friends, I would feel really sad and wish that my dad was young and could treat me in the same way. But my dad was a villager who did not look at me as a child, but rather in the way that an army commander looks at a soldier. I was one generation younger than all of my cousins. They should have been around my age, but instead I was the same age as their children because I was born so late. My oldest sister was older than my mother.

One of my cousins, Salah Mahmood, wanted his children to call him *Kaka*, which means "big brother," rather than Father, and Sheikh Salah really was like a big brother to his children. I was determined that when

I had children, I would be their friend rather than their authority figure, and teach them to call me *Kaka* rather than Father. So I tried to joke and play with them as though we were friends. I think they enjoyed it, but I was the one who was more excited. Just to have them jump on me, or ride on my back, or push me, or do any of the funny things that children do, gave me a great deal of pleasure. In my tradition, it was a shame for children to act this way, and a sign that they did not have respect for their father. I was not allowed to even talk in front of my dad without permission. There was no way to run or laugh or play in his presence.

Many times I would play with my children and other students in the *masjid*. This made some people angry, and they looked at me as though I was not the right person to be the Imam. According to them, an Imam should not allow children to play in the *masjid*. In my country, children playing in the *masjid* would have been beaten, and the Imam certainly would not have played with them. So apparently these people who objected thought that America had corrupted me, or that I was still in Iraq, or that I was a sign of the Final Hours.

One day when two brothers came into the *masjid* and I was running with the children and playing hide-and-seek, they started yelling at the children and made them sit quietly. I just stopped running and sat with the children. One of the brothers said that he would tell the Imam what the children were doing in the *masjid*—but one of the children told him that I was the Imam. The brother looked at me and asked if that were true. I went to him and shook his hand and told him I was serving in the *masjid*.

"But are you the Imam?" he asked.

"I lead the prayer too," I said.

"This means that you are the Imam," he said.

"People call me that," I said.

He shook his head and said, "If you are the Imam, what kind of people can there be here?"

I just smiled at him. I knew where he was coming from and I did not want to argue with him.

That Friday, I preached about the way we should deal with children, and I especially mentioned that not only was it OK to bring children to the *masjid*, they were even allowed to play as long as they behaved themselves when people were praying. I told them about how Mohammad, may peace be upon him, used to carry his grandsons Hasan and Hossain around, one on each shoulder. One day while the Prophet was prostrating himself in prayer, one of the grandsons came and jumped on his back. The Prophet stayed on the ground in prayer for a long, long time. After he finished praying, people asked him if something had changed in his prayers. "No," the Prophet said. "But you lay prostrate for so long," they said. "Oh," he responded, "my grandson was on my back, and I wanted him to take his time."

On another occasion while the Prophet was preaching, his grandson Hossain came to the *masjid*. When the Prophet saw him he stopped his preaching, went to him, picked him up, and returned to finish his preaching with Hossain still in his arms. Are we better than the Prophet, I asked them?

I did not listen to people who complained about the children. I knew it was just about culture and had nothing to do with religion. Thank God I received support in my attitude toward children, but a few people still believed that I was violating some precept of our religion. I used to remind these people of the Arab proverb, "If you have a kid, be a kid for him." I tried my best to be a kid when I was with my kids. I accepted the criticism from people, but I did not change my relationship with my children until the government took me away, locked me up in jail, and left them as half-orphans with no father and no one to play with. They had no one to take them to the park or to ride a bicycle with, and unless my neighbor took my children to school with his children, they would not have been able to go.

I will never forget the day that my daughter Dilnia was born while I was in jail, and I realized that she could know nothing about me. When they brought her to visit me for the first time, she was scared of me and did not know who this strange man was. Now when I call home, my older children all run to the phone yelling "Daddy, Daddy!", so Dilnia believes that "Daddy" means "phone." My daughter Alaa told me that when she asks Dilnia where her father is, she points at the phone. The phone is "Daddy."

I believe that one of the main reasons family ties are not strong in this country is because children do not grow up with their parents. My other children love me and miss me because they had fun with me in the past. But what will my baby Dilnia remember about me? What will she miss? She has no memories of me to start with. So let's go back to our nature. Let's build back the family so we will be happier, and when we get old our children will be happy to help us, as we helped them when they needed us.

One day in my cell I was listening to a radio talk show. A doctor was giving some advice to a woman who had not seen her daughter since birth, but was reunited with her when the daughter was twelve years old. The woman said that her daughter did not love her. The doctor advised the woman that every day she should put her daughter on her lap like a mother breast-feeding a child. Don't talk to her, the doctor said, but just look at her—make eye contact. This will imprint you in her mind as her protector and provider, and that will give her a sense of peace, and out of that will grow love. I said to myself, Glory to God and his natural laws. That is why human babies need their parents more than most creatures. In Kurdistan, they joke that when a child is not listening to his mom it is because he grew up on bottle milk and not breast milk. After I heard the doctor's advice, I realized that breast feeding must have an importance beyond just milk. It also provides love and security and the relationship between parent and child.

If we are not going to be part of our children's lives and we don't fill their minds with good memories and fun, we should not be surprised if they do not give any of this back to us. They do not owe us anything. We have to earn it by being real parents, real fathers and real mothers who help, teach, protect, love, and enjoy them. After that they will become adults who will love us back and serve others. God knows I was separated from my children against my will and put in jail for no reason. But what about you? Have you acknowledged your responsibility as a parent, and have you done something about it?

Do you want your children to be with you when you retire? I believe that the most beautiful part of the life of elderly people is to be surrounded by their children and grandchildren. They should not be alone in a nursing home. In the Middle East, it is traditional that when people get sick and old their children take care of them—and this is a beautiful tradition. Young men tenderly serve their grandparents, and the young man's parents will lovingly take care of his child. I believe we should all do this, and that Islam orders us to do it. Once a man was carrying his mother on his back in hot weather when he saw Ibn al Umar, one of Mohammad's companions. The man asked Ibn al Umar if he rewarded his mother by carrying her on his back. Ibn al Umar replied that the man's efforts were certainly worthy, but all of it was not enough to reward even one minute of his mother's pain in childbirth when she delivered him.

It really bothers me that people in the West leave their parents alone and go off to live separate lives. When I first came to the United States, I stayed in Mr. Paul's home. He was an old gentleman who lived with his wife in a huge, beautiful house and had to drive himself around with his two dogs in the car, speaking to them as though they were his children. It was fifty days before Christmas and the old man was literally counting the days because his only son had promised to visit him from Florida for the holiday.

"Is your son married?" I asked.

"No," Mr. Paul said.

"How old is he?"

"Forty years old."

I was surprised that an unmarried man would not want to live with his parents in this huge house so he could talk to them daily and help them around the house and make them more comfortable, just as they had done for him for at least eighteen years. Should we not give back to our parents at least a small part of what we owe them? In Kurdish culture, grandfathers and grandmothers are royalty, with all of the youth of all ages serving them. I believe that this relationship is normal and healthy and we should encourage it. Not every old thing is bad, and not every new thing is good.

Chapter Fourteen ◀
The Walls Can See and Hear

Keep Struggling

As long as we are alive, we have a responsibility to do our duty and do our best in whatever situation we may be placed. We have to struggle and work to achieve despite our concerns or fears, which put us under a lot of stress and pressure. This is the reality of life. Every person is going to have to face this struggle in different ways and in different amounts. It's impossible to not be concerned with this life struggle. Of course, the problems of presidents and prisoners are different, and Swedish problems are different than Iraqi problems, and the youth in the U.S. face different problems than the youth in Somalia. The Egyptian writer Taha Hussain wrote a story about two people complaining about their stomachs—one because he had eaten too much, and the other because he was hungry. Taha Hussain wrote that if the first had just given a little of the extra food that he had eaten to the one who was hungry, neither of them would have had stomach pain. So while we may have different, separate problems, we are united in pain, and if one of us worries about and helps another a little, none of us may suffer anymore.

People in third world countries are under stress because of daily violence, insecurity, hunger, unemployment, lack of medicine, electricity, clean water, phones, schools, etc. These are generally not the problems faced by people in the West. But Westerners have their own struggle for survival, and they get stressed in different ways. Westerners go to see a psychologist, or take anti-depressants or anti-anxiety medicines for stress, but in the East there is no medical care for such illnesses.

As we grow up, our needs also grow. We get something we need and we think that it will last forever, but soon afterwards another need comes along and we are just as needy as before. A person may say that he needs a radio to get the news broadcast, and if he could just get one radio he would not need anything more. But as soon as he gets a radio, he will think that if he just had a TV, he would not need anything more; and after that he would just need a computer, and after that entertainment, and then a laptop—and the list goes on forever. There is no end to a person's "needs" except self-satisfaction or death. In Arabic, it is said that a person is really rich when he achieves self-satisfaction. If you are satisfied with what you have, you are rich and you can enjoy it and have peace of mind. But if you do not have self-satisfaction, you will not have peace of mind no matter how much stuff you get. As the Prophet Mohammad, may peace be upon him, said, "The eyes of humans never get full except by the dust of the grave."

In Kurdistan and Iraq, my struggle for survival centered around two things: food and security for myself and for my family. Although many things changed as I moved from Iraq to Syria to the U.S., these two needs never changed. When I left Iraq, I thought that these problems would be over, but I had to struggle very hard for food and security in Syria. When I left Syria, I thought that these problems would be over, but I had to struggle very hard for food and security in the U.S. My struggle to feed my family was no less difficult in the U.S. than it was in Syria or Iraq. And my struggle to bring security to my family has actually been much greater in the U.S. than in either Syria or Iraq.

Many people are sick because they put too much food in their stomachs, and many other people are weak because they do not have enough food to put in their stomachs. When George Bernard Shaw heard people complaining that a growing population was causing people to go hungry, he supposedly put his hand on top of his bald head and brought it down over his face until he held his large bushy beard. The people looked puzzled, and Shaw explained, "I am bald not because I don't have enough hair, but because it is on my face instead of on the top." In the same way, the problem is not lack of food to feed everyone, but the way food is divided. If food were divided equally, there would be more than enough to go around, just as Shaw had more than enough hair to cover his entire head if it had not been all clumped up on his chin.

I am not an economist, but I still strongly believe that even though our planet produces much more food than humans can consume, the problem is in distribution. God's natural laws tie people together. They need each other for business and for exchange of natural resources. Some countries have oil; others have rice, or fruit, or grain. So they all need each other. When goods are fairly exchanged, life automatically improves for everyone and nations come to know and like each other.

In Iraq, people did not have enough food—not because grain was not grown, but because the government destroyed most of the villages and farms in the north and cut down the date palms in the south, while the Iraqi oil was used to finance war. The same is true about Sudan, Somalia, and many other places around the world. We pay a huge price for corruption and bad policy. Even in the Western countries, if you go to a big city you will see food going to waste in the garbage. What is thrown out in five-star hotels and restaurants is more than enough to feed all of the homeless and poor in the city. One of my friends told me that when he visited Florida, he saw a piece of land that was bright pink-orange, and when he came close he saw that the ground was covered with oranges. He asked his friend what this was all about and why they did not pick up the oranges. His friend said that the company that owned the orchard was trying to keep the oranges off the market so it could drive the price higher. Let the people suffer and struggle so that a big company can make money! And in the same way, you should not have been surprised when gas prices in the U.S. jumped to record levels—about $3 a gallon—while the oil companies made record profits.

I thought that by coming to the U.S., I would end my struggle for food to feed my family. I thought I would not have any difficulty making an easy income, and that I would have time to finish my master's degree and get a Ph.D. But after I arrived here, it took me six or seven months to find a job, and after I started working full-time at Albany Medical Center at minimum wage I could not make even $1,000 a month, which was not enough to feed a family of five. So I had to get a second job.

After several months, I got a part-time job as Imam at the *masjid*, but between the two jobs and helping with my children I had no time to sleep more than four hours a night. In order to be present in the mosque five times a day to lead prayer, I had to keep running back there from other activities. And so, although I spent a lot of time in the mosque, it was not a single block of time but rather an hour here and an hour there, five times a day. My day was very full. But from both jobs, I made only $1,500 a month, which still was not enough to pay rent and feed and clothe my family.

Eventually I was asked to work full-time as the Imam, for which I would be paid $1,500 a month. I was not making more money, but at least now I had more time—more time that I could devote to being an Imam. However, I still had the same problem of providing for my family.

Shamshad Ahmad, my friend and brother, had submitted a bid for me on a two-family house near the mosque that was being offered for sale by the U.S. Department of Housing and Urban Development. The required deposit was $500. I had been able to borrow only some of that from my friends in the U.S., so Shamshad had paid the difference and had helped me fix it up through various workmen that he knew. But I still needed to repay as much as $500 each month to Shamshad for the deposit and the repair work, and I did this over the years until the debt was paid.

These are all problems similar to those of millions of immigrants from third world countries with friends and relatives in the Middle East who are also struggling to survive in their own way, with their own problems. The friends and relatives believe that the one who has immigrated to the West has become rich and can help them—if he cares to. If you don't send money back to help them, they think you have forgotten them, now that you are rich.

Two of my brothers are still mad at me because I did not send them anything. One day my brother Mohsin called and was really angry. He said that it was no problem if I didn't want to help him or the family, but that I should at least do something for myself, since all of the other people who immigrated to Western countries had saved enough money in a year or two that they were able to buy a house or a store or property in the country they'd left. I told Mohsin that my income in the U.S. was not sufficient to cover my own basic needs. But he did not believe me.

"Why are other immigrants able to save money?" he asked.

"I can't do what other people do," I said. "Many jobs require that I do things that are not permitted in Islam, such as working with alcohol or pork, or working around gambling or in places where interest is charged. Zuhur cannot work because she is taking care of three children. It is hard to get jobs because I do not have a degree, I am not a professional, I do not speak good English, and I have to be in the mosque for prayer five times each day between 5 a.m. and 8 p.m. I cannot take a loan or use a credit card because interest is not permitted in Islam, you know that. It is difficult to be in the West and practice Islam."

"So why did you go to America, then?" he asked in exasperation.

"To live free and practice my religion," I said.

"Don't tell me that you still wear a beard and go to mosque five times a day," he said.

"Of course I do," I said. "I am an Imam."

"People go to the West to become a doctor or a scientist," Mohsin said. "If you want to be an Imam, why don't you come back to an Iraqi village like Hashazini? It would be much better for you."

"How would it be better?" I said. "If I became an Imam in Hashazini, I would be paid $5 a month. Here I am paid $1,500 a month."

"They pay you $1,500 a year?" Mohsin exclaimed, shocked at how much I was earning.

"No," I said, "$1,500 a *month*!"

There was a long silence as Mohsin tried to understand this incomprehensible statement. "So why can't you buy a house?" he finally asked.

"Because I can't support my family on $1,500 a month," I said.

This conversation made no sense to Mohsin. He did not understand it, and he could not believe me. (Note that if I sent home a mere $100 a year, it would be more than an Imam could earn in a year there. But to do that, I would have had to make more in America than I spent, and I was simply not able to do that.) I tried to explain to Mohsin that everything was different over here. He paid $10 rent in Iraq, but I had to pay $500. An electric bill was $2 in Iraq, and $100 here. The same was true for heat and insurance and phone and food. But Mohsin just could not understand that we lived on two different planets.

Many of my friends in Iraq used to call and ask me for a loan. My nephew wanted money to go to Europe. Most of them thought that life in America had changed me and made me forget them. They did not know that I felt sadder than they did when I told them I was sorry, but I had no money to give them. I could not sleep at night. Living in America made me feel constantly guilty, and it was no fun at all. I had no time for traveling, or for going to a hotel, or for visiting Disney World, or for seeing a zoo or a university. Every day was a struggle, and I worked every day, including weekends. And yet in seven years in America, I was never able to save the $7,000 or $10,000 necessary to pay for tickets to the Middle East to see my family. Many times I tried to save the money, but every time someone called and asked for help I could not lie and say I did not have the money. So I gave it all away. Slowly I came to believe what my friends who had immigrated to Europe used to tell me: that they had no rest in Europe. I did not believe them then, but I do now. They told me that with all the trouble and difficulty in surviving in the Middle East, it was more stressful living in the West. In the East, often people do not work, or do only simple things, and somehow they manage to survive; but in America I found myself running day and night and working constantly, and still I could not cover my family's expenses.

One day on the phone I swore to Mohsin that since I had arrived in the U.S. I had never bought a single suit, that my house was smaller than his in Kurdistan, and that his furniture was better than mine. He was shocked. "Yassin," he said, "you never complained before when you were living in Kurdistan. Why are you talking like this now? Does this mean that when a person becomes rich he complains more than a poor person? Or are you just afraid that I may ask you for money?"

I did not know what to say to him. We lived on different planets now, and there was no way to communicate across the space between us. I could not tell him that since I came to America, I had bought all my clothes and furniture at garage sales, I had never bought a new TV or refrigerator, and I never had a car worth more than $3,000. Even my house had cost only about $12,500, and eventually I sold it to my tenant in order to raise money to spend on my family's needs. We were five people living in a two-bedroom apartment, and my children never had a backyard to play in. But I could not tell Mohsin any of this because he wouldn't have believed me. And how could I make my family and friends in Iraq and Syria understand that they were all in my mind and heart and that I had not forgotten them, but that I had no way to help them?

After I became a full-time Imam at the mosque, a man we called Haji, who owned the *halal** grocery store next to the mosque, told me that he was going back to Pakistan for two or three months and asked if I could look after the store for three or four hours in the morning while he was gone. His son could watch the store in the afternoon. I agreed, and he showed me all the things I was supposed to do. The next morning I had to open the store from 9 a.m. until noon. As soon as I started, I received a letter from my social worker that I had to appear for an appointment to have my food stamps renewed. I immediately called my social worker and thanked her, but told her that I did not want food stamps anymore.

"Why?" she asked.

"Because I just got a part-time job at a food store, and I will be able to take care of my family now," I said.

"How much more will you make in your job?" she asked.

"$300–$400 every month," I said.

"You are still eligible for food stamps," she said. "You are a refugee, and you can get food stamps for up to six years."

"But I don't want them," I said. "I am OK now."

My social worker must have thought something was wrong with me. Maybe she thought I had a mental problem. In a sense she would have been right. Living on welfare made me feel very uncomfortable. It was against my religion for a healthy young man who could work to take charity. She asked me some questions to make sure she understood what I was saying. I thanked her for her concern and assured her that

* *Halal* in Arabic means "permissible" under Islam; when referring to food and dietary laws, its meaning is similar to the Hebrew "kosher."

we could take care of ourselves, and that she should give the money to someone who really needed it.

"But it is your right," she said.

"I will be happy to give my right to someone who needs it," I said.

"So you are not coming for the renewal interview?"

"No ma'am," I said. "I don't want it."

"Well, OK," she said. "If you lose your job or something else happens, you can always come back."

"I hope I will never need it again," I said. "Thank you very much."

About a week later, I received a letter from her stating that at my request they were stopping my food stamps and were closing my case. Thank God I never reapplied. After I was arrested and after my wife gave birth to our daughter Dilnia, she was eligible for food stamps, but she refused to take any help from the government because of what they had done to us. If it had not been for the help of people all over the Capital District, they would not have had food to eat.

When Haji returned from Pakistan I left the grocery store, but then I had to find another part-time job so I would not have to go back on food stamps. I asked my friend Mohammed Hossain, who owned the Little Italy Pizzeria, if I could work for him three or four hours a night delivering pizza. He agreed, but I told him I would only do deliveries. He said that sometimes he had only a few deliveries at night and that he would like me to also work in the store when I did not have anything to deliver, but I refused. I said I would be glad to work around the store for free, but I only wanted to be paid for deliveries. He agreed to this. So I worked from 8 p.m. until midnight delivering pizza, which was very slow work. Most of the deliveries were to places that other stores did not deliver to at night because it was dangerous.

About the third or fourth month on the job, I made a delivery one night about 11 p.m. After I had delivered the pizza to the customer, I came back to my car and found three young people with a knife waiting for me.

"What do you need?" I asked.

"Money," they said.

"I only have $20 from this delivery," I said.

"We need $100."

Living in the Middle East and reading Aziz Nesin's stories taught me to never put all my money in one pocket. I always put it in three or four different pockets, or even in my shirt or socks. I pulled out my pants pocket to show them that I did not have any more money. They came very close to me. I started using my hands to protect myself, and I discovered that they did not know how to fight. I was like a *ninja* compared with them. I pushed them back and got in my car. One of them grabbed my car jack and said he would break the window if I moved. I said if he did that, it would cost me much more than $20, and I told him it was better for him to believe that all I had was $20. "If you put my jack back in the car," I told him, "I will give you the $20—so be nice."

"Do you promise?" he said.

"I am not kidding you," I said.

He put the jack back in the car and I threw the money to him and drove off.

Back at the store, Mr. Hossain asked me why I had taken so long, and I told him what had happened. I said I did not want to deliver pizza anymore. He tried to change my mind but I refused. He accused me of being afraid. I told him that in fact I was afraid. If something happened to me, what would become of my children? And why should an Imam bring shame on his community by taking such work? It was difficult at that time for Middle Eastern people to find jobs because of 9/11. People looked at us as different and dangerous. Moreover, many people did not understand why an Imam would do such work. They thought it was greed, even though God knows I was only trying to feed my family.

Driver

After I stopped delivering pizza, I asked people at the mosque if they knew of any jobs. One person said that he had a small company, AMA Transportation, which drove people to the hospital for treatment. I asked if he could give me a job, but he said most of his work was in the area of Catskill and Hudson, some forty or fifty miles south of Albany. I said that if I took a job there, I would not have time to come back for prayers at the mosque. However, the owner said that he might try to take some orders in Albany, and if any came in he would give them to me. He told me that I would have to take a Red Cross emergency first-aid course, which I did.

After about two months, he gave me two people who had to go for dialysis three days every week—one from Albany and one from Ravena, fifteen miles south of Albany. The lady from Ravena was Spanish and did not speak much English, but she was very nice. I helped her walk and carried her baggage as much as I could, and she loved me and treated me like her son. Then one day my boss told me one his drivers was unavailable and that he needed me to pick up two people, in Castleton and Ravena, south of Albany, and take them to a hospital in Rotterdam, west of Albany. I picked up the first woman about 8 a.m., who said she had to be at the hospital by 9 a.m.

We were headed for Exit 25. I followed my directions to go north on the Thruway (I-87) to Exit 25, but at Exit 24 the Thruway turned west and became I-90, while I-87 (at that point called the Northway) continued north. I understood that my directions required me to stay on I-87 and not go west on I-90 (Thruway), so I got off the Thruway at Exit 24 and headed north on I-87 (Northway). The exits began again at number 1, and we drove for two hours until we came to Exit 25 of the Northway. It was somewhere in the middle of the Adirondack Mountains. The woman kept asking me where I was taking her and why it was taking so long this time. I told her I did not know, but I was already driving over the speed limit.

When we finally reached Exit 25 of the Northway, I could not find any sign for the hospital that was supposed to be there. I went to a gas station and asked the owner about the hospital. He told me that I should have gone to Exit 25 of the *Thruway* (which at that point was I-90 and was west of Albany).

"I just came from that direction," I said. "It took me two hours. Isn't there a shortcut I can take?"

"Sure," the man said. "You can take this road west," and he showed me the road on a map. We started out, and soon it looked like we were in the mountains of Kurdistan. There were few cars around and I was driving very fast. The woman kept asking me, "Where are you taking me?? Why are we in these mountains? Why are you driving so fast?"

"Sorry," I said. "I went to the wrong place. We have to go back."

The woman became very upset and began to say many things that I wished she would not say. But I did not answer her, because I knew it was my fault. I just told her to be patient and we would be OK. After two more hours of stopping here and there for directions, we finally found the hospital. Her appointment had been for 9 a.m., and it was now 1 p.m. I told her we were in the right place and she should see what the doctors could do for her. But she returned, cursing my company because she had been told to come back tomorrow.

"Sorry," I said to her. "It was all my fault. We will bring you back tomorrow."

"No, absolutely not," she said. "I don't want you to bring me back tomorrow."

"Sorry. Maybe they will send somebody else tomorrow," I said hopefully. She did not respond.

It was after lunchtime, and neither of us had eaten. I stopped at a gas station, filled the car with gas, and bought juice and a snack for the woman. I told her that I was very sorry and I knew she was tired and maybe a little food would help. I asked her to forgive me, I had just started this work and I was new to the company.

"So why did they send you?" she asked. "To lose customers?"

I explained about the confusion as to whether her destination had been Exit 25 of the Thruway, or the Northway.

"You're supposed to have a map," she said.

"Actually, I have a map," I said. "But I thought I was going in the right direction."

She was really angry, and I was really sad for what had happened.

My boss called me on the cell phone. "Yassin," he said, "where are you? You were supposed to pick up a lady in Ravena."

"I'm sorry," I said. "I got lost and now I have to take this lady back to Castleton."

"Where are you right now?" he asked.

"I am on the Thruway headed south, near Albany," I said.

"Just stop at Exit 23," he said. "I'll send someone to bring the customer back to Castleton. You need to go and pick up the lady in Ravena."

I stopped at Exit 23, and after about twenty minutes another car came to take the lady back to Castleton.

"I'm sorry," I told the lady once again. "This man will bring you home. I have to go pick up another customer."

"So!" she said. "You're going to lose someone else!" But then she smiled and said, "Please don't come and pick me up tomorrow."

"Certainly I will not," I said. "I am just working in Albany. Please forgive me."

"You're very polite," she said. "You've said 'sorry' and 'forgive me' enough times. Really, I forgive you. Just use a map next time."

"Thank you," I told her.

As I drove to pick up my customer in Ravena, the lady's words kept repeating in my mind: *Use a map.* I told myself, *Yassin, this is not Iraq. This is not Hashazini. Use a map. You are a villager living in the U.S. now—use a map!*

When I got to my customer in Ravena, I found her lying down. She said she was very tired. "Are you OK?" she asked me.

"Sorry I'm late," I said.

"I was just worried about you if you were OK," she said. "I was scared. God forbid something happened to you, because you never came late before."

I told her how I had gotten lost with the other customer.

"That happens all the time," said the woman.

"This was my first time getting lost," I said, "and the customer was really angry."

"She didn't have to be angry," the lady said. "You didn't get lost on purpose."

"I wish everyone thought like you do," I said.

"Son, I wish everyone was as helpful as you," the lady said. "This is my fifth year of dialysis, and I've gone through twenty or thirty drivers. None of them were as helpful as you."

"I don't have a busy schedule," I said. "I have time to help you, and you are like my mom." Then I saw that she had tears in her eyes and she couldn't talk anymore.

My Dear Brothers and Sisters of Color

One of my close friends in Albany is Abdulbarr. He is really my big brother who has always been here for me when I've needed him. I learned a lot about the culture of America from him, especially about the African American community. He is proof that you should never judge a man by his color. Some people think that a person acts because of his nature, but most of our actions come not from our nature but from our habits. Our actions are not imprinted on us at birth, like instincts that cannot be changed, but are habits that are learned, and can be unlearned. People can change themselves, but they need a sincere intention and a clear plan, an alternative to the path they are presently on.

Most of my friends are African American, and I have done many reconciliations for them. From my experience, I can say that no group pays a greater price for destructive customs and habits than the African American community. This community is really struggling to survive. Life for most African American brothers I have met in the U.S. is hard and tough—like Kurdish life. The problems are different, the causes are different, but the result is the same: suffering and poverty, having no equality, and feeling all the worst things about being a minority.

One day I saw a big scar on the back of Abdulbarr's head. I asked him what had happened.

"Forget it. It's a long story," he said.

"Will you please tell me how this happened?" I said.

"Let me tell you one thing first," he said.

"Yes, please," I joked. "In fact, tell me two things. We have time."

"Islam saved my life," he said.

"What do you mean by that?" I asked. I just wanted to help him tell his story.

He said, "I used to deal drugs. I bought them, I sold them, and I took them. I used to get drunk almost every night, and I changed women like I change clothes. I fought with girlfriends, friends, and the police. I stole money for drugs. I told lies and I cheated friends for drugs and women. I had no rest in my life and no peace in my heart. I had no joy. I went back to jail over and over, repeating the same bullshit each time. I hated white people and considered them evil. I never opened a book. But once when I was in jail, I studied Islam, and I decided to become a Muslim. Since then I have not touched alcohol, I have avoided drugs and even cigarettes, I have not committed any crimes, I married and stayed faithful to my wife, I work hard to support my family, I will not lie, I do not cheat, I do not steal. I will never again engage in violence. I do not hate anyone and do not believe that anyone is evil by color or race. If Islam had not changed me, I would have been dead or homeless. All the people I used to hang out with have either been killed or are in prison. I am here only because of Islam."

I was really excited by what he said, and I had many stories and dialogues with him. I mention Abdulbarr's experience because it is a perfect illustration of the fact that we are not guided by instincts but by habits. We can change. My experience in jail is that 95% of the prisoners here are victims of drugs and sex. They may have other charges against them, like robbery or assault or even murder, but most of the problems started with drugs and bad sexual relationships—especially in the African American community.

My dear brothers and sisters of color: please let me tell you something from my experience. I am Kurdish. For decades, if not centuries, we have blamed all of our problems on our enemies. After all we went through, we still found ways to excuse ourselves. It is true that much of our suffering came from our enemies, who caused us many problems, but the bigger truth is that we ourselves caused our own problems. Many things would have been different if not for our ignorance and arrogance. We ignored our responsibilities, we made excuses for our bad behavior, and we refused to change. The same is true of Arab and Muslim societies throughout the Middle East. For decades they blamed all of their problems on Israel. I believe Israel caused them problems, but in reality most of their problems had nothing to do with Israel, or America, or the West.

Israel did not tell Saddam to kill millions of his own people; America did not tell him to occupy Kuwait; Europe did not order Muslims to commit torture and keep silent about it; enemies did not cut down our trees or destroy our farms or close our universities. We did it to ourselves, but we blamed them. We must find out what causes our problems and why we are not getting what other people have. It is easy to pardon ourselves and to blame others for God's decree, but that will not bring about any change.

Please do not repeat our mistakes. Do not put the blame for all your problems on others. I believe you have a great system and a big opportunity here in America. You can use both to end your suffering forever. Let me be honest with you. I believe drugs and guns are threatening to destroy your communities. You must act to remove these poisons yourselves. Bad sexual behavior is also causing serious problems like HIV, AIDS, unwanted pregnancies, children growing up without fathers, poverty, and family stress. You must teach people in your community to control themselves. It's not worth ten minutes' diversion to be in jail for ten years. As you care about your bodies and you build your muscles, also build your minds. Don't be proud just because you have muscles and you can fight, but use your minds and wisdom to do things better and to serve the community.

If you do the following things, I guarantee that your children will grow up in a different kind of community, they will live more wholesome lives, and they will not have to live the kind of life that you went through. Take guns and drugs out of your communities. Control your sexual relations and stay in your marriages. Do not let other minds use your muscles, but educate yourselves and your children. These things are the keys. If you follow them, suffering and poverty will disappear from your communities and you will not be prisoners anymore; you will be one community of leaders.

I am just like you. I paid a high price for racism. Ignorance caused me great suffering. But when I saw you and your troubled condition, I forgot my own situation. I hope you will believe me and take my simple, sincere advice seriously to bring Martin Luther King's dream to reality.

Security Concerns

We used to say in Iraq, "Be careful, because the walls can hear." But in America you have to be even more careful, because the walls can see as well as hear. In Kurdistan while I was growing up, I expected at any time to be arrested by the government—not because I did anything wrong or broke the law, but simply because I was Kurdish. We used to shake from fear whenever we saw someone in uniform. Police, security forces, soldiers—all could arrest you and make you "disappear." They did not need a court order or a warrant.

I have no personal problem with anyone in the world. I have never fought with anyone in my life. Of course I have had many disagreements and argued with many people, but I never hated them, or looked on them as the enemy, or directed physical violence toward them, and so far as I know no one has ever hated me. I never broke any laws or committed any crimes or was a suspect by any group or government anywhere in this universe. I have my opinions about many groups and governments, and I have freely given my opinions and criticized groups and governments when I thought they deserved it. But I have never called for violence against them, nor was I ever violent. I say this to reassure anyone who reads this book that my problems were never personal problems against individuals or governments.

I suffered in Iraq simply because I was a Kurd. And when I finally came to America, I hoped to end this persecution in the land of freedom, the country of diversity, the place of peaceful life. I thought that by leaving the Middle East I had left security problems forever. No longer would I be afraid of the police or worry about government investigations. No longer would I be watched just because of my nationality. No more walls listening to conversations—I could say whatever I wanted. There was no charge or tax for talking in America. That was why the UN sent us here—to have our rights, to be safe from the government, and to live without fear. My brother Issa used to say that we Kurds were created to suffer. If we went to the ocean to get water, it would dry up. Issa went to Holland to end his struggle, but he was forced to stay there for almost eight years while his wife and children in Kurdistan waited for him to get papers to bring the whole family to Holland. It never happened. After eight years of suffering, he went back to Kurdistan with empty hands to suffer more. Still, his situation is better than mine. At least he was free in Holland.

Security problems followed me to the U.S., not because of any personal wrongdoing—I never had any problem with anyone in America, and I never committed any crime or broke any law. But after 9/11, I was waiting to be picked up by the FBI for investigation just because I was a Muslim. In the same way that we were under the watch of the Iraqi government in Kurdistan because we were Kurds, I was under the watch of the American government because I was Muslim. In America I have had to be as careful of what I say as I was in Kurdistan.

In Iraq, you could not trust whether or not a stranger was an informant; in America, it is the same—even in the mosque you could not trust anyone because you did not know who was carrying a tape recorder. In Iraq they could jail you without evidence. In America, they jail you based on secret evidence they say is "classified." In Iraq they told the Imams that they were not allow to preach on certain topics. In America, they say that everyone is free to speak, but when you criticize the government you are accused of being anti-American and anti-Semitic. In Iraq there was no mail service and no international calls. In America there is mail and phone service, but the FBI will open your mail and wiretap your telephone. So feel free to write and say whatever you want, but be 100% sure that the FBI will read what you write, listen to what you say, and will arrest you if you are too truthful in criticizing the government. In Iraq they search your house right in front of you without a court order, but in America they break into your house after you have left for the day. The parallels between civil liberties in Iraq and America go on and on.

I will never forget what my lawyer told me at my trial: that the government proved nothing against me and I did not have to testify, but he wanted me to testify only to show the jury that I was just a normal human being and not a terrorist. I told him that all our lives as Kurds, we have had to prove we are human beings because our enemies put out propaganda against us and said we were wild animals living in a jungle. So even in America, I must prove I am not a wild savage, rather than prove I am a human being and a Muslim. It is really sad that history repeats itself, and that someone can be accused just because of his nationality or color or religion. This should not happen in this country.

I do not want to overstate the problem. For many Americans, there is greater freedom in America than in Iraq, but for Muslims after 9/11 there is really no big difference between America and the Middle East. In my case, the safety and security of my family was actually better in Iraq and Syria. There, the governments never concocted a tricky plan to try to entrap me; they never arrested me; they never searched my personal belongings in my home and in the mosque; they never interrogated me and my wife for eight hours with repeated threats and bullying; they never put me in jail. All the time that I was in Iraq and Syria, I was speaking out against the Iraqi government and supporting the Iraqi opposition, and I wrote many poems against the Iraqi government and in support of Kurdish freedom. But after I came to America, I never supported any opposition to the American government. So in my case, I was safer in the Middle East than in America. I was far more critical of the government in Iraq than in America, and yet I was arrested in America, not Iraq. I believe strongly that what has happened to me is wrong, and that this administration has done many things to Muslims that are not fair. I hope that I will be the last victim for such a policy, and that all foreigners in this country will get their rights back.

Since the night the FBI attacked us, arrested me, and took my wife for interrogation, she has not been normal and is afraid of everything. She does not trust any human being, including me, and she believes that anyone who speaks to her is recording her voice for the FBI. We are still scared, and we do not know what else they want from us. Nothing is clear to us. We do not know what this is all about, or what our crime is, or how we are guilty. We are just losing our minds. We cannot understand what happened or how it happened. Sometimes we think that the UN sent us to the wrong place for free people. I hope the courts will prove me wrong and show my wife and children that this is a country of law and justice for all people, including Kurds and Muslims. In Kurdistan we say that if you ask a blind man what he needs, he will tell you: *two eyes*. If you ask me and my wife and children what we need, we will answer: *justice and freedom*.

Abass and Me

After I had dinner with my friend Abdulbarr one evening, it was time for him to go to work at St. Peter's Hospital, and I told him that I would drive him there. We came out of my home at 44 West Street in Albany, and the police were parked next to my house. I told Abdulbarr, "Look at that—Abass is here." He smiled and said, "It is your personal bodyguard."

I call the police Abass because of a story I once read. In Boston, a police car pulled over another car with four Arab youths inside. The youths were mad that the police officer would give them a ticket, and they began cursing him and making fun of him in Arabic. After the police officer finished writing the ticket, he asked them where they were from. They said that they were born in the U.S. The officer said, "No, I mean your parents." Some of the youths said Syria, some said Jordan. At this point the policeman began to tell them in Arabic that his name was Abass and that his parents were from Lebanon. The youths were all shocked, because this meant that the officer must have understood what they had said. They apologized for it, and he smiled at them and said, "No problem. You can take your ticket back, along with everything else you said. You did not insult me—you insulted yourselves. I am just doing my job." Since I heard this story, whenever I see the police I say to myself, *Look, it is Uncle Abass.*

As soon as I started my car, the police car drove behind me. After I crossed Washington Avenue and drove down North Lake Avenue, I put on my signal light to go to Albany Medical Center, but Abdulbarr reminded me that he was going to St. Peter's Hospital and to just go straight. I turned the signal light off and said, "Sorry. Since I worked at Albany Medical Center, my car just goes there automatically!" As soon as I turned off the signal light, the police car behind me pulled me over. The officer asked for my license and registration. I handed them over.

"Where are you coming from?" he asked me.

"The place where you were parked," I said.

"What?"

"44 West Street," I said. "You saw me when I came out of my house, and you can also see my address on my license."

"Where are you going?"

"I am driving my friend to his job."

"Where does he work?"

"At St. Peter's Hospital."

"So why did you have your left turn signal on?"

"Because I forgot and thought that he was going to Albany Medical Center. He told me to go straight, so I turned off the turn signal."

The officer looked at Abdulbarr as though he did not believe that this man with a long beard was working at a hospital. Abdulbarr knew why he was looking at him, and showed the officer his ID.

"You're OK," he said to Abdulbarr. But he took my license and said he would be back in a minute. After about five or ten minutes, he came back and returned my license without a ticket. "You're OK," he said to me.

"So why did you pull me over?" I asked.

"Because your signal light was on," he said.

"But I just turned it on for a moment and then turned it off," I said. "Is that a crime?" I was getting mad because Abdulbarr was going to be late for his job.

The officer said, "Drive off or I'll give you a ticket."

"Goodbye, Uncle Abass," I told him.

I started driving and apologized to Abdulbarr because I made him late. "Don't worry," he said. "It's OK."

I said, "In Iraq the motto for the police is 'Police Serving People.' It is written everywhere, even on their uniforms. But the people read it as 'Police Scaring People.' So tell me, which reading is correct for the American police?"

Abdulbarr smiled. "Here in America, both are correct. Police serve people who are white, and they scare people who are black and Muslim."

"But how do they scare you?" I asked him.

"Like what the police did to you right now. It happens hundreds of times when they stop me for no reason—and after that they let me go. Before 9/11 I was stopped just because I was black. After 9/11 I was stopped because I was black and Muslim."

I laughed and said, "So all of them are your friends? You are in double trouble. One, you are black, and two, you are Muslim."

Abdulbarr took a deep breath and said, "You don't know what we have been going through for decades."

I smiled at him and said, "Be strong, brother, and keep the faith. King dreamed that one day his dream would come true and we will all be equal."

"*Insha-Allah* (By God's will)," he said. I drove him to the hospital and apologized again for making him late. "I'm OK," he said. "Be safe. *Assalamu-Alaikum* (Peace be with you)."

On another day, after I did the grocery shopping with my family, I was driving home on Central Avenue and stopped at a gas station to get gas. It was really cold, and when my children wanted to get out of the car I told them no. As I filled the car, I was jumping up and down to keep from freezing. I remembered that my friend Idris Jaff, who lives in Ohio, told me that early one cold morning he had taken a bottle of water outside with him when he went to warm up his car on the other side of the street. By the time he had started the car and gotten back to his house, the bottle had frozen. So I remembered to thank God that my blood had not yet frozen like that bottle of water.

After I filled the car and drove back onto Central Avenue, I saw a police car fall into line behind me. I immediately made a mental check of everything I was doing to make sure I was driving correctly and not going too fast. The police car stayed behind me for awhile and then turned on its lights, so I pulled over. The officer asked for my license and registration, and I handed them over. The officer took such a long time to examine them that the children began to harass me and say that they had to use the bathroom. I begged them to be patient and quiet. After twenty or twenty-five minutes the officer returned. I asked him why he had stopped me.

"This will explain," he said, and handed me a ticket.

"A ticket for what?" I said.

"You changed lanes without using your turn signal," he said.

"Sir," I said, "I have been driving in the same lane since I left the gas station and you have been behind me the whole way. I never changed lanes."

"And this is your second ticket," the officer said, handing me another one, "because you were not wearing a seat belt."

"Sir," I said. "God knows I was wearing my seat belt, and my wife and children wear seat belts, and you saw a seat belt on me when you stopped me."

"No," he said. "You put the seat belt on after you saw me behind you."

My children started saying, "No, no, no." My daughter said that I put the seat belt on in the gas station and that I made sure all of them were wearing seat belts before I drove off. Even my wife's patience was exhausted at this point and she said to the officer, "It is not true what you say."

I told them to please be quiet and I asked the officer to take the tickets back. The officer said that he saw me put the belt on when he was driving behind me. I said that the back window was frosty and there was no way he could have seen me through the window from behind. The officer just left the tickets on my lap and told me to go.

I told him, "Sir, this first ticket is for my beard. I will take it and say *Okhay* (I like it). But please tell me what the second one is for. Is wearing a moustache a crime also? Please give me another ticket if you want to."

The officer turned and went back to his car as though he was going to give me another ticket. My wife said, "Yassin! Please go!"

"No," I said. "Let him bring one more."

"Yasseeeeen!!" she said. "Just go!"

I started to drive off. The officer followed me to the next traffic light, and after that I saw him make a turn. "Thank you, Uncle Abass!" I shouted.

"Who is Uncle Abass?" the children asked, and I started telling them the story.

On another day, I was driving the AMA car while taking my lady customer back from the dialysis center in Albany to Ravena. As I was helping her down from the car and carrying her oxygen bottle and bags, she said, "Look. Your front license plate has come loose." I saw that the front license plate was hanging by just one screw. After I brought her into the house I tried to fix the plate, but I did not have another screw. So I took the plate off and put it on the dashboard of the car where it could be seen, until I could get back to the company office and reattach it.

I started driving back to Albany. After a few minutes a police car came up behind me, and after awhile he pulled me over. The officer asked for my license and registration, and once again I handed them over. "What is wrong?" I asked the officer. But he only said that he would be back, and walked to his car. I said to myself, *I already have two tickets at home. How much is he going to cost me this time?*

In about five minutes, the officer returned. Thank God, at least he was quick and did not have a ticket in his hand. He gave me back my license and registration.

"Why did you stop me?" I asked.

Suddenly he saw the plate sitting on the front dashboard. "Give me back your license and registration," he said. He took them and went back to his car. A few minutes later he came back with a ticket.

"What is this for?" I asked.

"New York State law requires that you have two license plates."

"I have two. One in back, and this one in front."

"No, it has to be on the front of the car, not on the dashboard."

"Sir, the license plate just came loose and I had no screw to fix it. I put it here until I could get back to Albany. This is a company car and they will fix it."

"Sorry," he said. "It is still illegal."

"Sir," I said, "will you at least write on the ticket that the license plate was on the dashboard and could be seen from outside through the window? It is not correct to say 'No Front Plate' on the ticket. I have a front plate, but it is in the window."

"Are you telling me how to do my job?"

"No sir. But you should write it exactly as it is. I have a front plate, and it is showing in the window."

"You can explain that to the judge when you go to court," he said.

"So why did you stop me?" I asked.

"I just told you. You don't have a front plate."

"But at first you did not give me a ticket until you saw the plate on my dashboard, and only after that did you take my license back and give me a ticket. What I am asking is why you stopped me in the first place."

"Because you have no plate," he said.

"But how did you know that before you stopped me?"

"I saw it."

"Good," I said. "You saw my front license plate from behind my car, and so I must have had a front license plate that was clearly visible to everyone, even from the back."

The officer put his hand over his mouth to hide a laugh and said, "You can go."

"Thank you," I said, "but I will tell the judge that you gave me this ticket because of my beard."

I started driving home. I had not paid for the first two tickets yet. I made barely $100 a week driving for the company, but I was paying more than that in tickets. I did not even know how many points were left on my license. I thought maybe it would be better if I stopped working. But even if I stopped working, I would still get tickets as long as I kept driving. I was really working for Uncle Abass. I felt as though I was back in Iraq, where the police just harassed people all the time and scared them.

These are just some examples of my encounters with the police. I have had countless other similar encounters. I am not telling you this to turn you against the police or to lessen your appreciation of the great job they do to keep the community safe. There is no comparison between the police here and in Iraq. I really believe that without the law, our lives would be like the jungle, and without the police the law would never work. But I just want to tell you about my experiences. I did not become a refugee just to be safe from the security forces. I wanted to live free, as humans have a right to be. It bothers me to be treated this way just because I have a beard and look like a foreigner. I believe that such things should not take place in this country.

All of these incidents with the police took place before my arrest. After my arrest, I saw different cars following me. I had been accused of being dangerous and a terrorist, but they gave me bail and I was released for about thirteen months. For at least nine months of my release, I never felt that anyone was following me, and I saw nothing suspicious. But after about nine months, I had three or four cars following me every morning when I took my children to school and when I went to pick them up. I was like the president being followed by four beautiful, expensive cars wherever I went.

Sometimes they waited for me at the school. This game continued for four or five weeks. They used to come around 6 or 7 a.m. and leave by 3 or 4 p.m. I never saw them after 4 p.m. Often, just to find out if they were still there, I would go out and drive around, but they were not to be seen after 4 p.m. After several months they disappeared and never followed me again.

Then about two weeks before the government brought more charges against me, they appeared again, this time for twenty-four hours a day. When I came out of my house, they opened the windows of their cars so I could see them. I did not know what this was all about. I asked my lawyer about it and he said he did not know. My friend said that it was all psychological and that the government just wanted to scare me, that they hoped that I would get mad and do something that would cause me to lose my bail. I said they were not scaring me so much as terrorizing my wife and children. Every morning it became a game for the children to look out of the car and tell me if the government was following us. The children knew their license plate numbers and the make of their cars.

One day I was taking the family to a restaurant in Latham for my son Raiber's birthday. Usually I took them to another place, but Raiber wanted me to take him to this new restaurant. I had to stop several times to ask for directions, but I could not find the place, and still I had two or three government cars following me. Finally I said that I was going to ask the government how to get to the restaurant and suggest that maybe they could send a car in front that I could follow, because I could not figure out where the restaurant was.

My wife said, "Please just leave them alone!"

When I said I was going to ask them, my wife stated crying, so I didn't do it. Finally we found the place and went in. The children were happy, but my wife kept crying for two hours until we finally left.

"Zuhur," I said. "Please stop crying. This is Raiber's day. Let him feel good." But she was too emotional to even speak. I ate pizza with the children, but she was too upset to even eat.

It is part of our faith to always think positively about people and to interpret their words in a good way, and over and over at dinner I reminded her of this. In reply, she said, "Do you believe that everyone has a pure heart, like an angel of God?"

"No," I said. "I don't believe that everyone is like that. But still we should try to see people this way and trust them—until we see something different from them."

"How many lives do we have?" she said. "And how many tricks must we take?"

"God brings only the good," I told her.

"That is true," she said. "But not in times of corruption like this. You remember what they say in Arabic: 'Beware of evil in the person for whom you did good.'"

"Zuhur," I said. "We can never feel good and have peace in our minds until we look at everyone in a positive way. If we believe that people are plotting against us, we will destroy our own hearts. If we take their words in the worst way, we will never see any beauty in life."

"Good," she said. "Pretend that the people following you are there to save your life rather than destroy it. Think positive!"

"Well," I said, "it is better to let them waste their time on things that do not put us in any danger. A birthday party is nothing to be secret about, and I never did anything they can get me for."

We drove home from the restaurant, the government following us all the way. Since then, my wife has tended to see everything as an attack by the government. She is scared of everything and she does not trust even me. Since they targeted us and took her out of our apartment at 2 a.m. for a five-hour interview, she has not lived normally. Her life has changed. There are always tears in her eyes. She will not respond to me if I ask her a question unless I ask her again and again. The government has really destroyed my family. I don't know how my wife can learn to trust again, or how my children can have a normal childhood, or how I will get my freedom back. But the government is certainly responsible if my wife loses her mind, or if anything happens to my children.

I did not understand why the government was following me until the day I went to court to receive additional charges, and the government asked the judge to cancel my bail. The judge said that I had been out on bail for thirteen months and that I had done absolutely nothing wrong, nor had I violated the conditions of my release. Why should my bail be revoked? But the government said that I did nothing wrong only because I knew that they were watching me all the time. In fact, they said they had followed me for only about three months out of the thirteen I was free. They usually only followed me for one shift, and left the rest of the day unsupervised. I was wearing a leg band at the time as a condition of my release, and so they knew where I was in any event.

The judge should have asked them, *Why were you following him? What did you suspect? Who did he talk with? Why did you have cars following him to his children's school and back every day? Why did you terrorize his family wherever he went, in whatever he did, in front of whomever he met? What about his private life and his rights?* But instead the judge just accepted what the government said and revoked my bail.

Freedom from Tears

In Kurdistan there is a saying, "Do not believe in women's and children's tears." I do not know from where or from whom Kurds learned this erroneous philosophy. My guess is that they think they cry for simple reasons, and that after a minute or so children will forget the cause of their tears and laugh, and that women cry because they are considered (in my culture) to be kind and soft and emotional, and people believe that tears are a woman's only weapons.

For me it is nonsense to say that we should not trust tears, and we Kurds have paid a very high price for it. I lost my mom because we never cared about her tears. And logic should tell us that children do not cry without a reason. Even babies express something with their crying, such as pain or hunger or fear, and it is very dangerous to ignore these expressions. In Kurdistan, sometimes a baby or child would cry for hours, but his mother was busy working on the farm and just let him cry. As a child, many times I was given an extra beating by my father when I cried because he said I was not tough enough. If I cried in front of a guest, he said I brought shame on the family and made the guest uncomfortable.

Living in hard conditions makes people's hearts hard. But many times people act as though they have no hearts at all. Because of what happened to my mother, I understand now that women's tears should not be ignored. Tears that are ignored will destroy the mind and heart of the one who cries, and this will destroy the family, which is the cornerstone of the community. Two of my wishes have always been to keep my children happy, and to allow my wife freedom from tears.

Living in the Middle East makes many people take their dreams with them to the grave. Like most Middle Eastern men, when I married I did not have any experience with women. And in my home while I was growing up, there were no women, other than my sick mother. We young men were not taught to be soft or to act kindly towards others, which is very important in developing a relationship with women. We were taught just the opposite: to be tough. In my culture, young men were very attracted to beautiful eyes—blue eyes were popular, as well as eyes that were deep black. But no matter how much beautiful eyes may have affected us, I used to tell my friends that I loved a red eye most, but at the same time I wished never to see it. Red eyes tell the story of a bitter life. Eyes become red from chemical weapons or crying, from dust or fatigue or insomnia, and that is the reality for Kurdish women. Red eyes are the reality. But I wanted to save my wife from that.

My brother Issa used to say that we are created to suffer, and philosophers warn that history repeats itself. By my dreams and hard work, could I keep history from repeating our suffering? Could I keep my wife from suffering as my mother had? Could escaping to America save my wife from a life of tears?

Now I see how difficult it is. Since we came to the U.S., and especially since the government targeted us over these last three years, there has not been a day when I have not seen my wife crying. Many times when she visits me in jail, she spends the entire hour crying. When I call home for fifteen minutes, the same thing happens—she only cries. She is the real victim of the government's plot and the unfair, nonsensical charges against me, and she is paying for it more than I am, or anyone else. We thought that by coming to America the time of tears would be over, and the fear would go away, and the suffering would become history, but we have seen exactly the opposite. And the hardest part of it is, we do not know why. What did we do that we should go through all of this?

Zuhur, I am really sorry. I did not bring you to America for this. I did nothing to cause you all these headaches. I never wanted to see your eyes red. I did not want you to suffer. I did not want you to be left alone to raise our children. I am really sorry, and there is not much I can do for you. I am helpless. I pray that you will be stronger and feel better. I wish to see your eyes with no tears, and I want you to understand that tears will not help us. I hope you will be patient and face the reality of this situation. Please forgive me. I want you to take care of yourself and our children. May God help and protect you and the children.

Does History Repeat Itself?

In 2004 I was arrested, locked up in jail, and falsely charged with various counts associated with terrorism. The hardest part of this ordeal was being separated from my children and realizing that if I were sent away for a lengthy jail sentence, I would never be able to be a loving father to them and guide them in a way different from my own father.

The main reason I came to America was for my children's future. I wanted them to get the best education, to have fun while growing up, and never to see what I saw in my life. Now, sitting in jail, I have the feeling that history is repeating itself despite my best attempts to change it. Already my children have lost so much. It seems as though they are going to lose their childhoods at an early age and will have to start working hard very young, the way I did.

One night when I called home from jail, my youngest son, Kotcher, who is seven years old, said, "Daddy! I worked today and I made two dollars." He was really excited.

"Where did you work?" I asked him.

"In your friend's store."

My friend sometimes took both my sons to his store to spend time there so they could run off some of their energy. That day, to stop them from running around and making the customers uncomfortable, he told them that if they fixed a shelf for him, he would pay them one dollar for each hour they worked. They each worked for two hours, and each made two dollars.

But it troubled me to hear that my sons were "working," because I strongly believe that children should not work at a young age, as I had to. They should be in school, learning and playing. I reacted by saying to Kotcher, "Good. When you come to see me next time, could you bring me some of that money? I have nothing in my commissary account."

"Oh, sorry, Daddy," he replied. "I spent all of it already."

"What did you buy with your money?"

"Candy."

I said, "No problem, dear. Don't worry. I will get some money."

"Daddy," Kotcher said, "I promise you that if your friend lets me work for him again, I will keep the money for you."

"Thank you," I said.

A few weeks later, when I called home one day to tell Kotcher that his name had been approved for a visit the next day, he said with excitement in his voice, "Daddy, one of your friends gave me five dollars and I saved it for you. Tomorrow I will bring it for you."

I thanked him, but told him there was no need now, that someone had already deposited some money to my account. Later, after the visit with my son was over, I received a receipt from the jail guards that Kotcher had put five dollars in my account anyway. I kissed the receipt and asked myself, *What were you so afraid of that you needed to take five dollars from your son's pocket money? It is you who should be giving money to him.* I raised my face to the heavens and said, "God, please, give them a better life than I had. Don't let all of this suffering repeat itself."

Starting work at the age of eight was one of the reasons I lost my childhood, but other reasons were the lack of opportunity to play and have fun and the lack of a proper education. Of course, lack of good food, health care, and proper clothing, and a general atmosphere of fear, also contributed to my lost childhood. Now I am afraid that what the government has done to me will cause my children to lose their childhoods too. I am sure that my children live in fear when they see what the government had done to me. They are afraid that I may no longer be a part of their lives, and they are probably afraid that they will not have enough food, because I was the only person in the family to earn an income.

Under these conditions, how can my children have fun in their lives? I feel especially bad for my daughter Alaa. Kotcher and my other son Raiber can run down to the mosque and play with their friends there, and some of the men from the mosque can take them to the park or to ride a bicycle, but Alaa has no one she can play with. My wife Zuhur is still under great stress and shock from what happened, and does not often feel comfortable venturing out of the house to go to the park or the museum or the library. I was the one who used to do this with the children. I used to play with them at home and give them piggyback rides and ride bicycles with them, and our lives were beautiful and happy even though we were poor. Now I am sure they have lost at least 90% of the fun in their lives, and instead will face many difficulties just to get their basic needs met.

One day I told my lawyer that just my children alone were enough to prove that I had no intention whatsoever to do anything wrong, break the law, or cause harm to anyone. My lawyer said, "How do your children prove that?" And I said, "More than 90% of the terrorists and suicide attackers have been emotional youth who had no wives or children. If I were coming to attack America, would I bring my wife and children with me to suffer after I committed my crime? Why would I do that?"

Usually I call home from jail once a day around 6 p.m. Many times when I call, especially in the winter, Kotcher and Raiber are asleep. If they are having any fun, why are they asleep at 6 p.m.? Alaa told me that they wake up at 3 or 4 a.m. because they have slept ten hours, and they have nothing to do until morning. I remember that my mom used to say, "Yassin is like a chicken. As soon as the sun sets he is asleep, and he wakes up with the first rooster cry in the morning." Chickens sleep from sunset until dawn, and I did too, because I got so tired during the day and there was nothing to do at night. But I feel bad that this pattern has to be repeated, because my sons have nothing more exciting to do after the sun goes down than sleep.

It is not fair to compare the kind of education my children are getting today with the education I received in Iraq, in Hashazini. My children attend an Islamic-run school that is one of the best schools in New York State, and I am confident that the teachers are all well qualified. They do much more than is required for all the students, and maybe they even give my children a little more attention because they know there is no one at home to help them.

I spoke to Raiber, who was really unhappy about school, many times from jail. When I asked him what the problem was, he said that he wanted help with his homework. "Sorry," I said. "I cannot help you here in jail. Can you call one of your friends to help you?" I knew he was too shy to do that. Last summer, the school gave some summer homework to the students that they had to do in the library. In two months, my children were not able to go to the library more than once, even though the library is just a ten-minute walk from my house. My wife has Dilnia, our baby who cannot be left behind, and in addition she is still uncomfortable about going out in public places. When I called my children from jail the day before school started in the fall, all of them were crying because they did not have uniforms or book bags or school supplies and because they had not done their library homework. I did not know what to say. I told them that the teachers knew our situation and that they would be OK, and tomorrow I would make sure they got everything.

Immediately I called my friend Abdulhaqq and asked him how this could have happened. I was really upset. Abdulhaqq cried harder than the children and said he would fix everything in one day—they would have all that they needed for school. I am blessed with many good friends who look after my children, including him. If I didn't have my friends, it would be a true disaster.

I came to America because I did not want my children to live as I did, but it seems that my brother Issa was right when he said that God created humans to suffer. History really does repeat itself. My grandfather, my father, myself—at different times and places, from East to West, we have all had to face the same problems. Our childhoods were no fun, no food, no education, hard work, and fear, just because we were Kurds. And now my children's childhood will be the same, just because of the crime I did not commit.

PART FOUR:
THE WALLS

Yassin Aref after his arrest in 2004.

Photo by Philip Kamrass. Courtesy of Albany *Times Union*.

Chapter Fifteen ⚡
Jail Stories

Life Without Sun

I grew up in a Kurdish village. Many times my friends and I walked at night along paths so dark that we could not see five feet in front of us. We did not know if a wolf would come to eat us, or whether a soldier would shoot at us. Sometimes we walked in rain so heavy that we could not see if we were about to fall into a hole, or hit a tree, or trip on rocks. When the rain was really heavy, we used to wait for a flash of lightning so we could see which way to go. Those nights were very scary, but none of them were as hard for me as the night of August 4, 2004 in America, when they locked me up for the first time. That was the hardest, darkest, and longest night of my life.

It began as a night like many others. Night prayers at the mosque had started at 10 p.m., and I left the mosque around 10:30 to go home and get some rest because morning prayers were at 5 a.m. My home was just one block behind the mosque, and I always walked rather than drove.

As I approached my house, a man called to me: "Yassin Aref!" I was very surprised that someone so late at night knew my name, and I walked over to him. There were several men with him. I recognized one or two of them as FBI agents.

"Do you know us?" one of them asked.

"Yes," I replied. I knew them because they had interviewed me four or five times before. Twice they had come to my home and had taken me to their office.

"We need you to come with us to answer some questions," one of them said.

"Sure," I said. "Do you want me to tell my family?"

They spoke among themselves for a minute, and then said that I did not have to.

"Do you want me to bring my car?" I asked.

"No, we will bring you back," they answered.

They put me in one of their cars. As soon as the door closed, they told me that this time they did not intend to just question me, but had orders to arrest me. They showed me a paper. They asked me to put my hands behind my back so they could handcuff me. I said, "No problem," but I was shocked. I thought they were coming after the wrong person, but I said nothing.

They took me to the FBI building. Until we got there, I talked to myself: *Orders to arrest me? Why? What did I do?* They did not tell me what was wrong or what the charge was. As soon as we arrived, they asked me to take off my long shirt, which was cut in the Arabic fashion, and they brought me a chair and told me to sit. Then they opened my hands and chained me to the chair. They chained my feet as well.

Two agents began questioning me. One of them spoke very roughly to me; he yelled and shouted and threatened me. Sometimes he stood very close to my face as though he wanted to punch me, but he never did. He kept saying, "Tell me!"

"Good," I said. "What do you want me to tell you?"

He would ask me a question and let me answer. Then he would get angry, shout, and ask me the same question again. I would answer the question again as best I could. Then he would shout, "LIAR! Tell me the truth. We have a video. I can show it to you."

"So show me the video," I said. "Prove I lied to you. After that, give me the death penalty and hang me. I will accept it. I am not allowed to lie and I have nothing to lie about."

The agent would ignore me and ask me another question. When I answered, he would call me a liar again and threaten that it would be forever until I saw my children.

This continued for awhile, and then he left and another agent came in. He had a completely different manner. He spoke softly, talked nicely, and showed respect for me. He used some Kurdish words and was very friendly. "Aref, listen," he said. "That other guy is really tough. I'm telling you that the only way to help yourself is to tell them everything. If not, you will be in big trouble. We have a lot of evidence, but we would like you to tell us first. Don't lose your family."

"Good," I said. "What do you want me to tell you? Ask me anything and I will tell you whatever I know about it."

The agent asked me the same questions that the tough agent had asked me. I gave him the same answers, which were true.

"No. Please," the agent kept saying to me, "give me the truth."

"I'm not lying," I said.

"We have a video," he said.

"Go bring it," I said. "Show me where I lied. If you find any wrong answers, hang me."

"No, no," the nice agent said. "Before my friend comes back and yells at you, tell me now. It will be better for you. You have family and children, and I want to help you."

"I told you," I said. "Ask me whatever you want."

He asked his questions again, and I answered them. But he disapproved of my answers, and said that I did not want to help myself. He left the room and the tough agent came back in and started asking me the same questions.

"Look," I said. "I have already told you the truth."

"LIAR!" the tough agent shouted.

"No!" I said. "I am not allowed to lie. It is against my faith, and I have nothing to lie about."

"Now I'll show you," the agent said.

I said, "I will be happy and thankful and I will accept any punishment if you can prove that I lied to you."

The agent ignored me and kept on yelling and shouting and scaring me with threats. He told me that I would never see my children again and that I would go to jail forever. I kept responding that this was not Iraq, that the law protected me, and that I had done nothing to be in jail for.

"You'll see!" the agent shouted.

"Yes, I will see," I responded.

"We have the evidence!"

"Good," I said. "Let us go to court and you can show your evidence there."

I cannot remember exactly, but after about two hours of scaring and threatening me he told me that I had the right to ask for a lawyer and that I didn't have to answer questions until a lawyer arrived. I told him to ask me whatever he wanted, I didn't want a lawyer because I had done nothing to worry about. Around 3 a.m. he brought two papers for me to sign, so they could search my house and the *masjid*. He asked me if there were any weapons or explosive materials there.

All this questioning continued until about 6 a.m. I was tired, frightened, and very worried about my family. I was also really mad and upset at what all this could possibly be about. They never told me why I had been arrested or what the charges against me were. I had been afraid many, many times in Iraq, but I was never as frightened as on this night. It was the first time in my life that I had ever been placed in such humiliation and seen my hands and feet in chains. The whole night I was not allowed to close my eyes for one minute, and I was exhausted and fearful and uncomfortable on the chair all at the same time. In particular, I was very concerned about what would happen to my children and how this experience would affect my wife, who was already very fearful.

Around 6 a.m., the agents announced that the interrogation was over. They even said that they could not keep me any longer because they had only a limited amount of time and they had already spent seven hours interrogating me, and I needed to be taken to court at 8 a.m. They told me that they would keep me the next two hours here at their offices, rather than take me to jail before going to court.

Then all of a sudden the whole atmosphere changed. The agents began to laugh and joke and talk nicely to me. Even the tough one began joking with me and said, "Don't be scared. You will be OK," and wished me good luck. It was more of their scare tactics. All of this friendliness was scarier than the shouting. I asked them if I could do my morning prayer, and they said sure. They freed my hands but not my feet. They let me use the bathroom to make ablution and to pray.

One of them even brought me a Qur'an. Now it looked as though I was with my friends, joking and talking—no more threats, or questions, or shouting.

At 8 a.m. they took me to court. When they brought me in, I was astonished. I could not believe my eyes. The road was blocked off by police cars, the place was full of police, and the media and TV camera crews were everywhere. I said to myself, *What is this all about? How can this be about me? Is this who I have become?* Yesterday at this time I was a simple man serving in a small mosque and driving for a medical company to help support my family. Few people had heard of me, and even fewer knew me. Now, in one night, my picture and name were everywhere—not only in Albany, but throughout the U.S. and even around the world. What could I have done that was so important? Did they know that I was just a driver with fifty cents in my pocket, a simple Imam and a poor farmer? Why was I suddenly famous? It made no sense to me.

I went in front of the judge. He denied bail for me but he did enter a plea of not guilty. Then the FBI agents put the chains back on me and drove me to the Rensselaer County Jail, with three police cars in front and three behind. All the roads were blocked and there were ten or fifteen TV cameras. It was just like one of Saddam's motorcades in Iraq.

But the drama outside was overwhelmed by the drama of the questions that were going on in my head. I could not understand how this had happened. Why did they take me to jail? Why were all the media present? I had come to America to avoid tyranny and to live freely, and I simply did not expect that such things could occur here. I was very worried about my wife and children. What would happen to them? How would they handle this situation, especially without my being there? What would my friends and other people who knew me think? How would the Muslim community react to this attack by the very government that was supposed to treat all groups equally?

They took me to jail and locked me up by myself. From the window in my cell door, I could see the TV in the hall where the jail officer was sitting. My picture was on every channel, but I could not tell why.

After two or three days, someone brought me a newspaper. My picture was on the front page—and then I understood. They were saying that I was not a religious, peaceful Imam but an extreme, dangerous commander of a terrorist group in charge of a "sleeper" cell. I had no idea how that could be so. Because it wasn't true.

With Spider

After my trial was over and the jury started its deliberations, every day at 6:30 a.m. they used to take me out of my cell at the jail and put me in a small "holding" room in the courthouse that had no windows or any decoration, and keep me there until 5 or 6 p.m.—around ten hours. It was Ramadan and I was fasting, so I told them I did not want any food. As a result, nobody came to me and I was all alone, unless the jury had a question and I had to be brought up to the courtroom. Most of the time I did not have contact with anyone, and I did not even know what time it was. It was a really hard time for me because I was worried about the jury's decision and about my family. I also had a headache from the stress and the fasting, and there was no bed to lie down on—only a metal stool that made me cold when I sat on it. So for hours I just stood and waited. It was odd to remember how, in Iraq, I often worked for long, hard hours in the hot sun and longed for just a few minutes to relax in the shade. And now that I had a whole day to do nothing but wait in a small room with no work to do, how agonizing was the inactivity and the loneliness.

One day, while I was standing in the room letting my mind run again over all my worries and questions about how this could have happened to me and where it would lead me, I saw a spider moving from one corner of the room to the other. I smiled with relief that there was some other living thing in the room besides me. I wondered how the spider had gotten into the room. Was it a criminal spider? Why else was it in jail?

To comfort myself, I walked close to it and followed it. It walked very fast, as though it was fleeing from something or rushing to do something. It did not look like it was a prisoner. It was very active. So why was it here? Maybe it was here to spy on me? I had heard about tiny cameras and recorders that are so small they are virtually invisible. Did it have one, and was it watching me?

I looked around to find its web, but I could not see anything. Probably it did not live here, but then, how did it get in? What was it going to find to eat? Where would it find water? I was confused as to whether it was spying on me undercover like the FBI, or whether it was simply an innocent creature and my only friend in this small lonely room.

I remembered that once I had destroyed a spiderweb back home in Hashazini. My mother cried and was mad at me.

"Don't you know that a spider is a holy animal?" she said. "No one is allowed to harm it."

"It is dirty," I said.

"No. It is holy," she said.

"Why, Mommy?" I asked.

"Because it saved the Prophet's life," she said.

"How, Mommy?" I asked. But she did not know the story.

Later that day my father told me the story. When the Prophet Mohammad, may peace be upon him, had to flee from Mecca to Medina, the people of Mecca, who wanted to kill him, started searching for him everywhere along the road to Medina because they knew he planned to immigrate there. To escape from these enemies, at one point the Prophet and his friend Abu Bakr had to hide themselves in a small cave. The enemies approached the cave, but a spider wove a web across the entrance and closed it. One of the enemies asked his friend, "What about this cave? He may be hidden in there." The friend replied, "What are you talking about? Don't you see the spider's web on the mouth of it? Nobody has been here for decades." So they passed on by.

Abu Bakr said, "Oh, God's messenger! Look where their feet stood. If one of them had just looked down, he would have seen us." The Prophet told him, "Don't worry. God is with us." Because of this story, many Muslims, including my parents, believe that spiders are a holy creation and should never be harmed.

This recollection of a story long ago made me ask myself, *is this spider in my room to harm me or help me?* But still I could not understand how it had come into the room and how it was able to live without any food or water. I started talking to it as though I was Solomon talking to an animal. I told the spider my name and described my situation. I told it that I was in jail because I followed the Messenger whose life the spider had once saved. I asked if the spider could do the same for me by praying for me, so that the jury would make the right decision and let me go home to my family.

I hoped the spider would respond to me, but it did not. I thought that maybe it could not understand me, and I clapped my hands close to it, but it had no reaction. I thought, *Maybe the spider cannot hear, or at least perhaps this one is deaf.* I brought my finger close to its eyes, but still it had no reaction. *Could it be that a spider also cannot see? How can that be? How can it find food?* It didn't appear to be blind—it had plenty of eyes.

At this point I touched the spider's leg with the tip of my finger. It jumped and started running fast—first right, then left, as though it was really frightened. "I'm sorry," I told the spider. "I did not mean to scare you." It continued to run fast around the room. There was no hole or crack in the room where it could hide itself, and no way to get out.

A guard opened the door and said they had to take me to the court-room.

"Do they have a verdict?" I asked.

"We don't know," the guard said. "It may be just a question."

I thought that at least I would know what time it was. On some days I thought the time must be around 9 a.m., only to find out that it was noon. On some days I prayed the noon prayer, and afterwards I found out that it was only 10 a.m. I am not like my dad, who was always right in his estimates of the time. I cannot estimate time at all. Time goes fast on some days, and on other days it is painfully slow. Today I was surprised. I thought the time must be 10 a.m., but it was 2:30 p.m. and I had missed the noon prayer.

The jury just had a question. They did not have a verdict yet. The guards brought me back to the room. I looked around for my friend the spider, but he was not there. I felt really sad. Today my time was running like I lived in a palace. I had someone to talk to and make contact with. But what happened to the spider? Where did it go, and how did it get out of the room? I could see no way. Maybe when I was out of the room the guards picked it up or swept it out. My dad told me many times to think only good things about others, and my mom told me that spiders were holy. I could not believe that my spider was not. I wished that my dad could know that I was in trouble—trouble because I tried hard to think positive thought about others, and because I believed that others had pure hearts and good intentions.

Daddy, Why Are You in Jail?

I grew up in a culture where children were not allowed to ask for anything. Many times when we broke tribal law and we asked a question, especially when we had a guest present, we were answered with a stern look or a yell to be quiet, or a slap on our cheek, or we were ignored. In reaction to this upbringing, I treated my children just the opposite and always told them not to do something unless they knew why they were doing it. Make sure you understand everything, I told them. Ask about anything you don't understand.

Because my children have grown up in the U.S., they have learned to ask questions. This is one of the many beautiful things about this country—that children are allowed to ask all the questions they want, and allowed to say how they feel about things so that they have a sense of independence. I was always very happy when my children asked me questions, and I was happier when they made fun of my answers and proved me wrong. In fact, I was helpless to answer many of their questions because they knew more than I did about many things, and my language ability in English was never enough to satisfy them. One of their middle school English teachers said that after he came to the U.S. and his children learned English, the children always made fun of him and laughed at him when he spoke English. I know what he means. I can never pronounce English words the way my children can. I told the teacher I speak Kurlish—half Kurdish and half English.

The questions that my children directed at me were a big test of my own lack of knowledge. Many times I had to admit that I did not have an answer for them, but I never gave them a wrong answer. In fact, I was proud to say, "I don't know." It is said about Imam Malik, the founder of the Maliki school of thought in Islam, that when he was asked forty important questions about Islam, he answered thirty-nine of them by saying, "I don't know." When his followers asked how it was that he did not know the answers to these questions, Imam Malik said that it is a danger and a misrepresentation to give answers that you are not sure are true. It is not a shame to not know something, but it is a shame to mislead people. As the Prophet Mohammad, may peace be upon him, said, "If you do not know something, ask—because asking questions is the cure for ignorance." Many of the Prophet's teachings came through answering his companions' questions. Many times the Prophet did not have an immediate answer to their questions, and only after the companions had left for awhile and then returned did he give a revelation concerning the question.

The most difficult questions I faced from my children were from my son Kotcher and my daughter Alaa. (My son Raiber is quieter and keeps everything in his heart; even when something is bothering him, he is not as likely as his sister and brother are to talk about it, and I have to find out what it is that he doesn't want to talk about.) Just before they canceled my bail, my wife was seven months pregnant, and Kotcher was five years old. We were talking about the baby, which we expected to be a daughter. All of a sudden Kotcher asked me, "Daddy, how will the baby come out?" Immediately I remembered that I had asked my pregnant mother the same thing when I was seven years old—but I did not want to mislead my son with her answer. So I told Kotcher that when the time came for the baby to be born, which is normally nine months and nine days, God will send her out in the normal way; but if the birth cannot happen in the normal way, then the doctors will do surgery and cut the womb open and bring the baby out. Thank God Kotcher accepted my answer and did not ask me what I meant by the "normal way."

When I was seven and asked my mother how babies were born, she told me that she would throw up and the baby would come out with the vomit. I believed that until I was at least twenty years old. There were no discussions in school about this, there were many "warning lights" about certain topics that nobody could ask about, and I never had any contact with a woman until I was twenty-four, when I married. It is really sad that people think Islam prevents such questions. Even the Prophet praised Ansar's women, because bashfulness never prevented them from asking questions about things they needed to learn, including private situations such as menstruation.

My daughter Alaa's question, however, was harder. Until now I have not answered her, and I have come to believe that I will never have an answer to her question. The first time when they arrested me and took me to jail, they allowed me to call home and tell my family where I was. My wife was so upset that she could not talk to me, and just cried. The FBI had taken her and questioned her for at least five hours. So I spoke with Alaa instead, and told her that I was in jail. And she asked, "Why?"

I have always taught my children to ask why, because that is the key to knowledge, but this time I simply did not know how to answer my daughter's question. Why was I arrested? Why was I in jail? What did I do? What crime did I commit? What law did I break? I did not believe that I had broken any law or committed any crime, or that there was any lawful reason that I should be in jail. But should I tell her some other reasons that maybe I was in jail—that I am an Imam; that I have spoken out about foreign policy mistakes; that I am a religious Muslim; that I am a stateless Kurd; that I am not an American citizen; that I wear a religious beard? I believe that these are the reasons I was put in jail. But if I told her this, I also believed that she would be confused. So I told her that I truly did not know why I was in jail. And I promised her that I would give her an answer when I knew it myself.

Since then, I have been looking to fulfill that promise to Alaa, and I have tried to find out why I am in jail. When my lawyer came to visit me for the first time, I told him to go and find out. Look at the government's evidence, I said. If you believe that any of the charges are true, and I committed a crime, come back, tell me which one it is, and I will explain it for you. If you do not believe 100% that I am innocent, don't defend me. I do not want you to make a criminal innocent. If I did something wrong, I must pay for it. If my punishment is not in this life, God will certainly charge me in the next life, but I will be happy to pay for my crimes here and now and not later. I used to tell a friend who was a lawyer, "Fear God, for money will not make a guilty criminal innocent. Let justice prevail." He used to tell me that he only defended people so they could get their rights back.

After about three weeks, the government acknowledged that they had mistranslated an entry in an address book found in northern Iraq, which they had relied on to prove my "dangerousness." In the notebook was my name and first address in Albany (which I left in January 2000, three years before the Iraq War), and the word *Kak* in front of my name. The government had first translated *Kak* as "commander," but later, when the judge ordered them to turn over the page to the defense, the government acknowledged that they had mistranslated the entry: that the word literally translates as "brother," and that it is used in a manner similar to the English word "Mister," as a sign of respect. In fact, the word *Kak* is probably the most common word in the Kurdish language, because in our culture it is important to show respect to people. Because of the government's misrepresentation to the court, I was released from jail and remained under house arrest, wearing a monitoring cuff around my ankle for the next thirteen months. I told my daughter that the government had made a mistake, and that everything would be OK.

After thirteen months, the government brought nine additional charges based on the same evidence, and even accused me of making three false statements to the government. The new charges created a "presumption of dangerousness," and so the judge had to cancel my bail even though the case was still based on the same evidence as before and I had been free for thirteen months without any incident. I went back to jail.

When I called home and spoke to my children, they again asked, "Daddy, what happened? Why did they cancel your bail? Why are you in jail?" And again I had no answer for them. I just told them that I did not know. I did nothing, and so eventually I will be released: this is what I told them.

The next time I met with my lawyer I was really mad. I told him he had to do one of two things: either give me an answer for my children and let me know why I was in jail, or if he really believed what he kept saying to me—that I was completely innocent—go back to the judge and prove that I did nothing wrong. I told him it was not right for him to say that I was innocent and yet let me sit in jail. I argued with him a couple of times about this. One day I saw a big headline in the newspaper that said, "Nothing is harder than to be in jail for a crime you never committed." I showed the article to him, but he had nothing to say about it, except that I should wait for trial.

After about five months of waiting, on Martin Luther King's birthday I wrote a letter to the judge and asked him for a bail hearing. I said that I had a dream that I was back home with my family, and that in this country the people's dreams are supposed to come true. In response, the judge wrote to my lawyer and told him to do something. My lawyer put in a bail application, but he did not attack any of the government's arguments that suggested that I was "dangerous." Instead he showed that I was the victim of illegal wiretapping, and so I should get bail. I told him I did not want this motion. I did not care about any illegal wiretapping. If I was illegally wiretapped, it would only prove that I did nothing wrong. What I wanted was for him to answer the three claims by the government that caused my bail to be cancelled: that Yassin met with terrorists in the Middle East; that Yassin had contacts with terrorists after coming to the U.S.; and that Yassin believed in the goals of the terrorists. These three claims were the basis for the government's assertion that I was dangerous. But these three claims were completely untrue, and were based on complete misrepresentations and distortions. I wanted my lawyer to prove that none of these three claims were true.

At my bail hearing, my lawyer did not mention anything to refute the misrepresentations of the government. I lost my chance for bail, and I received no answer for my children as to why I was in jail. In the courtroom I begged my lawyer that at least I should be allowed to speak for just five minutes, but he said that I could not. The law did not permit it. I am in jail for seven months, and I am not allowed to speak for even seven minutes in court to defend myself? Why?

After that, I told my lawyer: stop telling me that I am innocent and that I am like your son. How can you sleep if you believe your innocent son has been denied bail, which even murderers are allowed to get? My lawyer stopped visiting me, but he said that at trial everything would be different and the truth would come out. I said, "If you are not able to prove to the judge that I am not a dangerous person, how are you going to prove that I am innocent?" He said the trial would be different.

I waited six more months for the trial to get my answer. I looked closely at every single piece of evidence that the government produced. I did not find any answer. I did not see any evidence of a crime that I was a part of. Much of the evidence against me that the government produced—my poems and speeches and diary entries between 1994 and 1999—had nothing to do with the so-called plot. In Iraq, such unconnected writings would not have been allowed in evidence, and it is hard to understand how a country like America that believes in free speech could permit it. I asked to testify at my trial, and I was allowed to answer questions from my lawyer and from the prosecutor, but I was never asked about, and so could not explain, that I never supported JEM, supposedly a terrorist organization; that I never had any information or idea about any plot in New York City; and that I did not know and was never told about any code words that were supposedly used in the plot. My lawyer said that the government had not proved any of this, and so I did not have to refute it. He assured me that we did not have to prove that it didn't happen and that I was innocent; rather, the government had to prove that I was guilty, and they had not done this.

The jury found me guilty of ten of the charges, including three conspiracy charges associated with each of the charges, although the jury dismissed the other twenty of the thirty counts. Oh God, what can I say now to my children? Now my lawyer is telling me to wait for the appeal, and that the appeal is different. But how long will that take? In what way will an appeal be different or better? Will an appeal ever give me an answer? I really doubt that I will ever see justice.

Dear reader, please: I want you to do me one favor. Find an answer

for me to my children's question: why am I in jail? What did I do or say
that was against the law? I will be very happy and thankful to you if you
can tell me why. Please go and study all the government's evidence, and
when you find out anything that proves any of the ten charges, send
me a letter and tell me that I am guilty of the charge because of the
evidence. If I cannot make clear to you 100% that I am innocent, I will
accept my prison time and I will promise to give your answer to my children so that they will finally understand. Please do that for me. Really,
it is true—there is nothing harder than to be in jail for a crime you have
not commited. And it is especially hard when you came to this country
to live free from the oppression in Iraq, and instead you find yourself in
jail, and your wife and children are suffering for no reason.

Letters to Judge McAvoy

Dear Your Honorable Judge McAvoy,
    Peace and blessings be with you. My name is Alaa Yasin
Muhiddin. I'm the daughter of Yassin Aref. I'm writing this
letter to you to ask you for some leniency in your sentencing.
Some reasons why I miss my dad are: 1) I don't go out as
much, which I really couldn't take at first. I was used to going
to Crossgates or Wal-Mart every weekend. After my dad was
put in jail I just didn't go out as much. It was like I was a prin-
cess in a castle. 2) I miss playing with him. My dad's really
not an adult. That's his secret. He might say he's 36 but he's
12 at heart. Or, at least, he acts like that. He used to race me,
play soccer with me and yaddy-yaddy-ya. 3) I miss arguing
with him. I know it sounds pathetic but it's true. We argue
about everything—once even about if you put the water in, or
the oil first when cooking rice. When I told him I got my arguing skills from him, he denied it. He said he doesn't argue so
we argued about whether he did or not. When I pointed out
we were arguing just then he denied that too.
    "No, no, no," he said. "You see, as long as no one is con-

cealing the truth it's not called arguing."

"So what is it called?" I demanded.

"It's called discussing." When he said that I laughed in his face.

"Well, one of us has to be concealing the truth," I said. "So we are 'arguing' and not 'discussing.'"

"No, no, no, you see, as long as no one thinks they're concealing the truth it's still called discussing." Can you believe him?

4) He's my dad—duh. Why else would I miss him. He was good, and the whole neighborhood knew it too. Besides—don't you think I would know it if he was a terrorist? I mean, I've known him for 11 years.

Thank you for your time and thought.

> Sincerely,
> Alaa Muhiddin

In the name of God most
Gracious most Merciful

Dear Judge McAvoy,

My name is Azzam Muhiddin. I miss my dad Yassin Aref. He gave me everything I wanted. He was really fun. I really want him to come back. He didn't do any harm. I don't know why he's in jail but I know he didn't do anything wrong. So please bring him back.

> Sincerely,
> Azzam Muhiddin

Dear Judge McAvoy,

My name is Salah Muhiddin son of Yassin Aref. I am writing this letter asking you to please let my dad out of jail. Ever since he left the fun days of the years got boring. Without him my life is not nearly as happy. I can't even think of what will happen to me without him. Days are going by. Still waiting for the sentencing, still waiting for the charges to drop off, still waiting for him to get out of jail. They are punishing him, but ask yourself why. It is only for a crime he has never done, so why do I have to wait for him to get out of his punishment, when there is no reason for him to get punished. Your Honor I am asking you to please get him out of jail. It is very hard for me to live without him. I can't live a day not thinking about him. I want him back. So can you please just think about why he is in jail, and why everyone wants him out of jail, and why is he and I are suffering. I am suffering because my father is in jail. Without him my life is ruined. I don't know how they found him guilty all I know is he isn't guilty. I miss him, he gave me what I wanted and gave me a fun life. He is the most innocent man I ever saw. He never did a crime, he never will do a crime, and he will never even think about or plan a crime. He is innocent, and he will always be innocent. He is not guilty and he will never be guilty. I miss him. Everyone misses him. I want him home. Everyone wants him home. I know he is innocent. Everyone knows he is innocent. I know he is not guilty. Everyone knows he is not guilty. I don't know why he is in jail. I don't know if anyone knows why he is in jail. He is just a regular innocent man. He didn't harm anyone. He didn't harm anything. He didn't do any harm. If any person is innocent, it will be him. He didn't even harm a plant. He didn't even help someone harm a plant. He didn't help someone harm or harm himself. He didn't do anything that should take him to jail. I miss him. He is my father. He deserves to be home. Just think—he didn't do anything. Why is he getting punished? There is no reason. Why isn't he free? I don't know. I am asking you to please be nice on him and give him no time.

He didn't even do anything wrong. He makes my life fun. Without him my life is boring. He always wants me to have fun. He makes me have fun. How can I have fun when my dad is locked up. If I have fun, it won't be nearly as much fun as I would have with him. He never supported anything that would do harm. He is what I need in my home. I miss him. He makes everyday fun. He is fun. He is innocent. He does deserve to be out. Please take him out.

Sincerely,
Salah Muhiddin

American Jail

I don't believe that it's right for me to talk about torture because I personally never saw it, and I have not myself been tortured. Being in jail in America is the first time I have ever been in prison. To be honest, the jail in Rensselaer County is not bad. I feel safe here. No one is harming me or threatening me, or scaring me, or abusing me. I would like to be out of protective custody, but the jail itself is not bad. I have actually received more rights and consideration in jail than I expected.

One thing I promised to do in Iraq, if God ever gave me the chance—because God loves the truth—was to build an organization to defend prisoners' rights and to work against torture. I have heard a lot about Abu Ghraib and Baghram and Guantanamo, all of which made me remember things that I heard from my friends about Iraqi prisons. People can be held in jail during investigations for years until the prisoner finally gives up and tells the investigators anything they want to hear, even if he never did what they accused him of. Or sometimes the prisoner is simply tortured to death. All of these stories made me thank God that I am not in that situation, and that I am in an American jail instead of one in the Middle East.

But it really troubles me that America, which should be leading other countries to abolish torture, instead has helped to oversee and encourage other regimes to continue the practice in jails in Iraq, Afghanistan, and Cuba. This has made many other regimes in the

Middle East abuse human rights. One day I heard a radio program about what was happening between Khalilzad, the U.S. ambassador to Iraq, and Abdul Aziz al-Hakeem, one of the Iraqi leaders. When Khalilzad told al-Hakeem that they should not torture prisoners, al-Hakeem just looked at him and laughed! So I ask: who is teaching us? Iraqis say they don't need America to preach.

People only get many human rights after a long period of struggle. After World War II, for instance, abolishing torture, freedom of speech, and the Geneva Conventions had all been disregarded or broken and cost America dearly, and many fascist regimes went back to their old-fashioned ways. America cannot claim that it wants free nations and civilizations, and a moderate Middle East, by abusing human rights by means of secret evidence, secret CIA jails, torture, and bombing. It should give the world a "life example" if it wants to lead.

Yet despite all of the advantages of an American prison, in many ways I feel that I have been treated differently than other prisoners, just to make me feel uncomfortable. In fact, being a prisoner and losing your freedom and your rights is enough to make anyone feel uncomfortable. I believe that my Imam's beard has caused the authorities here to treat me differently. It is something that they should not do. They put me in protective custody—PC—and lock me up in my room for twenty-three hours a day. Usually PC is at the prisoner's request. But I never asked for it, and I have repeatedly asked—five times—to be released from PC, and they will not let me out. I have asked them if this is the judge's order, and they say no. I have asked if it is the FBI's request, and they say no. So I ask, on whose order am I being held in PC? They just say it is for my safety, but I don't want that protection and I am certain that no one is going to harm me. The other prisoners love me, and now Muslim Americans also love and respect me. I am a peaceful person. I believe in love, not fighting, and I can promise that I will never open my hand to fight with anyone, even if someone tries to fight with me. I will simply avoid problems. This is not hard to do. I used to preach it regularly in the mosque. Now I can practice it.

There are other ways in which I am treated differently. I am an

Imam but they will not let me say prayers at the main Friday prayer service. Many times they have searched me after a visit with my lawyer, which normally they would not do. For five or six months they used to search my room five times more often than other prisoners in the same program. Several times they opened letters from my lawyer, which usually they do not do. If I send letters to my children, sometimes it takes two weeks for the letters to arrive. For one year I was not allowed to visit the law library (under no law that prohibited me!)

When my daughter Dilnia was born, my friend came to the jail the same day to visit me. Unfortunately they would not let him see me. Under jail rules I am allowed only two visits a week, and they must be approved in advance as to the person and the time. My friend's visit had not been approved in advance. So he gave the guards some pictures that he had brought of my new baby girl, to show me that she was healthy and that everything was OK (thank God). The guards told my friend that they would give me the two pictures. To this day, I have never seen them.

Muslims are not allowed to show their private parts to anyone, but many times when the authorities searched my room they took all my clothes off. They usually do not do this with other prisoners. One day they took me for a classification interview and they made me wait for half an hour. Then without classifying me, they brought me back to my cell. During a break, my friends told me that while I was gone, the guards went into my room and took all of my papers.

"So what is wrong?" I said.

"By law, you are entitled to be present when your room is searched," they said.

"I am an exception to the law," I said, and they all started laughing.

My experience in jail has taught me that even here in America, with all its riches and freedom, there are too many people suffering. Many people I have seen in jail believe that with just a little help they could become very good people and serve their communities. Will jail help them reform their lives, or cause them to lose their lives? Many young people in jail are really more victims than criminals, because they never had any positive role models to help them through their teenage years. Will jail give them positive role models, or negative ones? Many African Americans especially are afflicted in their communities by drugs, no child support, lack of education, and unemployment—in other words, by poverty. Will jail help lift this burden of poverty that was placed on them at birth, or will it become a new burden they must carry around with them? Please, all you peace seekers, justice lovers, human rights supporters—bring attention to these problems and seek solutions. This United States, the greatest country, should be able to change jail into schools for saving the community.

One Year in Jail
(My first year in jail by myself in a small room)

When I was very young, I used to argue with some of my friends about the morality of putting a bird in a cage. I was strongly opposed to that. When I came to Albany, my children wanted me to buy a bird and some fish for them, but I objected. Well, I did buy three baby fish. I used to wake up in the night and look at them. They tried to tell me that they wanted a bigger tank and more friends. They seemed to be saying, "We want to be free." I told my children that this would be the last time I would make an animal captive.

Now I live as a captive myself in a small room, with nothing to do and nowhere to go. The only things that I am allowed to do are read, exercise, and pray. I have no one to speak to. Twenty-three hours out of twenty-four, I sit by myself. Sometimes two or three weeks go by without any visits or letters or anything happening. I grew up in the Middle East where social relationships are very strong and people visit each other daily. Plus, I was an Imam, and in my culture an Imam is the most social person in the community. People go to the Imam daily for all kinds of matters, and it is very rare for an Imam to be alone, even for one hour. Being deprived of contact with other humans over a long period of time is cruel, and a form of mental torture that makes life very painful and difficult.

Most of all, I am a Kurd born in Iraq, and no one loves freedom like we do because we know what it means not to have freedom. All this has made jail really hard for me to accept, especially because I have done nothing to be in jail for.

Life is an opportunity for everybody to express the meaning of their existence by their actions. Life should be more than just sitting, eating, drinking, and nothing else. Some inmates have described themselves as "half-dead"—but many people outside are completely dead. Inside prison is a different planet, yet there are so many interesting stories happening all the time. I want to share some of them with you so you can get an idea of what life is like in here. Maybe these stories will move you to do something to end such suffering.

Good and Bad Apples

Wherever you go, you find people who love truth and are ready to sacrifice for it. Any human being who has not been corrupted should, by his nature, love the truth. And because of this, many people have supported me. If not for the truth, why would people be supporting me? Who am I? What can these people get from me? I had no relationship with them before this happened, so why are they supporting me now? These people know that not only will they not get any benefit from me, but their support may cause them problems and perhaps make them suspects to the government, or cause them to appear on some governmental list. But this is the beauty of humanity—to provide meaning for our existence and to see that, as human beings, we should stand up for justice and support the truth.

Even in jail many people have shown me support in many different ways—not only the inmates, but also many jail officers. They have all told me that they do not believe the charges against me are true, and that they know what is going on. The first time I was brought to jail after I was arrested on August 4, 2004, one officer told me, "This is just propaganda by the Bush Administration. They need it for the presidential election."

One day I wanted some hot water to make tea, but I was not sure whether I should ask my unit officer or not, because he didn't look pleasant. I thought he might be angry at me. But then I thought that the worst he could say was no. So the next time he passed my cell, I said, "Officer, please…"

"What do you want?" he said.

"Can I get some hot water?" I said.

Immediately he opened my door with his key. This was unusual, because the guards usually go back to the desk and open the cell door from the computer. He said, "Listen. I know you are a good man. I wish all the other inmates were like you, so we would not have any problems here." Another day, when another officer took us out of our cells into the "backyard" for our one-hour break, he called me over and said, "It doesn't matter what they say in the news. You have been here for almost one year. There is no way for me to believe that you are the person the government claims. Be patient. God will help you."

The jail decided to keep me in protective custody, which is like solitary confinement except that I am allowed to listen to the radio. Otherwise protective custody is essentially the same as solitary confinement. Solitary is used for punishment—usually for a period of time not exceeding thirty days. I do not believe they have any reason to punish me for even a short period of time, and I certainly do not want protection from the other inmates. The only reason for keeping me in what amounts to solitary confinement so far as I can see is to impose a form of punishment on me. One day one of the officers asked me what had happened to my latest request to be released from solitary. When I told him that my request had been denied, he said that it was not just, and that I should not be in jail at all, much less in protective custody.

On another occasion, one of the officers in our unit was friendly, and when we went for a break he told me that an officer in another unit had asked him about me. "I told him you were OK," he said. "My friend said that he couldn't understand how they could call you a terrorist. He said, 'He seems to be quiet and humble, and there is just no way he could be a terrorist.'" Many other officers have spoken to me in the same way, and said that what happened to me was not fair and wished me good luck. Of course, there are a few guards that show hostility and racism and have narrow views, but these guards are like that with other inmates as well, and no one in the jail likes them. They are the bad apples that you can find on any tree or farm.

Sky's Sons

When they cancelled my bail on September 30, 2005 and sent me back to the Rensselaer County Jail, there was one other person in protective custody too, named L. Every day we had a one-hour break together. He was a very quiet and peaceful person who seemed to have no idea about this universe. He asked me once where I came from, and I said Iraq. He did not know that there was a country called Iraq. After three years of war, apparently he was not aware that Americans were fighting and dying over there.

But L. was quite an amazing person, and his life gave me a different picture of America. He was forty-seven years old. When he was five his father had left him, and he never knew anything about him. He thought his father might be in a prison in North Carolina. L.'s wife had an order of protection against him, so he could not write to her or to his three children. He was in jail for abusing his mentally retarded daughter and he was prohibited from seeing her until she was eighteen years old. His mother had died, and he had a sister, but he could not get in touch with her; he had written her many times but she had not responded, and he was not sure if he had her correct address. He told me that he had spent five years "in the box" on an earlier occasion when he was in prison, and that is why he did not mind being in protective custody now. He told me many stories about prison and prisoners that I found hard to believe could happen in America in the twenty-first century.

L. was really alone. He had no one at all. My brother Issa used to say that it seemed as though our family had fallen from the sky, and we had nobody to help us, but if Issa had seen L. he would have met someone who really had fallen from the sky. Nobody ever sent him anything. Nobody sent him money for his commissary account so he could buy coffee or tea or shampoo or batteries for the radio. Nobody sent him letters. Nobody sent him news about what was happening outside. And he never sent a letter to anyone. He never made a phone call except to the public defender's office. No wonder he did not know anything about Iraq—he spent twenty-three hours a day by himself in his room without access to any information at all. He used to give away bits of the food he received at mealtime in order to get coffee. He loved to drink coffee, and he drank as much as he could. It seemed to be his one passion.

It was hard for me to understand someone who was so completely alone. Where was his family, his brother, sister, aunts, uncles? Where were his neighbors? Where were his friends? He had been living in America for forty-seven years. Is it possible that in that time he had not made one friend who would contact him or visit him, or write him, or put some money in his account?

L. told me that in prison there are thousand of prisoners like him. Some people spend five to ten years in the box without any contact with the outside world, like radios or news or TV or newspapers or letters or commissary money. Is that a life? How can someone live without love, without someone else to have contact with just to know that he is alive? How can someone be released from such an experience in prison and return to society as a normal human being?

One day another prisoner came to me and asked, "Brother, how are you doing?"

"Good, thank you," I said. "What about yourself?"

"Fine," said the man. "Let me warn you of one thing. Be careful not to trust anyone. Don't talk to them. I am forty-five years old and I have spent twenty-five years of it in prison. I care about you and I know what goes on—so be careful."

"Careful about what?" I said.

"Just don't trust anyone," he said.

"Sorry," I told him. "We cannot feel good until we trust people and think positively about them. If you really want peace in your heart, love people and be happy when you see them."

"But not in prison," he said.

"Yes," I said. "Especially in prison. Every human lives by his heart. Just because I am in jail doesn't mean I am evil. We live together and we should be like a family."

"You are amazing," he said.

"I want you to be the same," I told him. "Do you have children?"

"I have fifteen children," he said.

"Where are they now?" I asked.

"I don't know," he said. Only two of his daughters had sent him a birthday card this year. The rest had no contact with him.

"What is going to happen to you when you get out?" I asked.

He said that he had to go back to prison for another twelve years on another charge.

"God help you!" I told him. I gave him two bags of tea and a piece of candy. He became very happy with these small gifts—happier than I used to be when I was a child and could get a piece of candy back in Hashazini.

I thought for days about those fifteen children whom he knew nothing about, nor did he know where they were. He was forty-five years old and had spent twenty-five years in jail, and still he had time to father fifteen children. By the time he finishes his twelve-year sentence he will be fifty-seven and will have spent thirty-seven years in jail. It seems almost impossible.

Kids' Unit

My unit has two parts—a big part for those who get medicine daily, and a protective custody part. There was a boy in the cell next to mine who was around twenty years old, but he was at least 250 pounds and very fat. Since he was not in protective custody, he spent most of the day in a chair front of the TV eating snacks. He did nothing. He did not even move, except to get fatter and fatter. One day someone made fun of him and they got into a fight. They sent him to the box for four weeks.

During those four weeks, I used to think about him: *Someone should tell him to sit farther back from the TV so he does not hurt his eyes. Someone should tell him to get some exercise. Someone should tell him to eat less. Someone should tell him to go for a walk during his hour break and get some fresh air.* He was still very young. Maybe he had done something wrong, but that should not mean he has to lose his life because he has abused his health so badly while he is in jail. If he stays this way in jail for five or ten years, his health will be ruined and his life will be over.

I have heard about many young people between sixteen and twenty years old in the jail, in a special unit for minors that I am not allowed to visit. All of these kids should be in school, or at least should be taught while they are in jail. I feel so sad for them. I believe that they are all victims of corruption on the street and in the jail too. Who is thinking about them and about their future? What is the best way to save the communities from which they came?

One day in the visiting room I saw a very young boy on my left side. After about twenty minutes, I heard him crying. After that he stood up and said, "Mom! No! Please don't leave! Please don't go! Mom! Mom!" But his mother got up and left him. I do not know what happened. What made his mom so mad that she left him? I don't really want to know, but I am troubled about how a mother could do that. Did she not hear something in the way he said, "Please don't go!" that suggested there was more to be said? Couldn't she see that her son was very young and had a lot of growing still to do, and needed guidance from someone older like her? Did she not understand that her son would go back to his cell with a broken heart, and that he would be alone in that cell, and that he might even harm himself? Did she not realize how hard it would be for her to establish contact with her son after that, and that maybe she would never be able to make contact with him again? Did she not see his tears? Did she not understand how hard it was on her son when he was rejected in front of everybody?

Who will be the loser if her son becomes worse? Who can help her son change his behavior? Who will show her son some love? I should have stood up and asked her to please not leave her son, but I was sure the rules did not allow me to do that, and I was not the right person to intercede. But then, who is? Even now I cannot forget what happened, and still deep in my heart I say over and over to his mother, *Please don't leave him.* I felt so sad for that young man that I told him to be patient and she would come back. I wished him the best as they took him back to his cell, and then I started crying. How many youth like him are suffering?

Who or what has caused this to happen? How can this behavior be corrected and prevented? He is just a teenager, and he can still be saved.

Prisoners' Dignity

Living with nature is the most beautiful thing in life: different seasons, different weather, different places. Sometimes you are cold, sometimes hot; you see the birds, the trees, the water, the rocks. But jail prevents you from seeing and feeling all of that. You have no contact with the outside world except through a tiny window in the cell door. If it were not for that window and the small radio that I am allowed to have, I would not know if it was day or night, cold or hot.

Prisoners have just one hour to go to the tiny "backyard," which is what the jail recreation yard is called. Because that is the only time we can see the outside world, we seldom care what the weather is, as long as we can get out in it.

One day last winter when I was scheduled to go out for my hour in the backyard, I saw it was snowing, and my radio said it was five degrees below zero. Three of us were supposed to go outside at the same time. I asked the other two what they wanted to do. They said they would ask to stay in the recreation hall in front of the TV. Usually the guards will let prisoners stay inside during heavy rain or extreme weather, but this depends on the guard. Some guards also let us get hot water for tea or coffee, or make a phone call, and some do not. So we asked the officer if we could stay inside.

"NO!" he yelled at us. "You go outside, or you go back to your cells. This is not an inside break."

One of the other prisoners asked me if I wanted to go outside. I said, "This is the only hour outside that we have. Even if it were raining rocks instead of snow, I would want to go out and get some fresh air." So the other two agreed to come out, and we told the officer that we were ready to go.

"Then let's go, let's go, hurry up," he shouted at us. He opened the door—and it was as though someone had thrown needles on our face. We had not realized from our small windows how windy it was, and how it was driving the snow. We started to walk around in circles, as we usually did.

One of the prisoners was not wearing sneakers and had on only his jail slippers, which were like socks and did not protect his feet from water or the cold. The man said that his feet were freezing, and he stopped walking. The other prisoner and I were still walking in a circle.

Suddenly I heard the first man say, "Oh shit!"

I looked behind me and saw him looking at his pants. He had wet himself. I forced myself not to look, and pretended not to see anything so as not to embarrass him. I knew that he was a diabetic and a coffee drinker, and I was not surprised that in the severely cold weather he was not able to control his bladder. I told him that if he wanted to go back to his room he could ask the guard to let him in, and we would come back inside also, since it was not much fun being outside today.

But he said, "If I freeze here and die, I will not ask this guard to let me back in."

"Why?" I asked.

"He is not worthy to be asked," the man said. "Not every human being is worthy to be asked for favors."

"You can try," I suggested.

"No," he said. "I am not going to honor such a guy with a request for a favor."

"I don't think you are going to honor him," I said.

"Yes," he said. "There is nothing more honorable than to serve human beings and help them when they need you. If I ask him, and he says no, which I believe he will, it would be a humiliation for me. And if he says yes, it will be an honor for him to serve us and give us a favor. So I will take the cold and accept death rather than honor him or be humiliated by him."

I was shocked. I had no words to say to him. From my deepest heart I wanted to hug him and kiss him like a child, but I knew I could not do such a thing in this place or in this culture. I told him, "You are a great man. May God bless you and make you free so you can have your dignity restored."

"I can be patient," he said.

We still had a half an hour more outside, and so we started walking in circles again. It was really punishment, and not a break. We were each shaking like a tree in the wind, and we were wet through and through. Time did not fly by like other days, but still we had a glow inside because we had challenged the weather and the guard, and we had all agreed to keep our dignity.

Shako Mako

One day I was lying on my bed reading a book, which I usually do since there is nothing else to do. Sometimes I go deep into my book and forget the time, and even where I am. I vaguely heard the unit officer making his hourly check of the cells. I was so absorbed in my book that I had not paid attention to how many checks he had made, but this time as he passed I heard someone say, "*Shako Mako*" (Iraqi Arabic for "Hey, what's new?")

I jumped from my bed and ran to the window in my cell door to find out who had said that. I only saw the unit officer, and when he saw me looking out the window, he grinned. But I couldn't believe he had said it. How would he know Arabic? And how would he know how to pronounce Arabic with an Iraqi accent? I started talking to myself. *Maybe there was a new inmate who knew Arabic, and he walked past my door…but how would he know that I am Iraqi?*

I could not figure out who had greeted me, so I went back to my bed and began reading again. But "*Shako Mako*" kept running through my mind. The answer to this casual greeting—"What's new?"—is usually "Nothing," and so I answered *Nothing* a number of times in my mind. In jail, the answer is really true. Nothing is new: the same room, the same program, the same bed, the same sink, the same blanket, the same light, the same food. Nothing new goes on at all. When inmates explain what jail is like, they say, "Different day, same everything else." And after awhile, we can say, "Different year, same everything else." But my mind kept ringing with those words.

For the last fifteen years I had not heard "*Shako Mako*" spoken to me. It reminded me of my army friend, Raid, who taught me the phrase when I was ten years old, and he was the first person to whom I ever said it in return. *Shako Mako*: on my bed I was holding my book and pretending to read it, but I really did not comprehend any of the words on the page because I was back in Iraq, talking to Raid.

Then suddenly I heard it again, right outside my door: "*Shako Mako.*" I ran to my door window and I saw the same unit officer. Now I knew that it must be him, but how did he know these words?

When noon came and he brought my lunch, I asked him. He said that he had been in Iraq in the military for a year and had learned a few Arabic words. A few days later, he took us out for our one-hour break in the backyard, and I asked him about Iraq and what he had seen. He said he did not want to talk about it, but that it was terrible.

I said, "It is a different planet, no?"

And he said, "Exactly." He was deeply troubled about the way people were forced to live, especially the children. He said it really bothered him, and it was hard for him to forget what he had seen. "It has even affected my life now," he said. "It has made me a different person. I have trouble controlling myself. I get mad very easily, often for no reason."

And I said, "You were just there for one year. What about the people who live there?"

After that, I saw him many times, and he occasionally said two or three Arabic words to me with an Iraqi accent. One day when I went to get some hot water for tea, he said, "*O-guf! Tera armeek.*" I stood up immediately, and he laughed and came over to me. "What does that mean?" he asked.

"Repeat it," I said.

"*O-guf! Tera armeek,*" he said, and after he repeated it a few more times I understood.

"It means, 'Stop! Don't move or I will shoot,'" I said.

He seemed pleased that I had figured out exactly what he wanted to say.

"How many people did you shoot there?" I asked him.

He refused to tell me. I took my hot water and went back to my cell, but I really felt sad. I thought, *How many innocent Iraqis may have been shot because they could not understand what he was saying?* I myself had not understood him until he had repeated it two or three times, and if I had been in Iraq it could have cost me my life. I thanked God that I was not in Iraq, and that I had not met the guard with a loaded gun in his hands.

I Wish I Was Your Mom

If you have mercy upon those living on earth, the one in heaven will have mercy upon you. This is what Mohammad, peace be upon him, told his followers when he said that kindness will make anything more beautiful, and the absence of kindness will make everything ugly. In their busy lives today, people are searching for kindness and mercy because they live so much alone. They did not grow up in a family where people showed love and respect to each other in a kind way. Loneliness causes stress for many people, especially when they are forced to suffer alone without anyone to support them or show them compassion.

I have seen many people in jail who are really unhappy. They do not see the beauty of life. If it were not for their faith that God loves them, and the medicine they take for depression, I think many people would lose their minds and try to end their lives. It has been really sad to see this in America. In the East people think that the West is paradise, and Western people do not know the stresses and suffering of the East because they have material goods and no wars or embargos or torture or hunger. So why should people in the West be sad? They have beautiful houses, nice cars, good food, electricity, mail, telephones, computers, the Internet, satellite TV, and so much more. But I never would have believed that people in the West did not live in families, or were forced to face their problems by themselves, or that so many would be victims of self-inflicted diseases like drug and alcohol addiction.

Nothing is more beautiful than helping people when they are really needy, have problems, or are in trouble. Prisoners are really needy, but many of them do not get help. Some have no one to visit them, or write to them, or send something to them, and it is not easy to get any love in jail. Some guards make a prisoner feel really bad when he asks them for something; sometimes they just glare. Often prisoners hear only profanity from them, like "Shut your fucking mouth," which never helps anyone.

In Kurdistan we used to say, "Jail is a school," not because there were any educational programs for prisoners but because in jail prisoners learned patience and the real meaning of love. I believe that a jail should be like a school, where prisoners are actually taught a better way to live based on kindness and mercy and where they can change their behavior. There are many programs in American jails that prisoners can take advantage of to improve themselves. This was not true in Iraq. There the jails were also torture centers. They were dirty, there was no electricity, prisoners did not get enough food, and maybe once a month they could take a shower. In Iraq, 95% of the prisoners were in jail because of politics and their beliefs. They were seldom there because they had committed real crimes; they were there because they opposed the government's policies, loved their country too much, and worked too hard to achieve freedom.

In America it is different. 95% of the prisoners in America have actually committed crimes and broken the law. But which one of us is sinless? Who among us has never done anything wrong? Maybe people who walk on the street have broken the law more often than those in prison, but no one saw them do it. I have seen many people in jail who I believe are really great people—kind and full of compassion for others. They really want to live different lives, and if they could gain their freedom they would become self-sufficient and a help to the community. But the system does not show them any mercy.

In my culture we say that besides God, nobody shows mercy like mothers. A mother is the source of love and mercy; her heart is deep, like the ocean. For myself, I saw how my mom's love helped me forget many hardships and made me see the beautiful side of life. I lost my mom too soon, and I never received the same amount of love from anyone else. Many people talk about love. They claim that they love all human beings, and they believe that they must love even their enemies. But how many of them really practice their beliefs and show this love in daily life?

In the Rensselaer County Jail there is an officer named J. who I believe has nothing in her heart but love. Never in my life have I seen someone like this officer, who can love even her enemies. Whenever she comes into the jail, prisoners crowd around her asking different things, and she shows her pleasure in serving them. She talks to everyone; she listens to everyone; she smiles at everyone; she makes everyone happy; she gives hope to everyone. The day she comes to the PC unit is a day of celebration. I have found that J. performs her duties better than many of the other officers, and she follows the law in everything she does. But the only difference is that she does her duties with a smile. If you ask a guard for permission to get some hot water, some of them will not even answer you, but J. will always say "Absolutely," with a big smile. Nothing affects people like smiling, and nothing makes them feel good like a kind word. J. provides this for everyone, one at a time. Maybe a guard is kind to you, but not to other prisoners. Or maybe a guard smiles at you from time to time, but not always. But J. is kind to everyone all the time. When she sees a prisoner who is sad, she always talks with him. Many times she told me to be patient—"God will bless you," she would say. She feels sorry for me and prays for me. She is like a mother for all the inmates, God's mercy in the jail to give prisoners hope and the belief that they are still human beings who are worthy of love.

Before my sentencing, one day J. came to our unit and told me that she had read something about my life—part of this book—and that she was really affected by it. She said that no child should live like that. She told me how sorry she was for me, and she said, "I wish I had been your mom." I told her she really was. Since I lost my mom in 1986, I have not encountered anyone like J. who showed me such mercy. I did not ask her why she wanted to be my mom, but I believe it is either that she wished she could have protected me when I faced all of this difficulty, or she was proud of who I am. I have no doubt that she gives hope to all of the inmates in the same way and makes every one of them feel better. But maybe she does not know how much I wish to have a mom like her, or how I hope she is my mom. God knows I respect her as I would respect my own mom.

I Never Thought It Would Be Like This

After sixteen months in jail, and after I lost my trial and was convicted, I was interviewed for the first time by a journalist, Carl Strock. I had spoken to him when I was under house arrest, and I had no doubt that he was a fair man and a man of courage. I knew that he had written a couple of articles about my case, and I had often seen him at the trial. He had seen all of the evidence and had written that the jury's decision was a mistake. Some people had criticized him for being on the side of the defense, but I believe he was just doing his job professionally and was defending his country's Constitution and the freedoms and justice that it protects.

In his interview, Mr. Strock asked me about my life in jail. He asked me what I did in my cell all day and how I spent my time. I gave him the same answer that I wrote to my children about how I spend my time. I have four major things and four minor things that I do every day. The four major things are reading and writing, praying, sleeping, and listening to the news on a small radio. The four minor things are singing, exercise, eating, and crying. Mr. Strock was surprised when I mentioned singing, and repeated it two times to make sure I really meant it. I proved to him I could sing. After that, I thought to myself that maybe I had gone too far and it would be on the news tomorrow—"The Singing Imam"!

It may surprise some Muslims to hear that an Imam can sing, especially in jail. Singing in Kurdish culture is just a way to express your happiness, and you would not expect someone who is sad to sing. But for me it is different. Just as my mother used to sing at night by my grandfather's grave, grieving over the death of her two children, I express my grievances by singing rather than by tears. Kurds have many tragic songs, which are our way of expressing grief, and I know some religious chants for the same purpose. Maybe most people sing when they are happy, but certainly I sing when I am sad, following my father's theory that singing is the best way to defeat Satan the devil.

One of Mr. Strock's questions to me was about food. I told him what my dad used to say all the time, that anything softer than a stone he would eat as long as it helped keep him alive. I told him I only wanted to be my father's son. I never complain about the food here, and I never will. I come from a third world country, and poor families there are not concerned about the quality of the food they eat as long as they are not starving.

After three or four days, Mr. Strock published the interview and wrote that I said I would eat anything softer than a stone.

One day, as I was going to get my breakfast, someone called to me: "Aref, Aref!" I turned and saw it was R., the man in cell next to me. He said, "Anything softer than a stone I will eat, as long as it keeps me alive."

"Where did you get that from?" I asked him.

"I read it in the article," he said.

He told me that before he read the article, he would not eat breakfast because he did not like cereal, but the article made him think about why he ate food and what it meant to be alive. The article changed his life! He realized that he needed food to be alive. The food itself was not as important as the life. In Kurdistan, we say that we eat to live; we are not living to eat.

Another young boy named E. used to come with us during our one-hour break in the "backyard." I knew he was confused about me. He saw me as a different person than the character he had seen on the news. Although I did not usually talk about myself with other people, I opened myself up to him, and E. became my friend.

One day I gave him two chapters of my life story that I had been writing for this book and told him that I hoped it would help him to know something about his new friend. I did not believe he would read it, or that, if he did read it, he would get any benefit from it. But the same day, he surprised me by sending me a letter. He said that he was very sorry I had gone through so much trouble in my life. He said that he cared about me and was supporting me 100%; my story really touched his heart and he cried when he read about the people fleeing into the mountains to escape the Iraqi army, and about a woman so terrified that she threw her baby off a cliff. He said he would pray for me and wanted to be my brother. I saved his letter.

E. wrote all of this after reading only two chapters of my book. Really, his response made me care for him and to change my mind about him. He is not a lost boy, but a smart and kind human being. I felt sorry for him and for many other youth like him who pay for the corruption that has damaged their lives and our society. E. told me that his father had left him when E. was a year old, and that when he was five the police had taken him and his sister from their mother, and he never saw his mother again. He grew up in shelters, and he is now nineteen years old. Who was supposed to teach this youth or show him love, or protect him, or pay for his college education? He is a smart young man. He is kind and has a great deal of mercy in his heart. He cried when he read the story of the woman who threw her baby over a cliff. These are all signs of goodness. But how can a nineteen-year-old depend only on himself for everything? How can he survive with no family? How can he tell the difference between a good friend and a bad one? Who can help him control his strong teenage desires? How can he learn to feel good about himself when he is constantly told in jail, "Shut your fucking mouth! Go to the fucking lockup!"

When he has finished his sentence after two months, where will E. go? With whom will he live? He has no contact with his mother or his father or his family. He does not have a house or a job. His girlfriend is twelve years older than he is. She already has a husband, and has had an order of protection against E. for eight years. But still she wants to keep him around when he gets out. She has written to him that she loves him, but when she gets mad at him in the future she will call the police to arrest him again, because according to the order of protection he cannot be with her. And so for E., when he gets out of jail, his girlfriend's house will be the only place that he can go, and she will be the only person that he can live with, and he will not have any peace in his life.

E., I am sorry—it is not all your fault. You are really a victim of the corruption and sickness that eats at this society. You should have a dad you can count on. You should have a mom you can live with. You should have a family of brothers, sisters, aunts, uncles, grandmothers, grandfathers, nieces, and nephews who can help support you; you should have a chance to go to college; you should have someone to remind you, and advise you, and direct you, and help you, and love you, and protect you. You are too young to be alone. There are many wolves outside in the night. It is not easy to stand on your feet without help. Life is expensive here, and the system is not built for everyone.

I am sorry that I am helpless. I cannot do anything for you from my jail cell, but I really worry about you and about the thousands of youth like you. Please listen to me. Leave your girlfriend alone. She is somebody else's wife who is much older than you and has an order of protection against you. She put you in jail before, and she can put you in jail again if you do not change. This world is wider than anything you can see now. Don't make it so narrow that you miss the beauty and possibilities that are waiting. You are too young and you are too worthy to have your life smothered out. Leave alcohol alone, and avoid drugs if you are using them. I will promise to do whatever I can from here to find someplace for you to live, and a job, and some direction in life, and I want you in college. Good luck, my brother. Please, will somebody out there hear us!

Note: E. attached a statement in his own handwriting, which reads as follows:

I met Aref in January of 2007 while going to recon M-1, PC [recreation in the M-1 section of the Protective Custody Unit]. He was the only person that I trusted to talk to. He was very kind hearted and wise. He gave me lots of good advice that would help me get through my time here in RCJ [Rensselaer County Jail]. We wrote many letters to each other every day to help each other feel better. We became real good friends; I consider him my brother and he does the same. We would exchange pictures of our kids. I opened myself up to him and let him know everything that bothered me and he made me feel better about myself and my problems. I have learned one major thing about the people on this earth. "I can't judge a book by its cover," meaning that it does not matter what culture you come from—some people are good and some are bad and I can't judge them by their appearance. I pray to the lord that he will guide Aref out of this jail soon so he can be with his family where he belongs. I will remember and keep Aref close to my heart forever. Thank you Aref for everything.

E. also attached a statement about his family background and about his hopes for the future.

Why Are You Happy All the Time?

One day an inmate said to me, "Can I ask you something? Why are you so happy all the time? What is your secret?"

"Who told you I am happy?" I said.

"Whenever I see you," he said, "you are smiling. Your face is always happy."

"Well, let's see," I said. "I am in jail for no reason. I have four children and I have no way to take care of them. My wife is under terrible stress. I face 400 years in jail. I'm locked up in a room for twenty-three hours a day. I can't get any news from my family in Iraq, and I have no way to contact them, and I don't know which of them are still alive, and the government continues to claim I am a dangerous person and attacks my personality."

"But all of that should make you sad, not happy."

"So what can gloominess and crying do to help my situation?"

"Nothing."

"Then why should I do something that brings no benefit?"

"But how can you laugh?" the inmate said. "What is your secret for smiling?"

"I believe in God," I said. "That is all the secret there is. I smile to people to make them feel good and happy, and I complain and send all my grievances to my Lord."

"I wish I could be like you," he said.

"You can do much better," I told him. "Try smiling."

"Thank you," he said with a half-smile.

"No, not like that," I said. "A big smile—with your teeth—like this."

We both started laughing.

"Now you look excellent," I told him.

Now, whenever he sees me, he shows me his teeth. It always makes me laugh, and then he laughs back at me.

Chapter Sixteen ⊰≫⊱
Beyond the Walls

The Eve of Eid ul-Adha, December 30, 2006
New Year's Eve

My dear friends—justice lovers, peace seekers, and truth tellers—you are all in my heart.

Another year has passed into history, and for some it was full of enjoyment, while for others it was very difficult, and for still others it was a mix. When you try to remember how it went by, it seems like a dream. We look forward to the coming year but soon it will be over too. This is the nature of life. The earth is spinning fast through the sky, bringing night and day in cycles. Every year, every day, every minute, every second that passes takes a part of us away. Time is spending us, and it will never bring us back.

How many more years will we have? What will they be like? What do they carry for us? It is hard to know except that everything will eventually change with time. The poor will get rich, the sick will get well, the child will grow, the weak will obtain power, and the opposite is also true. As individuals, each of us will get older and we can expect to get weak or sick. We will not get our youth back. Last year we saw many people lose their power. Some of them died, some declared bankruptcy, some went to jail. A Kurdish poet once said, "Life will not raise anyone too high except to put him down harder." This is the reality, but humans still have a tendency to become proud and arrogant when they get a little power.

The new year should remind us that we are travelers going toward our end, and every day we get one step closer to it. None of us knows how long our journey will be, but we have to continue walking step by step because if we stop, time will not stop for us. Now last year is over. Many people lost what they valued most. There is no way for them to get it back. The only way to regain what we lost in our lives is to not waste a minute of what remains. If we do each day and each hour what we should do—what we need to do—we will take advantage of every minute and we will be successful. If we don't, no excuse is going to help us. The one who loses time is the loser.

God created us for some reason. He gave us minds to think, hearts to feel, eyes to see, hearing to listen, a tongue to speak, and made us the best of his creations on earth. We have the duty and responsibility to build this universe. God sent messengers with a catalogue for how to do it—and he warned us that if we don't follow the directions, we are going to pay for it. It is our planet that we will be destroying. To save our planet we not only must act responsibly ourselves, but we must stop others from destroying it. Most African countries contribute only a small percentage of the world's pollution, but global warming will cost them more than the countries that created the pollution problem in the first place. A majority of people in the Middle East do not support their governments and leaders and reject their policies—but they are the real victims for it.

We need to look at all people as though they were our family. As the Prophet Mohammad (peace be upon him) said, people in this life can be compared with travelers on a ship, in which some of the travelers have taken their places in the upper parts, and some on the bottom. When those on the bottom need water, they will say to the people on the top, do you mind if we make a hole down here so we can get some water to drink? If the people on the top don't stop them from acting foolishly, the ship will fill up with water and all will drown. Those on top need to draw water and pass it down to the people on the bottom so that all may be refreshed and saved.

We must take responsibility as human beings to feel for those who are suffering, and to work for justice and peace in order to build our universe.

We should feel compassion for anyone who dies from AIDS or HIV in Africa and work to see that medicine is made available in order to build our universe.

We should feel concern for those who lost their houses and are refugees because of wars or earthquakes or floods, and we should work to see that relief is provided in order to build our universe.

We should help children who don't have a chance to study and educate themselves, and we should work to improve their future in order to build our universe.

All of this is exactly what Moses and Jesus and Mohammad were teaching about. If we do not care about this, and we do nothing about it, we must ask ourselves, Who are we? Why do we live? What does it mean to be a human being?

We all live on one planet. Corruption anywhere will affect other parts of the world as well. Global warming and bird flu are just waiting to wake us up! Waiting for other people to provide leadership is useless. Each of us must say, "I will start. I will set an example. Let me remind people—let me warn them—so that if they will not do their duty, at least I did mine. I will do it for myself, my children, my country, and my planet."

We all know that it is more fun to give than to receive. So we must be happy when we work for the benefit of others. We must be ready to sacrifice our time, be willing to stand for peace and justice, and have the courage to speak out. I believe that all of you are doing this. That is why I am really so thankful for all of you. I am thankful not because you are defending me and supporting my family, but because you are standing for justice and defending your nation's values. You are standing for a better future and a peaceful planet.

I am just one person—not better than any of the 600,000 innocent Iraqis like me who have died for no reason. If the government puts me in jail or gives me the death penalty, and that makes them proud and happy for destroying my family and making my wife and children suffer—let them do it. But still I would ask: Why? What did I do? What is my crime? Where is the justice? Where are our rights?

Thank you very much for your support.

Thank you very much for your time.

Thank you very much for your feeling.

GOD BLESS YOU ALL.

From the bottom of my heart I wish every single one of you, and all peace-seeking, justice-loving, and truth-supporting people, happy Holy Days and happy new year. I wish you all long, healthy, and joyful lives. Glory to God in the heavens and peace for all people on earth.

For Martin Luther King Day Commemoration
Saratoga Springs, New York, January 15, 2007
Read by May Saffar

Martin Luther King

History is full of kings
Who sought power,
And all that power brings—
Palaces, food, women,
Drinking and pleasure.
I do not love these kings,
And put my faith only
In the King of heaven,
While on earth, humans need
A leader to serve—not enslave.

Martin Luther King was different.
He was a real king—a leader who
Served, and taught, and gave, and never
Took favors from others,
Or sought power for himself.

He was a victim of racism,
But still he kept faith
In his vision that all people
Are equal as brothers
Having the same father.

He had a dream to one day
See them all gathered together

Living free with dignity
Supporting one another
As equals under the law
Now and forever!
I love now two kings:
The great King in heaven
And my brother Martin Luther,
Who struggled on earth to bring
God's justice and peace to all.

The day before sentencing — March 7, 2007

My Dear Friends, Justice Lovers, Peace Seekers, and Truth Tellers,

You cannot know how grateful I am for what you have done and for what you are doing—not just because you are supporting me, but because you are also serving your country and defending its values. You want to prevent those in power from taking America back to the Dark Ages and to stop them from demolishing what has been built through decades of struggle. The freedom that we have in America is the fruit of the efforts of people like you and the sacrifices of people like Martin Luther King. I was very proud of all of you, and prayed for you when I heard what you had done.

In the last five months you challenged severe weather, cold, and snow to participate in vigils in front of the courthouse asking for justice and freedom for me and for Hossain and refusing to accept what has been done to us and to our families. Your signs, letters, and articles were perfect tools and weapons for defending the Constitution from being violated or destroyed. Your support for me and my family helped us believe that we came to the right place after all, and gave us a lot of hope that we will eventually get our rights back. It is still possible that justice and truth will be served.

Thank you very much to each and every single one of you. You are true soldiers fighting for freedom, justice, equal rights, a peaceful life, and human dignity—the very values for which millions of people like me immigrated from third world countries to have, and which are the honor of America. I grew up in Iraq under a dictator's rule as a second-

482 ⊰⊱ Son of Mountains: The Walls

class citizen, and I saw the situation in the Middle East. I understand what happens to life in such countries when the government takes over the judicial system and controls the courtroom, especially when narrow minds and biased men are rulers. I hope everyone understands this and works hard to keep the courts in America independent and decisions based on the best of the evidence and nothing more. If not, I will not be the last victim. My case will just be the beginning of the disaster to come, which could end the rule of law and turn the justice system into a tool for corrupt leaders to enforce their policies.

You may think that Yassin is just being emotional. Perhaps you think that I have not been in this country long enough to make such conclusions, and that I am over-reacting. I cannot say that such a disaster to our judicial system will certainly occur, but I see that the process has started. I hope that you can stop the process before it is too late. It is my life experience that when people let wrong things happen, even a few times, it often becomes too late to control.

If, in Iraq, we had stopped Saddam when he executed Barzani's family in 1982, Saddam would not have been able to gas Halabja in March 1988; if we had stopped Saddam when he destroyed Halabja, he would not have been able to launch the Anfal genocide in July and August of 1988 that killed 180,000 Kurds; if we had stopped Saddam when he launched the Anfal genocide, he would not have been able to occupy Kuwait. And so on. But instead, many people praised him or were too scared to say no to him, until we reached the point where we had lost everything, the country was destroyed, and millions of people had been killed.

Since 9/11, the American government has brought disaster after disaster upon the people in the name of defending them, and whoever opposes the government is accused of not being patriotic or entitled to citizenship. The administration claimed that Iraq had weapons of mass destruction and was supporting terrorism. They fabricated maps, pictures, and stories that they showed to the world through the UN. Look what happened as a result. More than 3,000 Americans have died; over 700,000 Iraqis have been killed; billions of dollars have been wasted; and no benefit has been achieved.

In America since 9/11, more than 20,000 Muslims have been deported or left the country. Hundreds of Muslims are in jail on trumped-up charges for which they were wrongly convicted; billions of dollars have been wasted; the Constitution has been violated and damaged; and as a result the whole world has lost faith in America. People who want to live in a real democracy with freedom, justice, human rights, and dignity have been attacked and made to feel unsafe in their own country. I am not crying for myself. I went through many difficulties in my life and I saw many tragedies. Jail is not the worst for me, but I am worried about you, and I know that if nothing is done and things continue in the same direction, this nation will lose its place among others.

The prosecutors and the government may be proud for jailing innocent people like me and for destroying my family. They know well that I never did or said anything against this country, and I have no idea about any plot to harm America. What do they achieve by putting me in jail? I believe it is the government that is the loser. The government broke the law and violated the Constitution; the government made thousands of citizens lose faith in its judgment and honesty; the government wasted millions of dollars for no reason. They concealed the truth, killed justice, destroyed the peace, and divided the community just to frame an innocent person like me. Putting me in jail will not help them win the war in Afghanistan; it will not make them successful in Iraq; it will not make America safer in any way; it will not improve relations with other countries; it will not bring down gas prices; it will not prevent global warming; it will not take drugs off the streets of America; it will not end child abuse; it will not prevent crime; it will not improve the educational system. Putting me in jail will only affect my wife and children and cause them to suffer for no reason. The only thing that the government will get out of putting me in jail is a short propaganda statement that it can give to the media, telling the people that they are busy finding terrorists and that the war on terror is still going on. The government knows that I had nothing to do with terrorists, and I believe that two-thirds of Americans now know that they are liars.

My dear friends—I would like to remind you about a few things, which I believe it is my duty to say from the deepest part of my heart and from the love and respect and concern that I hold for you and for all the people in this country. As God is my witness, I assure you and all of the American people that I did nothing against them, and I had no will or intention to harm them in any way. I came to this country only for my children's future.

I believe that I was convicted for being a Muslim. That is the only thing the evidence showed, and I am proud to admit it. It does not matter if they give me the death penalty, I am not going to call for revenge or teach my children or the Muslim community to hate this country. It is against my faith to hate people for their color or language or nationality. The prophet Mohammad never took revenge for himself. I will never give up my hope because I believe in God, and I did nothing wrong and I know thousands like you are asking for justice. I still believe in the justice system of this country, and I do not want the government to corrupt it.

I want you all to continue your support and to never give up. It is not for me or my family, but for this country, America, and its people. The freedom and equal rights in this country and in Western countries are the fruit of the struggling and sacrifice of many people like you. If it were not for the horrors of the World Wars, the Geneva Conventions would not have been written; if it were not for the sacrifices of the civil rights movement, Dr. King's vision of equality for all would still be just a dream. As long as life continues on this earth, there will be struggle. Be happy and proud that we can be part of it, and that we can work to achieve something good for everyone.

After spending the last eighteen months in jail I now realize that it is not just me, but many people, who are suffering. Many youth are victims of drug and alcohol abuse that is destroying America from the inside. Sexual relationships between men and women need to improve and provide for more stability and sensitivity. If not, the children will be the victims and the family will be lost. We need to rebuild families in this country. Many children do not know their parents; many couples are separated.

I have many things I would like to say, but soon by God's will I will be able to publish my book and it will all be in there. I hope to help construct something beautiful—not a castle, but a strong nation. Please forgive me, I have taken too much of your time. I love you all and I will never forget your help. Keep the faith. Stay firm. Be strong. Keep working. Have patience. And never give up. God bless you all, and God bless this country.

The Muhiddin (Aref) children,
Thanksgiving Day, 2007. At top: Alaa;
from left: Raiber (Salah), Dilnia, Azzam (Kotcher).

Photo by Huma Ahmad.

EPILOGUE

On March 8, 2007, Yassin was sentenced to fifteen years in prison. Because of the outpouring of community support for him and for his co-defendant, Mohammed Hossain, Judge Thomas McAvoy reduced the sentences for both men from the recommended thirty years. With time served and good behavior, Yassin will probably serve eleven years.

In May 2007, Yassin was sent to the Communication Management Unit (CMU) at the federal prison in Terre Haute, Indiana. This special medium-security unit, created in December 2006 by the U.S. Department of Justice to isolate Muslim prisoners with terrorism-related convictions, severely restricts all communication with the outside world. Prisoners are limited to one fifteen-minute, English-only phone call per week, which the warden has the power to reduce to three minutes a month. All incoming and outgoing letters must be written in English and are read and copied by prison authorities, often with a substantial delivery delay. The communication privileges of anyone on the outside can be terminated by the prison at any time without notice. Except for legal visits, all other visits, including from family members, must be approved well in advance, and to date have been disapproved for anyone who has not had "a relationship with the prisoner prior to this incarceration." All visits are limited to two hours, twice a month, are non-contact, and must be conducted via in-house telephone; a Plexiglas window separates visitor from prisoner at all times. Since his arrival at the CMU, Yassin has had one legal visit (from one of his appeal lawyers, Kathy Manley) and one visit from his two sons, who were accompanied by Steve Downs.

Yassin's appeal will be heard by the 2nd Circuit Court of Appeals in New York City in March 2008.

You can write to him at this address:

Yassin M. Aref

12778-052

Federal Correctional Institution

P.O. Box 33

Terre Haute, Indiana 47808

Visit Yassin's website at

http://www.yassinaref.com

for updates on his case

and to read his new writing from prison.

Visit the Muslim Solidarity Committee website at

http://nepajac.org/Aref&Hossain.htm

to learn about continuing support activities on behalf of Yassin,

his co-defendant Mohammed Hossain, and their families.

After production expenses, all proceeds from the sale of this book will go directly to the Aref Children's Fund to benefit Yassin's children. For more information about the fund, to send additional donations, and to contact the editors, please write to:

Aref Children's Fund

c/o Law Office of Stephen Downs

26 Dinmore Road

Selkirk, New York 12158

PROFILE OF A FRAME-UP
by Stephen Downs

Yassin appeared in chains, squinting and dazed as though he had suddenly been exposed to light from a dark place. I put my arms around him and held him tight for a few seconds, aware that he could not hug me back as he usually did because his wrists were chained to a belt around his waist. The guard helped him sit in a chair across the table from me. He looked abused.

"Are you all right?" I asked him.

"They don't beat me," he mumbled. He tried to say something else, but didn't seem to know where to begin. Finally he said, "How did you find me? I could not write or even make a call."

"They listed you on the prison computer directory as being here at Ray Brook," I said. "You're only allowed a visit from your lawyer, so I couldn't bring the family."

It was April 11, 2007, and I had not seen Yassin Aref for almost three weeks, one of the longest periods during the year that I hadn't seen him. On March 8, he had been sentenced to fifteen years in prison from his conviction in October 2006 on terrorist-related charges: support for a foreign terrorist organization, conspiracy with a weapon of mass destruction, money laundering, lying to the government. In early April, the Federal Bureau of Prisons had started him toward his destination, Terre Haute, Indiana—but with a "stopover" at Ray Brook, near Lake Placid, New York. We didn't know that the bureau would subsequently "stop" him for a week here and two weeks there in three more federal prisons in Massachusetts, Brooklyn, and Oklahoma City, or that his trip to Terre Haute would take over a month and a half.

"I am in the box, in solitary," Yassin said. "I have no radio, nothing to read, and nobody to talk to. I cannot call anyone or write to anyone. They let me out of my cell for exercise one hour a day, but the exercise yard is smaller than my cell, three steps across. The only exercise I get there is shivering. I asked a guard how I could get some things that the other prisoners had, like soap. He told me to fill out a request form—addressed to S.H.I.T. He said he would roll it up into a ball, shove it up my ass, and wait to see what kind of a response I got." He trembled. "Why would he say something like that to me? I told him he should fear God. He said I better get used to it because it would be worse in Terre Haute."

Yassin looked at me and began to tear up. "I can hold out for six to eight months of this," he said. "But I do not know how much longer than that. Please file the appeal as soon as possible."

In April 2006, I became part of Yassin's defense team. Being a lawyer recently retired from a New York State job, I volunteered to help Terry Kindlon, Yassin's court-appointed lawyer. In the cinder-block conference room at the Rensselaer County Jail in Troy, Yassin and I discussed the charges against him that grew out of a "sting," in which a government informant, pretending to be an arms merchant, had tried to involve him in a plot to assassinate the Pakistani ambassador with a missile. Yassin emphatically denied that he knew anything about a plot. He challenged me to find anything he had ever said, in the hours of secretly tape-recorded conversations with the informant, that showed he was told of or knew anything about a plot, or that he had ever said anything supportive of terrorism. But he had a more immediate problem: he wanted a new bail hearing, since his most recent application on March 24, 2006 for release on bail would probably not be granted. "It was just tricky by the government," he said in his still-evolving English, "and my lawyer did nothing to show their tricky." Clearly he was upset with both the result and his legal team, and he didn't hesitate to tell me so. I agreed to help him draft a new bail application.

Yassin was very worried about his wife, Zuhur, and his four children, who ranged in age from 1 to 12; the youngest had been born while Yassin was in jail. Zuhur had no source of income except charity from the mosque, and she had never worked at a job in America. Although the family seemed to have no resources, attempts to provide them with money or supplies met with Zuhur's resigned response, "All is fine. We have everything we need." The children were very smart, active, and Americanized; the affection that they gave so readily to regular visitors like me made the destruction of the family doubly painful, and kept me working on what could be done to get Yassin out of jail. Yassin wanted to file the bail application in part to give Zuhur some hope that he might be released. Even if this were unlikely, hope was all he had to give her right then.

Because of his deprived childhood, Yassin wanted his children to have everything that he'd missed: fun and play, education and security. "That is why I came to America," he said. But he was haunted now by the possibility that they would grow up under the same fear and deprivation he had suffered, and that history would repeat itself: "For myself, I don't care that they put me in prison. In Iraq they would call this prison a hotel, and people would fight to get in where you had three regular meals and a safe place to sleep. But it is for my wife and children that I am afraid. They are the ones who are suffering, not me. What did they do to deserve this? Why should they suffer?"

Yassin told me that after he became the imam at Masjid as-Salam, he would play tag or hide-and-seek in the mosque with the children. Some people were shocked to see a grown man cavorting like that in a house of prayer—with a group of children, no less—and would demand to see the imam about this outrage. Yassin would then introduce himself as the imam and explain that Allah loved children to play and have fun—and what better place to play than in a mosque? His eyes sparkled with the memory. "You see," he said, "I am a radical Muslim imam—just not the kind of radical Muslim the government thinks I am."

Yassin was especially upset that the government would claim he was a terrorist. He had repeatedly told Malik the informant, in conversations secretly recorded by him, that he was not interested in terrorism. "I always denied it," Yassin would say in exasperation. "Here, look at the January 14, 2004 conversation. I told Malik that when we came to America we promised to obey the law—and a Muslim always obeys his promise. I told him that my duty in America is to build the community, to teach and marry couples and counsel people with their problems, and I had no interest in anything else. I told him that bombing buildings in America will not give any benefit. I told him that suicide was forbidden in Islam. I told him that if he wanted to help liberate Kashmir he should send his money to the women and children who were hiding in the mountains without food or shelter, and that way he did not have to help the terrorists. I told him that I have no plans for *jihad*, I am not in that situation. Where did I say anything that supported terrorism? You have to write about all this in the bail application." I did, and after each draft he wanted even more material and arguments added, until the application approached the size of a small book.

The passage of the Patriot Act right after 9/11 signaled that the Bush Administration was preparing to fight a tough, if possibly unconstitutional, war against terrorism. New paradigms were introduced to law enforcement. Vice President Cheney urged the government to use the "One-Percent Test," whereby if only a 1% chance existed that a situation might result in a terrorist attack, the government must respond to prevent it. Department of Justice and FBI officials indicated that their post-9/11 strategy required them to prosecute suspicious individuals *before* a crime was committed—a kind of "preventive conviction" designed to remove anyone who, in their view, presented even a 1% chance of being sympathetic to terrorism. Now, six years later, what has emerged is just how unconstitutional the "war on terror" has become, and what devastation it has wrought on innocent people with no connection to terrorism.

On August 6, 2004, Washington journalist Mark Helm's article in the Albany *Times Union*, "Goal Is To Break Up Conspiracies Early," described this new strategy with comic delicacy:

> Prior to the September 11 terrorist attacks, federal agents in counterterrorism cases were more at ease following evidence trails until arrests were *appropriate*. But in the wake of the attacks, with multiple inquiries focusing on law enforcement failure to figure out that a major strike was brewing, authorities are placing renewed emphasis on breaking up terrorist conspiracies before they *ripen*. (Italics added.)

When we were still operating under the Constitution, arresting someone before the evidence indicated that a crime had been committed would have been both *inappropriate* (to put it mildly) and illegal. But now authorities were arresting people before they had evidence that a crime had *ripened*. The euphemisms disguise what amount to the practices of a police state.

There have been hundreds of such arrests and convictions all across the country. Many cases, like those of Hamid and Umer Hayat in Lodi, California, Sami Al-Arian in Florida, and Maher Arar of Canada, generated widespread publicity and criticism of the government. Other cases simply passed by with little media attention. Many of these started with overblown press conferences, in which the government proclaimed that it had broken up "terrorist cells" and described in lurid detail the plots that the cell members intended to inflict on the U.S., only to quietly acknowledge later that the defendants were not real terrorists. They had merely been lured into participating with a government informant by money or friendship—or in some cases, the defendants had not actually participated at all. The violent plots, the criminal intent, were found only within the *government agents'* minds, not the defendants'.

The government first claimed that Yassin was a dangerous terrorist "commander" based on a mistranslation of notebooks found in Iraq.

After admitting that its translation was wrong, the FBI then seized Yassin's 1999 diary, as well as some old poems and speeches from the time he was living in Syria, and concocted a fantasy of misrepresentations to create the illusion that he was "dangerous" and part of a terrorist plot against America. The government essentially claimed that in 1999, Yassin had been sent to America by an Islamic organization, the IMK (Islamic Movement of Kurdistan), as "our representative" to start a "center abroad" for Mullah Krekar, one of the leaders of IMK who was now a notorious terrorist leader intent on carrying out a "plan in America." The government's position was summed up at the bail hearing by prosecutor William Pericak, who said of the 1999 diary, "It's cryptic notes. But we get the idea what they're talking about. [A] Mullah Krekar Center abroad and 'our representative' coming a couple of months later to the United States here."

In fact, the opposite was true. In 1998, Congress passed the Iraq Liberation Act, which made the overthrow of Saddam Hussein's government in Iraq official U.S. policy. The act provided that various organizations—including IMK—would be allies of the U.S. in this effort, and would also be eligible to receive American aid. Neither IMK nor Mullah Krekar were considered by the U.S. to be associated with terrorists at that time. It was not until 2003, long after both Yassin and Mullah Krekar had left IMK, that the government decided to classify a new organization with which Mullah Krekar was associated, Ansar al-Islam, as a terrorist organization; Yassin had no contact at all with Ansar al-Islam or with Mullah Krekar after he left IMK in 1999 and came to the U.S. The term "plan in America," scattered throughout Yassin's diary, was also mistranslated by the government from the correct term "America's Plan," which the diary made clear was the U.S. plan to topple Saddam Hussein from power. In 1999, the IMK had been working to support this plan, and Yassin as a minor employee in IMK had been helping in the effort. The "Mullah Krekar Center abroad" referred to in the diary actually involved a debate within IMK as to whether to open a *European* office of IMK, not an American office. In the diary, Yassin clearly opposed the Krekar Center abroad because he did not trust Mullah Krekar. As for the letter from IMK designating Yassin as "our representative," it bore the letterhead not of IMK but of another harmless and unrelated organization, and in his diary Yassin clearly indicated that when he learned about the letter in 1999, he told the organization involved that he did not want to be their representative.

In short, the basis upon which the government claimed that Yassin was "dangerous" was either wholly false or a gross distortion of the truth, and it had to know that what it was telling the Court was untrue. I began to understand why Yassin was so upset. Our motion to reconsider the order of bail was filed on June 6, 2006, and the Court eventually denied it. But significantly, the government's response to the motion did not contest most of what we claimed were outright lies and misrepresentations. I began to realize that the government was just throwing mud at Yassin and hoping some of it would stick. They were just making it up.

Under the Bush administration, the Justice Department had become highly politicized. An extraordinary amount of money had been channeled to the FBI and the Justice Department to hunt down and remove terrorists from our national domestic life, and yet compelling independent evidence showed that there were few, if any, actual terrorists in the U.S. after 9/11. The "Terrorist Trial Report Card," published by The Center on Law and Security at New York University School of Law (http://www.lawandsecurity.org/publications/TTRCComplete.pdf), reports on the terrorism cases brought by the Department of Justice in the U.S. between September 11, 2001 and September 11, 2006, and concludes: "The overall record revealed in these charts suggests the presence of few, if any, prevalent terrorist threats currently within the U.S."

Given these circumstances, how did Justice Department officials prove their loyalty to an administration that demanded terrorists when there were no real terrorists to prosecute? The answer was to simply create some: manufacture plots and try to draw innocent Muslims into participating. From the government's point of view, this exercise in fear not only justified a bloated counterterrorism budget

496 Son of Mountains

and satisfied a political agenda; it also worked. Even if the defendants were not real terrorists, their convictions were success stories because these prosecutions reminded Muslims in the U.S. that the government was always watching, always infiltrating, always ready to strike at anyone it chose.

It was also becoming increasingly apparent that satisfying a political agenda was a primary criterion for U.S. Attorneys to retain their jobs. Karl Rove and the Bush White House seemed to have wanted these attorneys to undertake vigorous prosecutions against voter fraud in the run-up to the 2006 elections, notwithstanding clear evidence that there was little, if any, voter fraud in the country. Targeting Democratic candidates with voter fraud charges served a political purpose, and the prosecutions by themselves were believed to hold down the votes of minority voters, who were more likely to vote Democratic. By 2007, the ploy was overt: U.S. Attorneys who were not perceived to be loyal Bush supporters and who did not follow this political imperative were threatened with replacement, fired, or forced out.

In the same way, it seems clear that the Bush Administration viewed prosecuting terrorists as having important political payoffs. Proving that terrorists were living in American communities reassured the body politic that the Republicans were indeed defending the country. U.S. Attorneys who did not bring such prosecutions were perceived as politically disloyal and were in danger of being replaced; those who could not find any real terrorists to prosecute were under pressure to "create" them. John McKay, a former U.S. Attorney in Washington State who was one of those replaced by the Bush Administration, reported that Glenn Suddaby, the U.S. Attorney for the Northern District of New York, was on the list to be fired but somehow escaped the political pressure. Suddaby was responsible for two major "terrorist" prosecutions in upstate New York: the Aref/Hossain case, and the case of a Syracuse oncologist, Dr. Rafil Dhafir, and four other co-defendants. These prosecutions apparently were considered top priority in Washington, and it may well be that they saved Glenn Suddaby's job.

While I was working on Yassin's bail application, something strange began happening. Starting in the fall of 2004, the government had begun to secretly show material to the presiding judge—secretly, because the government claimed the material was classified—without the defense being allowed to know what the material was or why it was being shown to the judge. The defense would receive copies of letters or briefs from the prosecutor to the judge related to Yassin's case, but all of the substantive information had been deleted on grounds of national security.

In December 2005, the *New York Times* revealed that the National Security Agency (NSA) was conducting warrantless searches and eavesdropping in apparent violation of the Constitution. NSA officials were subsequently quoted as claiming that the NSA program helped catch some terrorists, specifically including an imam in Albany, New York. In "Spy Agency Data After Sept. 11 Led FBI to Dead Ends" in the *New York Times* on January 17, 2006, reporters Lowell Bergman, Eric Lichtblau, Scott Shane, and Don van Natta Jr. wrote that "[s]ome of the officials said the eavesdropping program might have helped uncover people with ties to Al Qaeda in Albany; Portland, Ore.; and Minneapolis." The article later stated that "different officials agree that the NSA's domestic operations played a role in the arrest of an imam and another man in Albany in August 2004 as part of an FBI counterterrorism sting investigation. The men, Yassin Aref, 35, and Mohammed Hossain, 49, are awaiting trial on charges that they attempted to engineer the sale of missile launchers to an FBI undercover informant."

A color picture of Yassin in chains accompanied the article.

The defense seized on this statement and demanded to be shown what information had resulted in Yassin being "uncovered." Eventually the judge issued a decision but immediately "classified" it—meaning that the defense could not see it, even though the defense lawyers had obtained security clearances. An appellate court ruled that it would not decide the legality of classifying a judicial decision until after the trial was over. None of the secret information was ever given to the defense for the trial, nor has it been seen to date by anyone (including the jury) other than the government and the trial judge.

After filing the bail application, I began a search for character witnesses to present at trial. I met many people who spoke about Yassin's charisma and how he had been a positive influence in their lives. One African-American man who had met Yassin after being released from prison said, "He told me that as a Muslim I had made promises, and that a Muslim always keeps his promises. I had promised to obey the law, and now I had to do it. I had to tell the truth. I had to be faithful to my wife and take care of my children. I had to pray. I couldn't just say I would. I had promised to do these things, and so I had to do them. That is what it meant to be a Muslim—to give yourself over completely to God. It saved my life." Everyone I spoke to told me that both Yassin and his co-defendant Hossain were peaceful people who were not involved in any way in terrorism.

People also told me stories about Yassin's comic generosity and his naiveté regarding financial matters. He seemed incapable of saying no to people looking for help. People learned that all they had to do was tell him a story about a tragedy and he would immediately give them all the money in his pocket. As a result, he was perennially short of money. Their descriptions reminded me of Yassin's stories about his grandfather and uncle in their small village in Kurdistan— two beloved imams who were so simple and humble that they would rush out of their houses to share their suppers with a poor person wandering in the street.

I began work on the criminal charges themselves. Malik, the government's informant/actor, was a Pakistani who had recently been convicted of felony fraud in connection with 80–100 separate criminal acts. He took bribes to give the correct answers to foreign applicants during the written test for motor vehicle learners' permits, under the guise that he was translating the tests for the applicants. He also worked with corrupt Motor Vehicles employees to provide drivers' licenses with false identification information and photographs to foreign applicants. He was scheduled to serve a long prison sentence and then be deported to Pakistan, where he was said to be facing a murder charge. But the government offered to make all of his legal troubles go away, and to allow him to remain free in the U.S., if he could bring about Yassin's conviction by involving him in a fictitious terrorist plot. So in 2003, Malik began to follow a carefully crafted script that would provide Yassin with just enough information to secure a conviction, but not enough to alert him that something illegal might be happening. The FBI set Malik up with all the trappings of a rich importer, including a store and merchandise. Then he began sniffing around Yassin's mosque to find a co-conspirator. (Under federal law, a government informant cannot engage in a conspiracy with the target, so another individual was needed as the co-conspirator.) After several false starts, Malik settled on a man named Mohammed Mosharref Hossain.

Hossain was originally from Bangladesh. He and his wife, Fatima, had been naturalized American citizens for nearly twenty years; they had six young children. Hossain ran a small pizza shop in Albany, and at the time he badly needed money to fix up some rental properties he had just purchased. Malik spent a long time winning Hossain's confidence by small talk and displays of concern for the family and by bragging about the wealth he'd made through his import business. Then he offered to loan money to Hossain. Malik claimed that Hossain was such a dear friend that he would allow Hossain to keep $5,000 of the loan for himself. (Malik described this as his *jihad*, or struggle, to help a fellow Muslim with a gift of money.) Malik would loan Hossain $50,000 and Hossain would pay back $45,000 in installments of $2,000 every month.

Malik then began a long series of conversations in which he explained to Hossain that he obtained the money for the loans by selling "ammunition" to a listed terrorist group, JEM. The ammunition included missiles. On November 20, 2003, Malik even pulled out a SAM missile that he had in his store (supplied, of course, by the FBI) and showed Hossain how it worked. JEM was supposedly trying to liberate Kashmir, a predominantly Muslim state, from India.

Hossain had no awareness of JEM; according to the secretly recorded tapes of his conversations with Malik, Hossain initially thought that JEM was a musical group. And even the government conceded that Hossain was not a terrorist sympathizer and was only used as a way to get to Yassin. Nor did freeing Kashmir from India have any obvious connection to the U.S. or threaten any U.S. interests. One can understand how Hossain might believe that it was none of his concern how Malik made his money in a struggle between Pakistan and India over Kashmir. But if Malik wanted to give him $5,000 as a gift, why should he refuse, especially if it would save his business?

Eventually, on February 3, 2004, long after the loans had started, Malik suggested to Hossain that his group might try to assassinate the Pakistani ambassador during a visit to New York City, providing a possible connection to the U.S. But so strong is the power of rationalization that Hossain, who was by now full of gratitude to his wealthy benefactor, apparently did not see the trap and was still ready to accept Malik's money. Certainly Hossain never intended to be involved in an assassination of the Pakistani ambassador—he just wanted a loan to fix up his properties. It was a classic (and illegal) entrapment, in which the only party with any criminal intent was the government.

Under Islamic law, loan transactions had to be witnessed and recorded in much the same way that a notary is used, and both parties decided to use Yassin as their witness, since this was a traditional role performed by an imam. Once Yassin was selected to be the witness, Malik was supposed to give information to Yassin that the money for the loan was made from an illegal source (the sale of a missile), that it was part of a terrorist plot to assassinate the Pakistani ambassador in New York City with the missile, and that the loan was intended to launder the proceeds of the illegal missile sale so it could not be traced by the government (money laundering). Theoretically, that is how Yassin, the target of the sting, should have been informed, so he could make a choice about whether to participate or not. But Malik did not do this. He simply failed to give Yassin information from which Yassin could have deduced that there was any illegality or any plot.

The government claimed that simply witnessing the loan transactions (which Yassin, as an imam, was willing to do for free as a service to his community), coupled with knowledge of the plot, was a criminal act, as long as Yassin did it with the intent to conceal the illegal source of the money in order to protect Malik so that Malik could make additional illegal arms sales in the future. The crucial question was whether Yassin ever received enough information to understand the illegality of an otherwise innocent act (witnessing a loan). If he was given enough information, the operation was a sting (stings are legal). But if he was not given enough information, it was not a sting: it was a frame-up.

On four occasions, Malik inserted vague, confusing statements during his secretly recorded conversations with Yassin that suggested he was involved with missiles or that there was going to be a missile attack in New York City. But with one notable exception, Yassin never reacted to any of these statements to indicate that he had either heard them or understood what Malik was talking about. For example, on January 2, 2004, while Yassin was witnessing one of the loan transactions, Malik handed Yassin a wad of paper money to count. While Yassin was looking down and counting the money, Malik leaned over to Hossain, held up a handle-device that looked like a mechanism for putting price labels on products in supermarkets, and said, "This is the part of the missile [mizz-aile] I showed you." The government acknowledged that Malik always mispronounced the word "missile" as "mizz-aile." In his opening statement to the jury, prosecutor William Pericak said, "...the cooperating witness will take out the trigger mechanism for the surface to air missile...and he'll say this is part of the missile (mi-syl) I showed you—and the court reporter may not be able to get down my change of pronunciation—but that's how the cooperating witness pronounced missile. This is part of the missile (mi-syl).... "

On the videotape it is clear that Yassin never looked up or reacted to Malik's statement in any way—and even if he had looked up, he would not have recognized the handle-device as anything related to a missile. Moreover, the mispronounced noun, even if heard, would not have conveyed any information about a plot. The government

argued that on January 2, Yassin was shown the missile (handle), but
it was obvious that Yassin had not seen it and had not understood its
significance, nor would anyone else who'd happened to be there. The
jury acquitted Yassin of the counts of the indictment related to the
January 2, 2004 conversation.

On January 14, 2004, Malik began telling Yassin about JEM and
Azar Mohammed's attempts to liberate Kashmir from India. In the
middle of this description, Malik stated:

> He is in Pakistan right now, and he's trying to liberate Kashmir
> from India. And, uh, he's been fighting the Holy War for
> almost now, so many years and we're, we are trying to help
> in that war. And this President Musharref, the President of
> Pakistan is, uh, is against him and, uh, against the Holy War
> because he's helping the Mushriq [idolators], uh, and uh, we
> are fighting him too. Uh, that's why, the missile, that we sent
> it to New York City to teach Mu, uh, President Musharref,
> the lesson not to fight with us. And I don't know how, how
> I do look at it in Allah's way. What do you think about that I
> mean, I want to make my mind clear with God.

Yassin responded, "Right brother, especial, I'm not talking about
that group and that organization." He went on to say repeatedly that
he did not know anything about JEM except that he had heard about
it on television.

The government argued that on January 14, Yassin was told that
a missile ("mizz-aile") had been sent to New York City to attack the
Pakistani government, but clearly Yassin made no comment or reaction
to indicate that he understood anything about the missile plot; instead,
he focused on his lack of knowledge of JEM. At trial, Yassin testified
that he did not know what the word "mizz-aile" meant, and had not
heard it used. The notion that a person could hear and understand that
a missile attack was being planned for New York City and not react
in any way to it is almost impossible to imagine—and yet the position of the government was that Yassin heard and understood Malik's
comment about a missile being sent to New York, and had no reaction

to it. (In any event, there was no connection between this comment and the loan transaction, which was a required element of the crime). Significantly, the jury found Yassin not guilty of the counts related to the January 14, 2004 conversation.

The third conversation occurred on February 12, 2004, when Malik and Hossain came to Yassin's house so Yassin could witness another repayment transaction. That night Yassin had a guest for dinner from Michigan, Kassim Shaar, who was not known to either Malik or Hossain. (For all Malik knew, Shaar might have been an FBI agent.) While they were sitting at Yassin's table discussing the loan, Malik abruptly blurted out something to the effect that it would be advisable to stay out of New York City next week because there would be an attack. It was not clear exactly what Malik said, because the tape recorder he was supposed to have been wearing "accidentally" fell out of his pants, and he allegedly failed to notice that it was gone. But whatever he said, it got Yassin's attention.

Yassin testified at trial that he told Malik to leave his house, and that he was 100% certain on February 12 that Malik was joking and was not serious about an attack in New York City next week, because nobody involved in such an operation would blurt out such information in the middle of a conversation with people that he did not know. Yassin also testified that he warned Malik on March 2, 2004 not to make such jokes, because they could be misinterpreted. Obviously, according to Yassin, Malik was not a real terrorist, but jokes like that were dangerous and would get people in trouble.

The government argued that in the tape-recorded March 2 conversation, Yassin had entered the conspiracy by warning Malik not to speak openly about the plot. But why would Yassin warn Malik not to compromise a missile plot when Yassin knew nothing about the plot? Malik's "attack" comment on February 12 conveyed no information about what was intended, or why, or by whom, or whether Malik was even involved. Moreover, Yassin told Malik that he believed that the FBI had bugged his house. If that were true, obviously the FBI would know from Malik's careless comment that a missile attack was coming in New York next week and would arrest everyone involved. Why would Yassin want to be part of a plot that had already been compromised? Indeed, what would have been Yassin's motive to enter into a missile plot at all?

Entering such a plot would not be undertaken lightly. Is it conceivable that someone working hard to provide for his wife and children in a new country, who had never before been involved in terrorism or plots or criminal activity, would suddenly one day hear a vague reference to a missile attack and casually decide to become part of it, without ever asking a single question about the plot, its chances of success, or the consequences—especially after he knew that the plot, if it existed, had already been compromised? In later conversations, Yassin never referred to the plot, or questioned what had happened to the missile attack, or said anything else to indicate that he understood anything about it. Surely if he had wanted to join a terrorist plot on February 12, 2006, he would have mentioned it to Malik at later meetings. The jury acquitted Yassin of the counts associated with the February 12 and March 2 conversations.

It was the government's apparent position that whereas most people would be unlikely to enter into such an ill-conceived plot, a Muslim would, because fanatical Muslims will jump at any chance, no matter how vague, impractical, or suicidal, to destroy this country— a racist assumption directed against a new victim population. If evidence this weak can be used to frame an innocent man based on the assumption that members of his "race" are all terrorists at heart, the whole U.S. Muslim community is in danger.

Finally, there was the fourth conversation on June 10, 2004 in which the word "missile" was mentioned—*but only in code.* On February 3, 2004 in a private conversation, Malik told Hossain that his people (JEM) had a code word for "missile"—and that word was "chaudry." Yassin was not present during this conversation, and the government basically conceded that Yassin was never told that "chaudry" referred to a "missile." (FBI agent Tim Coll testified: "Q: Again, my question is, Malik did not ever tell Mr. Aref that Chaudry was a code word for missile, correct? A: On tape, right....Correct.")

On June 10, during a conversation about the loans, Malik referred to his business of selling "chaudries," and of sending a "chaudry" to New York, but since Yassin did not know what "chaudry" meant the statements conveyed no information about the plot. Later in that conversation, Malik said that he might have to hide himself from the FBI. Yassin reacted with surprise, and said that for his part the FBI was welcome to investigate him because he (Yassin) was not doing anything except "eating, drinking and talking," and as a result he did not "have a problem." Obviously Yassin did not believe that he was doing anything illegal that the FBI would be interested in. Although no other significant information was exchanged on June 10, the jury convicted Yassin of all the counts and charges associated with that conversation, and it was only that conversation which gave rise to his terrorism-related convictions. Perhaps the jury had forgotten that he did not know the code word "chaudry."

The indictment also alleged that Yassin had engaged in money laundering—using the loan transactions and repayments to disguise the money from the illegal sale of the missile. At their first meeting on December 10, 2003, Malik explained the terms of the loans to Yassin and asked whether he believed the terms were legal according to Allah's laws, even though the loans might violate American laws. Yassin responded that he did not believe the loans violated American laws. At that point, if it had been a real sting, Malik would have clearly explained to Yassin that the loans violated American laws because the source of the money came from the illegal sales of missiles. Instead, Malik said something so misleading that it strongly suggests a deliberate frame-up. When Yassin said, "I don't believe it is against the law," Malik responded, "Because I don't pay taxes." In other conversations, Malik suggested that the loan transactions would provide documentation to help him pay his taxes and thus "legalize" his money. Malik never said anything about using the loan to hide the proceeds of the sale of a missile. The jury found Yassin not guilty for the money laundering counts arising from these discussions, although it found him guilty of money laundering for the counts surrounding the June 10, 2004 meeting, where Malik discussed the code word "chaudry," which Yassin did not know.

The government tried to explain away the lack of motive for Yassin to enter the "plot" by recycling its discredited arguments, based on Yassin's 1999 diary and other Syrian writings, and by suggesting that he was a radical Muslim who had come to America as "our representative" for the establishment of a "Mullah Krekar Center abroad." Yassin's poems, diaries, and writings were so old and out of context that they were obviously irrelevant to the sting charges and should have been excluded from evidence. But the government had cleverly foreseen this problem by including two extra charges that related to Yassin's life in Syria: one charge that he had failed to disclose his membership in IMK when he came to the U.S., and one charge that he had lied to the FBI when he said he did not know Mullah Krekar personally. Even though both charges carried only minor penalties compared with the others, they allowed the government to introduce large amounts of prejudicial evidence about the IMK and Mullah Krekar in the event that the judge limited its right to do so in connection with the character issue. The defense made a motion to strike the poems and other material as irrelevant and prejudicial, but the judge did not limit the government to any significant degree.

The trial began on September 12, 2006. Yassin was brought into court in chains in the middle of an absurd display of security that included posting snipers in buildings around the courthouse. (Whom were they planning to shoot?) The government desperately wanted the public to believe that it had captured a real terrorist. The trial followed the government's script, complete with an FBI agent parading a missile around the courtroom to intimidate the jury into believing that the defendants had posed a real terrorist threat, even though, by the government's own evidence, neither defendant had ever sought to use a missile for any purpose whatsoever.

On the morning that Yassin was scheduled to testify in his own defense, I spoke to him at the defense table. Perhaps I looked a little emotional when I told him that I hoped we had made the right decisions, because I didn't want him to suffer if we were wrong. He looked over at me and said, "Let me tell you a story. There was a man once who bought a beautiful vase. He warned his young son to be very careful not to knock the vase over and damage it. Daily he reminded the son of the horrible things that would happen to him if he broke the vase. But one day the son was playing in the house and knocked the vase off the table, and it broke into pieces. The son was terrified. He ran out of the house to hide, and ran straight into his father's arms.

'Why are you so upset?' the father asked his hysterical son.

'I broke your vase,' the son sobbed.

'So what?' said the father. 'If it is broken, we can just buy another.'

'But you said that you would do horrible things to me,' said the son.

And the father said, 'That was yesterday, when we still had the vase. Now it is broken, and we just have to start over from here.'"

Yassin looked at me closely. "I know you did your best," he said. "If the vase breaks, we will just have to start over from where we are."

Yassin's testimony was riveting, and he impressed everyone with his honesty. The defense felt that he had successfully refuted the charges. So powerful was his testimony that during the summation, prosecutor William Pericak felt forced to acknowledge:

> ...we are not proving that Mr. Aref is a terrorist. Mr. Kindlon [Yassin's lawyer] was wrong to say that's what the government is trying to prove. But we are trying to demonstrate to you on these charges that he knew a fact, he knew where the money came from and that he intended to help, he intended to help Malik disguise where that money came from...That is all we are trying to prove here. All we are offering that evidence for. And that is all you should consider it for.

The secret, classified aspects of the case continued to cast a shadow over the trial. At the end, the judge instructed the jury that the government had "good and valid" reasons for targeting Yassin with the sting, but that the jury need not consider this issue. The instruction seemed to tell the jury that there was other evidence of Yassin's guilt that the prosecution had not been allowed to present. This was unsuccessfully objected to by the defense.

Hossain was convicted of all of the counts against him. And in addition to convicting Yassin of the counts arising from the June 10, 2004 conversation, the jury also convicted him of the charge that he lied about knowing Mullah Krekar personally. It was a shock to the defense, because nobody had expected that the June 10 conversation would pose any problems. It seemed obvious that Yassin would not have understood Malik's use of the code word "chaudry," and the government's witness had conceded that without knowing it, the conversation would not have amounted to much. The charge that Yassin lied about knowing Mullah Krekar personally seemed ridiculous because it was so obvious that he was telling the truth. Yassin was a low-level office worker at IMK in Syria, while Krekar was a senior IMK official living in Norway. Krekar came to Syria on just one occasion, for a one-month visit, and during that time Yassin met him on a few occasions at group functions involving IMK. How was this knowing someone "personally"? It was like having a candidate for national office fly into a city to thank the local campaign workers for their efforts. Did shaking hands with the candidate on several occasions mean that the campaign workers knew the candidate personally?

On the day after the verdict, I visited Yassin in jail. He was trying hard to put a brave face on the conviction, but he was obviously very worried about his wife and children. Still, he tried to smile and joke with me, even when both of us had tears in our eyes. He related how, whenever his father hit his head on the low rafters of the family barn, he would say, "*Okhay*," which meant "I like it," because he did not want Satan to derive any satisfaction from his suffering. We both said "*Okhay*" several times and laughed, as though to confirm that the government would not derive any satisfaction from our pain, either.

An analysis of the evidence raises serious questions about the fairness of Yassin's conviction. Is it fair to expect a target like Yassin, who was only notarizing (witnessing) financial transactions as a favor, to remember a few casual comments out of hours of conversations, which were held over a six-month period in an imperfect, mispronounced, third language (English)? Is it fair to expect the target to later connect these conversations up and understand that there was an underlying criminal aspect to the financial transactions that transformed the otherwise praiseworthy act of being a witness into a crime? The government, the judge, and the jury apparently believed that this was a reasonable expectation. For the rest of us, it seems more like a frame-up.

Indeed, the government was quite open about the frame-up. On October 12, 2006, two days after the conviction, Albany *Times Union* reporter Brendan Lyons wrote an article in which he quoted various FBI agents about the "sting":

> In the eyes of the FBI, Yassin Aref was cunning and cautious. If the bureau's undercover informant was too aggressive and pulled out a shoulder-fired missile in front of him, Aref might see through the trap and the sting would be over. So the agents were patient. They reeled him in slowly, ordering their informant to engage Aref in discussions on Islam and terrorism, and the profits it could bring, before flashing a less-sinister-looking triggering device during a secretly videotaped meeting...Yet not once during the yearlong sting was Aref ever shown the missile tube, easily recognizable to the average citizen as a potential weapon of mass destruction. "There was a lot of debate on that issue," said an FBI agent, who spoke to the *Times Union* this week on the condition he not be identified...If Aref saw the missile, the agent said, he may have been "spooked."

In other words, if the agents had shown Yassin a missile, he might have recognized it and called the police, which would have ruined the frame-up. But if they just flashed the handle of the triggering device, Yassin would not be likely to recognize it, and they could argue that they had shown him the missile (mispronounced as mi-syl) without much possibility that he would realize what was happening.

The fingerprints of a frame-up are all over the evidence. The only time Malik ever suggested that the money for the loan came from the illegal sale of a missile was at the end of the sting, on June 10, 2004, but Malik used the code word "chaudry" for "missile," which Yassin did not know, and so Yassin would not have learned anything from the conversation about the plot or its connection to the loan—an indication of a frame-up. Malik constantly mispronounced the word missile as "mi-syl" or "mizz-aile"—another indication. Malik showed only the handle of the missile to Hossain when Yassin was counting the money—a third indication. Malik claimed to have lost the tape recorder during the crucial conversation with Shaar about the attack in New York City—a fourth indication. Malik misled Yassin about the legality of the loan by saying the repayment checks were necessary in order to pay taxes—indication five. Yassin never used the word missile in his discussions with Malik; never said anything to suggest he knew about the sale of the missile; and never said anything to show he believed there was a serious plot for an attack in New York City, or that there was anything illegal about the loan transaction, or that he was involved in any illegal activity. The government knew all this, and never attempted to fill in the blanks for him—another indication. In short, the government spent a great deal of time, money, and effort making sure that Yassin never learned anything about the "plot" so that he would not be "spooked" and could be convicted without ever knowing why. These are the parameters of a classic frame-up.

The government began its investigation of Yassin by using the Patriot Act (and the new law enforcement paradigm of preempting a "crime" before it "ripened") to install listening devices in Yassin's house and in the mosque; by wiretapping phones; by sending informants to the mosque; and by using the NSA to obtain information without a warrant. At one point during the trial, defense counsel asked FBI Agent Tim Coll on cross-examination, "Was Mr. Aref under 24-hour surveillance at this point [December 10, 2003]?" The

prosecutor immediately objected, and stated in a lawyer's conference with the judge that Coll's answer could implicate classified evidence. Defense counsel replied, "What if I say constant *physical* surveillance?" This was acceptable to everyone, and back in front of the
jury, defense counsel asked, "And, after the December 10, 2003 conversation, was my client under constant physical surveillance?", to
which Agent Coll answered, "No." Thus it was quite clear that Yassin
was under constant *non*-physical surveillance at this time, i.e., warrantless—illegal—bugging. December 10, 2003 was just a few months
before various Justice Department officials rushed to then-Attorney
General Ashcroft's hospital bed in a fruitless attempt to get him to
recertify the illegal NSA bugging program. As was widely reported,
Ashcroft and Acting Attorney General James Comey refused to do so
for a period of at least a few weeks, which would have coincided with
the time period Yassin was recorded. It seems clear now that the NSA
warrantless wiretapping/eavesdropping program was illegal and a
violation of the FISA laws during its entire existence, not just during
those few weeks when DOJ realized it was.

The government also interviewed such a large number of
Muslims in Albany, and its presence was so heavy, that Muslims in
the community commonly reminded strangers that conversations
were likely to be recorded. In a police state, people routinely remind
each other to be careful what they say because the government is
listening everywhere, and they treat even friends with suspicion
because they may be government informants. Muslims in the U.S.
are living in just such a state.

After Yassin's conviction, a Muslim friend of mine described a
conversation that he had with a casual acquaintance who was going
to Afghanistan to visit. When my friend asked the reason for the
trip, the acquaintance laughed and said, "Why, to join bin Laden, of
course." At the time, my friend understood it as a joke; if the man was
serious, he certainly would not have said such a thing to someone he
hardly knew. But later my friend began to wonder if maybe the man
was working with the FBI. Perhaps this was a test. What should he

do? He certainly could not report the man to the FBI for making a bad joke, but he did not want to be targeted by the FBI in some sort of sting, either. He had many sleepless nights until he was finally able to satisfy himself that the man was not working for the FBI. If this is the fear that the government wants to create, it has succeeded very well—but at what price?

Destroying Muslims and their families and communities by framing the innocent does not make America safer from terrorism, but more vulnerable to it. Muslim communities in the U.S. have the greatest possible interest in preventing terrorism. Many of their members came to the U.S. to escape chaos in their native countries; they love America and know that a terrorist attack would, in the end, hurt American Muslims more than any other group. But trumped-up charges and phony allegations understandably breed resentment; they know that if respected Muslims like doctors, teachers, and imams can be unfairly framed by the government, then none of them are safe. And if the rule of law that made America a beacon to other nations and cultures is shown to be nothing more than the machinations of a third-world dictatorship, nobody is safe.

Eventually, when the government's massive surveillance and interrogation program failed to turn up any criminal activity, U.S. Attorney Glenn Suddaby and his bosses must have considered the enormous investment of time and money in the investigation, as well as the intense political pressure to convict Muslim terrorists at all costs, and the 1% possibility that Yassin might be open to radical activity, and they must have decided to send in Malik with instructions to say just enough to get a conviction but not enough to "spook" the target by suggesting an actual crime. So the frame-up began.

This "preventive conviction" campaign tramples on centuries of fundamental freedoms that are part of the fabric of America. It's a lawyer's trick to try and make an unthinkable idea (jailing someone before he commits a crime) into a perfectly reasonable proposition ("All we're trying to do is prevent another attack like 9/11"). If the government could lock up everybody who it believed was likely to commit a crime in the future, the crime rate might drop in the short run, but the country would be thrown into true terror from the fear of arbitrary arrest and prosecution. The fact that this terror is now directed at the Muslim community in America does not make it right, nor does it guarantee that the practice will not be directed against other groups in the future. In fact, the government cannot foresee future criminal activity with any certainty, and any such system will inevitably collapse under the weight of its own injustice.

During World War II, the U.S. government ordered over 100,000 Japanese-Americans held in concentration camps because their loyalty to America was suspect, based on nothing more than their ethnicity. Not until 1988 did the country formally apologize for this maltreatment of its own citizens. Today it seems shocking that we could have engaged in such blind, irrational bias. But prejudice has accompanied virtually every conflict in our society. Native Americans were driven off their own lands. Colonists loyal to Britain were driven out of America after the Revolution. The government turned a blind eye to the lynching of African Americans after the Civil War. German-Americans were persecuted during the First World War. And in between, the Irish, the Italians, the Jews, the Chinese, the Latinos, and many other ethnic and religious groups all had their turn at being second-class citizens and subjects of hysteria and prejudice. In fact, the dark side of our history is littered with unjust laws and judicial decisions that reflected our fears and hysteria rather than our commitment to justice. Now it is the Muslims' turn. In due time, we will apologize for our present excesses against our Muslim neighbors, just as we have apologized for our excesses of the past. But wouldn't it be better if we learned from the past and reversed our folly now, while our apology might still do some good for the victims?

After the verdict, I watched Terry Kindlon interview new clients. I understood that he had to take new cases to keep his practice going;

I had done the same in my career. But this time I found that I could not move on. I had never before in my professional life encountered a deliberate frame-up. I was familiar with prosecutorial abuses that led to innocent men being convicted—sloppy police work, concealment of errors, hubris and arrogance—but what happened to Yassin was something quite different. The government had deliberately plotted to convict a man who they knew had not committed a crime. There was no sloppiness, no incompetence, but rather a cold, calculating plan carried out over a long period of time, costing millions of dollars and involving dozens of agents, prosecutors, and the acquiescence of high-level officials, to convict two men of terrorism who had no involvement or interest in terrorism. This frame-up was a basic shift in my experience as a lawyer. I had practiced law for over thirty-five years with certain assumptions about the rights of individuals and the limitations of government, but I could not adapt my assumptions to this new reality. For me, Yassin's case would not be over until the injustice was corrected. Besides, he was now my brother.

I continued to visit Yassin in jail and encouraged him to write about his life in Kurdistan. By the time he and Hossain were sentenced, five months later, to fifteen years each in prison, Yassin had written this book about his life and I was involved in plans to get the book published. His wife and children needed legal advice and personal attention to deal with his absence. The Muslim Solidarity Committee had been formed to protest and raise awareness of what had happened to the defendants and to the whole Capital District Muslim community. So many activities revolved around the case that they absorbed most of my time.

One day I stopped in at Little Italy, Hossain's pizza shop on Central Avenue, for a late lunch. I had taken Yassin's oldest son, Raiber, to the doctor for a bad cough, and we decided to have some of Hossain's famous pizza. Fatima, Hossain's wife, was running the shop now. In the shop, and later on the street, I became aware that people were smiling and nodding to me. Most of them were Muslims who lived or worked in the area, and normally they would have passed by without comment or recognition. But today something was different; it was as though I was one of them. And then I realized what was different—Raiber was with me. People knew him. They knew what had been done to his father; they knew that his father was not a terrorist but a respected imam who had been framed by the government. And if I were with Raiber, I must be OK; I must be on their side.

It made me realize that this case would not move on, either. The children and the families of Aref and Hossain continue to live in the community as silent witnesses to what happened, and no one who sees them and cares about justice can walk by without a sign of recognition or remembrance. Injustice, even if we cloak it in euphemisms like "Patriot Act" or "war on terror," is still injustice, and it will not be forgotten.